CW01095372

UNCOVERING MEDIEVAL TRIM

Uncovering Medieval Trim

Archaeological excavations in
and around Trim, Co. Meath

Michael Potterton & Matthew Seaver

EDITORS

FOUR COURTS PRESS

Typeset in 10.5 pt on 12.5 pt Ehrhardt by
Carrigboy Typesetting Services for
FOUR COURTS PRESS LTD
7 Malpas Street, Dublin 8, Ireland
www.fourcourtspress.ie
and in North America for
FOUR COURTS PRESS
c/o ISBS, 920 NE 58th Avenue, Suite 300, Portland, OR 97213.

A catalogue record for this title is available
from the British Library.

ISBN 978-1-84682-169-1

ACKNOWLEDGMENT

This publication received funding from the Heritage Council under the 2009
Unpublished Excavations Grant Scheme. It is an action of the County Meath Heritage
Plan 2007–2011, supported by Meath County Council and the Heritage Council.

Printed in England
by MPG Books, Bodmin, Cornwall.

Contents

Figures, tables & plates

TABLES

COLOUR PLATES
(between pages 160 and 161)

Abbreviations

AFM	*Annála ríoghachta Éireann: annals of the kingdom of Ireland by the Four Masters from the earliest period to the year 1616*, ed. & trans. John O'Donovan (7 vols, Dublin, 1851; repr. New York, 1966)
AMS	Accelerator Mass Spectrometry
B	burial
BABAO	British Association for Biological Anthropology and Osteoarchaeology
BP	before present
Bd	greatest breadth at distal end
Bp	greatest breadth at proximal end
cal.	calibrated
CF	calculation factor
CJR	*Calendar of the justiciary rolls in the court of the justiciar of Ireland … 1295–1303 [etc.]*, ed. James Mills (2 vols, Dublin, 1905, 1914)
cm	centimetre(s)
CPL, 1198–1304 [etc.]	*Calendar of entries in the papal registers relating to Great Britain and Ireland: papal letters, 1198–1304* [etc.] (London, 1893– ; Dublin, 1986–)
CRDS	Cultural Resources Development Services
DEHLG	Department of the Environment, Heritage and Local Government
DHB	disarticulated human bone
DJD	degenerative joint disease
ed.	editor(s); edition; edited by
ESH	estimated shoulder height
Excavations 1971 [etc.]	*Excavations 1971* [etc.]: *summary accounts of archaeological excavations in Ireland*, ed. T.G. Delaney (1971–6), Claire Cotter (1985–6), Isabel Bennett (1987–) [1977–84 incorporated in *Irish Journal of Archaeology*]
F	feature
fig./figs	figure/figures
GL	greatest length
GLI	greatest lateral length
IAC	Irish Archaeological Consultancy
IAPO	Irish Association of Professional Osteoarchaeologists
IAWA	International Association of Wood Anatomists
IFA	Institute for Archaeologists [formerly Institute of Field Archaeologists]
indet.	indeterminate
intermed.	intermediate
JRSAI	*Journal of the Royal Society of Antiquaries of Ireland*
Juv.	juvenile
m	metre(s)
ml	millilitres

MNE	minimum number of (anatomical) elements
MNI	minimum number of individuals
Ms[s]	manuscript[s]
n.a.	not applicable
NA	National Archives (of Ireland)
NGR	National Grid Reference
NISP	number of identified specimens present
NLI	National Library of Ireland
NMI	National Museum of Ireland
NRA	National Roads Authority
NUI	National University of Ireland
OD	Ordnance Datum
OPW	Office of Public Works
OS	Ordnance Survey
path.	pathology/ies
pers. comm.	personal communication
pl./pls	plate/plates
prep.	preparation
PRIA	*Proceedings of the Royal Irish Academy*
RDKPRI, i [etc.]	*First* [etc.] *report of the deputy keeper of the public records in Ireland* (Dublin, 1869–)
repr.	reprint; reprinted
RIA	Royal Irish Academy
RMP	Record of Monuments and Places
RSAI	Royal Society of Antiquaries of Ireland
s.a.	*sub anno*
ser.	series
SMR	Sites and Monuments Record
sp./spp	species (sing./pl.)
trans.	translation; translated by
TVAS	Thames Valley Archaeological Services
UCD	University College Dublin
UJA	*Ulster Journal of Archaeology*
unid.	unidentified
upr	upper

Contributors

FIONA BEGLANE is primarily a freelance zooarchaeologist and also lectures part-time at the Institute of Technology, Sligo. She is the author of a number of published faunal reports.

JOHN BRADLEY is a senior lecturer at the Department of History, National University of Ireland Maynooth.

SARAH COBAIN is a freelance archaeobotanist specializing in charcoal and plant macrofossil identification and analysis.

JENNIE COUGHLAN is a freelance osteoarchaeologist based in Dublin. She has worked on a range of skeletal assemblages, ranging in date from the Bronze Age through to the medieval period and is published in *Blood red roses: the archaeology of a mass grave from the Battle of Towton, AD1461* (2000).

DOMINIC DELANY has over twenty years experience in Irish archaeology. He was a contributor to *Archaeological investigations in Galway City, 1987–1998* (2004), which included his excavation of a medieval castle and hall in the hearth of the city.

CARMEL DUFFY is a freelance consultant archaeologist based in Co. Meath.

DONAL FALLON was a project manager and site director for CRDS Ltd between 2002 and 2006. He is now a practising barrister.

LINDA FIBIGER is a consultant osteoarchaeologist. She is currently completing her PhD on violence and conflict in Neolithic Europe at the University of Oxford.

ALAN R. HAYDEN is director of Archaeological Projects Ltd, archaeological consultants and contractors. He directed excavations at Trim Castle in 1995–8.

MARK KELLY is a senior supervisor with CRDS Ltd. He has supervised excavations at Finnegan's Way/Townspark South, the Black Friary and Loman Street and has taken part in numerous monitoring projects in Trim.

EOGHAN KIERAN is a marine archaeologist from Co. Meath. He is currently employed as a senior archaeologist by Moore Group.

CAMILLA LOFQVIST is an osteoarchaeologist with Moore Group.

PATRICIA LYNCH is a consultant archaeologist and osteoarchaeologist (human and fauna) based in Dublin.

SUSAN LYONS is a freelance archaeobotanist specializing in plant macrofossil and wood identification.

CLARE McCUTCHEON is a freelance ceramic researcher and archaeologist, specializing in medieval pottery. She is the author of *Medieval pottery from Wood Quay, Dublin* (2006).

ROSANNE MEENAN is currently employed as field monuments advisor for Meath County Council. She is a specialist in medieval and post-medieval pottery.

CLARE MULLINS is a consultant archaeologist. She is a graduate of University College Cork.

CONOR NEWMAN is a lecturer in archaeology at NUI, Galway. He directed the Discovery Programme's Tara Survey and is chairman of the Heritage Council.

FINOLA O'CARROLL is a company director of CRDS Ltd and has excavated sites in Trim and throughout Co. Meath.

EAMONN O'DONOGHUE has a long-standing interest in medieval castles and aerial photography.

BRIAN O'HARA has been a senior archaeologist with Dominic Delany & Associates since 2003.

MICHAEL POTTERTON is a senior research archaeologist at the Discovery Programme. He is the author of *Medieval Trim: history and archaeology* (2005).

MATTHEW SEAVER is a senior archaeologist with CRDS Ltd and has excavated extensively in Co. Meath.

DENIS SHINE is a graduate of University College Dublin and a licensed archaeologist with CRDS Ltd.

MANDY STEPHENS is a licensed archaeologist with CRDS Ltd. She has conducted excavations in Trim and the Bend of the Boyne.

CIARA TRAVERS is an MA graduate of Southampton University and an osteoarchaeologist with CRDS Ltd.

Foreword

This book marks an important step in the development of urban archaeology in Ireland because it is the first time that the archaeology of a small town has been the subject of such intensive study. Publications in urban archaeology have tended to concentrate on the larger cities, such as Cork, Dublin, Galway and Waterford, but little is known about the archaeology of the small market town, which in many ways was more typical of urban life in medieval and post-medieval Ireland.

The development of urban archaeology in Ireland has followed much the same pattern as that of the rest of Western Europe, with the difference that the absence of Roman remains lessened the tempo of exploration. It began in the seventeenth century with scholars such as Sir James Ware (1594–1666) and Bishop David Rothe (1573–1650) speculating on the origins of Dublin and Kilkenny, recording medieval tomb inscriptions and noting discoveries such as the burials in a sepulchral mound (perhaps the Thingmote) removed prior to the construction of Nassau Street, Dublin, in 1646. This pattern of incidental and partial recording continued throughout the eighteenth into the nineteenth century when the foundation of antiquarian societies in Kilkenny (1849) and Belfast (1853) provided a forum for discussion and publication. Attention focused primarily on surviving medieval remains such as houses, friaries, castles and churches but there was also interest in what was below ground. Thomas Matthew Ray (1801–88) collected objects from the trenches dug to accommodate Victorian Dublin's sewerage and drainage facilities, while James Graves (1815–86) conducted the first excavation of an urban house (it happened to be post-medieval) at Newtown Jerpoint in 1868. The eighteenth and nineteenth centuries also saw the publication of several scholarly urban histories: Ledwich's *Irishtown and Kilkenny* (1781), Ferrar's *Limerick* (1787), McSkimmin's *Carrickfergus* (1811), Hardiman's *Galway* (1820), Ryland's *Waterford* (1824) and Gilbert's *Dublin* (1854–9) among them. By the end of the nineteenth century, at least among the educated classes, a sense of the depth of Irish civic culture had developed.

Towns, however, were largely written out of the history of independent Ireland, which, for ideological reasons, tended to privilege the richness of the Irish rural tradition. With the prominent exception of O'Sullivan's *Old Galway* (1942), little new scholarly work was published on Irish medieval towns in the first forty years of independence. Modern urban archaeology began in 1961 with the excavation of the east wing of Dublin Castle, which was carried out after its destruction in a fire. Following nineteenth-century thinking, the work was conducted as an investigation of the castle itself but it had the surprising result of revealing Viking-age deposits underneath. The subsequent excavations at High Street and Fishamble Street (1968–72) demonstrated the richness of Dublin's Viking-Age archaeology. It was the Wood Quay excavations (1974–81), however, that marked a real turning point in public awareness, when thousands of people took to the streets to protest against its destruction. In retrospect, one can see that the public outcry was largely a plea for a pluralist rather than an insular Ireland; an Ireland that valued all of its traditions equally, rather than just privileging one. Caught on the hop and anxious to avoid a repeat of the public demonstrations, the government commissioned an Urban Archaeology Survey (1982–94), with the aim of identifying the zone of archaeological potential in every town within the Republic. With a few notable exceptions, the climate at local government level was generally hostile to archaeology at this time and so the argument for a zone of archaeological potential had to be indisputable and, accordingly, it was defined as tightly as possible. In the intervening period since the 1980s, excavation has shown that in some towns, such as Drogheda and Kilkenny, there were extensive thirteenth-century suburbs extending far beyond the zone of archaeological potential.

Between the 1960s and 1980s archaeological excavations concentrated on the larger cities and towns, although substantial excavations occurred in Carrickfergus in the 1970s and the occasional friary or castle was investigated in smaller towns. During the 1990s, however, an increasing amount of archaeo-logical work was carried out in smaller towns, when for several years over fifty per cent of all excavations in Ireland were urban in nature. The initial work in smaller towns yielded very little surviving archaeology and, for a time, it was feared that no archaeological evidence, other than sub-surface pits and trenches, might survive in small Irish towns. The importance of Trim is that it is one of a handful of small towns with an archaeology rather than just a list of incidental, unconnected discoveries.

The archaeological study of Trim has largely followed the national trend. Heraldic shields within St Patrick's Church attracted the attention of scholars in the seventeenth century; some of the monuments within the town were recorded by Beranger and Cooper in the eighteenth century, while in the nineteenth century the ancient character of Trim inspired a remarkable historian, Richard Butler (1794–1862), to produce four editions of his *Notices of Trim Castle* (1835, 1840, 1854, 1861). Butler also collected and preserved artefacts found in Trim and its environs, most of which he presented to the Royal Irish Academy, from whence they entered the collection of the National Museum of Ireland. Butler's book remained essential reading until 2005 when Michael Potterton published his magisterial volume *Medieval Trim: history and archaeology*, which elevated the study of medieval Trim to an entirely new level. Incidental archaeological finds, including the occasional burial, were made in the course of the twentieth century but scientific excavation only commenced in 1974 when work began at Trim Castle in advance of conservation. The Urban Archaeology Survey of County Meath (1984) defined the zone of archaeological potential for Trim and three years later, in 1987, the first excavation took place within the town, an investigation of a site on High Street carried out prior to the construction of the library. It was not until 1998, however, that archaeological excavation became a regular occurrence, and since then excavations have taken place every year.

The results of archaeological work at Trim are important, not only because of the factual information they provide, but also because of their relevance to modern life. This book gives us an insight into a forgotten part of Irish history, the lives and experiences of the occupants of a small town in medieval and post-medieval Ireland. It was only in 2001, according to the census, that a majority of the Irish population was found to live in towns. This pattern will continue and, as we search for new identities to cope with a changing Ireland, interest in the story of Irish towns will increase. So, in examining the archaeology of one Irish small town, this volume makes an important contribution not only to knowledge but also to the exploration and discovery of Irish identity.

JOHN BRADLEY
Kilkenny
Easter Monday 2009

Preface

As a consequence of the construction boom in the latter part of the twentieth and early twenty-first century, archaeologists have been involved in over a hundred excavations in Trim. Much of this work has only been visible to the wider public through hoardings. In 2008 Meath County Council and CRDS Ltd organized a conference on the growing body of archaeological evidence for Trim and its hinterland through the ages. The conference was designed to bring the information from archaeologists and specialists on artefacts and environmental remains to the public and to give meaningful feedback on interpretations of the past. It also allowed different archaeologists from a range of consultancies to focus on the overall direction of research in the town. The conference was held in the Knightsbrook Hotel in November 2008 and was well attended by archaeologists and by members of the public from Trim, and from elsewhere in Co. Meath and further afield. Such was the success of the conference, that it was decided to publish the papers presented, and to issue a call for further contributions from those not able to present on the day. This includes the important work of specialists who contribute massively to the archaeological narrative and who are not always as visible to the general public. This publication, while not intended to be a definitive statement on the archaeology of Trim and its environs, aims to present important information on the origins and evolution of the town.

The editors would like to thank a multitude of people who have given their time and energy towards the creation of this book. This volume aimed to examine the archaeology of Trim town through recent excavations carried out by a range of archaeological companies and individuals. The editors are especially grateful to all of the contributors for their hard work in providing stimulating and informative papers. We are delighted that John Bradley agreed to write the foreword. In particular, we would like to thank Loreto Guinan, Heritage Officer with Meath County Council, for her enthusiasm, organizational skill and energy from the outset, both in making the initial conference possible and for supporting the whole publication process. It is a pleasure to thank Rosanne Meenan, the National Monuments Advisory Officer in Co. Meath, and Louise McKeever and Alesandro Cruiciani of the Heritage Office, Meath County Council, for their work throughout the project. Finola O'Carroll and Steve Mandal of CRDS Ltd provided backing for the project from the start and were extremely encouraging and tolerant of the scale of commitment required. The staff of CRDS Ltd, particularly Niall Lynch, Catherine Bishop, Joanne Gaffrey, Ciara Travers and Milica Rajic, provided enormous amounts of skill in finalizing illustrations, editing and co-ordinating specialist information for many of the papers. Patrizia LaPiscopia of the School of Archaeology, UCD, also gave of her time to assist with image-scanning, and Christiaan Corlett and Tony Roche (DEHLG Photographic Archive) were helpful in sourcing photographs. New photographs were taken, at short notice, by Mark Condren, Richard Johnston and Clare Mullins. Kevin O'Brien was very generous in allowing one of his magnificent reconstruction drawings to be used as the cover illustration. Many other individuals, particularly specialist archaeologists, were involved in preparing the papers for publication, often giving extensively of their free time and knowledge, and are thanked at the end of individual papers within.

The authors and editors would like to thank the various institutions and individuals who have given permission for their images to be reproduced here. In particular, we are grateful to Aideen Ireland and the National Archives of Ireland, Amanda O'Brien (Meath Local Authorities), Dominic Cronin (Ordnance Survey Ireland), Sarah Gearty (Irish Historic Towns Atlas; Royal Irish Academy), Frances Tallon (Meath County Council Library Service), Raymond Refaussé (Representative Church Body, Library), Colette O'Daly (National Library of Ireland), Waterford Museum of Treasures and Trinity College Dublin Map Library. We are thankful for the assistance from Anthony Corns, Mary Shackleton, David Sweetman, Irene D'Arcy, Rosemary Ryan and William Jerald Kennedy.

This volume would not have been possible without the support of Meath County Council. We are especially grateful to the Heritage Council for financial support through the Unpublished Excavations Grant Scheme 2009. The editors are also grateful to Four Courts Press for agreeing to take on this project, and particularly to Martin Fanning for his advice and patience. We are thankful to Michael Ann Bevivino for her suggestions and counsel. Thanks also to the people of Trim for showing such an interest in the initial conference and the subsequent walking tour in November 2008. Finally, our sincere thanks to family members and friends who had to tolerate the absence of the editors for significant periods of time during 2008 and 2009.

This book is not intended as a final statement on excavations in Trim, and the archaeological narrative continues to evolve over time. It will hopefully contribute to the understanding of this important town and its development through the ages, and provide some direction for future research in and around the town.

MICHAEL POTTERTON
& MATTHEW SEAVER
Midsummer's Day 2009

Introduction: understanding Trim through the ages

MICHAEL POTTERTON

This paper consists of three parts. The first outlines briefly the state of knowledge regarding prehistoric and medieval Trim in advance of the excavations that are reported on in this book. The second part highlights the significance of the archaeological work that has been carried out in recent times and the ways in which this has thrown light on previously poorly understood or misunderstood aspects of Trim through the ages. The final part outlines some of the questions that remain to be answered and suggests ways in which these might be approached.

PART I: WHAT WAS ALREADY KNOWN

Trim is located 40km to the northwest of Dublin, on the banks of the river Boyne, one of the major natural route-ways connecting the inland plains with the Irish Sea (Potterton 2005). Well-drained by the Boyne and its tributaries, the land surrounding the town is relatively low-lying and flat, generally ranging from 60m to 70m above sea level. Trim lies towards the eastern edge of the largest continuous stretch of carboniferous limestone in Europe (Aalen et al., 1997, 7). In the countryside surrounding the town, this limestone bedrock is generally concealed beneath highly productive soils which are ideally suited to the cultivation of grass, but can also produce good yields of root-crops, cereals and vegetables. The area around Trim is among the best agricultural land in the country, for both pastoral and tillage farming (Finch et al., 1983, 51; Aalen et al., 1997, 18).

The name Trim derives from the Irish *Áth Truim(m)*, meaning 'ford of the elder tree', and it seems that one of the attractions for early settlers at Trim was the fact that they could cross the river at this point (Hogan 1910, 71). Prehistoric finds indicate that farming communities sought out the fertile lands on which to graze their cattle and cultivate crops, while the river supplied fish including salmon, trout and eel. An important communication route, the Boyne was also a source of water for washing, cooking and drinking, and a means of disposing of waste, while the shallows at Trim made crossing possible for much of the year.

The earliest known reference to Trim appears in an eighth-century document that was later incorporated into the ninth-century codex known as

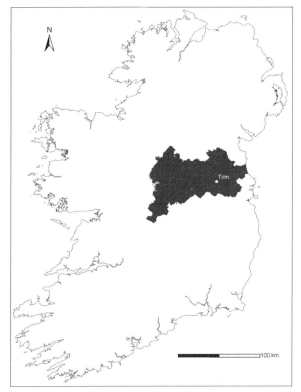

1.1 Map of Ireland showing the extent of the medieval lordship of Meath and the location of Trim. The lordship, which covered over 325,000 hectares, extended from the Irish Sea in the east to the River Shannon in the west. Trim was located at the furthest navigable point inland on the River Boyne

the Book of Armagh (Gwynn 1913). The narrative account describes the foundation of the church at *Vadum Truimm*, 'the ford of Trim', by the British missionary Lommán, who was, according to the text, a nephew and disciple of Patrick. Early Medieval Trim was home to both ecclesiastics and scholars. At one time or another the religious community numbered abbots, bishops, *princeps* and anchorites, while its poets achieved high renown and its scribes kept records of political affairs and family alliances. The early Irish annals record the deaths of ecclesiastics, scribes and poets at Trim in the eighth and ninth centuries, as well as the burning of churches, while further information on the inhabitants of the site is recorded in genealogies and martyrologies. From all of the documentary evidence, it appears that Trim's Early Medieval profile was at its highest in the eighth century. After that its significance gradually faded until the twelfth century.

In 1172 Henry II granted to Hugh de Lacy the whole of the ancient kingdom of Meath and the right to appoint officers for its government. De Lacy selected Trim as the caput of his new lordship and it was to become the administrative centre of Meath (fig. 1.1). The focus of control and organization was at the castle, which must have been built soon after Henry II made his grant to de Lacy. The land was fertile and productive, there was an established crossing point on the river, the location was known to traders and merchants, and a certain level of organization was already in existence. Trim Castle was built on land belonging to the church, and rent for the site of the castle, town and bridge was paid to the church from the twelfth to the nineteenth century.

Much of what we know about the earliest Anglo-Norman fortification at Trim comes from the epic Norman-French poem known as *The Song of Dermot and the Earl* (Orpen 1892, ll 3222–41). Here it is said that 'Hugh de Lacy fortified a house at Trim and threw a trench around it, and then enclosed it with a stockade'. It was long believed that this early fortification was a motte, but archaeological excavations have revealed that it was in fact a ringwork (Sweetman 1999, 4–5). The ring-work was quickly replaced by the first phase of the masonry structure, however, and two further phases were to follow in rapid succession.

The development of Trim from the 1170s cannot be fully understood in isolation from the lordship of Meath. The importance of the town necessitated a strong emphasis on fortification and defence, the location there of government officers called for appropriate facilities, and the development of the town as a focal point attracted settlers, traders, religious orders, and of course thieves, cripples and beggars. Trim's central location and its prominent position politically also meant that it was a suitable venue for parliament, which convened there on no fewer than ten occasions in the fifteenth century alone.

Trim was a dual-purpose town. On the one hand, it functioned as the caput of a rich and extensive lordship, while on the other it developed as a fortified market town with extensive mercantile connections and an independent administration. The castle was the hub of the lordship's government, housing the chancery, exchequer, treasury, prison, garrison and hall as well as functioning as the repository for all documentary records. It housed a chapel and chaplain's quarters and served as the primary residence of the lord and his inner household. The government of the town itself had its own responsibilities for, among other things, the upkeep of the town, the maintenance of the walls (from 1400), the collection of taxes, accounting to the exchequer and keeping the peace.

The lordship was held successively by three important families: the de Lacys; de Genevilles (pl. 3); and Mortimers, before being inherited by Richard, duke of York, in 1425. Throughout this time the lordship was periodically under pressure from various quarters. Geographically adjacent to a generally antagonistic Dublin administration that persisted in its efforts to seize the lands of the lordship and particularly its revenues, the extraordinary rights and privileges enjoyed by the lords of Meath also attracted envious attention and required constant defence. Sharing lengthy borders with Ulster, Connacht and

Leinster also engendered unease while, from within, instability was heightened by the actions of 'Irish enemies' and 'English rebels'. The running and defence of the lordship was further unsettled by frequently absent lords and especially by periods of minority and forfeiture. Interestingly, however, it is during such unstable periods that records are fullest; the Dublin administration kept detailed accounts on aspects of finance, property, crime and punishment and building projects. Some of these records survive, but most of those produced by the Trim administration disappeared mysteriously towards the end of the fifteenth century.

As with most medieval towns, Trim was enclosed by a fortified wall. In addition to its role in defence, the wall served as a highly visible division between the town and the countryside. It was a physical expression of the legal separateness of the town, the civic identity of its inhabitants, and the power of the community. Gates served as collection points for tolls and represented for many incomers the first contact with town government, reminding them of the organization and regulations they could expect to find within. Visible from afar, the walls and gates symbolized the internal order of the town. Their construction was expensive and as such they embodied substantial collective effort and investment. It is estimated that the combined walled areas at Trim, north and south of the river, enclosed an area of between twenty and twenty-three hectares, making it Ireland's eleventh largest walled town, similar in area to medieval Waterford and Wexford.

Within the walled area, the unusual street pattern is a reflection of the various phases in the evolution of the town. Although Trim does not adequately fulfil Bradley's criteria for inclusion as a monastic town (Bradley 1998; Bradley 1988–9, 30, 41–2), the curving nature of the streets almost certainly follows the line of at least one ecclesiastical boundary. The dominant curving pattern, from which most of the subsequent development stemmed, may be a case in point. It may also simply be the result of the gradual and organic growth of the settlement and its network of laneways and streets. The streets extending from the west and north of this curve represent later expansion, and the regular intervals at which they occur on this curve suggest that this was an organized development. South of the Boyne, the linear nature of Market Street (the widest street in the town) and the streets associated with it clearly marks an important phase of planned urban expansion. The most rigidly linear section of the town is extra-mural and this may be the location of Trim's earliest suburb, in the area centred on what is today Emmet Street and running south to Patrick Street and Newhaggard Road. The town's streets were cobbled and the surfaces were repaired periodically and sometimes re-laid completely. Some of the streets may have been kerbed.

It is a feature of most towns of medieval origin that contemporary property boundaries follow the lines of medieval divisions. The initial plot pattern was a

1.2 The 'Yellow Steeple' was the belfry of the Augustinian priory from the fourteenth century. The remains of a stretch of the town walls can be seen in the foreground

remarkably stable element of the town-plan, due, in part, to the logistical difficulties involved in altering established divisions, but especially to the legal attributes of burgages. Unfortunately, no specific records relating to the medieval burgages of Trim survive in documentary form, and the best source of information is the town-plan itself.

The parish church was a key component in any medieval town, and in this regard St Patrick's Church in Trim was no different. Its primary role was religious, but it also served a range of social and administrative functions. It was a diocesan as well as a parochial centre, and as such it hosted meetings, court sittings, visitations and elections, as well as more regular religious ceremonies, services and worship. It was patronized by the local merchant classes and by successive lords of Meath and Trim, while, as an exceptionally wealthy prebend, it attracted clerical incumbents of high standing. Its rectors studied at Cambridge, Oxford and Rome, and some went on to become bishops and archbishops or to hold high secular offices.

By the late fifteenth century, the rectors of Trim were regularly absent. Interestingly, the architectural evidence suggests a period of wealth, apparently fuelled by endowments, followed quite quickly by a period of decline. The medieval ecclesiastical remains consist of a tower, a chancel and a collection of memorial monuments and miscellaneous masonry fragments. The evidence from these features indicates an important phase of construction at the end of the fourteenth or beginning of the fifteenth century. The representation of a series of armorial shields on the piscina, a plaque on the wall of the tower, two plaques now within the tower and several other heraldic shields, now lost, demonstrates that the Mortimers were important benefactors of this church. It also appears that Richard, duke of York, was a patron and it is likely that the declining fortunes of the church coincided with York's death in 1460 and the subsequent transfer of Trim to crown hands.

While the Mortimers clearly patronized the parish church, the de Lacys and de Genevilles had earlier been major benefactors of religious houses in the town. Hugh de Lacy appears to have re-founded the Augustinian priory that had first been established in the 1140s, while Geoffrey de Geneville founded a Dominican friary in 1263. It was probably also at about this time that the Franciscan community was first established in Trim, in the shadow of the castle, near the bridge. These three orders played a highly significant role in the medieval town, treating the sick, looking after the poor, and attending to the spiritual needs of the townspeople. St Mary's developed as an important place of pilgrimage and attracted many visitors. Each of the religious houses had an impressive array of buildings and some managed extensive estates nearby. Members of the communities wore distinctive clothing and would have been readily identifiable as they walked through the market or visited the ill or infirm. The sound of pealing bells would have been a continual reminder of the monastic presence in the town and, as the tallest building in Ireland, the Yellow Steeple dominated the skyline for many miles around.

Neighbouring the Yellow Steeple, Talbot's Castle is one of two medieval fortified townhouses in Trim. It is likely that at least some of this structure formed part of the monastic complex of the Augustinian priory, and it was probably transformed and enlarged after the dissolution. Immediately to the north of Talbot's Castle is Nangle's Castle, which is now ruinous, but its location and some of its features suggest that it may once have been home to a wealthy merchant and his family. Before that, it too was probably part of the monastic complex.

In addition to the medieval structures represented by the upstanding remains at Trim, the documentary record attests the presence of a frank-house, a guildhall, orchards, gardens, water mills and an eel weir. There was a weekly market and an annual fair that attracted merchants from around the country. Trade in cloth appears to have been particularly important, and there is evidence for merchants travelling from England and Flanders. Despite the town's inland location, a range of seafood and foreign merchandise were traded in addition to locally produced commodities and processed goods. Trade was strictly regulated, weights and measures were checked and taxes were levied

1.3 The drawing room in Talbot's Castle. A range of architectural features here and elsewhere in the building appear to have been adapted from original elements of the monastic buildings. This photograph was taken in 1902–3, and is part of an album that originally belonged to a certain F. Hemingway of Kells, Co. Meath (courtesy of Mary Shackleton)

and collected systematically. There is evidence that a variety of occupations were practised within the town: millers, bakers, butchers, goldsmiths, carters, weavers, tanners, shoemakers and leather-workers are all attested, in either the documents or the archaeology, while carpenters, masons, metalworkers and other craftsmen were frequently employed in a range of construction projects.

Situated at the southeast corner of the town, Trim Castle is the most extensive and best documented of the town's medieval buildings. It is strategically sited on a limestone outcrop on the south bank of the Boyne, and is one of the oldest Anglo-Norman fortresses in the country. Thirty-six towns in Ireland are associated with Anglo-Norman castles, and just like many of these (such as Athenry, Carrickfergus, Dublin, Kilkenny and Limerick), the castle at Trim is located at the periphery of the town. The situation of the castle at an extremity was strategic – it was close to the town and people and yet still peripheral, while the necessarily massive defences of the castle doubled as defences for the town. The position of the castle in an angle of the town walls facilitated its protection – both against extramural attackers and from the townspeople themselves in the event of a rebellion.

The relationship between castle and town was mutually beneficial, however, and it played a key role throughout the middle ages. The extent of the lordship was reflected in the scale of the castle, while the security provided by this fortification facilitated the establishment of three religious houses and enabled the town to grow and prosper. The protection afforded by the castle was also a factor in the transfer, by Bishop Simon de Rochfort, of his cathedral from Clonard to Newtown Trim in 1202 (*CPL, 1396–1404*, 74–5). Clonard had been attacked and burned two years earlier (*AFM, s.a.* 1200), and Rochfort's new site was strategically located, less than two kilometres to the east of Trim, within clear view of the castle (fig. 1.4). Nonetheless, the fact that the cathedral was two kilometres away, and not in the town itself, meant that Trim was lacking one important component. This missing link is almost certainly part of the reason that Trim did not develop into a major medieval town or city.

The conventional picture of medieval Irish towns shows a period of general decline and contraction after *c.*1320, but for Trim this was not the case. Trim and Drogheda dominated the hierarchy of Meath towns, and their wealth is reflected by the fact that, in 1300, Trim paid two hundred marks to the town subsidy levied by Edward I to finance the war in Scotland, while Drogheda on the side of Meath paid sixty (*CJR, 1295–1303*, 303–4; *Berry 1907*, 232–3; *RDKPRI 38, appendix*, 70). At Trim, a period of sustained growth and consolidation was maintained throughout the fourteenth century, and this period witnessed a number of major construction projects. Murage grants were issued in 1290, 1308 and 1316; repairs were carried out at the Franciscan friary after 1330; the bridge (fig. 1.8) was built sometime between 1330 and 1350; the Yellow Steeple was erected soon after 1368; parts of the parish church were rebuilt and several episodes of construction took place at the castle. Most of the fourteenth century seems to have been a boom period for Trim, marked by strength and prosperity. The decline in the fortunes of the town, anticipated elsewhere in urban Ireland one hundred years earlier, did not begin until the fifteenth century, and even then it was not until the second half of the century that a nadir was reached. Richard, duke of York, died in 1460 and the lordship passed to the crown for the rest of the middle ages. Without a powerful lord with a personal interest in the town, without a benefactor of the parish church and religious houses and, most especially, without an administrative presence at the castle, Trim slipped from significance. The symbiotic relationship between the castle and the town was such that the fate of one was intimately tied up with the fate of the other.

By the close of the fifteenth century the pressures on the lordship had become unbearable. Declining revenues and the contraction of the area under government control meant that maintaining a lordship as extensive as Meath was simply unfeasible. Even to govern such a large county became impossible, and its inevitable partition in 1541 signalled the end of an era. When the lordship suffered, the town suffered, and with the declining fortunes and final

1.4 Aerial photograph of some of the upstanding medieval remains at Newtown Trim,
including the parish church (left) and the cathedral (centre right)

abolition of the liberty of Trim, the wealth and importance of the town also
faded. Although parliament was to sit there once more in the year after the
county was divided, Trim was no longer a centre for anything more than local
administration – and even that was considerably reduced by 1541. By this
time, Trim was weak and depopulated. Buildings were in ruins and the town's
defences were in need of repair. At the time of the dissolution the monasteries
were already in decline and their communities were small. The county was
partitioned and the town was impoverished. In 1541 it was found that Trim's
portreeve and burgesses were entitled to the rents and petty customs of the
town and that the annual fee farm was worth just four pounds (Mac Niocaill
1992, 57). Compared with the substantial returns accounted for in the early
thirteenth century, this is a stark illustration of how the fortunes of the town
had dwindled. Trim had been central; by 1541 it was an outpost, on the very
furthest reaches of the lands administered by the Dublin government.

PART II: WHAT'S NEW?

Until relatively recently, most of our knowledge and understanding of the
development of Trim through the ages was derived from historical sources and

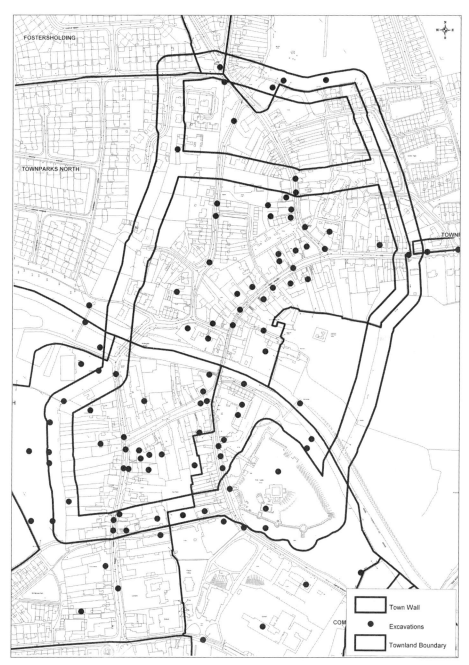

1.5 Location of over one hundred licensed archaeological excavations that have taken place in Trim. The line of the medieval town defences is shown, with a buffer-zone on either side (Map researched and prepared by Rosanne Meenan, Amanda O'Brien, Irene D'Arcy and Michael Potterton; base-map courtesy of Ordnance Survey Ireland, Permit 8565 © Ordnance Survey Ireland/Government of Ireland)

upstanding remains. Apart from the two major campaigns of excavation at the castle, and a handful of smaller excavations at other locations in the town, very little information had come from the remains that lie beneath the ground's surface. Over the past decade or so, however, major changes and developments in and around the town have necessitated advance archaeological investigation (fig. 1.5, pl. 1). It is remarkable that the excavation that began at Trim Castle in 1995 was only the fifth licensed archaeological dig in the town (fig. 1.6). Since that year, over one hundred licensed excavations have taken place, averaging over ten a year for the last decade (1999–2008). The massive expansion of archaeological intervention has generated a significant corpus of data. Some of this has shed a great deal of light on aspects of Trim's past that were previously poorly understood. Much of the data has added to what was already known, while some of it has forced a rethink of other assumptions and interpretations. The papers in this volume present details of some of the most significant excavations and their findings. In this part of the paper, I will give some examples of how this work has contributed to our overall understanding of the development of Trim through the ages.

Prehistoric Trim

Archaeological evidence indicates a human presence in Trim from as early as the Neolithic period, with activity increasing during the Bronze Age. It is still not possible to say whether the Neolithic presence was permanent or transitory, however, but the Bronze Age evidence suggests both occupation and ritual activity. The first evidence for Iron Age activity at Trim was found during excavations directed by Mandy Stephens outside the east curtain wall of the castle and close to the river (Stephens, 'Empty space', this volume; fig. 1.8). This remarkable find consisted of a hoard of young pigs' forelegs dating to the second or third century BC (Beglane, 'Long pigs' feet', this volume). At least twenty-eight pigs were represented, as well as three cattle. Fiona Beglane carried out detailed analyses of these enigmatic remains and concluded that they were deposited in autumn and that they are unlikely to be butchery off-cuts. Could they be the remains of a large feast or part of some votive offering? In this regard, their deposition in autumn – at the time of the equinox or at Samhain? – and their proximity to the River Boyne could be significant. The discovery of this hoard might also indicate that the lords of the castle were not the first high-status individuals to inhabit this site.

Early Medieval Trim

The location of the Early Medieval ecclesiastical site at Trim has generated a great deal of speculation. Various suggestions have been put forward, but in the last few years several commentators have concluded that the site now occupied by St Patrick's Church of Ireland Cathedral is the most likely

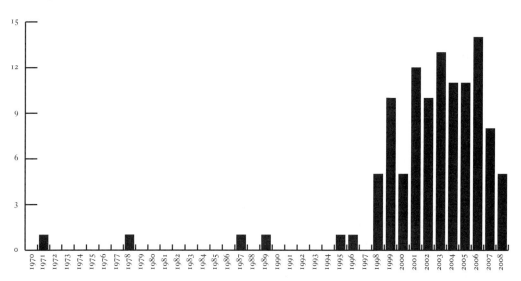

1.6 Graph showing the increasing number of archaeological excavations carried out in Trim annually, since 1970. Excavations that extended beyond one calendar year are recorded in the year in which they began only (for example, the excavations that took place at Trim Castle in 1995–8 are included under 1995 only) (sources: *Excavations 1971* [etc.]; DEHLG)

candidate (Hennessy 2004, 1; Potterton 2005, 350). This is the highest ground in the town, it is the site of the medieval parish church, the present church retains a dedication to St Patrick, and traces of a curving boundary can be detected in the modern street plan. Until recently, however, the physical evidence for a pre-Anglo-Norman church-site here was scant. Recent excavations directed by Eoghan Kieran just outside the churchyard wall at the east end of St Patrick's Cathedral uncovered the remains of over thirty human burials (Kieran, this volume). Their presence at this location indicates that the graveyard formerly extended beyond the modern perimeter, in the direction of Haggard Street. Indeed, the curve of Haggard Street at this location may preserve the original line of the cemetery, or (one of) the church enclosure(s). Of particular significance is the fact that the one burial that has so far been dated has produced a calibrated radiocarbon date of AD780–1030 (Table 1.2). This demonstrates that burials were taking place here from the ninth or tenth century, if not earlier. Even if this goes no way towards proving a fifth-century origin for the church site at Trim, it certainly gives very strong support for the identification of this location as the site of a pre-Anglo-Norman church, and probably the one that was in use at the time the *Additamenta* to the Book of Armagh were being composed in the late eighth century. Further dates are keenly awaited from this site, and the results of the analysis of the human remains will also be of great interest.

Elsewhere on Haggard Street, Clare Mullins directed excavations that uncovered the remains of a sequence of road-surfaces of medieval date (Mullins, this volume). The earliest cobbled surface identified seems to be older than those found anywhere else in the town, and this is particularly interesting in the light of Kieran's discovery just a hundred metres away. Mullins suggests that the cobbled surface and its associated walls, pits and gullies could be the remains of a pre-Anglo-Norman complex. Combined with the discovery here of a probable eleventh-century copper-alloy pin, this is further evidence for the Early Medieval development of this part of Trim. This is the third recorded pin of this type from Trim. One was found in 1842 and the second was recovered during excavations at the site of the Franciscan friary in 1999 (Pryor 1976, no. 63, pp 82, 86; Purcell 2000; Potterton 2005, 360–1 (fig. 10.5), 341).

It is likely that Haggard Street developed from a laneway that skirted the edge of the early ecclesiastical enclosure and that a secular settlement grew up under the shadow and protection of the church. It is possible that a church boundary continued in an arc that would have taken it through the point at which Church Lane and High Street now meet. If this trajectory is correct, then there should be no surprise that excavations directed by Alan Hayden on High Street uncovered evidence for pre-Anglo-Norman activity in this area (Hayden, 'High Street', this volume). It seems that pre-1170 occupation ended at this site some years before the arrival of the Anglo-Normans here acted as a catalyst for more intensive settlement and industry. Elsewhere on High Street, a section of ditch excavated by Claire Walsh in 1987, and interpreted by her as 'earlier than the Anglo-Norman occupation' (Walsh 1991, 46), could yet turn out to be part of an early church enclosure.

It is unlikely that Early Medieval settlement was confined to any one part of Trim, and evidence has recently been found for possible pre-Anglo-Norman activity at a number of other locations, including Emmet Street, Market Street and Trim Castle (Stephens, 'SubUrbia', this volume; Fallon, this volume; McCutcheon & Meenan, this volume).

Excavations are also beginning to shed light on the Early Medieval landscape in the vicinity of Trim. Burials of fifth-/sixth-century date were revealed at Peterstown in 1997 (Murphy 1998) and, more recently, Dominic Delany directed the excavation of twenty-four inhumations at Iffernock, 2.5km to the southeast of Trim (Delany & O'Hara, this volume). While no firm dates have been established for this burial ground, Delany and O'Hara believe that it is Early Medieval. Iffernock is one of surprisingly few places around Trim that retains its pre-Anglo-Norman name. The discovery of a possible Early Medieval cemetery is potentially more significant now, in the light of a recent discovery by Conor Newman and Eamonn O'Donoghue. Using aerial photography, Newman and O'Donoghue have identified a dense complex of inter-related earthworks in the townland of Iffernock, in the field adjacent to the excavated cemetery (Newman & O'Donoghue, Appendix 4.1). For now, little is known about these features, but they are probably Early Medieval in date, with possible Iron Age or older antecedents. Based on a preliminary examination, Newman and O'Donoghue are of the opinion that this could be a high-status site of some significance. Could this possible high-status Iron Age site be linked in some way with the above-mentioned second-/third-century BC hoard of pigs' feet on the banks of the Boyne at Trim, just 2km away?

Medieval Trim

Town defences Little is known about Trim's earliest urban defences. The enclosing stone wall, of which only fragmentary stretches survive, was the latest incarnation of a fortified boundary that probably began as a ditch and bank, topped by a timber palisade. Even the line of the defences is likely to have fluctuated over time, in some areas at least. Donal Fallon directed the excavation of a substantial ditch that ran east-west along Emmet Street, and he believes that this was an early town boundary (Fallon, this volume). The ditch was at least 2.2m deep and 5–6m wide and remained open through the thirteenth century. The section investigated by Fallon may be a continuation of a large ditch discovered by Rosanne Meenan extending east-west across the northern end of Market Street (Meenan 1996, 6–8). If such a town boundary existed, it would be on a significantly different line to that of the later stone wall. The difference between the two lines would also indicate the extent to which the town had expanded by the end of the thirteenth century, if indeed that is when the stone wall along the back of the Emmet Street plots was originally built (at the time of the 1290 murage grant). Fallon confirmed that the ditch was filled-in deliberately, possibly with the remains of its internal defensive bank. This would have cleared the way for the westward expansion of the town and the carefully-planned layout of new property plots towards the end of the thirteenth century.

The stone walls that were eventually built around the town were punctuated by at least five defended gates. The Sheep Gate (fig. 1.8), on the east side, is the only surviving example, but photographs survive of one other – the Water Gate (fig. 1.7; Potterton 2005, 186–7). The site of the so-called Dublin Gate, on Emmet Street, is known, while the former location of two other gates is recalled in the place-names Athboy Gate and Navan Gate. Excavations at Navan Gate recently uncovered the remains of a ditch, two pits and a small wall (Shine et al., this volume). While no physical remains were found of the gate itself, the ditch came to an end at the site on which it is thought to have stood. More definitive evidence for another town gate was identified by Matthew Seaver at Athboy Gate (Seaver, 'Porta Via', this volume). Here, a ditch measuring 4.6m in width and 1.6m in depth was radiocarbon-dated to 1280–1400 cal. AD, based on a bone sample recovered from a deposit within it (Table 1.2). Thirteenth-/fourteenth-century pottery was also recovered, as

1.7 The Water Gate, viewed from the south. This photograph, by J.W. Shackleton, was taken at Easter 1890 (courtesy of Mary Shackleton)

well as a fragment of human skull. Waterlogged deposits in the ditch suggest that it may have been water-filled. A curving stone structure was built into the southern terminal of the ditch, and a large wall-base was almost certainly part of the town wall.

In the southwest corner of the town, the curtain wall of the castle must have doubled as town defences. Outside this wall was a water-filled moat, which provided an extra measure of security. The span of the arch at the barbican gate gives a false impression of the scale of the moat, and recent excavations in this area indicate that it was at least ten and possibly twenty metres wide, and up to two and a half metres deep (Stephens, 'Empty space', this volume). Further excavations by O'Carroll (this volume) on Castle Street suggest that the moat was 15–17m wide. It is not clear how the castle wall and the town wall joined, if indeed they connected at all. Perhaps the town wall running eastwards from Dublin Gate simply ran up to the edge of the moat, with spiked bars or timbers projecting over the side of the moat from the end of the wall. It is also possible that chains were hung across the moat from wall to wall (John Bradley, pers. comm.).

A large twelfth- to early thirteenth-century ditch excavated by Alan Hayden at the east end of Market Street was at least 3–5m in width and up to 2m in depth (Hayden, 'Market Street', this volume; fig. 1.8). It is possible that this feature marks the outer defences of the castle at its north-western extent. Perhaps the ditch (partly?) enclosed land that was subsequently granted to the Franciscans for their friary some time in the second quarter of the thirteenth century.

The streets Clare Mullins' excavations on Haggard Street indicated that the cobbled street surfaces of the medieval town were periodically re-levelled and re-surfaced (Mullins, this volume). The chronology and characteristics of this street parallel the sequences revealed elsewhere in the town, as on High Street, Mill Street and Navan Gate Street (see, for example, Shine et al., this volume). Mullins also found evidence for a phased northward expansion along Haggard Street, in the direction of Athboy Gate. Among the artefacts recovered were horseshoes, horseshoe nails, a rowel spur and fragments of leather shoes, all of which were probably lost or discarded during the day-to-day hustle and bustle on a busy street. The dating evidence suggests that Haggard Street was at its busiest in the thirteenth century, and this ties in well with the other indications that Trim was a prosperous and expanding town at this time. Interestingly, there appears to have been another period of heightened activity in the sixteenth century. Throughout the middle ages, the general pattern suggests that domestic refuse and weeds were allowed to accumulate on the street surfaces in Trim (Shine et al., this volume).

Housing Recent excavations have uncovered the remains of several medieval houses in Trim. An excavation directed by Donal Fallon on Market Street revealed the stone foundations of a possible sill-beam house (Fallon, this volume). The narrow end of the building would have faced onto the street, while the area behind the house included a cess-pit, refuse pits and a dry-stone well. The pits contained pottery of late thirteenth- and fourteenth-century date, as well as a ceramic roof-tile and macrofossil remains reflective of domestic waste. Further east on Market Street, Alan Hayden excavated the remains of a probable fourteenth-/fifteenth-century building (Hayden, 'Market Street', this volume). Little of the house survived, but the hearth was located, and the discovery of various tiles indicated the manner in which the building had been floored and roofed. Outside, the remains of a possible cess-pit and well were identified. The house seems to have been abandoned in the sixteenth century.

Hayden's excavation of the vestiges of several houses on High Street has provided further evidence for the manner of construction and the appearance of domestic building in the town in the thirteenth and fourteenth centuries (Hayden, 'High Street', this volume; Hayden 2001). Among the finds were line-impressed floor-tiles, peg roof-tiles, fragments of curved roof-tiles and a fragment of green-glazed cockscomb ridge-tile. There was a hearth and a cess-pit, as well as a possible kiln and evidence for extensive metalworking. The impression is that the metalworking areas were focused on the street-front, rather than behind the properties, and this is unusual. Hayden concludes that High Street was little developed at the time. Nonetheless, Carmel Duffy excavated the remains of another house on High Street, which, on the basis of the assemblage of ceramics, was also thirteenth-to-fourteenth century in date (Duffy, this volume). The house appears to have been stone-built, with a slated roof. Several roof-tiles were also recovered. The refuse pits contained cereal remains, animal bone and, unexpectedly, fragments of human bone.

Two houses of late thirteenth- to fourteenth-century date were excavated by Mandy Stephens on Emmet Street (Stephens, 'SubUrbia', this volume). One was 7m by 6m and the other measured 5m by 3m. Beneath these structures there was evidence for earlier, post-and-stake-built structures. Before the later houses were built, the ground was built-up and levelled out. The houses appear to have been roofed with tiles and floored with stone, although some floor-tiles were also recovered. They were probably timber-framed. A wooden latch that was recovered probably came from one of the doors. Behind the houses were ancillary buildings that may have functioned as toilet facilities. One cess-pit appears to have had a wooden toilet seat. The yards behind the houses provided evidence for various industrial activities (discussed further below).

In general, our understanding of the appearance of Trim's medieval houses is still sketchy, but we are now starting to fill in some of the gaps. Even the occasional discovery of architectural fragments adds to our knowledge. Take, for example, the stray window mullion and a decorated floor-tile from Market Street (Fallon, this volume), the pieces of wood, roof-tiles and slates from Haggard Street (Mullins, this volume), or the perforated roofing slate from Athboy Gate (Seaver). Curved ceramic roof-tiles have been found in several locations on Market Street (Hayden; Fallon, this volume). The lime-pit found on the same street may have served in the preparation of mortar to render the exterior of wooden buildings, while the presence of small, sharp-edged fragments of wood suggest that carpentry took place here, perhaps as part of the construction or maintenance of the houses.

Industry The expanding corpus of archaeological evidence for medieval Trim continues to throw light on the extent, range and importance of industry in the development of the town. Many households appear to have operated at least some small-scale domestic industry at the back of their property. Beglane has interpreted the cattle horn-cores and goat horn-cores from Market Street as a likely indication both that slaughter and primary butchery were taking place on-site and that a tanner or horn-worker was based there (Beglane, 'Meat and craft', this volume; Fallon, this volume). The age of the animals at death also suggests that horn was being imported onto the site from elsewhere. On High Street, evidence for metalworking included nails, horse-shoes, knives, much iron and copper slag and fragments of copper alloy (Hayden, 'High Street', this volume). Metal-production was only one of the activities performed at Emmet Street, where bone-, wood- and leather-working, as well as linen-processing were also carried out. Horn-working and tanning or bleaching may also have been practiced here. The discovery of a loom-weight and shears indicate that wool may have been processed on-site, and fragments of wool cloth with a herring-bone weave were found at Athboy Gate (Seaver, this volume). Elsewhere in the volume, there is evidence for dying, button-making, flax-processing and possible vellum-production.

It has long been recognized that a distinctive local wheel-thrown pottery-type was in use in Trim in the late thirteenth century. It is similar to other later-thirteenth- and fourteenth-century finewares found in Dublin and Kilkenny (McCutcheon & Meenan, this volume). Despite the fact that Trim-type ware is regularly found on excavations (for instances, see in this volume, Stephens, 'SubUrbia'; Mullins; Duffy; Seaver et al.; McCutcheon, Appendices 12.1, 15.3, pl. 13), the location of its production remains unknown.

Despite the fact that no kiln has yet been found, there is increasing evidence that cereal-drying was being carried out within and outside the town. Carbonized grains, and weed seeds associated with arable crops have been found at a number of sites. Cobain concluded that the charred barley and oat grains in samples retrieved from Navan Gate Street were likely to have 'originated from rake-out waste from the stoking areas of a corn-drying kiln or

1.8 Aerial photograph of Trim, showing the castle and the southwest quadrant of the town. The general locations of some of the excavations reported on in the present volume are marked (A: Stephens, 'Empty space'; B: Hayden, 'Market Street'; C: O'Carroll, 'Castle Street'). The bridge (D) and the Sheep Gate (E), with a partially surviving section of the town wall, are also shown. The origin and function of the tree-topped semi-circular earthen bank (F) remain to be established

from a domestic fire used to dry or process grain' (Appendix 7.1). Deposits at High Street contained oats, barley, wheat and rye, as well as chaff, suggesting that primary cereal-processing was carried out here (Lyons, Appendix 12.3). Elsewhere in the town, such as at Athboy Gate, Market Street and Kiely's Yard (Seaver; Fallon; Stephens, 'SubUrbia', this volume), the absence of chaff in samples that contained other cereal remains, suggests that cereal-processing did not take place at these sites, and that it was carried out elsewhere, perhaps at dedicated locations. The Dominicans would almost certainly have been self-sufficient, and the discovery at the Black Friary site of 'rake-out waste from stoking areas of the corn-drying kiln' was not a surprise (Cobain, Appendix 15.1). Oak and ash charcoal in the same samples is likely to derive from kiln-fuel, while the fragments of wild cherry, willow, holly and alder/hazel are probably the remains of kindling. Chaff may also have been brought into the town separately, perhaps in cart-loads, as it had an economic value in its own right (John Bradley, pers. comm.), probably as a fuel or as bedding.

Trade There can be little doubt about the importance of trade to the development and expansion of Trim through the middle ages. Its location on the banks of the Boyne in the heartland of fertile Meath lands, just 35km by river from Drogheda and 40km over land from Dublin, gave it a strong platform from which to increase its wealth and to expand its commercial contacts. The river provided Trim with an important trade-artery and a link with Drogheda and the Irish Sea. This is underlined by the frequent discovery of the remains of salt-water fish and marine molluscs in medieval contexts in the town (Stephens, 'SubUrbia'; Beglane, 'Meat and craft'; Fallon, this volume; Duffy, this volume).

A range of documentary sources, but especially murage grants, provide a good overview of the types of items that were bought and sold at the weekly market and the annual fair. The picture can now be supplemented with information coming from recent excavations. In particular, there is increasing evidence for overseas contacts. The discovery of a grape-seed on High Street suggests that certain luxury foodstuffs were being imported, probably in a dried form, from countries such as France or Spain (Lyons, Appendix 12.3). Similarly, fig seeds have been recovered from medieval contexts on Market Street and at Athboy Gate (Cobain, Appendix 10.1; Seaver, this volume). Like grapes and walnuts, figs are likely to have been imported into medieval Ireland.

The most frequently found indicator of trade is pottery. The overall assemblage from Trim is now extremely substantial (McCutcheon & Meenan, this volume). In the late twelfth and early thirteenth century, most of the wares used in Trim were imported. Ham Green ware from England and Saintonge ware from France are the most commonly encountered imported ceramics in Trim (Fallon; Hayden, 'Market Street'; Hayden, 'High Street'; McCutcheon & Meenan, this volume). Further English wares, including Minety, Redcliffe and Chester wares, were found during excavations at the castle. The clay for the roof-tiles at Trim Castle may also have been English. Imported wares were quickly overtaken by locally-produced vessels, however, and the vast majority of the medieval pottery found in Trim was locally-made or brought in from Dublin. Smaller quantities of Drogheda-type ware have also been recovered, as well as Leinster Cooking Ware (Hayden, 'High Street'; Mullins; Seaver; McCutcheon & Meenan; pl. 14). In later contexts at the castle, sherds of Normandy ware and Merida-type ware from the Iberian Peninsula were also found. Of course, the recovery of these imported wares in various contexts and at various sites in Trim does not necessarily mean that the townspeople or even the residents of the castle were in direct contact with sources in England, France, Spain or elsewhere – although they may have been – but it does underline the fact that Trim was part of an extensive trade network and that other goods from these locations may also have ended up in Trim.

Religious houses There were three major religious houses in Trim in the middle ages – Augustinian, Franciscan and Dominican. Little survives at any of these sites, but the Yellow Steeple and parts of Talbot's Castle originally formed part of the Augustinian house on the north bank of the Boyne. The location of the Franciscan friary – on the site now occupied by the courthouse – is well-attested, but the position of the graveyard and its extent remained matters of conjecture until very recently. Excavations directed by Finola O'Carroll on Castle Street have helped to clarify these matters (O'Carroll, this volume; fig. 1.8). The discovery of a series of formal burials under the street indicates that the friary cemetery was located to the southwest of the main complex and that the present line of the street does not reflect its medieval antecedent. While the burials included adults, children and infants, all of those that could be sexed appear to have been male. Little is known about the architecture of the friary, but fragments continue to come to light. The heads protruding from a cottage beside the old bridge, the pieces of arch recovered from the river, a window mullion excavated in 2000 and various other disparate pieces all seem to have once formed part of the monastic complex (Potterton 2005, 340–2). A fragment of line-impressed tile unearthed by O'Carroll may have been part of a floor in the friary (fig. 14.4, pl. 5).

The site of the Dominican friary, outside the line of the town walls, was the subject of a campaign of geophysical research in the 1980s. While the results were inconclusive, they provided a useful base-line for future research. Recent excavations at the Black Friary, as it was known, have been able to build on this initial survey (Seaver et al., this volume). The regularity and uniformity of medieval religious houses make it possible to anticipate the location of the various components of the monastic complex once one or more parts have been identified. The 2008 excavations identified a series of twelve or more burials to the southwest of the former site of the main friary buildings. One grave contained multiple burials. At least one individual (the only one so far radiocarbon-dated) died in the fifteenth or sixteenth century, probably before the friary was dissolved in 1540 (Table 1.2). As with the burials at the Franciscan friary, all of those that could be sexed appear to have been male. Also uncovered during the excavations were a gully and a series of post-holes, a possibly timber-lined well and indirect evidence for a cereal-drying kiln. There were seventy-two acres of land attached to the Black Friary, and much of this would have been in arable production. Indeed, samples from the well included grains of wheat, oats and barley (Cobain, Appendix 15.1). It stands to reason that the friars would have had a kiln to dry the damp grains brought in from the fields. Cereal crops were an important resource that provided thatch, bedding, fodder, fuel, flour and beer. The orchard at the friary was probably the source of the crab-apple seeds and cherry wood fragments that were also retrieved from the well.

More death and burial In addition to the burials associated with St Patrick's Church and with the Franciscan and Dominican friaries, human remains have been recovered at a range of unexpected locations, outside formal burial grounds. A skull fragment was found in the ditch at Athboy Gate (Seaver, this volume), while bones from at least four individuals were identified on one of the sites at High Street – one child aged between eight and ten years at death, one female aged between seventeen and twenty-five, and two other adults (Lynch, Appendix 12.2). Outside the curtain wall of the castle, the remains of six individuals were found in an informal cemetery of late thirteenth- or fourteenth-century date (Coughlan, Appendices 5.1–5.3). All of those whose sex could be determined were male, and all appear to have been under twenty-five years of age at death. Several of them bore the marks of wounds and other injuries. Could these young men have been victims of the Plague? Or perhaps they were prisoners who died while in captivity in the castle prison? The deaths of several prisoners at the castle are recorded in the fourteenth century (Potterton 2005, 93, 225, 226, 413–14).

Landscape and environment Refined sampling strategies and improved techniques of laboratory analysis have facilitated a revolution in the depth and range of information that can be deduced from the study of palaeo-environmental remains from archaeological sites. It is because of this that we are now able to piece together an image of the natural environment and the agricultural landscape in and around medieval Trim (Cobain, Appendices 7.1, 10.1, 15.1; Lyons, Appendices 8.2, 12.3). The image that is emerging shows that there were orchards producing apples and cherries and gardens producing fruit, vegetables (including cabbage) and herbs (including fennel) within the town. Wild fruit, berries (hawthorn, elder, blackberry) and nuts (hazel) probably grew on the outskirts of the town, while more extensive woodland consisted of oak, ash and willow trees, with an under-storey of alder, hazel and holly. There may have been stretches of alder-carr scrubland along the banks of the Boyne. Agriculture in the hinterland seems to have been divided between animal production and arable cultivation. Wheat, barley and oats, and to a lesser extent rye were grown. In addition to agricultural produce, the hinterland of the town provided timber for construction and manufacture and other wood for fuel and craft, as well as other resources such as moss, stone and clay.

The range of animals represented in the archaeological record from Trim is normal for medieval sites in Ireland (for examples, see Lofqvist, Appendix 8.1; Beglane, 'Meat and craft', this volume). Cattle normally dominate the assemblages, with smaller numbers of sheep, goats, pigs, horses, dogs and cats. The frequency of sheep increases in the later thirteenth century, perhaps as a result of a growing export trade in wool. At Athboy Gate, there was an unusually high proportion of horse, one of which was an older individual with evidence that it had served as a draught-horse or for carrying loads. Cut-marks on cattle bones from the same site were most likely associated with the slaughter process, and the chopped up diaphyses suggest that marrow had been extracted. Deer bones of medieval date are most frequently found on high-status sites (Beglane, 'Meat and craft', this volume), but recently they have also been recovered from sites on High Street (Duffy, this volume) and Market Street (Fallon, this volume). The different parts of the deer that are represented in different parts of the town can be used to inform a discussion of the roles, functions and status of these places and their inhabitants, and the inter-relationships between them (Beglane, 'Meat and craft', this volume). It is possible that the deer were gifted to the residents of High Street and Market Street, but it is more likely that they were poached from the park. The remains of duck, geese and other birds are occasionally found, as well as fish and shellfish.

Diet and health Recent analyses of the contents of medieval cess-pits and refuse dumps, and the close study of human remains is fleshing out our understanding of the diet and health-status of the inhabitants of Trim in the middle ages. Most of the animals mentioned above would have been exploited for their meat (as well as other resources and by-products), and the various vegetables, cereals, fruits and nuts would also have formed part of the diet. Wealthier individuals appear to have had access to imported foods such as figs and grapes, as well as seafood and venison. At the other end of the scale, skeletal evidence indicates that at least some individuals suffered from iron-deficiency and poor nutrition during childhood (Stephens, 'Empty Space', this volume; Coughlan, Appendices 5.1–5.3).

Osteo-archaeological studies have also demonstrated the range of illnesses, injuries and other health problems suffered by the town's inhabitants. There is a general pattern of relatively poor oral hygiene, with calculus, caries, abscesses and tooth-loss noted in several instances, even in young individuals (Coughlan, Appendices 5.1–5.3; Fibiger, Appendix 14.1). Some individuals, notably males, suffered from degenerative joint disease and wear, probably related to physical stress, heavy lifting and/or manual labour. One individual buried at the Franciscan friary was found to have suffered from Legg-Calve-Perthes disease. This person would surely have walked – if he or she walked at all – with a pronounced limp.

Among the individuals excavated by Stephens outside the castle walls, one male was suffering from an infection that affected the ribs, while another had congenital or traumatic fusion of two vertebrae (Coughlan, Appendices 5.1–5.3).

There was evidence for a well-healed leg-break, but another individual suffered a severe blade-wound to the skull. The absence of any signs of healing indicates that this wound was fatal. A man buried at the Dominican friary suffered a similar wound, but this appears to have healed for several weeks before death occurred (Travers, Appendix 15.2). He was also one of several individuals who had suffered a broken arm, one of which had healed badly and must have affected the victim in a serious way. On the other hand, one broken wrist had healed very well, and may even have been splinted.

It is known that there was a leper hospital in Trim from at least the fourteenth century, and there was another hospital at Newtown Trim, but little is known about the care and treatment that patients received. Sarah Cobain has identified a range of plant species in samples from Market Street – opium cannabis, poppy, fennel, flax and drug fumitory – that may have been used as pain-killing drugs and as cures for other ailments such as cuts, bruises, liver disorders and eczema (Cobain, Appendix 10.1). However they may have been treated, it seems that despite some run-of-the-mill accidents and the odd dramatic attack, the population of medieval Trim was fairly healthy, and most enjoyed a reasonably balanced diet. The majority of those for whom calculations could be made were of average stature for the time. You understand the point she is making when Cobain states that the 'individuals were in relatively good health at the time of death'.

Post-medieval
There is an increasing body of archaeological evidence to supplement the documented history of Trim in the post-medieval period. While this is not a focus of the current volume, it is a subject that will be returned to in future publications. Post-medieval pottery and tiles are regularly found on excavations in the town (for instance, see Duffy; Hayden, 'High Street', this volume), and some post-medieval structures and features are reported on in brief below (Fallon; Seaver et al., 'Black Friary'; Shine & Seaver; Stephens, 'Empty space'; Stephens, 'SubUrbia', this volume). Outside the town, one of the cemeteries excavated by Dominic Delany at Iffernock may be post-medieval in date, and the results of this investigation provide information on a community living and dying in the hinterland of Trim at this time (Delany & O'Hara, this volume).

PART III: WHAT WE STILL DON'T KNOW, AND HOW WE MIGHT FIND OUT

Even in the few years since the publication of the *Irish Historic Towns Atlas* for Trim (2004) and *Medieval Trim: history and archaeology* (2005), there has been significant progress in our overall understanding of the development through the ages of this small market town. And of course, an improved understanding of the evolution of Trim contributes to an appreciation of urban development right across the country. Trim is unique in many respects, but it is also typical in many others.

While some questions have been answered, many others remain to be addressed, and the answers to the first set have generated a whole new series of enquiries. It is clear that the final word on the story of Trim can never be written. But to advance our knowledge further, it is also clear that a broad, collaborative and inter-disciplinary approach has to be taken. Archaeology is central to this. All future construction and infrastructural projects need to be carefully monitored, and comprehensive archaeological excavation will continue to be essential in many cases. Many of the papers in the present volume demonstrate the importance of carefully-planned sampling strategies and the indispensability of specialist analysis in extracting the greatest amount of information from even small archaeological excavations. The role of the specialist should begin even before the excavation starts, and not just after it has ended. Methods and formats for the recording and presentation of all sorts of data need to be standardized to facilitate comparative analysis.

Close dating of the archaeological vestiges revealed through excavation is not always possible, but the nature of the damp, alluvial and waterlogged soils in and around Trim is such that organic remains can sometimes survive very well. Several of the papers in the present volume demonstrate the importance of radiocarbon-dating in establishing a chronology for the major phases of development in the town (Table 1.2), and it is essential that all future archaeological investigation involves a programme of systematic organic sample retrieval and dating. Indeed it may also be possible to send for dating some samples that have been retained from excavations that took place within the town before the use of radiocarbon-dating was as widespread as it is now. Dendrochronological analysis was central to determining the sequence of construction of the keep of Trim Castle (Condit 1996), and it is likely that this dating method will also have an important role to play in cases where larger oak timbers survive elsewhere in the town.

The prospect of development should not be the only driving force behind archaeological investigation, and research-led approaches ought to be taken at sites that would otherwise be unstudied. In particular, targeted campaigns of geophysical prospection should be carried out at the Black Friary, around the Yellow Steeple, and indeed right across the Porchfields. While it is a great pity that so little survives aboveground at these locations, it is fortunate that they survive as green-field sites. Trim is in an enviable position in this regard, with great opportunities for future programmes of research, especially around its former monastic complexes. Outside the town, Newman and O'Donoghue have identified a complex of earthworks in the townland of Iffernock. For now, these have been signalled at least, but they need to be carefully surveyed and studied, and protected from future development that might damage them or impinge upon their integrity.

Other questions that remain to be answered relate to the nature and extent of prehistoric activity and settlement in the area, and the location and form of the Early Medieval secular site. Now that the site of an early church has been located, we can start to think more about what it may have looked like, and whether or not there were cross-slabs and high crosses and other such features. Was there a round tower (Potterton 2005, 60–1)? In terms of medieval Trim, there are hundreds of questions to be answered. There is no obvious way to organize these questions, but they seem to fall into a series of categories:

1) Precise topographical questions
These questions relate to the location and form of buildings and features, such as the town walls, gates and mural towers; the road through the Sheep Gate linking Trim with Newtown Trim; the market cross; the documented mills on the Boyne; and the ford. What was the origin and function of the semi-circular tree-topped earthen bank next to the river to the east of the Sheep Gate (fig. 1.8F)? Where were the frank-house, the tholsel and the guildhall? Where was the 'Park of Trim' located? Where did the annual fair take place? What was the arrangement at the points where the town walls met the river? What was the layout of the Augustinian priory? It is likely that the answers to these and other similar questions will be discovered through excavation and non-invasive archaeological prospection.

2) General topographical questions
More general questions relate to the whole question of the origins and evolution of the town of Trim, and of its various components – the castle, the parish church, the religious houses, the streets, the domestic buildings, the industrial features, the urban defences. What were the main stages of growth? When did the town begin to decline and what are the indicators of this? Issues such as these are best approached in an interdisciplinary manner, especially through the research of archaeologists, architectural historians and historical geographers.

3) Environmental questions
There is increasing interest in the development of urban landscapes, and also in the natural landscape in the vicinity of towns. How extensive was the woodland in the vicinity of Trim? What are the indications of climate-change over time? How different was the Boyne from today, and how often and how extensively did it flood? It is clear from several of the contributions to the present volume that answers to many of these questions can be found through

the careful scientific analysis of palaeo-environmental remains retrieved during excavation.

4) Economic questions

It is evident that the inhabitants of medieval Trim were self-sufficient in many respects. It is also clear that there was a great deal of interaction between the town and its hinterland. The town was supplied with food, fuel and raw materials from the countryside, and rural-dwellers were able to sell their surpluses at the market, and to provision themselves for the week ahead. The range and scale of urban industry is becoming clearer, but it is not entirely clear what Trim derived its economic livelihood from. Nor are the nature and extent of its trade networks fully understood. What was the extent and nature of river traffic on the Boyne? How far outside the town did Trim-type wares penetrate? What was the zone of circulation of coinage from the Trim mint in the fifteenth century? Questions like these underline the importance of research outside the town, and the ways in which the work that is being carried out in one area is of importance to researchers in another.

5) Demographic questions

In many respects, population figures are closely tied to the other sets of questions. But estimating population sizes is a notoriously difficult task – so much so that there is still no satisfactory figure for the size of medieval Dublin, the most intensively studied town in the country. How many people lived in Trim in the middle ages? How did the population fluctuate? What areas of the town were densely inhabited and when? The answers to these questions relate directly to other issues such as the scale of local industry, the role of the market, the size of the parish church, fuel and food consumption, the provision of water, and standards of living. The best approach might be theoretical, and it will surely involve careful metrical analysis of the property plots in the town and its suburbs. This should be combined with a study of the excavated evidence for house sizes and the identification of their most intensive periods of usage. Perhaps the most important factor will be the estimation of household sizes.

6) Social questions

A more careful analysis of the demographic make-up of medieval Trim is necessary. What were the ethnic divisions through the centuries? What was the role of the betaghs and where did they live? Who were the wealthiest members of society and where did they live? Who were the poor and how were they treated? The answers to some of these questions have so far been elusive, but key indicators may be found through artefact studies, place-name analysis, and the systematic listing of personal names recorded in documentary sources relating to Trim.

7) Historical questions
Even some of the watershed moments in the development of Trim remain
shrouded in uncertainty. Little is known about the transition from monastery
to Anglo-Norman town, or the impact of the Black Death, or the ways in
which the town was affected by the dissolution of the monasteries. There
seems to be some evidence for a revival in the town's fortunes in the sixteenth
century. If this is the case, why? And what were the consequences? There is
more primary documentary source material for the history of medieval Trim
than many people realize. Much of this has already been looked at, but the
nature of the documents and the fact that so many of them are not in Ireland
have meant that a lot of historical source analysis remains to be carried out. A
systematic trawl through all of the sources relating to medieval Ireland would
be an enormous task, but it could prove to be worthwhile. In the mean time,
chance discoveries of references to medieval Trim do continue to be made.

8) Cultural questions
It is clear that religion played an important role in the daily lives of the
townspeople in the middle ages, but the details of this are not clear. Even less is
known about the role of art in the town. Were the sculptures in St Patrick's
Cathedral produced locally? Were there others like them? What do these
carvings reveal about the sculptor and the patron? Who was responsible for the
other medieval carved stone heads that survive near the bridge, at Nangle's
Castle and at the leper hospital? What was the role of music and song in the
town, or in the religious houses? Where were the taverns and inns, and what
were they like? What is the origin of the names 'Yellow Steeple', 'Rogues'
Castle' and 'Sheep Gate'? What was the mix of languages spoken on a daily
basis, and how did this change over time? Answers to some of these questions
can be hinted at through archaeology, but this is one of those groups that
would be best approached from an interdisciplinary perspective.

There are ways in which aspects of the corpus of archaeological data can be
inserted into a historical framework, and many examples of how documented
events can be used to explain archaeological discoveries. This is all very well.
On the other hand, there are times that archaeological approaches are best
embarked upon in isolation from an established narrative. An example might
be using archaeology to reveal the environment of medieval Trim, or investigating the population make-up more closely through osteoarchaeology, or
tracing the development of animal-husbandry, or charting the evolution of
diet, health, hygiene and sanitation.

In the meantime, while we are mulling over these and other questions, there
needs to be a comprehensive and coherent strategy for dealing with the
archive, the finds and especially the data recovered from past, present and

future archaeological work, in all its forms. This would include architectural surveys and post-graduate theses, graveyard studies and chance finds. A worthwhile project in the short-term would be the compilation of a complete catalogue of all known medieval architectural fragments in the town. There needs to be a forum for the discussion and presentation of research results.

Trim is a member of the Irish Walled Towns Network. Within the past year, Conservation and Management Plans have been drawn up for the town walls (Meenan, this volume). These documents address the preservation, maintenance and presentation of the town's medieval defences. They identify the primary threats to the fabric and integrity of the walls, prioritize necessary works and recommend the establishment of a management group to take charge of the future conservation, management and presentation of the walls.

There is a clear appetite for knowledge relating to the development of Trim through the ages. It is imperative that this healthy curiosity is matched by a determination to conserve what remains of the town's ancient character and heritage. The explosion in infrastructural development is over for now, and there has been a steady decrease in archaeological excavation in Trim over the past three years (fig. 1.6). It seems that the heady days of ten or twelve excavations a year in Trim have come to an end. Now is a time to gather together the results of the one hundred or so excavations that have taken place, and to reflect on what it all means. It is a time to present the results of this research to as wide an audience as possible and to plan where to go from here.

ACKNOWLEDGMENTS

I have discussed various aspects of this paper with a number of individuals and I would like to thank the following for their assistance in one form or another: Chris Corlett, Noel Dempsey, Martin Fanning, Loreto Guinan, Steve Mandal, Conor McDermott, Rosanne Meenan, Margaret Murphy, Kevin O'Brien, Finola O'Carroll, Kieran O'Conor and Rob Sands. I am especially grateful to Michael Ann Bevivino, John Bradley and Matthew Seaver for their comments on an earlier draft of this paper.

Table 1.1 Radiocarbon dates mentioned in the text. The Loman Street site is still being excavated (24 April 2009), and is not reported on in the current publication. The table was prepared by Matthew Seaver; all dates are calibrated using Bronk Ramsey 2005

Paper/ excavation	Lab. code (68.2%)	Sample (95.4%)	BP date	Context dated	1 Sigma cal.	2 Sigma cal.
Beglane, 'Pigs'	Wk-22788	Pig metacarpal	2172±37BP	Peat deposits	360–170BC	370–110BC
Beglane, 'Pigs'	Wk-24915	Cattle pisiform	2089±30BP	Peat deposits	170–50BC	200–40BC
Kieran	LuS 7860	Human bone	1105±50BP	Skeleton 26	AD880–990	AD780–1030
*Seaver, Loman St	Wk-25840	Human proximal phalange	1500±30BP	Burial	AD540–600 (68%)	AD430–640
Stephens, 'Empty'	Wk-21543	Human bone	685±30BP	B142	AD1581–1665	AD1535–1680
Stephens, 'Empty'	Wk-21542	Human bone	647±34BP	B33	AD1280–1390	AD1280–1400
Stephens, 'SubUrbia'	Wk-22840	Unid. seeds	580±32BP	Phase 2b hearth deposit F547	AD1315–1410	AD1290–1420
Stephens, 'SubUrbia'	Wk-22839	Unid. seeds	364±32BP	Phase 2c stone-lined pit F601	AD1450–1630	AD1440–1640
Stephens, 'SubUrbia'	Wk-22838	Hazel	855±35BP	Phase 2b F659 fill of pit F766	AD1155–1225	AD1040–1270
Stephens, 'SubUrbia'	Wk-22837	Hazel	809±33BP	Phase 2 pit with lime	AD1210–1265	AD1160–1280
Stephens, 'SubUrbia'	Wk-22836	Hazel	884±36BP	Phase 1 hearth F550	AD1050–1220	AD1030–1220
Stephens, 'SubUrbia'	Wk-22835	Pomoideae	782±32BP	Phase 2 pit with lime	AD1220–1270	AD1205–1285
Stephens, 'SubUrbia'	Wk-21540	Hazel	920±32BP	Phase 2a fill F744 of gully F743	AD1040–1160	AD1020–1190
Stephens, 'SubUrbia'	Wk-21541	Pomoideae	870±32BP	Phase 2a F795 fill of cess-pit F825	AD1050–1220	AD1040–1260
Shine & Seaver	Wk-25659	Animal bone	678±30BP	Deposit within ditch	AD1270–1390	AD1270–1390
Seaver	Wk-23891	Unid. bone	625±30BP	Organic deposit at base of ditch	AD1295–1395	AD1280–1400
Fallon	Wk-25661	Cattle tibia	885±37BP	Lower ditch deposits	AD1050–1220	AD1030–1220
Fallon	Wk-25660	Cattle horn-core	925±30BP	Metalled surfaces under bank	AD1040–1169	AD1020–1180
Seaver et al.	Wk-24840	Human bone	519±30BP	Burial cutting well	AD1415–1490	AD1390–1530 (87.3%) AD1550–1630 (8.1%)

* This date was received as the book was going to press.

BIBLIOGRAPHY

Aalen, F.H.A., Whelan, K., & Stout, M. (eds), 1997, *Atlas of the Irish rural landscape*. Cork.
Bartlett, R., & Mackay, A. (eds), 1989, *Medieval frontier societies*. Oxford.
Berry, H.F. (ed.), 1907, *Statutes and ordinances, and acts of the parliament of Ireland, King John to Henry V*. Dublin.
Bhreathnach, E., 1999, 'Authority and supremacy in Tara and its hinterland *c*.950–1200', *Discovery Programme Reports* **5**, 1–23. Dublin.
Bradley, J., 1988–9, 'The medieval towns of Meath', *Ríocht na Midhe* **8:2**, 30–49.
Bradley, J., 1998, 'The monastic town of Clonmacnoise' in King, H. (ed.), *Clonmacnoise studies* 1, 42–55.
Bronk Ramsey, C., 2005, 'OxCal progam v3.10'. Online: http://www.rlaha.ox.ac.uk/O/oxcal.php (accessed 22 April 2009).
Condit, T., 1996, 'Rings of truth at Trim Castle, Co. Meath', *Archaeology Ireland* **10:3** (autumn), 30–3.
Curtis, E., 1936, 'Rental of the manor of Lisronagh, 1333, and notes on "betagh" tenure in medieval Ireland', *Proceedings of the Royal Irish Academy* **43C3** (February), 41–76.
Finch, T.F., Gardiner, M.J., Comey, A., & Radford, T., 1983, *Soils of Co. Meath*. Soil Survey Bulletin, 37. Dublin.
Gilbert, J.T. (ed.), 1884, *Chartularies of St Mary's Abbey, Dublin*. 2 vols. London.
Graham, B.J., 1980, 'The mottes of the Norman liberty of Meath' in Murtagh, H. (ed.), *Irish midland studies: essays in commemoration of N.W. English*. 39–56. Athlone.
Gwynn, J. (ed.), 1913, *Liber Ardmachanus: the Book of Armagh*. Dublin.
Hayden, A., 2001, '01E1146ext: excavation report, High Street, Trim'. Unpublished excavation report lodged with the National Monuments Service.
Hogan, E., 1910, *Onomasticon Goedelicum locorum et tribuum Hiberniae et Scotiae*. Dublin.
Hunnisett, R.F., 1961, *The medieval English coroner*. Cambridge.
Mac Niocaill, G., 1964. *Na buirgéisí xii–xv aois*. 2 vols. Dublin.
Mac Niocaill, G. (ed.), 1992, *Crown surveys of lands 1540–41, with the Kildare rental begun in 1518*. Dublin.
McNeill, C. (ed.), 1950, *Calendar of Archbishop Alen's register, c.1172–1534*. Dublin.
Meenan, R., 1996, 'Archaeological monitoring of excavations for Trim Water and Sewerage Scheme: licence no. 96E0175'. Unpublished excavation report.
Meenan, R., 1997, 'Trim' in Bennett, I. (ed.), *Excavations 1996: summary accounts of archaeological excavations in Ireland*, no. 315, p. 89. Bray.
Mills, J., & McEnery, M.J. (eds), 1916, *Calendar of the Gormanston register*. Dublin.
Murphy, D., 1998, 'Peterstown' in Bennett, I. (ed.), *Excavations 1997: summary accounts of archaeological excavations in Ireland*, no. 431, pp 143–4. Bray.
Orpen, G.H. (ed.), 1892, *The song of Dermot and the earl*. Oxford.
Orpen, G.H., 1911–20, *Ireland under the Normans, 1169–1333*. 4 vols. Oxford.
Otway-Ruthven, A.J., 1951, 'The organization of Anglo-Irish agriculture in the middle ages', *Journal of the Royal Society of Antiquaries of Ireland* **81**, 1–13.
Otway-Ruthven, A.J., 1968, *A history of medieval Ireland*. New York.
Potterton, M., 2005, *Medieval Trim: history and archaeology*. Dublin.
Pryor, F., 1976, 'A descriptive catalogue of some ancient Irish metalwork in the collections of The Royal Ontario Museum, Toronto', *Journal of the Royal Society of Antiquaries of Ireland* **106**, 73–91.
Purcell, A., 2000, 'Trim courthouse, Manorland, Trim' in Bennett, I. (ed.), *Excavations 1999: summary accounts of archaeological excavations in Ireland*, no. 721, pp 250–1. Bray.
Sheehy, M.P. (ed.), 1962–5, *Pontificia Hibernica: medieval papal chancery documents concerning Ireland, 640–1261*. 2 vols. Dublin.
Sweetman, P.D., 1978, 'Archaeological excavations at Trim Castle, Co. Meath, 1971–4', *Proceedings of the Royal Irish Academy* **78C**, 127–98.

Sweetman, P.D., 1999, *Medieval castles of Ireland*. Cork.

Tresham, E., 1828, *Rotulorum patentium et clausorum cancellariae Hiberniae calendarium*. Dublin.

Walsh, C., 1991, 'An excavation at the library site, High Street, Trim', *Ríocht na Midhe* 8:3, 41–67.

Wood, H. (ed.), 1932, 'The muniments of Edmund de Mortimer, third earl of March, concerning his liberty of Trim', *Proceedings of the Royal Irish Academy* 60C7 (May), 312–55.

Long pigs' feet from Iron Age Trim

FIONA BEGLANE

An enigmatic find of animal bones dating to the Iron Age was recovered from peaty deposits in the castle lawn area of the town of Trim (fig. 2.1). This consisted almost entirely of pig forelegs, a few bones from the forelegs of cattle and a small number of other animal bones. This paper considers the material with reference to the results of excavations at other prehistoric and Early Medieval sites, and in light of early documentary sources.

INTRODUCTION

According to the ninth-century Book of Armagh, Trim was the site of a monastery founded by St Loman, possibly as early as the fifth century, on the site of the royal residence of *Cenél Lóeguire Breg*, but little is known of what went before that, and even this may be more mythological than a record of actual events. There are no recorded prehistoric monuments in the immediate area of the town or its surroundings, although a number of Neolithic and Bronze Age artefacts have been found. Three Neolithic stone axes, two Middle Bronze Age palstaves, a Late Bronze Age looped spearhead and a gouge from the same period, were all chance finds. Excavation at the castle revealed some prehistoric pits and stray flint artefacts, a flint flake was recovered from the Library site on High Street, and recently two burnt mounds were excavated on the Athboy Road, one of which yielded a Late Neolithic or Early Bronze Age leaf-shaped arrowhead (Hayden 1997; 2003; Potterton 2005, 34, 36–7, 41, 357–69; Walsh 1990–1). These show that while no evidence for major prehistoric settlement activity has been discovered in Trim, there are indications for periodic human presence in the prehistoric period.

Excavation carried out in advance of water and sewerage works yielded animal and human bones from a variety of contexts (Stephens, 'SubUrbia', this volume). The majority of this material appeared to date to the medieval period, although a peaty deposit that covered much of the excavated area proved to be an interesting exception, containing a large quantity of animal bone that has been radiocarbon-dated to the Iron Age.

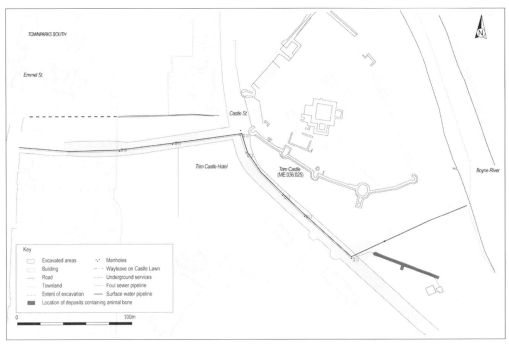

2.1 Location of deposits of animal bones south of the castle (base-map courtesy of Ordnance Survey Ireland, Permit 8565 © Ordnance Survey Ireland/Government of Ireland)

FAUNAL REMAINS

In the castle lawn area the natural subsoil consisted of grey sand overlain by a natural deposit of water-rolled stones, which in turn was overlain by a highly organic peaty material that was probably formed due to intermittent flooding of the area by the River Boyne (O'Carroll & Stephens 2007). This context of peaty material extended over almost the entire excavated area of the castle lawn, typically to a depth of 20cm, and contained a substantial quantity of animal bone. Although the majority of this animal bone was found scattered within the peat, some formed a discrete deposit in a single location and all came from a single trench that ran in a south-easterly direction for 70m across the castle lawn. Initially, the discrete deposit was thought to be a disturbed human burial, but on-site examination by an osteoarchaeologist confirmed that the bones were non-human and excavation proceeded (Mandy Stephens, pers. comm.). There were several disturbed medieval burials and sherds of medieval pottery within this peaty layer, which also included frequent roots, wood and charcoal (O'Carroll & Stephens 2007). If this peaty layer was laid down as a result of intermittent flooding, this would explain the disturbed nature of the human and animal remains and the mixing of medieval and prehistoric material within the peat.

Table 2.1 Details of faunal remains in the peaty layer

Bone	Cattle			Sheep/Goat			Pig			Horse		
	L	*R*	*U*	*L*	*R*	*U*	*L*	*R*	*U*	*L*	*R*	*U*
Loose mandibular tooth	–	–	1	–	–	–	–	–	–	–	–	–
Loose maxillary tooth	–	–	–	–	–	–	–	–	–	–	–	1
Humerus dist.	–	–	–	–	2	–	–	–	1	–	–	–
Radius prox.	2	1	–	–	–	–	20	21	–	–	–	–
Radius dist.	2	1	–	–	–	–	8	11	2	–	–	–
Ulna	3	1	–	–	–	–	23	28	–	–	1	–
Metacarpal 1 prox.	1	1	–	–	–	–	–	–	–	–	–	–
Metacarpal 1 dist.	1	1	–	–	–	–	–	–	–	–	–	–
Metacarpal 3 prox.	–	–	–	–	–	–	19	12	–	–	–	–
Metacarpal 3 dist.	–	–	–	–	–	–	12	7	–	–	–	–
Metacarpal 4 prox.	–	–	–	–	–	–	9	8	–	–	–	–
Metacarpal 4 dist.	–	–	–	–	–	–	7	7	–	–	–	–
Pelvis: pubis	–	–	1	–	–	–	–	–	–	–	–	–
Tibia prox.	–	–	–	–	–	–	–	–	–	1	–	–
Tibia dist.	–	–	–	–	–	–	–	–	–	1	–	–
Metapodial U prox.	–	–	–	–	–	–	–	–	1	–	–	–
Metapodial U dist.	–	–	–	–	–	–	–	–	15	–	–	–
Phalanx 1	–	–	2	–	–	–	–	–	16	–	–	–
Phalanx 2	–	–	3	–	–	–	–	–	15	–	–	–
Phalanx 3	–	–	2	–	–	–	–	–	3	–	–	–
Carpals and lateral/medial metacarpals and phalanges	–	–	2	–	–	–	–	–	86	–	–	–
NISP	20	–	–	2	–	–	285	–	–	3	–	–
MNI	3	–	–	2	–	–	28	–	–	1	–	–

This peaty layer yielded a total of 343 animal bone and tooth fragments including the material from the discrete deposit. Of these, 310 were identifiable elements, with the remainder being unidentifiable fragments and rib fragments. It is possible that most or all of the material started off in the discrete deposit, and was moved around as a result of flooding, but this cannot be confirmed. The bones identified were almost entirely from the forelimbs of pigs, and when the minimum number of individuals (MNI) was calculated, they were equivalent to fifty-one pig forelegs (representing at least twenty-eight individual pigs), four cattle forelegs (representing at least three cattle), a small fragment of cattle pelvis, two sheep humeri (representing at least two sheep), two horse bones (one of which had a different colour and is likely to have been intrusive), and a horse tooth. One of the pig metacarpals was radiocarbon-dated and yielded an early Iron Age date of 370–110BC (Wk22788), while a cattle pisiform gave a date of 200–40BC (Wk24915), both at 95.4% probability. In combination these firmly indicate an Iron Age date for the material.

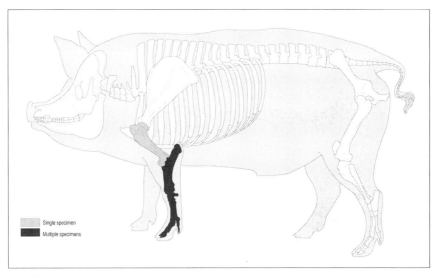

2.2 Graphical representation of pig body parts present

All of the identifiable pig bones were from the front limbs (Table 2.1; fig. 2.2). Only a single pig humerus was found, with all other bones being from the lower part of the limb or from the foot. Elements from the left and right sides were represented in approximately equal numbers. Several of the pig elements showed signs of butchery: two left and two right radii had evidence of cut marks on the dorsal side of the shaft, close to the proximal ends. This is the point at which the carcass was dismembered to separate it from the humerus above (fig. 2.3). Similarly, twenty of the fifty-one ulnae were broken at the *incisura semilunaris*, again as part of the dismemberment process (fig. 2.7), suggesting that after cutting through the flesh, ligaments and tendons, the ulna was twisted and broken to separate it from the humerus. In human terms, this is equivalent to being dismembered at the elbow.

The age distribution of the pigs was not typical of that expected for efficient production of pork and bacon. Since pigs do not produce any secondary products the majority are usually killed for meat as they approach full size and relatively few are retained into adulthood for breeding. A peak of slaughter is therefore expected between eighteen and thirty-six months. Unfortunately, since the range of elements for analysis was limited to those of the lower forelimbs, this meant that only relatively wide age-groups could be examined. In this case 37% of the pigs were aged under twelve months and a further 23% under two years, with very few bones of adult pigs. This pattern infers that most pigs were being killed when they were smaller than the optimum size to maximize meat production, but this would result in very tender meat being available. If an assumption is made that all the bones were deposited either on a single occasion or at a particular time of year, then the season of deposition

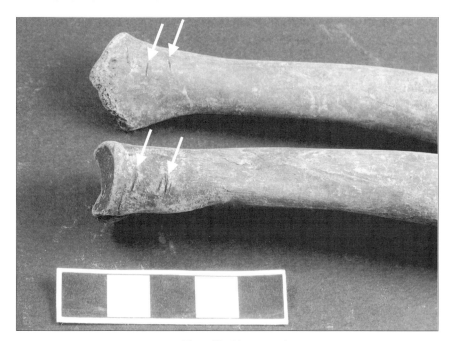

2.3 Pig radii with cut-marks

can be inferred. If it is assumed that pigs were generally born in April–May then, since the bones of the youngest pigs were not excessively small, it is unlikely that the bones were deposited in spring or summer. Given that they must be under twelve months old this means that the time of deposition can be narrowed to autumn, winter or early spring. As 10% of the pigs were in the range of twenty-four to thirty months, then, on the same assumption of spring farrowing, this would tie the deposition to a range of April to November. Taking these timescales in combination, the assemblage as a whole can be assumed to

Table 2.2 Fusion states of pig elements

Skeletal element	Age at fusion (months)	Number fused	Number unfused
Metapodium proximal	Pre-natal	48	0
Radius proximal	12	21	18
Phalanx 2	12	13	2
Humerus distal	12–18	1	0
Phalanx 1	24	5	9
Metapodium distal	24–27	13	32
Ulna proximal	36–42	1	13
Radius distal	42	1	16

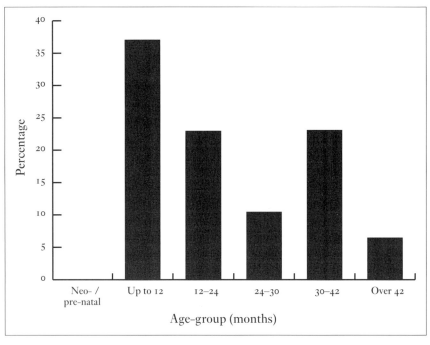

2.4 Pig age at slaughter, based on fusion data

relate to the September–November period. The other age-groups are too wide to give any useful seasonal information. Autumn is the season that slaughter would be expected, however the younger group of pigs should be a year older than they actually are in order to optimize meat production (Table 2.2; fig. 2.4).

A further point of interest in this assemblage was the presence of the forelegs of several cattle. Unusually for cattle bones, they were all substantially whole, rather than being broken open to access the marrow. With the exception of a small fragment of a cattle pubis they again included only radii, ulnae, carpals, metacarpals and phalanges, so that generally only the bones of the lower part of the front leg and foot were present. Unfortunately, it is not known where the individual bones were found within the context, and the number of cattle bones is much smaller than the number of pig bones. These cattle bones could have been deposited on the same occasion or occasions as the pig bones or as a result of entirely separate events during the Iron Age.

BUTCHERY PRACTICE

As described above, the pigs were dismembered at the joint between the distal humerus and the proximal end of the radius and ulna. The radius and ulna are

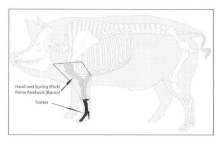 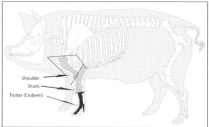

2.5 (left) Modern British cutting of pig carcass, adapted from Davis (1987, 25)
2.6 (right) Irish cutting, based on discussion with E. McGettigan, butcher, Donegal Town

known as the shank, while the same part on the back leg is called the hock. Today, the shank and the hock are routinely separated from the trotter. The usual practice in modern Irish butchery is for the meat of the shoulder and humerus to be sold 'off the bone' for boiling, and to sell the 'shank' or radius and ulna as a separate piece 'on the bone' (Ernan McGettigan, pers. comm.). In contrast, in Britain, the humerus, radius and ulna are retained in one piece as the 'hand and spring', in the case of pork, or the 'prime forehock', in the case of bacon (Davis 1987, 25), and both are commonly roasted (McGettigan, pers. comm.). These cuts are shown in figs 2.5 and 2.6. In both cases the trotter is then used for making processed meat products such as sausages; however, in the past these were used to make a popular dish known in Irish as *crubeens* or *crúibíní*, in which the trotters were wrapped with string to prevent them disintegrating before being boiled for several hours (Allen 2005). In the context of the Trim assemblage, it is interesting to note that the front trotters are believed to be sweeter and more succulent, while Allen (2005) suggests that those of the hind feet should be used for pie meat. In Trim, however, the trotter and the lower part of the foreleg have been kept as a single piece that would have had considerable meat on it, but would have been of lower quality than the upper part of the forelimb.

From consulting of a range of recipe books and websites, it is apparent that pigs' feet are part of the traditionally 'edible' portion of the pig in most cultures, and that while the inclusion of the lower limb bones with the trotter is not common, it does occur, being known in the US as 'long pig's feet' (100wordminimum.org 2004; chowhound.com 2007; mouthfulsfood.com 2007). The meat of the trotters is high in connective tissue and is very gelatinous, so many of the recipes use this to create thick stews or even jellies.

DISCUSSION

A number of potential interpretations for the deposit of pig and cattle long feet at Trim were considered. Attention was focused on the pig bones since these

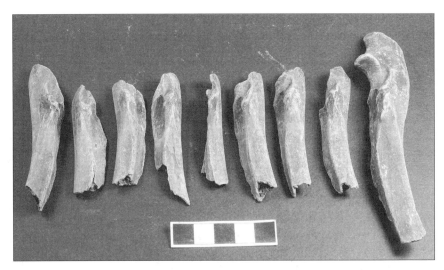

2.7 Broken pig ulnae, with one unbroken ulna to the right

made up the majority of the material. The potential interpretations considered were that the bulk of the faunal material represented either: a) primary butchery waste; b) glue-making waste; c) cooking or table waste or d) ritual deposition.

Butchery

When an animal is slaughtered, the first step in the butchery process is usually to skin it. Sometimes the feet are left on the skin to provide points of attachment for hide-workers needing to stretch the hide, and at the same time, to identify the species that it came from (Serjeantson 1989, 136–9). In this case, however, the shanks were also present, and as these are relatively high in meat it would be unlikely that these would be discarded when the skin was processed, even if the potentially edible trotters were disposed of. Having skinned the carcass, the next stage in butchery is to remove inedible parts and break down the carcass into manageable pieces for storage. One option is that meat was being de-boned as part of the butchery process and that the bones were then disposed of. This would be extremely difficult with raw pig trotters since many of the bones are small and tightly bound with connective tissue, whereas de-boning is very easily carried out on cooked trotters. It is therefore unlikely that these remains are from butchery.

Glue-making

Glue-making involves boiling bones and skin to extract gelatine. It is usual to smash the bones into small pieces to obtain the maximum amount of gelatine from the matrix (Schmid 1972, 48–9). Raw bones provide more gelatine than cooked ones and the difficulty of separating out the raw bones of the trotters has been discussed above. Therefore the evidence from the Trim site does not support an interpretation of glue-making waste.

Cooking or table waste

Having discounted primary butchery and glue-making, the possibility of this being food waste or a ritual deposit must be considered. Since these bones were found in a single layer within peat deposits in the floodplain of the River Boyne, it is possible that they were deposited on a single occasion. It is also possible that, prior to deposition, they were deliberately accumulated over a period of time. There is also the possibility that bones were deposited into this marshy area on a number of separate occasions.

If these bones were ordinary food waste from cooking or from eating, then a range of body parts and a more balanced representation of species would be expected, whereas in this case one species and one body part predominates. It is possible that these bones represent the accidental loss of a quantity of stored meat. For example, a container of salted or smoked long feet being unloaded from a boat may have broken open and the contents lost, although it would be expected that some attempt would have been made to retrieve the contents. Alternatively, if a container of long feet became rotten they may have been deliberately disposed of by being thrown into marshy waste-ground.

There were relatively few cattle bones in the assemblage, so that any inter-pretation is even more difficult, but again only the bones of the lower part of the front legs and feet were present (that is, cattle 'long feet'). Where fusion could be determined, the bones were all fused, so that they came from animals aged over twenty-four to thirty months, but unfortunately the olecrannon processes of the ulnae, which fuse at forty-two to forty-eight months, were all missing, so that it is not possible to be more specific. In the case of beef, no cut of meat includes the feet, which have much less meat than those of the pig, but they can be used to make stock and calves' foot jelly, although if either of these were the case it is likely that the bones would have been chopped into pieces to optimize the extraction of gelatine.

The few horse and sheep elements in the assemblage do not conform to the pattern of elements seen with the pig and cattle bones and are much less numerous. Since the peaty layer in which they were found also contained medieval human remains and pottery, it is likely that these bones are unrelated to the long feet and that they can be discounted from further discussion.

If the slaughter of at least twenty-eight pigs in order to obtain the front feet and shanks took place as a single event, this would have taken large-scale co-ordination to ensure that the remainder of the meat from the carcasses did not spoil prior to use. An Iron Age pig had an estimated live weight of around 80kg and gave around 64kg of meat (McCormick 2006, 165), while a shank and foot can be estimated to have a combined weight of approximately 2kg. Therefore, over 1,700kg of pig meat are unaccounted for in this assemblage and, even allowing for the majority of pigs being juveniles, an estimate of 1,000–1,500kg could be made. 1,500kg is equivalent to 6,000 portions of meat at a sedate 250g (or half a pound) each or 1,500 portions of a very generous 1kg of meat, suggesting that a substantial number of people were needed in order to consume the meat, so that several hundred people could easily be fed for a week with this quantity of food. Furthermore, a minimum of three cattle were also present and if the meat from these is included they would provide an additional 675kg, based on a live weight of 450kg (McCormick 2006, 165) (fig. 2.8).

2.8 Approximately one third of the faunal bone assemblage

It is possible that pigs' long feet were considered to be a delicacy to be eaten on a particular type of occasion. This cut would result in a portion-sized piece of meat that would be larger and of better quality than the trotter on its own. Since at least twenty-eight individual pigs were involved, and the remains of at least fifty-two actual limbs were recovered, it could represent a single episode of great importance to the community, incorporating a large feast, with subsequent disposal of the foot bones into marshy ground. In this case, the fate of the remainder of the body parts would be problematic, since the rest of the carcass would need to be consumed before it became spoiled.

Ritual deposition
The final option under consideration is that the bones represent a deliberate ritual deposition of animal long feet. Two possible scenarios will be considered. Firstly, that a mass slaughter of pigs and a few cattle took place. In this case the long feet may then have been ritually deposited as an offering, while the remainder of the meat was consumed. This consumption could potentially

have been part of a large-scale feast associated with a festival or religious event with the feasting waste disposed of elsewhere. A second possibility is that this was part of the routine autumn slaughter of excess beasts, and the preservation of their meat by salting or smoking. In this case, all of the long feet from the surrounding area could have been brought to a single location, in marshy ground by the side of the River Boyne, and again ritually deposited as an offering. In either case, it is possible that the bones were deposited on a number of separate occasions, with those found together representing one single event, and the remainder of the bones from other similar occurrences of the same activity.

Comparative examples of ritual feasting and deposition
During the Iron Age many animals had symbolic associations and were used in rituals. Since pigs produce many young they have long been associated with fertility and fecundity, and many mythological tales exist in which the supply of pork from a cauldron is inexhaustible regardless of how much meat is consumed, or in which slaughtered pigs miraculously reappear alive the next day (Green 1992, 119, 170). They were also associated with warfare, being seen as fearless and ferocious (Green 1992, 89) so that, for example, a La Tène boar figurine described by Mitchell et al. (1977) was probably originally mounted on a standard or helmet. McCormick and Murray (2007, 32) note that both Strabo – writing about the European Celts – and Irish mythology mention pork as a favoured food of the aristocracy, one example being the tale of the 'Feast of Bricriu', in which the guests argue about which warrior should receive the champion's portion of pork (Koch & Carey 1997, 64–95). During the Early Medieval period, pork was considered to be the preferred dish for feasting, with documentary sources giving details of how the various body parts should be distributed among the participants when a whole pig was being prepared (Kelly 2000, 358), thereby presumably attempting to avoid a repeat of the incident provoked by Bricriu.

Excavations of Iron Age material in Ireland and elsewhere in Europe have provided evidence for both feasting and ritual deposition. Faunal remains from Navan Fort (McCormick 1997) and Dún Ailinne (Crabtree 1990; Crabtree 2004) have been reviewed by McCormick and Murray (2007, 31–5), who compared the assemblages at these sites, which all had different characters. At Navan Fort there was a high proportion of pig, interpreted as high-status domestic food waste, whereas at Dún Ailinne there was a high proportion of cattle bone, with this being interpreted as food waste associated with feasting and the demonstration of status. Crabtree (2004) found that the domestic animals in the assemblage at Dún Ailinne were predominantly cattle (53.6%), with pig bones (35.5%) making up most of the remainder. Many of the cattle were under six months of age, so that their slaughter would have been uneconomic both in terms of the amount of meat they would have produced, and as a result of the loss of future dairy products due to the discontinuation of lactation by the mothers of the calves. This suggested that the extravagance of killing young calves was important in demonstrating wealth, power and prestige, by showing a disregard for the economic cost of losing the potentially larger meat and dairy source (Crabtree 2004). Looking at an earlier period, at Kilshane, Co. Dublin, McCormick identified that the articulated and disarticulated remains of fifty-eight cattle had been placed in the ditch of a Neolithic segmented enclosure (McCormick forthcoming; Moore 2007).

A parallel with the pig bones from Trim is a Late Bronze Age to Early Iron Age midden at Llanmaes in Wales, where many of the bones come from the right forequarters of pigs (Madgwick 2007). Madgwick (pers. comm.) has suggested that this may represent periodic ritual feasting in which the price of entry to the feast was the provision of a defined portion of this specific animal. Animal bones have been found in graves from various locations throughout Iron Age Europe, in the form of food offerings, the remains of ritual feasting, and animals to accompany the dead (Green 1992, 107). Examples of particular relevance to the Trim discovery are the sites of Mont Troté and Rouliers in the Ardennes region of France, where pigs were deposited with only one foot remaining on the skeleton and the other three missing (Meniel 1987, 101–43, cited by Green 1992, 107–8), and the site of Tartigny in Oise, France, where the pigs were missing all of their feet. These examples contrast with the bones from Trim, where only the feet and lower forelegs were present. Green (1992, 116–19) noted that pigs used in sacrifice were generally under two years of age, and that the pigs at Rouliers seemed to be associated with male graves. She also pointed out that, in many cases, even a single bone could be used to symbolize the whole animal (Green 1992, 107). There is archaeological evidence for pigs being used in ritual feasting in the Gaulish sanctuaries such as Gournay, also in the Oise region of France, where young pigs under two years of age were preferred, and at Hayling Island, Hampshire, England, where pigs and sheep were sacrificed (Green 1992, 118).

Votive deposition of metal objects in watery and boggy places is a feature of Irish Bronze Age and Iron Age archaeology but, in addition to metal artefacts, hoards could include items such as beads and boars' tusks (Eogan 1983, 151–2). Cooney and Grogan (1999, 161–2) have noted that the rate of deposition of known hoards of metal artefacts increased from an average of one every twelve years in the Early Bronze Age to one every three years by the final stages of the Late Bronze Age. They also note an increasing tendency over the Late Bronze Age for hoards to be associated with wet or boggy locations, reaching 58% by the Dowris Phase. Many hoards have been found at or near fording places, which they argue were recognized places for ritual deposition, although other interpretations have included casual loss and losses during warfare at strategic locations (Cooney & Grogan 1999, 167). Twenty-two Iron Age metal hoards have been identified, with the overwhelming majority coming from bogs, rivers and lakes (Cooney & Grogan 1999, 196–9). At both the King's Stables, associated with Haughey's Fort, Co. Armagh (Lynn 1977) and at the ritual pool of Loughnashade at Emain Macha (Warner 1986), animal bones were deliberately deposited in the pools, so that again it is clear that not only metal artefacts but also faunal material could be offered to the gods. Bog bodies have been interpreted as offerings to the gods, as human sacrifices and as executed criminals and deviants, with the ritual interpretations being the most widely accepted (Glob 1969, 190–2; Parker Pearson 1999, 70–1). In the case of bog butter, samples have generally been dated to the Iron Age and Early Medieval periods, and again a variety of suggestions for their existence have been made, including that bog butter was deposited in order to preserve it, to maintain emergency food supplies and as a votive offering (Synnott & Downey 2004).

Taking account of these other examples of late prehistoric and Early Medieval deposits, the most likely possibility is that the pig and cattle long feet from Trim represent a deliberate votive deposit of specific body parts, either as part of routine autumn slaughter or possibly in conjunction with a feast in which the remainder of the meat was consumed, and the food waste disposed of elsewhere. The long feet may have been considered to be an appropriate gift or offering to the gods. In favour of the feasting hypothesis, the unusual age distribution of the pigs, with animals older and younger than the economic optimum being selected for slaughter and ultimate deposition, suggests that this was not carried out as part of routine slaughter. The age-at-slaughter profile of the assemblage indicates deposition in the autumn, raising the possibility that the deposition was part of a festival associated with the autumn equinox in late September, or with Samhain at the end of October/beginning of November. The importance of pigs as a symbol of fertility and new life may be of significance here since the autumn equinox can be considered as a harvest festival and the end of the agricultural year, while in pre-Christian times, Samhain was the start of the new calendar year (Chadwick 1970, 181; Frazer 2006 [1922], 255–6).

CONCLUSIONS

This unusual and highly enigmatic assemblage included the remains of at least twenty-eight pigs, three cattle, two sheep and a horse deposited in the marshy ground now occupied by the castle lawn. It provides a unique insight into the Irish Iron Age, with the bulk of the assemblage probably representing a votive deposit of pig and cattle forelimbs to the gods. This deposition may have taken place on a single occasion or repeatedly over the years. In any case, the co-ordination required in order to obtain sufficient pigs and cattle for this activity, and the number of people needed to consume the meat, demonstrate that this was an event of major significance to the community.

ACKNOWLEDGMENTS

Thanks are due to Finola O'Carroll and Mandy Stephens of CRDS, who excavated the site, and to Trim Town Council, who funded the excavation. Thanks also to Richard Madgwick and Finbar McCormick for allowing me to use unpublished material, to Ernan McGettigan for useful discussions on butchery practice and to Marion Dowd, who commented on an earlier draft of the paper.

BIBLIOGRAPHY

100wordminimum.org, 2004, http://100wordminimum.org/archives/2004_03.html. Accessed 30 November 2007.
Allen, D., 2005, 'Darina Allen's letter and recipe of the week'. Saturday 17 September 2005. Cooking is fun. http://www.cookingisfun.ie/letters/2005/September/slowfoodcork fstival17th.htm. Accessed 2 December 2006.
Chadwick, N., 1970, *The Celts*. London.
chowhound.com, 2007, http://www.chowhound.com/topics/414002. Accessed 30 November 2007.
Cooney, G., & Grogan, E., 1999, *Irish prehistory: a social perspective*. Dublin.
Crabtree, P., 1990, 'Subsistence and ritual: the faunal remains from Dún Ailinne, Co. Kildare, Ireland', *Emania* **7**, 22–5.
Crabtree, P., 2004, 'Ritual feasting in the Irish Iron Age: re-examining the fauna from Dún Ailinne in light of contemporary archaeological theory' in Jones O'Day, S., Van Neer, W., & Ervynck, A. (eds), *Behaviour behind bones: the zooarchaeology of ritual, religion, status and identity*, 62–5. Oxford.
Davis, S.J.M., 1987, *The archaeology of animals*. London.
Eogan, G., 1983, *Hoards of the Irish Later Bronze Age*. Dublin.
Frazer, J.G., 2006 [1922], *The golden bough: a study in magic and religion*. South Dakota.
Glob, P.V., 1969, *The bog people: Iron Age man preserved*. London.
Green, M., 1992, *Animals in Celtic life and myth*. London.
Hayden, A., 1996, 'Trim Castle, Trim' in Bennett, I. (ed.), *Excavations 1995: summary accounts of archaeological excavations in Ireland*, no. 237, pp 73–5. Bray.
Hayden, A., 2006, 'Athboy Road, Trim' in Bennett, I. (ed.), *Excavations 2003: summary accounts of archaeological excavations in Ireland*, no. 1468, p. 392. Bray.
Kelly, F., 2000, *Early Irish farming: a study based mainly on the law-texts of the 7th and 8th centuries AD*. Dublin.
Koch, J.T., & Carey, J., 1997, *The Celtic heroic age: literary sources for ancient Celtic Europe and early Ireland and Wales*. Andover, MA.
Lynn, C., 1977, 'Trial excavations of the King's Stables, Tray Townland, Co. Armagh', *Ulster Journal of Archaeology* **40**, 42–62.
Madgwick, R., 2007, 'The animal bone from Llanmaes'. Unpublished report for Cardiff Osteoarchaeology Research Group.
McCormick, F., 1997, 'The animal bones from site B' in Waterman, D.M., *Excavations at Navan Fort, 1961–71*, 117–20. Belfast.

McCormick, F., 2006, 'Animal bone' in Armit, I., *Anatomy of an Iron-Age roundhouse: the Cnip wheelhouse excavations, Lewis*, 161–72. Edinburgh.

McCormick, F., forthcoming, 'The faunal remains from Kilshane, Co. Meath'.

McCormick, F., & Murray, E., 2007, *Knowth and the zooarchaeology of Early Christian Ireland*. Dublin.

Mitchell, F.G., Harbison, P., de Paor, L., de Paor, M., & Stalley, R., 1977, *Treasures of Irish art*. New York.

Moore, D., 2007, 'Kilshane' in Bennett, I. (ed.), *Excavations 2004: summary accounts of archaeological excavations in Ireland*, no. 612, pp 143–6. Bray.

mouthfulsfood.com 2007, http://mouthfulsfood.com/forums//index.php?s=5b14d33e2 ca3ee3e2270fc6aaa97b6e6&showtopic=2578&st=735. Accessed 30 November 2007.

O'Carroll, F., & Stephens, M., 2007, 'Archaeological assessment, monitoring and excavation at Trim Townparks: Consents C121 and C139: licence no. E2016'. Unpublished draft stratigraphic report 31/7/07, for CRDS Ltd.

Parker Pearson, M., 1999, *The archaeology of death and burial*. Stroud, Gloucestershire.

Potterton, M., 2005, *Medieval Trim: history and archaeology*. Dublin.

Schmid, E., 1972, *Atlas of animal bones*. Amsterdam.

Serjeantson, D., 1989, 'Animal remains and the tanning trade' in Serjeantson, D., & Waldron, T. (eds), *Diet and crafts in towns*, 129–46. BAR British Series 199. Oxford.

Synnott, C., & Downey, L., 2004, 'Bog butter: its historical context and chemical composition', *Archaeology Ireland* **18:2**, 32–5.

Walsh, C., 1990–1, 'An excavation at the library site, High Street, Trim', *Ríocht na Midhe* **8:3**, 41–67.

Warner, R., 1986, 'Preliminary schedules of sites and stray finds in the Navan complex', *Emania* **1**, 5–9.

Burials at St Patrick's Cathedral: new evidence for the Early Medieval ecclesiastical site at Trim

EOGHAN KIERAN

INTRODUCTION

The surviving references in the Book of Armagh suggest that the church of Trim may have been founded as early as the fifth century – before the founding of the church of Armagh (Byrne 1984, 316–19). This ninth-century text describes the foundation of a church at the 'Ford of Trim' (*Vadum Truimm*) by the British missionary Lommán (Potterton 2005, 37). He is said to have converted a local king who appears to have had a residence close to the ford. The successors of St Loman were variously described as abbots or bishops until the diocese of Trim was united with the diocese of Meath in 1152 (Lewis 1837, ii, 643). O'Keeffe suggested that the enclosure associated with the church was represented by the curve of Castle Street, High Street and Navan Gate Street (O'Keeffe 2000, 94). Hennessy postulated that although there is no trace of the original Early Medieval church, it 'was almost certainly located at or adjacent to, the present-day St Patrick's Cathedral' (Hennessy 2004, 1). He based this conclusion on a number of factors. The first of these was the dedication of the present church to St Patrick, which hints at its medieval origins. In addition to this, analysis of plot boundaries and street alignments in the vicinity of the church reveal two possible outlines of an early ecclesiastical enclosure. St Patrick's Church appears to have functioned as the parish church for Trim from at least Anglo-Norman times. It is now owned by the Church of Ireland and was elevated to the status of cathedral in 1955. Definitive evidence of the pre-Anglo-Norman origins of the church and an indication of the extent of the graveyard came with the archaeological excavation of a number of human burials on a site adjacent to St Patrick's Cathedral, behind Haggard Street, between 15 April and 11 May 2007.

SITE BACKGROUND

The site was located to the east of the present eastern boundary of St Patrick's Cathedral and was accessed from Haggard Street. The standing remains of the church consist of a substantial tower of probable fifteenth-century date along

3.1 Site location showing excavated features and position of burials. Skeleton 26 was radiocarbon-dated to AD780–1030. Burials recently discovered on Loman Street are also shown (CRDS and Moore Group. Ordnance Survey Ireland, Permit 8565 © Ordnance Survey Ireland/Government of Ireland. Inset from *Irish Historic Towns Atlas, no. 14: Trim*, by permission of the Royal Irish Academy © RIA)

with a rebuilt section of the nave, which re-opened in 1802. A ruined section of the chancel survives 8m from the site of the excavation. This chancel contains a fine fifteenth-century window inserted into a wall of probable thirteenth-century date. Sandstone fragments of a thirteenth-century window can be traced in the masonry of the chancel and these appear to be the oldest visible upstanding structural components at the site. Other parts of this and other such windows may survive among the various architectural fragments gathered together in piles around the ruinous chancel. The church is approached from the High Street side via the curving Church Lane, which runs along the backs of the plots on Loman Street and Haggard Street.

The site of the excavations discussed here was previously occupied by buildings marked on nineteenth-century maps. The name of Haggard Street has been recorded since 1571 and it was also referred to as Blind Lane in the eighteenth century (Hennessy 2004, 9), with various activities carried out on the street up to the twentieth century (ibid., 11). In the nineteenth century there were three forges and smithies (1846–94), a car manufacturer (1846) and coach manufacturers (1861–81).

3.2 Location of the excavation (beyond the tall trees in the middle) viewed from St Patrick's
Cathedral bell-tower (courtesy of Michael Ann Bevivino)

ARCHAEOLOGICAL TESTING

Three archaeological test trenches were excavated (fig. 3.1). The natural yellow
boulder clay rose considerably upwards from the east to the west of the site
towards the hilltop occupied by the church site at 62m OD. Trench One
uncovered a mortar-bonded wall close to the eastern end of the trench. A
hearth was found further west, as well as a southwest–northeast V-shaped ditch
(1.6m in width and 67cm in depth) containing medieval pottery. A further pit,
40cm in diameter, and a hearth were uncovered to the west, and a 2m-wide
north–south ditch, containing charcoal, stone and animal bone was exposed at
the western end of the trench. Trench Two uncovered a north–south wall, 1.8m
in length, at the street frontage. An east–west return for this wall was found
during monitoring of Trim Street Reconstruction works (Matthew Seaver,
pers. comm.). An east–west ditch, 60cm wide, containing bone, charcoal and
oyster shell, was uncovered, and this matched a similar ditch 10m from the
eastern end of Trench Three. It contained medieval pottery. A further ditch
was found 4m from the eastern end of the trench.

THE BURIAL GROUND

During the course of the programme of archaeological monitoring of ground-works, human burials were uncovered. Initially, the remains were identified as a group of three closely-spaced single inhumations, orientated in an east–west direction (with their heads to the west). They were *c.*20cm below the contemporary ground level on the south-western end of the site, close to its boundary wall with the present church. In total, thirty-one articulated burials were uncovered. Numbers were assigned to three other potential skeletons which, upon excavation were found not to be articulated burials. All of the burials were contained within the 30m^2 that formed the impact zone of the car park of the development. The area was cleaned by hand and all identified features were planned and recorded in detail. All graves and skeletons were drawn to scale and photographed and ordnance datum (OD) levels were taken. The skeletons were individually and systematically removed by component part, with each component bagged in pre-prepared labelled bags. All work was supervised by the site director and the on-site osteologist. The burials had no discernible grave-cuts and were contained within very compact, brown, silty clay with occasional pebbles and modern debris.

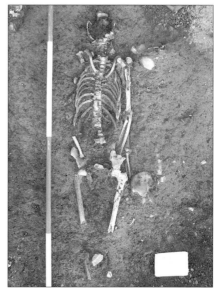

3.3 Skeleton 4 from east   3.4 Skeleton 6 from east

The human remains
The full osteological analysis of the human remains uncovered during these excavations has not yet been completed. In anticipation of that report, it is

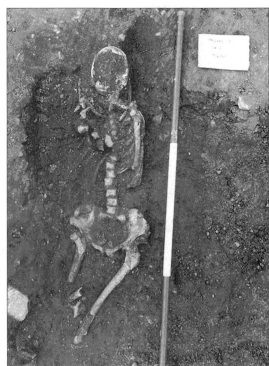

3.5 Skeleton 7 from east   **3.6** Skeleton 11 from east

possible to make some general observations about the burials. These are
presented below. In all cases where orientation could be established, the head
was to the west.

Skeleton 1 was a fully-extended, supine inhumation orientated east-west.
This skeleton was missing its entire left leg as well as its right tibia, fibula and
foot. The right hand and arm was placed over the individual's stomach, with
the left arm lying by its side. The skull was badly crushed.

Skeleton 2 comprised portions of what appeared to be an extended supine inhumation. The remains were orientated east-west. The skeleton was badly preserved,
with only the feet, tibia, fibulae, left femur, pelvis, ribs and a small portion of upper
cranium remaining. This grave was cut by a later burial and this may have resulted
in the destruction or removal of the missing portions of Skeleton 2.

Skeleton 3 consisted of a right and left femur and a left fibula. These remains
were in a poor state of preservation, and as a result little could be gleaned from
the remains.

Skeleton 4 (fig. 3.1) was a partially intact, fully-extended supine inhumation
orientated east-west. This skeleton was missing its lower legs and right arm,
which appeared to have been truncated.

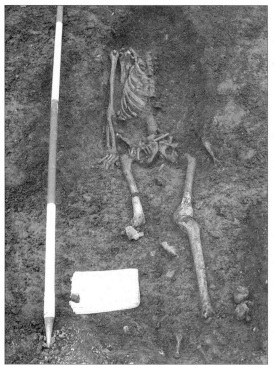

3.7 Skeleton 14 from east   3.8 Skeleton 15 from east

Skeleton 5 was represented by the left ribs, a portion of the spine and the pelvis. As a result of the poor state of preservation, little information could be gleaned from the remains.

Skeleton 6 (fig. 3.4) was an almost fully intact, extended supine inhumation, orientated east-west.

Skeleton 7 (fig. 3.5) was an almost fully intact, extended supine inhumation, orientated east-west.

Skeleton 8 comprised only the legs and hands of what appeared to be a supine extended inhumation. The remainder of the burial appeared to have been truncated by a modern drain.

Skeleton 9 comprised only the upper body of an extended supine inhumation. Its left arm was fixed across the body and the right pelvis and lower legs were missing.

Skeleton 10 comprised only the lower body of an extended supine inhumation. All that was present were the lower pelvis, right and left legs.

Skeleton 11 (fig. 3.6) comprised only the upper body and legs of an extended supine inhumation. Its left arm was fixed across the body and the right pelvis and lower legs were missing.

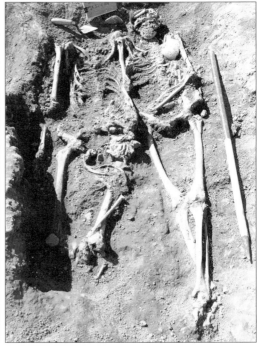

3.9 Skeleton 20 from east   **3.10** Skeletons 24 & 31 from east

Skeleton 13 was a very badly truncated inhumation. The burial of a dog (initially thought to be the remains of a human (**Skeleton 12**)) badly disturbed this burial. All that remained were two clavicles, the upper spine and lower legs.

Skeleton 14 (fig. 3.5) was an almost fully intact, extended supine inhumation, orientated east-west.

Skeleton 15 (fig. 3.6) comprised only the upper body of an extended supine inhumation. Its left pelvis and lower legs were missing. It was not possible to determine the cause of the removal of the legs.

Skeleton 16 was an almost fully intact, extended supine inhumation, orientated east-west. Both arms were bent at the elbow, crossing the body and meeting at the pelvis.

Skeleton 17 was an almost fully intact, extended supine inhumation, orientated east-west. The left arm was bent at the elbow, crossing the body to the pelvis. The right arm was absent.

Skeleton 18 comprised only the upper torso, left leg and right lower leg of an extended supine inhumation.

Skeleton 19 was a very disturbed burial. The only remains noted were the skull, portions of the left ribs and the right ulna.

Skeleton 20 (fig. 3.9) was a fully intact, supine extended inhumation. It was orientated east-west. This burial had folded arms meeting at the stomach. All bones were present.

Skeleton 21 was poorly preserved. The skeleton was badly truncated with no right side and only two pairs of ribs. The pelvis was badly damaged and there were no legs. The head and right arm were also absent.

Skeleton 22 was an extended inhumation lying slightly on the right side with the head in a poor state. The majority of the upper body was present, with the right arm buried under the body and the lower legs cut by a modern land-drain.

Skeleton 23 comprised the right side of a former extended inhumation. The majority of this skeleton was truncated by a modern land-drain. All leg bones were absent, as was the entire left side. All that remained was the upper right side and skull.

Skeleton 24 (fig. 3.10) was part of a double burial with Skeleton 31and was in a good state of preservation: it contained almost the entire upper body and upper legs of an extended supine inhumation. Its right arm was lying beside the body, with the left arm partially missing. The lower legs were truncated by a nearby land-drain.

Skeleton 25 was a fully intact, supine extended inhumation. It was orientated east-west. This burial had folded arms meeting at the stomach.

Skeleton 26 was an almost fully intact, extended supine inhumation. The burial was orientated east-west. All bones were present, with the exception of the left arm. A radiocarbon date was determined for this burial (see below).

Skeleton 27 comprised only the lower portions of a pair of tibia and fibulae and feet. It appeared that the remainder of the burial was truncated by a nearby trench.

Skeleton 28 consisted of the partial remains of what appeared to be an east-west orientated, extended supine inhumation. The head of this individual was in relatively good condition, together with an intact right arm, spine, ribs and pelvis. The remainder of the burial had been truncated by a drainage ditch.

Skeleton 29 contained only a very small number of human bones, comprising skull fragments, a clavicle, a small section of spine and three ribs.

Skeleton 30 contained only the torso and right side of an extended supine inhumation.

Skeleton 31 (fig. 3.10) was an almost fully intact, extended supine inhumation, orientated east-west. All bones were present with the exception of the lower legs. The right arm was bent at the elbow and passed over to the left elbow. The left arm was also bent and passed to the pelvis. It was within a grave containing Skeleton 24.

Skeleton 34 (fig. 3.11) comprised the lower right side of a former east-west orientated extended inhumation. The majority of this skeleton was truncated

3.11 Skeleton 34 from east

by the nearby land-drain. The right arm, leg, pelvis and lower spine were the only intact remains.

Skeleton 35 was a poorly preserved burial. The remains comprised the lower right and left legs, the upper left leg and pelvis, a portion of the lower spine and lower left arm, as well as a number of ribs.

It was not possible to excavate the full extent of **Skeleton 36**, as it lay under the site boundary wall. The portion that was excavated comprised the complete lower section of a fully extended supine inhumation.

CONCLUSION

The discovery of the remains so close to the church posed the question as to whether they were related to the early church site. The absence of any grave-goods, datable material, coffins or even shrouds or pins meant that radiocarbon dating was the only means by which a date for the remains could be recovered. In September 2008, a calibrated radiocarbon date of AD780–1030 (95.4% confidence) from a sample of human bone from Skeleton 26 was returned from Lund University, Sweden (LuS 7860). This indicates that the graveyard had its origins before the twelfth century and is the location of an Early Medieval ecclesiastical site. The burials also indicate that the medieval burial ground extended further towards Haggard Street than it does presently. It is likely that much of this area was not reclaimed for settlement until after the Reformation. The additional features found during testing indicate further complexity to the site, although their relationship with the burials is unclear. The presence of medieval pottery is an indication that at least some of the features relate to the boundaries of the church site. The paucity of evidence from the other postulated locations for the early church also supports the conclusion that the current St Patrick's Cathedral was built on the site of Trim's earliest church. The burials will be subject to full osteological analysis in the near future and a final report will be lodged with the statutory authorities. Further radiocarbon dates are awaited and these will no doubt contribute to our understanding of the chronology of the site. If similarly early dates are returned, then there can be little doubt that the site of the current St Patrick's Cathedral was indeed the site of the original monastic settlement in Trim.

As this book is going to press, excavations on Loman Street have uncovered human burials and bowl-furnaces underlying the footpath on Loman Street (fig. 3.1). A sample of human bone underlying medieval metalled street surfaces has yielded a fifth- to seventh-century date (Table 1.1). The burials were located immediately outside the eighteenth-century boundary wall of St Patrick's Cathedral. Together with the ninth-/tenth-century date, this suggests the presence of a large Early Medieval ecclesiastical site covering the hilltop. The full implications of this are a matter for future discussion (Matthew Seaver, pers. comm.).

ACKNOWLEDGMENT

I would like to thank the excavation team, particularly Camilla Lofqvist, the Moore Group osteologist, who supervised the excavation of all human remains.

BIBLIOGRAPHY

Byrne, F.J., 1984, 'A note on Trim and Sletty', *Peritia* **3**, 316–19.
Hennessy, M., 2004, *Irish Historic Towns Atlas No. 14: Trim*, Dublin.
Lewis, S., 1837, *A topographical dictionary of Ireland*, London.
O'Keeffe, T., 2000, *Medieval Ireland: an archaeology*, Stroud, Gloucestershire.
Potterton, M., 2005, *Medieval Trim: history and archaeology*, Dublin.

Two forgotten cemeteries at Iffernock, Trim

DOMINIC DELANY & BRIAN O'HARA

with a contribution by CONOR NEWMAN & EAMONN O'DONOGHUE

INTRODUCTION

In late 2005 two cemeteries were excavated prior to the development of lands at Iffernock, approximately 2km to the east of Trim town centre (figs 4.1 & 4.2). The lands are located within the former curtilage of Teaguestown House, a late-eighteenth-century dwelling that possibly occupies the site of an earlier house. The cemeteries were discovered some 200m apart during a programme of archaeological monitoring in a six-acre field (fig. 4.1). For recording purposes the cemeteries were identified as Site I and Site II. The burials at both sites were interred in the standard Christian fashion; supine in position and

4.1 Extract from Ordnance Survey orthographic aerial photograph of Iffernock townland (2005), showing site-locations (Ordnance Survey Ireland, Permit 8565 © Ordnance Survey Ireland/Government of Ireland)

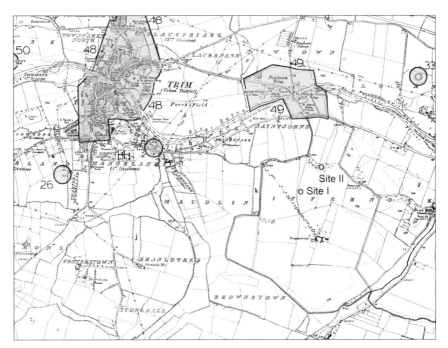

4.2 Extract from the 1959 six-inch Ordnance Survey map, showing Recorded Monuments and Places (shaded grey), and the development site at Iffernock, with Site I and Site II marked

orientated to face the rising sun. Site I was uncovered close to the field's western boundary and immediately east of the line of the original entrance avenue to Teaguestown House. A total of thirty-one burials, ranging in age from neonate to mature adult, were excavated at this site. The cemetery was sealed by a thick layer of topsoil and was well-preserved, with the majority of the burials being complete. There was little disarticulation of the skeletons. Site II was located on a gravel ridge known as the Trim Esker (Hennessy 2004, 1), a glacial ridge that runs east-west across the northern edge of the field. A minimum number of twenty-four burials were excavated from Site II. In contrast to Site I, this cemetery was very poorly preserved, with the majority of the skeletons being incomplete and severely crushed. The burials lay directly on top of the gravel, beneath a thin topsoil layer. As this field was used for cereal cultivation, it is likely that much of the damage to Site II is the result of plough action.

ARCHAEOLOGICAL & HISTORICAL BACKGROUND

The place-name Iffernock is derived from the Irish *Iath Fearnog* meaning 'land of the alders'. There are no known documentary references to Iffernock in the medieval period. There are significant archaeological sites of medieval date in the area, however, including an ecclesiastical complex on the banks of the River Boyne at Newtown Trim to the north, and a medieval complex comprising a motte, a church and graveyard, and a tower house at Scurlockstown, to the northeast (fig. 4.2). Archaeological testing and excavation at Scurlockstown in 2001 and 2003 indicated that this was the site of the medieval manorial settlement known to have been granted to John Scurlock by Hugh de Lacy in the latter part of the twelfth century (Hayden 2003; 2006).

The earliest known reference to Iffernock is contained in the Civil Survey of 1654–5, which was undertaken in the wake of the Cromwellian re-conquest. This survey records the townland name as 'Iffernocke', in the 'Parrish of Trym' (Simington 1940, 167). In 1640, the most significant land-holding in the townland belonged to one 'Gerrard Linch of Knock' and consisted of an estimated two hundred acres, 180 of which were classed as arable. There was also 'on the premisses one eale weare'. Larkin's Map of 1812 names the area 'Teaguestown', but for all other sources this name is only applicable to the house. The place-name probably derives from *Baile Téige* – townland of Tadhg – but its application here is uncertain. O'Donovan listed Iffernock as the property of Lord Longford (Herity 2001). It is recorded as covering an area of 489 acres, and is sub-divided into holdings ranging from thirteen to 180 acres. A mention of a range of low hills running east-west across the townland is presumably a reference to the Trim Esker. Griffith's Valuation for Co. Meath (1855) records Iffernock as being in the parish of Laracor. The largest single holding consisted of a house, old offices and land totalling 218 acres, which was leased to Hugh Hanbury by Honourable R.T. Rowley. There is also a reference to 'new farm offices (built 1853)'. All of these historical sources indicate the existence of a substantial land-holding at Iffernock, which is almost certainly co-extensive with the recent farm pertaining to Teaguestown House. This suggests that there was a 'big house' here from a relatively early date, and it is most likely to have been located on the site of the existing Teaguestown House, which is said to have been built in 1796.

The first edition Ordnance Survey six-inch map of Co. Meath (1836) depicts the Trim Esker as a winding road running east-west through the townland of Iffernock, towards Trim (fig. 4.3). The entrance to Teaguestown House is at the point where the main road ceases to follow the esker but turns sharply north towards Newtown Trim. A small lodge is marked at this junction, and from it the avenue leads southwards to the house, which is depicted as a modest structure with a couple of free-standing outbuildings to the rear. By the time of the first edition Ordnance Survey twenty-five-inch map (1908–11), a completely new entrance had been created further along the esker road to the west (fig. 4.4). A new lodge is marked at this location and an impressive tree-lined avenue leads directly south-eastwards to the house. The old avenue

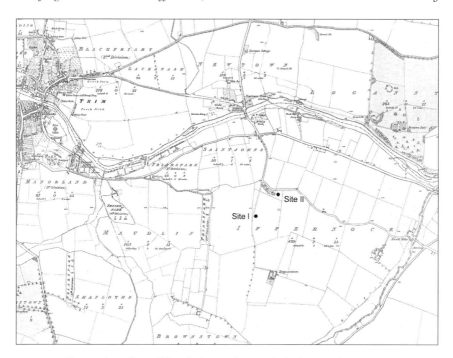

4.3 Extract from first edition Ordnance Survey six-inch map of Meath (1836),
showing Iffernock townland to the south of the River Boyne. The locations of
Site I and Site II are marked (reproduced with kind permission of the Board of the
University Library, Trinity College Dublin)

remains as a secondary entrance, but appeared as little more than a track-way
through the fields. The house itself had been enlarged, and a formal enclosed
courtyard complex had been erected on the site of the earlier outbuildings.
Presumably these are the new farm offices referred to in Griffith's Valuation of
1855. This courtyard was subsequently demolished and a series of modern
agricultural buildings now occupy the site.

SITE I CEMETERY

Site I was located in the southwest part of the field, immediately east of the
former avenue to Teaguestown House (figs 4.1, 4.2 & 4.3). The avenue is
clearly marked on the first edition six-inch and twenty-five-inch Ordnance
Survey maps and was still traceable on the field surface prior to topsoil
stripping. It runs parallel and in close proximity to the field's western
boundary at this point along its route. The cemetery contained thirty-one
burials and included eight adult males, nine adult females, three unsexed

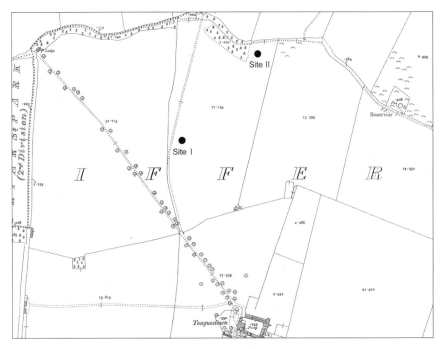

4.4 Extract from first edition Ordnance Survey twenty-five-inch map of Meath (1908–11), showing Iffernock townland to the south of the River Boyne (reproduced with kind permission of the Board of the University Library, Trinity College Dublin)

adults, three adolescents (probably one male and two female), four juveniles and four infants, including one neonate. The majority of the burials were interred in four well-ordered rows within a confined area measuring 12 by 15m, with the grave-cuts having a roughly equal distance from one another (fig. 4.5). The burials were in simple graves and conformed to the conventional Christian practice of being supine in position and orientated to face the rising sun. In order to conform to the latter requirement, the majority of Christian burials are orientated along an east-west axis, with the head to the west. At Site I, however, all but one of the burials was orientated from north-northeast to south-southwest. This may be due to ignorance of the convention on the part of those tasked with burying the dead, or as a consequence of a mistake concerning the true direction of east. The one burial that was at odds with the general pattern of the site was aligned along the expected east-west axis. The orientation of this burial suggests that it is not contemporary with the other burials, and most likely post-dates the general period of usage of the cemetery. One of the burials appears to have been re-interred as the long bones, skull, scapulae and some of the ribs were placed together in a small, shallow pit. There were just four instances of interments truncating earlier burials. The

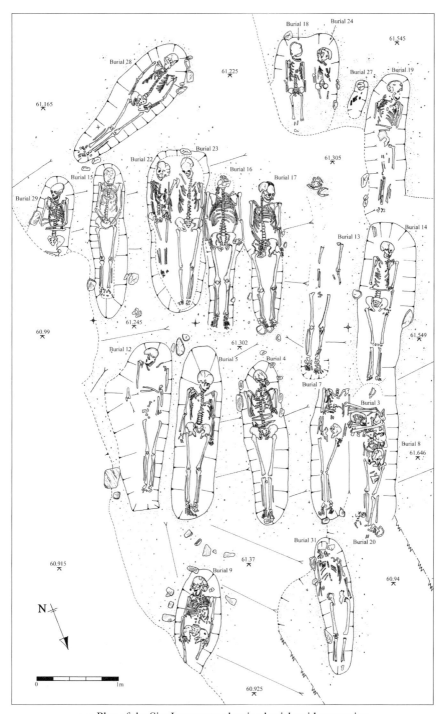

4.5 Plan of the Site I cemetery, showing burials mid-excavation

well-ordered layout of the cemetery (fig. 4.7) and the relatively few instances of truncated burials indicates that the location of the individual graves was visible or known during the primary period in which cemetery was in use.

The majority of the burials were situated to the immediate east of a gravel track marking the route of the original avenue to Teaguestown House. The four burials at the south-western extent of the cemetery, however, were covered by the track. Nonetheless, it is likely that the avenue pre-dates the cemetery and that subsequent to the cemetery going out of use the track was widened and re-surfaced with the four burials to the southwest being covered by the new gravel deposit.

The occurrence of three infant burials raises the possibility that the cemetery may have had a secondary period of usage as a burial ground for unbaptized children. Indeed the evidence indicates that this may well be the case. One of the infant burials was located some 12m to the northwest of the main part of the cemetery, suggesting that it is a later interment. The other two infant burials also appear to post-date the cemetery's main period of usage as they occur relatively high in the stratigraphic sequence and one slightly truncates an earlier adult burial.

Two double burials and two possible double burials were uncovered during the course of the excavation. The first recorded double burial consisted of an adult female aged 30–35 and a juvenile female aged 10–12. The arms of the skeletons were linked, indicating a close familial relationship (fig. 4.6). The second double burial consisted of two unsexed juveniles, one aged 18–24 months and the other 5–6 years. In both cases, the possible double burials consisted of an adult male and an adult female of similar age. Due to the looseness of the pea gravel into which the burials were inserted, it was not possible to ascertain the precise outline of the grave-cuts. The positioning of the skeletons side-by-side and in close proximity to each other, however, suggests they are simultaneous.

The location of the cemetery and its lapse from the community's collective memory raises the inevitable questions as to who was buried here and what was the cause of death. There was no evidence for any trauma or pathological conditions beyond the range one would expect with any sample population group. Consequently, one can only speculate, based on the evidence at hand, as to the likely cause of death. Determining the date of the burials is crucial to any attempt at speculating as to the potential causes of death. In the absence of artefactual evidence and in advance of any potential radiocarbon-dating of the bone, the date of the cemetery is unknown. There is other dating evidence, however. Although there was no evidence of trauma or recurring pathological conditions, it was noted that the instance of dental caries was high with eleven of the thirty-one skeletons exhibiting the condition to varying degrees. This suggests that the cemetery is post-medieval in date. Dental caries, more

4.6 Photograph of double burial with interlocking arms, from Site I

commonly known as tooth decay, are a recurring pathological condition in skeletal assemblages. An extensive survey of dental caries in archaeological populations in Britain by Moore and Corbett in 1978 established that prevalence rates escalated in the eighteenth and nineteenth centuries. This result is replicated in Ireland, where a survey of more than one thousand individuals

4.7 Photograph showing well-ordered layout of the Site I cemetery

from both historic and pre-historic populations (C. Power 1994, unpublished MA, quoted in Murphy 2007) has shown that the condition was absent in the Neolithic, rising to a 0.7% prevalence rate in the Bronze Age when cereal consumption began. From the Iron Age to the medieval period the prevalence rates remained broadly consistent, indicating a generally unchanging diet of meat, cereal and milk products (Iron Age 4.4%, Early Medieval 3.9%, Medieval 4.2%). During the post-medieval period, however, the prevalence rate increases dramatically to 8.7% (Murphy 2007). This rise coincides with the importation into Britain and Ireland of cane sugar from the Americas. Sugar arrived in increasingly large quantities from the seventeenth century. The consumption of gruel or porridge, which formed an increasingly significant part of the diet of the poor from the eighteenth century, is conducive to the development of the condition.

Having established a probable post-medieval date for the cemetery, and an apparent brief period of primary usage which included several double burials, it seems reasonable to assume that famine or epidemic is the most likely cause of death for the majority of the individuals interred in this cemetery. In the eighteenth and nineteenth centuries, famine and acute food shortages were recurrent in Ireland. Such events were generally caused by successive poor harvests, which reduced the capacity of poorer sections of Irish society to pay for alternative foodstuffs that rose sharply in price as demand increased. The famine of 1726–9 hit hardest in the north of the country, but was somewhat ameliorated by the fact that the poor harvest was local in scope and foodstuffs were still available from outside Ireland. The famine of 1740–1 was much more severe, as the poor climatic conditions that prevailed in Ireland were also witnessed across Europe. The onset of full-blown famine in the spring of 1741, and the outbreak of typhus and dysentery that summer resulted in very high mortality rates leading to 1741 becoming known as *bliadhain an air* (year of the slaughter). The period between the famines of 1740–1 and the Great Famine of 1845–9 has been termed 'the gap in the famines'. Though bad harvests were a relatively common occurrence during this period (leading to near famine conditions in 1756–7, 1765–6, 1769–70, 1774–5, 1782–4, 1799–1801 and 1821), major catastrophe was averted due to a degree of economic resilience created through the existence of cottage industries. The immediate cause of the Great Famine of 1845–9 was the failure of the potato crop in 1845, but the factors leading to the disaster had evolved in the preceding decades. The rapid expansion of Ireland's population in the first half of the nineteenth century resulted in a correspondingly rapid reduction in the size of the average farm holding. In order to make such small holdings viable, subsistence farming, which was almost exclusively based on the potato, became the norm in marginal areas.

The writings of Jonathan Swift, who was rector to a small congregation at Laracor Church of Ireland church from 1699 to 1745, suggest that the famine of 1726–9 had a severe impact on the locality. Best remembered for *Gulliver's Travels*, Swift was also a noted social commentator and pamphleteer. In 1729 he published the satirical essay 'A modest proposal', in which he proposed that the best solution to the problem of poverty in Ireland was for the poor to raise their children as food for the wealthy of England. The essay was written in the culminating year of the successive bad harvests of 1726–9, and undoubtedly the author was greatly influenced by the events that unfolded in his community. The local impact of the famine of 1726–9 identifies this as a possible date for the origination of the cemetery at Iffernock.

SITE II CEMETERY

Site II was located on top of the gravel ridge that runs east-west across the northern edge of the same field in which the Site I cemetery was excavated. This ridge is part of an extensive esker running southeast from Trim that is commonly referred to as the Trim Esker (Meehan & Warren 1999, 15–17; Synge 1950; Kilroe, 1907, 224). On the first edition Ordnance Survey six-inch map, a roadway is indicated running along this ridge from Trim to Knock Mills, which is situated at the eastern end of Iffernock townland on the road from Scurlockstown to Laracor. To the east of Iffernock, despite being much quarried out, the former line of the esker is partly reflected in the route of the local class road running southeast through the townlands of Adamstown, Mitchelstown, Foxtown, Windtown, Blackcut, Galtrim, Ballynamona, Collegeland and Arodstown, possibly terminating at church and castle sites in the latter townland. The use of glacial ridges as roadways is well-attested in Ireland, with the Annals of the Four Masters recording the names of forty-one such routes. The practice of burying the dead in glacial ridges is known from the Bronze Age through to the medieval period. Indeed recent archaeological work in Co. Meath has uncovered evidence bearing testimony to this practice. In 1997–8 two burial sites were excavated in the townland of Peterstown (Murphy 1998), 2.5km to the north of Iffernock. The first site was located on a gravel ridge and contained four burials, which were initially dated to the Early Medieval period by reference to the orientation of the skeletons and the relative lack of dental caries. Subsequent radiocarbon analysis established an Early Medieval date (AD414–532). The second burial was of a single individual and was radiocarbon-dated to the second quarter of the fifteenth century (AD1425–1461). In 2004, test excavations at Dangan (Breen 2007), to the southwest of Iffernock, uncovered disarticulated human remains near the surface of an elongated glacial mound that was partly truncated by the modern road running alongside the mound. The burials were preserved in situ and no further archaeological investigation was undertaken. In the same year eight burials were uncovered along the summit of a low glacial ridge at Sarsfieldstown in east Co. Meath. The site director interpreted the burials as pre-dating the medieval period (Deevy 2000).

A total of twenty-four individuals were identified from the skeletal assemblage excavated at Site II, of which twenty were found in situ. These burials were supine and orientated east-west, with the head to the west, suggesting that this is a Christian cemetery (fig. 4.8). All of the burials were those of adults or adolescents. They were interred in simple graves, which were very shallow and in some instances excavated only to the surface of the gravel. There were two groups of four burials, in which the interments were found to be placed in very close proximity to each other. This is suggestive of simultaneous burial, but the evidence was inconclusive due to the poorly-preserved nature of the remains. The burials were contained within a relatively confined area measuring 17m by 9m. The site was very disturbed, however, and disarticulated bone was scattered over a wide area. This scattering of bone was particularly evident to the north and south of the main part of the cemetery, and it is likely that this was a result of plough action, which would have run along the field's long axis from north to south. It may also have been a result of a more direct action in reducing the height of the esker. Two burials were truncated by a modern pit measuring 5m by 1m, which was back-filled

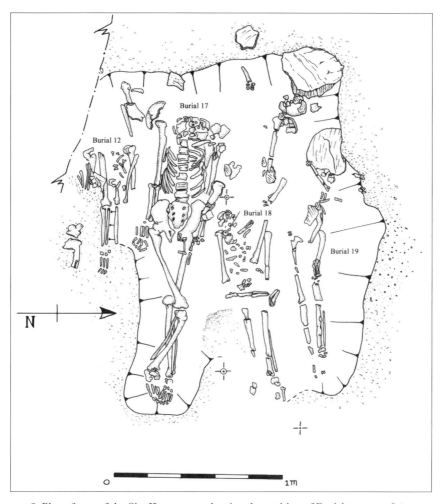

Burial 17

Burial 12

Burial 18

Burial 19

N

0   1m

4.8 Plan of part of the Site II cemetery, showing the position of Burials 12, 17, 18 & 19

with a single deposition of topsoil and sand. A substantial quantity of disarticulated bone was recovered from the pit fill. Plastic wrappings found at the base of the pit indicate that it is of recent origin and was presumably excavated for the extraction of gravel.

Unfortunately, the poor state of preservation of the burials at Site II prevents us from drawing many conclusions regarding the nature and origin of this cemetery. The orientation of the burials, however, and the evidence from other burials in glacial ridges suggests that this cemetery dates from the Early Medieval period.

ACKNOWLEDGMENT

Dominic Delany wishes to acknowledge the contribution of Philip Culleton, who carried out the osteological analyses of the human remains from the Iffernock sites.

BIBLIOGRAPHY

Aalen, F.H.A., Whelan, K., & Stout, M., 1997, *Atlas of the rural Irish landscape*. Cork.
Barry, T.B., 1987, *The archaeology of medieval Ireland*. London.
Bradley, J., 1984, 'The urban archaeology survey of County Meath'. Unpublished report prepared for the Office of Public Works.
Breen, T., 2007, 'Killahaushky, Killahaushkeen or Killasheen, Dangan' in Bennett, I. (ed.), *Excavations 2004: summary account of archaeological excavations in Ireland*, no. 1215, p. 304. Bray.
Brothwell, D.R., 1981, *Digging up bones*. Oxford.
Carlin, N., Clarke, L., & Walsh, F., 2008, *The archaeology of life and death in the Boyne floodplain*. Dublin.
Channing, J., & Randolph-Quinney, P., 2006, 'Death, decay and reconstruction: the archaeology of Ballykilmore cemetery, County Westmeath' in O'Sullivan, J., & Stanley, M. (eds), *Settlement, industry and ritual: proceedings of a public seminar on archaeological discoveries on national road schemes, September 2005*, 115–28. Dublin.
Deevy, M., 2000, 'Sarsfieldstown' in Bennett, I. (ed.), *Excavations 1999: summary accounts of archaeological excavations in Ireland*, no. 710, p. 244. Bray.
Edwards, N., 1990, *The archaeology of Early Medieval Ireland*. London.
Fibiger, L., 2005, 'Minor ailments, furious fights and deadly diseases: investigating life in Johnstown, County Meath, AD400–1700' in O'Sullivan, J., & Stanley, M. (eds), *Recent archaeological discoveries on national road schemes 2004*, 99–110. Dublin.
Rogers, T., Fibiger, L., Lynch, L.G., & Moore, D., 2006, 'Two glimpses of nineteenth-century burial practice in Ireland: a report on the excavation of burials from Manorhamilton Workhouse, Co. Leitrim, and St Brigid's Hospital, Ballinasloe, Co. Galway', *Journal of Irish Archaeology* 15, 93–104.
Hallissey, M., O'Sullivan, J., & Roberts, J., 2002, *Human remains in Irish archaeology: legal, scientific, planning and ethical implications*. Kilkenny.
Halpin, A., & Newman, C., 2006, *Ireland: an Oxford archaeological guide*. Oxford.
Hayden, A., 2003, 'Scurlockstown' in Bennett, I. (ed.), *Excavations 2001: summary accounts of archaeological excavations in Ireland*, no. 1051, p. 334. Bray.
Hayden, A., 2006, 'Scurlockstown' in Bennett, I. (ed.), *Excavations 2003: summary accounts of archaeological excavations in Ireland*, no. 1463, pp 390–1. Bray.
Hennessy, M., 2004, *Irish Historic Towns Atlas No. 14: Trim*. Dublin.
Herity, M. (ed.), 2001, *Ordnance Survey letters, Meath: letters containing information relative to the antiquities of the county of Meath collected during the progress of the Ordnance Survey in 1836*. Dublin.
Horner, A., 2008, *Mapping Meath in the early nineteenth century, with an atlas of William Larkin's map of County Meath, 1812*. Wicklow.
Kilroe, J.R., 1907, *A description of the soil-geology of Ireland*. Dublin.
Leigh-Fry, S., 1999, *Burial in medieval Ireland, 900–1500*. Dublin.
Mays, S., 1998, *The archaeology of human bones*. London.
Meehan, R.T., & Warren, W.P., 1999, *The Boyne Valley in the Ice Age: a field guide to some of the valley's most important glacial geological features*. Dublin.

Moody, T.W., & Vaughan, J., 1986, *A new history of Ireland vol. iv: eighteenth-century Ireland, 1691–1800*. Oxford.

Moore, W.J., & Corbett, M.E., 1978, 'Dental caries experience in man: historical, anthropological and cultural diet-caries relationship – the English experience' in Rowe, N.H. (ed.), *Diet, nutrition and dental caries*, 3–19. Ann Arbor, MI.

Murphy, D., 1998, 'Peterstown' in Bennett, I. (ed.), *Excavations 1997: summary accounts of archaeological excavations in Ireland*, no. 431, pp 143–4. Bray.

Murphy, E., 2007, 'Human osteoarchaeology in Ireland' in Murphy, E.M., & Whitehouse, N.J. (eds), *Environmental archaeology in Ireland*, 48–76. Oxford.

Nolan, J., 2006, 'Excavation of a children's burial ground at Tonybaun, Ballina, County Mayo' in O'Sullivan, J., & Stanley, M. (eds), *Settlement, industry and ritual: proceedings of a public seminar on archaeological discoveries on national road schemes, September 2005*, 89–101. Dublin.

O'Kelly, M.J., 1989, *Early Ireland: an introduction to Irish prehistory*. Cambridge.

Ortner, D.J., 2002, *Identification of pathological conditions in human skeletal remains* (2nd ed.), San Diego.

Otway-Ruthven, A.J., 1968, *A history of medieval Ireland*. Dublin.

Simington, R.C. (ed.), 1940, *The Civil Survey, AD 1654–56* (10 vols, 1931–61), vol. 5: Meath. Dublin.

Sweetman, D., 1999, *Medieval castles of Ireland*. Cork.

Synge, F.M., 1950, 'The glacial deposits around Trim, Co. Meath', *Proceedings of the Royal Irish Academy* **53B**, 99–110.

Uberlaker, D.H., 1978, *Human skeletal remains: excavation, analysis, interpretation*. Aldine Transaction.

Vaughan, J. (ed.), 1989, *A new history of Ireland vol. v: Ireland under the union, 1801–1870*. Oxford.

Waddell, J., 1998, *The prehistoric archaeology of Ireland*. Galway.

Wilde, W., 1849, *Beauties of the Boyne and its tributary the Blackwater*. Dublin.

APPENDIX 4.1: CROPMARKS AT IFFERNOCK

By Conor Newman & Eamonn O'Donoghue

The cropmarks at Iffernock townland were photographed from a fixed-wing light aircraft in August 2002 by Eamonn O'Donoghue and Conor Newman (figs 4.9 & 4.10). The field in question lies 2.5km east/south-east of Trim Castle (NGR 282600/255800) and was under ripe cereal (probably barley) at the time. The cropmarks appear as a result of plant height differentiation, which is picked up by raking evening sunlight. There is virtually no colour differentiation, and what appears as a C-shaped feature (highlighted by a dark green band of vegetation) along the eastern boundary towards the south end of the field, is merely the original edge of a natural indentation recorded on the first edition Ordnance Survey maps of the 1830s (see figs 4.3 & 4.4 above), which has since been back-filled and reclaimed. The eastern boundary of the field is defined by a steep and quite abrupt incline down to what is now a small steam running more or less north-south. The drop is about 4m, and it confers on this field a height advantage over the surrounding fields. The stream was dammed as a millrace and the mill-house buildings (Knock Mills) still survive in ruins nearby to the north.

What is revealed by the photography is a very dense complex of enclosures, buildings and inter-connecting paths, extending from north to south. All of the

4.9 Aerial photograph taken in August 2002 of cropmarks at Iffernock townland
(Photograph by Eamonn O'Donoghue & Conor Newman)

4.10 Aerial photograph of cropmarks at Iffernock townland,
with annotation of visible features

features are circular or curvilinear, except for what appears to be a square enclosure at
the southern extremity of the cropmark complex. It is not known whether this latter is
contemporary with the other structures, but if so, intriguing possibilities emerge. The
general contemporaneity of the remaining features is not in doubt, because they
intersect with one another. They include two apparently conjoined circular enclosures
of unequal size (A and B; the larger enclosure (A) being to the north), approached
from the south by a narrow, slightly curved pathway (C). Internal features (buildings?)

are evident in both enclosures, but in the interior of the larger, northern enclosure is another smaller, nearly complete circular feature, tangential to the northern side. Within this is a yet smaller circle feature, which is probably closer to the dimension of a domestic house.

To the west of the path approaching these two possibly conjoined enclosures is another large circular enclosure (D), which appears to be contained within its own rectilinear space, defined by a bank(?). This is approached by a path (E) leading from the north, which has the same narrow, arcuate footprint as the path (C) approaching the conjoined enclosures. There are hints that enclosure D is conjoined with another circular feature to the south, but the image loses definition at this point.

A greenish band of vegetation running roughly east-west across the mid-line of the field bears all the hallmarks of an older field boundary, but such does not appear on the first edition map, so it may be an earlier division. Regardless, to the south of it is a square or rectilinear enclosure (F). Though by no means unprecedented (for instance, moated sites of medieval date), rectilinear or square enclosures are somewhat unusual in the repertoire of early Irish enclosures; the general tendency being towards the round or elliptical; and particularly so when both forms are possibly juxtaposed, as here at Iffernock.

In all likelihood, the circular enclosures A, B, and D date from the Early Medieval period. Association with Cemetery Site II, dating from the fifth to early sixth century AD, is certainly possible, and it would be important to try to establish this in due course. What makes the cropmarks particularly interesting is the probability of contemporaneity, and the fact that enclosures A and B appear to be conjoined, because conjoined enclosures, just like conjoined buildings during this period, are most likely to have been high-status settlements. It is reasonably certain that this architectural motif derives its importance from a very ancient pedigree, for figure-of-eight or conjoined buildings and enclosures are a leitmotif of Iron Age architecture at the great so-called 'royal' sites of Tara, Emain Macha, Cruacháin and Dún Ailinne. This opens up the possibility, distant though it may be, that the Iffernock cropmarks signal the presence of much more ancient remains. It is against this backdrop that the existence of the nearby square enclosure becomes particularly interesting, because if it does date from this period it is unlikely to have fulfilled a domestic function.

Clearly, these cropmarks raise some very interesting questions. The clarity with which they appear suggests good sub-surface conditions and survival. The adjacent development, however, heralds the possibility of change, and it behoves us to anticipate this with further analysis, including field-walking and geophysical prospection.

Empty space: excavations outside Trim

MANDY STEPHENS

with a contribution by JENNIE COUGHLAN

In 2006, archaeological excavations on the castle lawn, east of the curtain wall of Trim Castle, revealed evidence of a previously unknown burial ground, the castle moat, an intriguing deposit of pig bones and post-medieval remains associated with land reclamation. This paper discusses issues of liminality and psychologies of space, with reference to this burial ground.

INTRODUCTION

Archaeological excavations were conducted by CRDS Ltd, on behalf of Trim Town Council, in advance of a scheme of infrastructural works that included upgrading the town's mains drainage and the construction of a new road, Finnegan's Way, to link Emmet Street with Castle Street. The pipeline extended from the south bank of the Boyne, across the landscaped green, to the Dublin Road, then on to Castle Street and the town car park (fig. 5.1). The development corridor lay in close proximity to Trim Castle and the town wall, both of which are National Monuments subject to preservation orders. The works were carried out under Ministerial Consent orders C121 and C139.

The following remains were identified along the pipe route: a) post-medieval and possible medieval structural remains on the Dublin Road side of the castle lawn, south of the curtain wall and barbican gate; b) a burial ground at the Dublin Road side of the castle lawn, south of the curtain wall and barbican gate; and c) a section of the castle moat, at Castle Street/Dublin Road, just outside the south tower.

A series of organic, peaty deposits were identified across most of the pipe route. These peaty deposits were interpreted as the remains of the Leper River (also known as the Water of Luppard). This natural watercourse, which rises at the west of the town, is believed to have been canalized in the medieval period, to feed the castle moat and to function as a town ditch, flanking the town wall.

Previous investigations in the vicinity of the Trim Castle Hotel indicate that ground conditions in that area were similar (Hayden 2006). Local sources suggest that peat-cutting was being carried out in the vicinity of the Garda Station (on the opposite side of Castle Street) up to the 1940s (Anthony

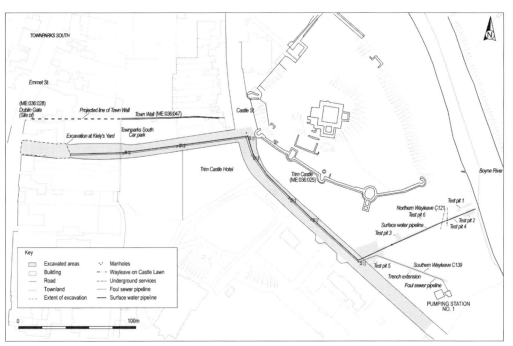

5.1 Plan showing location of excavations outside castle walls (base-map courtesy of Ordnance Survey Ireland, Permit 8565 © Ordnance Survey Ireland/Government of Ireland)

Conlon, pers. comm.). This natural watercourse links all of the areas of interest uncovered in the course of this project.

THE LEPER RIVER

The Leper River is important in understanding the utilization of natural watercourses for the defence of Trim and in the development of the street plan. It is believed to have run along the town wall between Emmet Street and Castle Street and might have been canalized to feed the castle moat (Potterton 2005, 176). Its natural course is believed to have run a little further south of the town wall, under what is now the Trim Castle Hotel, and into marshland on the south bank of the Boyne, directly south of the castle (fig. 5.1). The Leper River would have been a reasonably substantial watercourse, approx 70cm–1.4m in depth (Hayden 2006).

Marshland on the southeast of the castle, cut through and fed by the Leper River, would have served as a secondary 'moat'. Intermittent flooding of this area would have resulted in the formation of the peaty bog deposits that were identified during the excavations. In terms of castle defences, the curtain wall would have been supplemented to the east by the Boyne, to the north and east

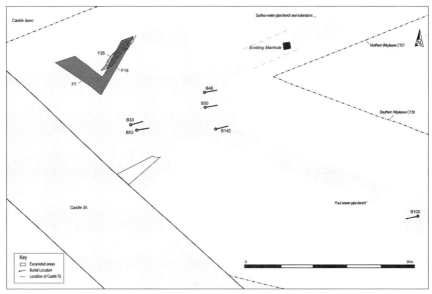

5.2 Plan showing location of burials and structural features mentioned in the text (base-map
courtesy of Ordnance Survey Ireland, Permit 8565 © Ordnance Survey Ireland/
Government of Ireland)

by the town wall, and to the south and west by marshland, the Leper River and
the town wall.

EXCAVATIONS ON THE CASTLE LAWN, PHASE 3: POST-MEDIEVAL

Archaeological investigations revealed a network of drains and culverts and the
foundations of two structures cut through a series of organic peaty deposits
(fig. 5.2). The drains and culverts relate to eighteenth- and nineteenth-century
public works – an attempt to reclaim marshy land in advance of the construction of a number of municipal buildings on this side of the town, including the
gaol, the Catholic church and the Dublin Road itself. The network of drains
and culverts was constructed to contain and channel the Leper River and to
direct its flow to the Boyne. The drains were excavated through bogland and
medieval remains. Finally, the peaty deposits on the green were sealed by
modern refuse and garden soil deposits associated with more recent landscaping of the area.

The foundations of a structure, dated to the post-medieval period on the
basis of cartographic evidence and pottery sherds recovered, were subject to
limited investigation. The structure appears on the first edition Ordnance
Survey map of the town (fig. 5.3). This structure was found to partially overlie
an earlier stone wall. The wall was linear, and composed of large cut-stone

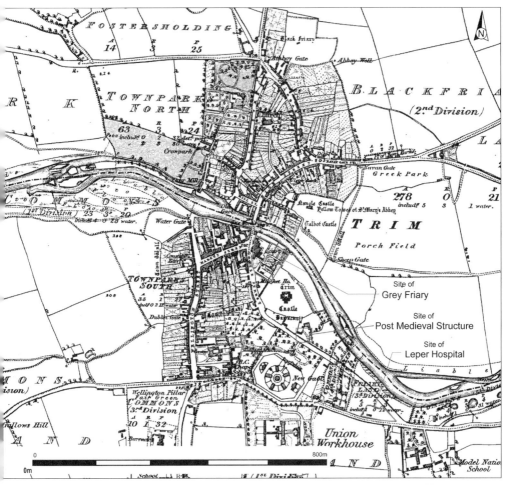

5.3 Extract from first edition Ordnance Survey map of Trim, showing post-medieval structure south of castle walls, and location of nearby medieval graveyards (reproduced from *Irish Historic Towns Atlas, no. 14: Trim*, by permission of the Royal Irish Academy)

blocks, packed with mortar. It measured 4.2m in length and 52cm–1m in width. This wall is believed to be of medieval date, based on its stratigraphic position and the pottery sherds found in association with it. It is not possible to comment further on these structures as the pipe corridor was relocated further to the south in order to facilitate their preservation.

EXCAVATIONS ON THE CASTLE LAWN, PHASE 2: THE BURIALS

Post-excavation assessment of the faunal remains from the peaty deposits produced an unusual assemblage that forms the subject of another paper in this volume (Beglane, 'Meat and craft'). Five human burials were identified within the pipe corridor on the castle lawn (fig. 5.2). The skeletal remains had been placed in the layers of organic peat that were indicative of marsh or boggy ground and all of the burials had been truncated to varying degrees; in one case all that remained was the skull (B50).

These were extended, supine, simple burials (figs 5.5, 5.6 & 5.7). The bodies appear to have been shrouded or tightly bound prior to burial, as indicated by the fact that their legs were crossed. The hands were crossed over the chest and/or pelvis in three cases. All but one were orientated north-west/south-east and the exception was very badly disturbed by later agricultural activity. On the basis of position, orientation and the absence of grave-goods, these individuals, or at least those who buried them, appear to have been Christian.

All of the human remains were analyzed by a specialist (Appendixes 5.1–5.3). The osteologist could not identify the cause of death of the individuals, but at least two cases exhibited evidence of nutritional stress in childhood. The specialist suggested that these were young adult males in cases where age could be determined based on pelvis and skull measurements (see below). Two burials were radiocarbon-dated to 1280–1396 cal. AD (B33) and 1267–1389 cal. AD (B142), suggesting that all of the burials were broadly contemporary.

Cemeteries in proximity

These people were not buried in any known cemetery. The nearest contemporary graveyards (fig. 5.3) were: a) the Grey Friary (ME036:024), which was located inside the town wall, on the site of the present courthouse, with a burial ground extending along Castle Street (O'Carroll, this volume); and b) a cemetery associated with the Leper Hospital of St Mary Magdalene (itself a holding of the Grey Friary), which was located to the south of the castle, the town wall and this development on the castle lawn. It is possible that these burials relate to the Leper Hospital, although they were north of the assumed limits of that cemetery. Their location suggests several possibilities. Firstly, it is possible (albeit unlikely) that the Leper Hospital cemetery was further to the north and/or was larger than previously thought. Secondly, while the Grey Friary was established c.1228 (Potterton 2005), the burials may relate to an earlier graveyard in the vicinity. Thirdly, these individuals may have been deliberately placed outside any known cemetery.

Trim witnessed a series of calamitous events in the thirteenth and fourteenth centuries. The Bruce invasion, poor harvests, famine, the Black Death, the destruction of the Franciscan friary by the great Boyne flood and of St Mary's Abbey by fire and the encroachment of Gaelic enemies were all factors in the decline of the town. These events would have been catastrophic for significant numbers of people both within and without the town walls

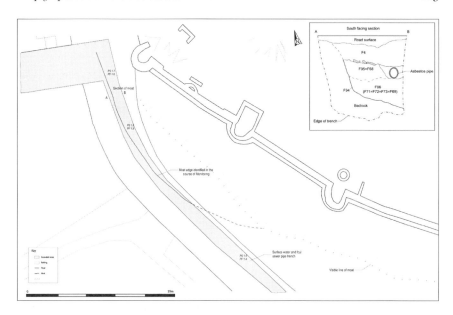

5.4 Plan showing line of moat and section through it (base-map courtesy of Ordnance Survey Ireland, Permit 8565 © Ordnance Survey Ireland/Government of Ireland)

5.5 Burial 33, mid-excavation

5.6 Burial 46,
mid-excavation

(Potterton 2005, 227). Politically, it was also a time of stress, with constant battles over control of the lordship between the crown and the de Lacys, de Genevilles and Mortimers.

   These conditions probably caused the deaths of significant numbers of people, both directly and indirectly. Any of these factors might have necessitated burial in unconsecrated ground. The bodies were placed in marshland, close to a townland boundary and in a marginal space between the town and the world outside its walls. Social status had an impact on medieval burial practice. Certain classes of criminals, the sick and sinners would not have been afforded full Christian burial rights. Those charged with burying them, however, would probably have done so in accordance with known traditions. As a result, practices such as positioning and shrouding may have been used, but without the complete package of Christian funerary tradition and ritual. The spatial arrangement of the burials is not particularly dense or organized and only five people were identified across a relatively large area, suggesting that this was not a formal cemetery or a mass-grave, such as a plague pit.

5.7 Burial 52, mid-excavation

Liminal burial?

The osteological assessment could not determine the cause of death of these young men, and their location is intriguing. The castle lawn would have been liminal space, in marshland that was prone to flooding from the Boyne and waterlogging from the Leper River. Furthermore, this area must surely have been considered a 'no-man's land' between the town and the rural hinterland, between the controlled order of the Anglo-Norman town and the countryside. These young men were deliberately buried in this liminal space, and in all likelihood this was an expression of their 'outsider' status, which may well have been related to their political beliefs, social status or criminal activities.

EXCAVATIONS ON CASTLE STREET, PHASE 2: THE CASTLE MOAT

Trim Castle is founded on an outcrop of bedrock, on a low hill overlooking the area beyond the town, south of the castle. A substantial moat would have been excavated during quarrying of rock for the castle construction, providing raw material for the building and a defensive feature outside the curtain wall. As the pipeline progressed up the Dublin Road, a section of the moat was identified in the trench as far as the junction with Finnegan's Way (fig. 5.1). The line of the moat is visible along the south curtain wall today, but these excavations revealed that this is unlikely to be the true edge of the ditch. The line identified during this project was wider than expected, and this is most likely a result of extensive landscaping of the area in the recent past.

The moat was clearly visible in section in the pipe corridor, but trench conditions were hazardous and this impacted on the recording of this feature. It was encountered slightly further south than expected, and 'curved' into the pipe-trench from the east for a distance of approximately 30m. The moat had been heavily disturbed by a variety of services, including electricity, gas and water mains, telecommunications cables and sewer lines (fig. 5.4).

The moat was fed by the Boyne on the north side of the castle and by a tributary or canalized branch of the Leper River on the west side. Based on these investigations, the projected width of the moat was between 10m and 20m, narrowing as it approached the tower on Castle Street. The moat had a potential depth in excess of 2.5m (the trench depth did not exceed that level). This is comparable with the moat at Dublin Castle (Lynch & Manning 1985–7).

Previous excavations
Previous excavations further to the north on Castle Street identified the line of the moat, where the projected line of the town wall should meet the castle curtain wall (O'Carroll, this volume). No evidence for the town wall was uncovered in the course of that project and the excavator suggests that the wall may have arched over the moat at this point. The castle wall has been disturbed at this point and the section visible today is a relatively modern insertion (Potterton 2005). These sections of the curtain and town wall may have been dismantled or quarried-out during the construction of Castle Street/the Dublin Road in the nineteenth century (ibid.; Hennessy 2004).

CONCLUSION

It is likely that further defence was provided by the marshland cut through by the Leper River on the south side of the castle. This liminal space on the south side of the castle provided not just defence but also a spatial and psychological barrier with the outside world. While the curtain wall certainly achieved this, the utilization (and, to an extent, the creation) of a 'secondary moat' to the south of the castle was not just a physical barrier but also a psychological one. The burials on the castle lawn of (predominantly young) males in a previously unknown, informal cemetery reflect this division of space. Those outside the town would have been defined as 'other' and these would have included the lower orders of Anglo-Norman society as well as the Gaelic Irish. Just as the fortifications were a physical display of wealth, power and dominance, the (presumably) empty space between would have expressed the distance between those within and those without the walls.

ACKNOWLEDGMENTS

I am grateful to Finola O'Carroll for her management of the project and advice throughout. I would like to thank Bernice Watts, Caoimhe Tuthill, Lisa McQuaid, Catherine Bishop and Greg Flanagan for their work on site. Niall Lynch provided illustrations from the site drawings. All post-excavation work was managed by Milica Rajic and Joanne Gaffrey. All site works were funded by Trim Town Council.

BIBLIOGRAPHY

Coughlan, J., 2007, 'The human skeletal remains from Trim Castle'. Unpublished specialist report for CRDS Ltd.
Beglane, F., 2007, 'Report on the faunal material from Townparks South, Trim, Co. Meath'. Unpublished specialist report for CRDS Ltd.
Hayden, A., 2006, '01E0145 ext'. Unpublished excavation report for the National Monuments Service.
Hennessy, M., 2004, *Irish Historic Towns Atlas, No. 14: Trim*. Dublin.
Lynch, A., & Manning, C., 1985–7, '15.4 : Dublin Castle E296/E297/E298/E323/E324'. http://www.heritagecouncil.ie/archaeology/unpublished_excavations/section15.html.
Moore, M., 1997, *Archaeological inventory of County Meath*. Dublin.
O'Carroll, F., 2003, '03E1484, Castle Street, Trim'. Unpublished excavation report for National Monuments Service.
Potterton, M., 2005, *Medieval Trim: history and archaeology*. Dublin.

APPENDIX 5.1: OSTEOLOGICAL ANALYSIS

By Jennie Coughlan

The osteological analysis of human remains is undertaken to establish, where possible, demographic information (sex, age and stature), and to identify skeletal changes that can be linked to occupational, pathological or nutritional stresses. The determination of age, sex and stature not only provide basic population data, but can also aid in the identification of age-related skeletal changes, gender differences in diet and occupation and the frequency of disease through different population groups. As only six individuals were recovered during this programme of excavation, it was not possible to produce a statistical analysis of either the demographic or pathological profile of the site.

Preservation

Assessment of preservation is important in the study of skeletal remains as it can impact on the level of information retrieved during analysis. Aspects affecting preservation include burial environment, disturbance after deposition and treatment of skeletal material both during and after excavation. The skeletal remains from this site were assessed on two separate aspects of preservation, namely completeness, recorded as a percentage of the skeleton present, and preservation, where consideration was given to the condition of the bone.

Burials were scored on a five-point scale, ranging from 'very good' through to 'good', 'moderate', 'poor' and 'very poor'. When assessing completeness, a score of 1 was assigned when over 85% of the skeleton was present, a score of 2 when 70–84% of the skeleton was present, a score of 3 when 50–69% of the skeleton was present, a score of 4 when 25–49% of the skeleton was present, and a score of 5 when less than 25% of the skeleton was present. When scoring for preservation, consideration was given to both the degree of surface erosion and post-mortem fragmentation.

All burials had been disturbed to some degree by the later construction of drainage systems in the area, resulting in only poor to moderate levels of completeness for all individuals (Table 5.1). Burial 50 and Burial 100 were the most incomplete of all the individuals, with Burial 50 surviving as the skull, cervical vertebrae and left shoulder only, and Burial 100 surviving as the fragmented and incomplete remains of the left arm and right and left legs. Preservation of the bone was variable throughout and ranged from poor through to good, with some surface erosion and fragmentation affecting all individuals.

Table 5.1 Preservation by individual

Burial	Completeness	Preservation	Comments
33	Moderate	Moderate	Lower legs and feet missing; cranium and vertebrae fragmented
46	Moderate	Poor	All elements represented, but incomplete and fragmented
50	Poor	Moderate	Skull, cervical vertebrae and shoulder only; some fragmentation
52	Moderate	Moderate	Severe surface erosion and some fragmentation
100	Poor	Moderate	Incomplete long bones; some surface erosion
142	Moderate	Good	Lower half only; some fragmentation at epiphyses

Assessment of age

Individual development is influenced by a number of factors, including population growth rates, environmental conditions and dietary influences (Whittaker 2000, 83). These aspects of development are difficult, and sometimes impossible, to predict in archaeological material and, as such, methods used in the ageing of skeletal remains can only provide broad age estimates.

Sub-adult age is assessed using aspects of both dental development (calcification and eruption sequences) and skeletal development (stages of ossification, long-bone length and epiphyseal fusion). As maturation in females occurs at approximately one to two years earlier than in males, the combined age-range for males and females is used where applicable. Although dental development is completed by approximately eighteen years, with the eruption of the third molar, skeletal development continues into early adulthood, with late fusing epiphyses, including the vertebral end-plates, the iliac crest and the medial clavicle, continuing to provide information on age. Once these elements have completely fused, however (by approximately thirty years of age), age assessment is based on processes of skeletal degeneration and dental attrition.

When ageing adults, primary consideration is given to degenerative changes to the pubic symphysis, based on the Suchey-Brooks scheme (Brooks & Suchey 1990; Suchey & Katz 1986), and found in Buikstra and Ubelaker (1994), and changes to the auricular surface as defined by Meindl and Lovejoy (1989), and again found in Buikstra and Ubelaker (1994). Although considered the most reliable indicators of age, these areas of the pelvis are often damaged or incomplete. In addition to skeletal changes, dental attrition (Brothwell 1981) can be used, where applicable, to provide a broad estimation of age at time of death.

In this population, the incomplete survival of the skeletons, combined with surface-erosion affecting a number of skeletal elements, meant that the most reliable skeletal indicators of age, namely the pubic symphysis and/or auricular surface, could only be used to age two individuals (Burial 33 and Burial 142). Age estimation for Burial 33 used a combination of the pubic symphysis and dental attrition, both of which gave a young adult age determination (17–25 years). Although only the lower half of Burial 142 was recovered, there was good survival of the pelvis and age estimation in this example was based on changes to the auricular surface. Age determination for this individual suggested a young adult age of 20–24 years.

Dental attrition could be used to age a further two individuals (Burial 46 and Burial 50). In both examples there was very little wear on any of the surviving teeth, suggesting that these individuals were young adult (17–25 years) at the time of death. The remaining two individuals (Burial 52 and Burial 100) could only be given the broad age determination of 'adult', due to poor and incomplete preservation.

Assessment of sex

Biological sex was determined using standard techniques as featured in Bass (1987), Buikstra and Ubelaker (1994), and Cox and Mays (2000). Sex determination is primarily used to provide population data, but also can affect additional aspects of osteological assessment, and both age and stature determination can be affected by the sex of the individual. Reliable sex differences in skeletal remains first appear at puberty, when increasing hormone levels begin to act on the body and skeletal structure.

Commonly, however, sub-adult remains, even those that have reached puberty, show little skeletal sexual differentiation.

In general, the pelvis is considered to exhibit the highest degree of sexual dimorphism, as it is adapted in females to allow for childbirth. Essentially, the broad pelvic structure in the female skeleton contrasts with the narrow and high pelvis in the male skeleton. In addition to the pelvis, the skull is also used as a primary indicator of sexual differentiation in skeletal material and it is often found that males display more robust or prominent features than their female counterparts. This, however, may not always be the case, and morphological variations, visible in living populations, may manifest in skeletal remains. It is therefore important to use a combination of criteria, where possible, in the determination of sex. In addition to the primary areas of the pelvis and skull, articular surface measurements, taken on specific points of the skeleton, can be used to provide information on sex.

Sex could be determined for five of the six individuals recovered during these excavations (Table 5.2). Three of the individuals were determined to be male, with two assessed as probable male. The poorly-preserved remains of Burial 100 were too incomplete to provide an estimation of sex.

Table 5.2 Age and sex by individual

Burial	Sex	Age category	Years	Criteria used in age estimation
33	Male	Young adult	17–25	Pubic symphysis and dental attrition
46	?Male	Young adult	17–25	Dental attrition
50	?Male	Young adult	17–25	Dental attrition
52	Male	Adult	–	Robusticity and development of skeletal elements
100	–	Adult	–	Long bones fused; robusticity of skeletal elements
142	Male	Young adult	20–24	Auricular surface

Stature
Stature is estimated using regression equations, developed by Trotter and Gleser (1952; 1958), that are applied to the length of the long bones. In this population, stature could only be estimated for a single individual due to fragmentation and incomplete survival of the skeletal elements. Stature for Burial 33, a young adult male, was estimated at approximately 164–6cm. This was based on measurements of the humeri and radii.

Dental analysis
Teeth are composed of three main elements: *dentine*, the soft inner component of both the root and crown; *cement*, the hard thin layer surrounding the dentine at the root; and *enamel*, the durable outer covering of the crown. Dental enamel contains a high mineral content that, importantly in the study of human remains, results in good preservation in most archaeological contexts. In addition to this property, teeth are both non-vital and non-reparable. This simply means that any changes to the structure of the teeth – developmental, pathological or cultural – will not be remodelled through time. Analysis

of teeth can therefore provide important information on aspects of diet, health and hygiene. Only three of the six burials from this site were recovered with dental remains, each of which is discussed individually below (see also Table 5.3).

Burial 33 This young adult male survived with a complete dentition. He was affected by two visible dental anomalies, including slight mesial rotation of the right mandibular canine and non-eruption of the right maxillary canine. In addition to these anomalies, the dentition was affected by a number of commonly occurring conditions. One of the most common forms of dental pathology encountered in archaeological populations is calculus. This hard deposit is formed on teeth through the mineralization of dental plaque and commonly occurs in the absence of dental hygiene practices. Calculus affected twenty-four (77.4%) of the thirty-one teeth in full occlusion. The deposits were most commonly found on the buccal and lingual surfaces of the teeth, and ranged in severity from slight to moderate through the maxilla and from slight to severe through the mandible.

In addition to calculus, carious lesions were identified on three teeth (9.7%). These cavities are defined as areas of localized destruction, occurring in the presence of dietary sucrose (Hillson 1996, 282). Although rates of caries increased after the introduction of refined sugars in the seventeenth century, the consumption of a high carbohydrate diet, commonly in the form of cereal crops, has also been linked to the development of dental caries. All affected teeth were from the left maxilla and included the second pre-molar (distal surface), second molar (origin obscured) and third molar (mesial surface). All three dental cavities were recorded as large and had resulted in the destruction of over approximately 50% of the crown surface. Although multiple factors, including diet and environment, can influence the development of caries, in this instance the presence of extensive calculus deposits in combination with the presence of multiple carious lesions suggests that poor dental hygiene practices may have contributed to the development of caries.

Associated with the caries were two large abscesses located at the second and third left maxillary molar positions. Abscesses occur subsequent to exposure of the tooth pulp or root to bacteria and they are most commonly found in association with caries or severe attrition. The cavities visible on dry bone form during the later stages of abscess development, allowing the accumulation of pus at the base of the tooth root to escape. These localized cavities would, most probably, have been the source of some pain to the individual. Attrition was slight throughout the dentition (Stages 1–3), but the pattern of wear on the maxillary incisors indicated that this individual had a slight overbite.

Burial 50 This young adult, of undetermined sex, survived with a total of twenty-six teeth and twenty-seven tooth sockets. Post-mortem tooth-loss had affected two of the tooth positions, with an additional one tooth (3.7%) lost ante-mortem. Loss of teeth prior to death can be related to a number of dental conditions, including periodontal disease, severe attrition, caries and localized trauma. In this example, however, it was difficult to determine the cause of the loss, although calculus and caries were both prevalent through the dentition.

Calculus affected 21 (80.8%) of the teeth and ranged in severity from slight to moderate. Calculus deposits were most commonly found on the buccal and lingual tooth-surfaces and were notably heavier and more frequent through the left side of the jaw.

Carious lesions were visible, affecting a total of seven (26.9%) of the teeth recovered with this individual. All affected teeth were molars. The majority of carious lesions were recorded as 'pin-point' or 'small', with the occlusal surface affected in five of the seven examples. In addition to the less severe carious lesions, both the right and left mandibular third molars had large caries on their occlusal surfaces. The right mandibular first molar was also affected by carious action, with total destruction of the tooth crown. A single buccal abscess was visible at the socket for the right third mandibular molar. As with Burial 33, the incidence of both calculus and caries throughout the dentition suggests that dental hygiene was poor.

In addition to caries and calculus, this individual was affected by slight periodontal disease. This is a process of inflammation of the tissues surrounding and supporting the teeth. This process of inflammation is called *gingivitis* when it affects the soft-tissues and *periodontitis* when it extends to involve the bony tissues. In archaeological material, it is recognizable as resorption of the margins of the alveolar bone. Slight periodontal disease was also observed affecting five (55.6%) of the nine surviving undamaged sockets.

Episodes of nutritional stress and/or pathological disturbance can cause a temporary cessation in enamel growth. This period of non-development is visible in teeth as a line, pits or a groove on the enamel surface and is termed enamel hypoplasia. While these lines can indicate periods of physiological disruption, it must be remembered that crown formation of the teeth is completed by approximately the seventh year of life in all but the third molar. As such, these hypoplastic lines can only be linked to periods of stress during childhood. Hypoplastic defects, visible on both the right maxillary canine and left mandibular canine, indicated that this individual had suffered a period of nutritional or pathological stress during childhood.

Dental attrition was slight throughout, with the majority of teeth affected by Stage 2 or Stage 3 attrition (Smith 1984). The most severe attrition (Stage 4) affected the maxillary central incisors.

Burial 46 A total of twenty-four teeth and two sockets were recovered with Burial 46, but no dental pathology was observed. Dental attrition was very slight, ranging from Stage 1 to Stage 2 (Smith 1984) through most of the dentition, with Stage 3 wear affecting the left maxillary first molar only. Small enamel pearls were visible on the roots of three maxillary molars. These are small nodules of enamel on the root of a tooth and are non-pathological.

Pathological analysis
There are, relatively speaking, only a small number of diseases that visibly affect bone. Most conditions that do affect the skeleton result from periods of long-standing disease and/or nutritional deficiency. In general, acute episodes of nutritional or pathological stress either resolve themselves, or result in death, before the bony elements become involved. An exception to this is seen in cases of trauma where direct insult to the bone is readily apparent.

Table 5.3 Summary of dental pathology by individual

Burial	No. of sockets	No. of teeth	No. of teeth lost post-mortem	No. of teeth lost ante-mortem	No. of teeth affected by calculus	No. of teeth affected by caries	No. sockets affected by abscesses	No. of teeth affected by hypoplasia	No. sockets affected by periodontal disease
33	32	31	–	–	24	2	2	–	–
46	2	24	–	–	–	–	–	–	–
50	27	26	3	1	21	7	1	2	5
52	–	–	–	–	–	–	–	–	–
100	–	–	–	–	–	–	–	–	–
142	–	–	–	–	–	–	–	–	–

Joint disease Normally one of the most commonly-encountered pathologies in skeletal material, this was only identified through the lower thoracic and lumbar vertebrae of Burial 33. Changes affecting this individual were associated with degeneration of the inter-vertebral disc. Visible changes indicative of degeneration of the inter-vertebral disc include osteophytes, which develop at the margins of the vertebral body as a compensatory measure, increasing the vertebral body surface during accumulated axial pressure, and Schmorl's nodes. Schmorl's nodes appear as depressions in the vertebral bodies and develop where sufficient compressive forces through the centre of the disc cause the nucleus pulposus to herniate. When this material enters the vertebral body, it causes death (necrosis) of the surrounding tissue. In dry-bone, Schmorl's nodes can take a variety of forms, from linear through to V- and L-shaped, and vary in both size and depth.

In this example, Schmorl's nodes were visible through the lower thoracic and lumbar regions of the spine, affecting T9 through to T11, and from L1 to L3. Joint disease can occur as a consequence of ageing, as a response to stresses at the joint through occupational activity, or secondary to trauma. In this example, the young age of the individual suggests that degenerative disc disease was related to physical stresses rather than age.

Metabolic disease Metabolic disorders result from a deficiency in, or an excess of, dietary vitamins or minerals. The most commonly encountered of all the metabolic diseases in archaeological populations is iron-deficiency anaemia. Changes associated with this disorder are termed *cribra orbitalia* when the orbits are affected and *porotic hyperostosis* when the cranial vault is affected. Although *cribra orbitalia* is found on the orbits of both children and adults, it has been suggested that the skeletal changes visible in adult individuals represent a period of childhood deficiency (Stuart-Macadam 1985; 1992). Lesions present on the crania of adults are often found to be in a healing or healed phase.

Causes of iron-deficiency are variable, ranging from a diet lacking in iron-rich foods and/or a diet rich in foods that inhibit the absorption of dietary iron, to blood loss through injury or disease. Iron-deficiency may also indicate that the body was fighting a high pathogen load, as when the body reduces the amount of iron present in the blood stream, it becomes a less suitable medium for bacterial development (Weinberg 1992; Stuart-Macadam 1992, 158). While it is therefore possible to identify signs of iron-deficiency on the skeleton, it is more difficult to determine the cause of such a deficiency.

Evidence for healed porotic hyperostosis was visible on the parietal and frontal bones of Burial 50 and Burial 52. Healing of the lesions indicates that the period of nutritional stress was not on-going at time of death.

Non-specific infection This is the term given to skeletal lesions that identify the presence of an infectious pathogen, but where the exact nature of the infection is unknown. These differ from specific infections where both the pattern of skeletal involvement and the nature of changes to the bone identify a specific type of infection.

Evidence for non-specific infection is common in archaeological populations and can result from a wide range of sources, including direct insult (for example, a blow to a limb with resulting infection) and transportation to the bone through the blood-stream from an unrelated source (Roberts & Manchester 1995, 127). As with most diseases visible on skeletal remains, infectious lesions only form if the infection is chronic and long-standing.

There are three main categories of bony involvement seen in infection, namely periostitis, osteitis and osteomyelitis. In this population, evidence for non-specific infection was limited to a single example of periostitis. New bone growth was identified on two incomplete rib shafts that were possibly associated with Burial 100, an adult of undetermined sex. The presence of woven bone on the external surface of the rib shafts indicates that infection was active at the time of death, but there were no additional osteological indicators that could be used to identify the cause of this infection.

Trauma The vertebrae of Burial 46 were very fragmented and incomplete, with considerable erosion affecting the surviving fragments. Despite this, two of the lumbar vertebrae were visibly fused through both the vertebral bodies and the apophyseal joints. It is suggested that this represents localized traumatic or congenital fusion, as there was no evidence for associated degenerative joint disease at either this point or through the rest of the vertebral column. An enthesopathy at the insertion of *latissimus dorsi/teres major* on the left proximal humeral shaft of this individual may represent the site of localized muscle trauma.

Burial 142, a young adult male, had a well-healed fracture of the left tibial shaft. The site of fracture was recognizable through slight expansion of the shaft approximately mid-way down the length. There was no evidence for associated infection and no displacement of the shaft fragments. The level of healing indicated that the trauma had occurred a significant time prior to death, although the cause of the fracture could not be determined.

In addition to the articulated human remains, a small quantity of disarticulated human bone was presented for analysis. Included in this group of material was an unstratified adult frontal bone from Trim Townparks. This bone presented the only evidence for peri-mortem trauma encountered in the skeletal remains. On the left side of the frontal bone, a shallow, roughly oval, blade-wound was clearly visible. This wound measured 25mm medio-laterally and 13.8mm anterior-posteriorly, and had sliced a thin section of cortical bone from the cranial vault. There was no healing of the injury, indicating that it occurred in or around the time of death. Unfortunately, as this bone was disarticulated, it is impossible to ascertain any further information on the individual affected, although it is clear that this person was subject to some form of violent encounter which, most probably, resulted in death.

DISCUSSION

Excavations at Trim Castle lawn uncovered the remains of six individual burials, all of which had been disturbed by later activity. In addition to the individual burials a small quantity of disarticulated bone was recovered and presented for analysis. The osteological evidence strongly suggests that a single sub-set of the population was interred in this location, with young adult males dominating the demographic. As excavations were limited in extent, however, and only six individuals were identified, it is difficult to establish the significance of this profile. Although it is possible that further excavation could identify additional burials, comprising a wider population demographic, the discovery of this small group of individuals in an area of boggy soil outside the limits of known burial grounds suggests that this group of young males was deliberately placed in this location.

There were no skeletal indicators that would suggest why this sub-set of the population was buried in this particular location and evidence for skeletal and dental pathology was minimal. Mild joint disease affected only the vertebral column of one individual, although this is hardly unusual, given the young age-profile of the individuals analyzed. Evidence for nutritional stresses was also limited, with two examples of healed porotic hyperostosis, indicative of a period of iron-deficiency in childhood, and one example of enamel hypoplasia, again indicative of childhood deficiency or stress. Evidence for trauma was limited to a small number of healed traumatic lesions, all of which could have resulted from normal occupational or environmental hazards.

The dental remains suggest that dental hygiene was poor, with high rates of calculus and caries affecting two of the three individuals with dentition. Dental attrition was slight throughout, supporting the young adult age determination for the majority of individuals in the group.

A single disarticulated frontal bone from Trim Townparks provided the only evidence for peri-mortem trauma, with a shallow blade-wound on the left side of the bone. This wound did not penetrate through the cranial vault, but rather represents the site of a shallow, slicing blow. There was no evidence of healing, indicating that this individual was involved in some level of conflict at the time of death. Unfortunately, there is nothing to directly link this cranial fragment with the articulated skeletal remains.

BIBLIOGRAPHY

Bass, W.M., 1987, *Human osteology: a laboratory and field manual*. Missouri.
Brooks, S., & Suchey, J.M., 1990, 'Skeletal age-determination based on the *os pubis*: a comparison of the Acsadi-Nemeskeri and Suchey-Brooks methods'. *Human Evolution* 5, 227–38.
Brothwell, D.R., 1981, *Digging up bones* (3rd ed.), London.
Buikstra, J.E., & Ubelaker, D.H. (eds), 1994, *Standards for data collection from human skeletal remains*. Arkansas Archaeological Survey Research Series 44. Fayetteville.
Cox, M., & Mays, S. (eds), 2000, *Human osteology in archaeology and forensic science*. London.
Hillson, S., 1996, *Dental anthropology*. Cambridge.
Meindl, R.S., & Lovejoy, O.C., 1989, 'Age changes in the pelvis: implications for palaeodemography' in Iscan, M.Y. (ed.), *Age-markers in the human skeleton*, 137–68. Springfield, Illinois.
Roberts, C., & Manchester, K., 1995, *The archaeology of disease* (2nd ed.), Stroud, Gloucestershire.
Smith, B.H., 1984, 'Patterns of molar wear in hunter-gatherers and agriculturalists'. *American Journal of Physical Anthropology* 63, 39–56.
Stuart-Macadam, P., 1992, 'Anaemia in past populations' in Stuart-Macadam, P., & Kent, S. (eds), *Diet, demography and disease: changing perspectives of anaemia*, 151–70. New York.
Stuart-Macadam, P., 1985, 'Porotic hyperostosis: representative of a childhood condition'. *American Journal of Physical Anthropology* 66, 391–8.
Suchey, J.M., Wisely, D.V., & Katz, D., 1986, 'Evaluation of the Todd and McKern-Stewart methods for ageing the male os pubis' in Reichs, K.J. (ed.), *Forensic osteology: advances in the identification of human remains*, 33–67. Springfield.
Trotter, M., & Gleser, G.C., 1952, 'Estimation of stature from long bones of American whites and Negroes'. *American Journal of Physical Anthropology* 10, 463–514.
Trotter, M., & Gleser, G.C., 1958, 'A re-evaluation of estimation of stature based on measurements of stature taken during life and long bones after death'. *American Journal of Physical Anthropology* 16, 79–123.
Weinberg, E.D., 1992, 'Iron-withholding in prevention of disease' in Stuart-Macadam, P., & Kent, S. (eds), *Diet, demography and disease: changing perspectives of anaemia*, 105–50. New York.
Whittaker, D., 2000, 'Ageing from the dentition' in Cox, M., & Mays, S. (eds), *Human osteology in archaeology and forensic science*, 83–99. London.

APPENDIX 5.2: SKELETAL CATALOGUE

By Jennie Coughlan

Burial 33

SEX	Male	COMPLETENESS	Moderate
AGE CLASS	Young adult	PRESERVATION	Moderate
AGE RANGE	17–25 years		
STATURE	164–166cm		

BONES PRESENT — Cranium; mandible; right and left scapulae, clavicles, radii and ulnae; right and left hands; vertebrae; sternum; ribs; pelvis and sacrum; right and left femora

NON-METRIC TRAITS	Mtopic suture; palatine torus; right supracondyloid process

DENTITION

| 18 | 17 | 16 | 15 | 14 | u | 12 | 11 | | 21 | 22 | 23 | 24 | 25 | 26 | 27 | 28 |
| 48 | 47 | 46 | 45 | 44 | 43 | 42 | 41 | | 31 | 32 | 33 | 34 | 35 | 36 | 37 | 38 |

DENTAL PATHOLOGY	Calculus (24/31); caries (3/31); abscess (2/32)
SKELETAL PATHOLOGY	Schmorl's nodes

Burial 46

SEX	?Male	COMPLETENESS	Moderate
AGE CLASS	Young adult	PRESERVATION	Poor
AGE RANGE	17–25 years		
STATURE	/		

BONES PRESENT	All elements represented, but fragmented and incomplete
NON-METRIC TRAITS	/

DENTITION

| | 18 | 17 | 16 | — | — | 13 | 12 | 11 | | 21 | 22 | 23 | 24 | 25 | 26 | 27 | 28 |
| | — | 47 | — | — | 44 | 43 | — | 41 | | 31 | — | 33 | 34 | 35 | 36 | 37 | 38 |

DENTAL PATHOLOGY	/
SKELETAL PATHOLOGY	Localized congenital/traumatic fusion of two lumbar vertebrae; probable muscle trauma on left humerus

Burial 50

SEX	Undetermined	COMPLETENESS	Poor
AGE CLASS	Young adult	PRESERVATION	Moderate
AGE RANGE	17–25 years		
STATURE	/		

BONES PRESENT	Cranium; mandible; cervical vertebrae; left clavicle, scapula and humeral head
NON-METRIC TRAITS	/

DENTITION

| | — | 17 | 16 | — | — | 13 | 12 | 11 | | 21 | PM | 23 | 24 | 25 | 26 | 27 | — |
| | 48 | 47 | 46 | 45 | 44 | PM | PM | 41 | | 31 | 32 | 33 | 34 | 35 | AM | 37 | — |

DENTAL PATHOLOGY	Calculus (21/25); caries (7/25); abscess (1/24); enamel hypoplasia (2/25); ante-mortem loss (1/24)
SKELETAL PATHOLOGY	Healed porotic hyperostosis

Burial 52

SEX	Male		COMPLETENESS	Moderate
AGE CLASS	Adult		PRESERVATION	Moderate
AGE RANGE	/			
STATURE	/			

| BONES PRESENT | Cranium; left clavicle and scapula; right and left humeri, radii and ulnae; right and left hands; small number of vertebral and rib fragments; pelvis and sacrum; right and left femora, tibiae and fibulae; right and left feet |
| NON-METRIC TRAITS | Ossicles in lambdoid (right); auditory torus (bilateral); supra-condyloid process (bilateral) |

DENTITION

— — — — — — —   — — — — — — —
— — — — — — —   — — — — — — —

| DENTAL PATHOLOGY | / |
| SKELETAL PATHOLOGY | Healed porotic hyperostosis |

Burial 100

SEX	Undetermined		COMPLETENESS	Poor
AGE CLASS	Adult		PRESERVATION	Moderate
AGE RANGE	/			
STATURE	/			

| BONES PRESENT | Incomplete left clavicle, scapula and humerus; incomplete left femur and left and right tibiae and fibulae; small number of vertebral fragments |
| NON-METRIC TRAITS | / |

DENTITION

— — — — — — —   — — — — — — —
— — — — — — —   — — — — — — —

| DENTAL PATHOLOGY | / |
| SKELETAL PATHOLOGY | Rib periostitis on two associated rib fragments |

Burial 142

SEX	Male		COMPLETENESS	Moderate
AGE CLASS	Young adult		PRESERVATION	Good
AGE RANGE	20–24 years			
STATURE	/			

BONES PRESENT   Incomplete cranium; lumbar vertebrae; pelvis and
sacrum; right and left femora, tibiae, fibulae and feet

NON-METRIC TRAITS   Hypotrochanteric fossa (left), third trochanter
(bilateral)

DENTITION

— — — — — — — —   — — — — — — — —
— — — — — — — —   — — — — — — — —

DENTAL PATHOLOGY   /

SKELETAL PATHOLOGY   Healed left tibial fracture

APPENDIX 5.3: DISARTICULATED BONE REGISTER

By Jennie Coughlan

Table 5.4 Register of disarticulated bones

Feature no.	Sample no.	Notes	Description	Comments
F54	87	Assoc. B: 52	2 x partial lumbar neural arches	Adult
F54	87		3 x spinous processes	Adult
F54	87		1 x incomplete rib shaft	Adult
F54	87		1 x partial proximal radial shaft	Adult
F54	87		1 x incomplete right navicular	Adult
F54	82		2 x small rib shaft fragments	
F54	82		1 x partial proximal radial shaft	Adult
F54	82		3 x incomplete intermed. hand phalanges	Adult
F54	82		1 x incomplete prox. hand phalanx	Adult
F54	82		1 x partial MC	
F54	82		2 x vertebral neural arch fragments	
F54	82		1 x incomplete MC/MT head	
F54	82		Small shaft fragments	
F102	172		1 x spinous process	
F102	172		1 x long bone fragment	
F102	172		1 x ?pelvic fragment	
F101	156		1 x neural arch fragment	
F101	156		Small number of additional fragments	
F31	18	Assoc. B:33	3 x distal hand phalanges	Adult
F31	18			
F31	10	Assoc. B:33	2 x small neural arch fragments	
F31	10		1 x fragment of rib	
F31	10		Small number of additional fragments	

Feature no.	Sample no.	Notes	Description	Comments
F31	98	Below B:53	1 x incomplete distal right fibula	Adult
F31	98		1 x small neural arch fragment	
F31	98		1 x fragment of fibular shaft	
F31	98		Small number of additional fragments	
F54	88		Small number of pelvis fragments	Adult
F49	42	B:46	1 x left lunate	Adult
F49	42		1 x neural arch fragment	
F49	42		1 x rib fragment	
F49	42		1 x pelvic fragment (ilium)	
F49	42		Small number of additional fragments	
F54	58		1 x very small cranial fragment	?Human
F31	61	Cranial area of B:50	Small number of sphenoid fragments	
F31	81		1 x very small shaft fragment	?Human
F31	38		Small number of cranial vault fragments	
F31	38		2 x unidentified fragments	
F49	33	B:46	1 x premolar – root damaged	Stage 1 attrition
F49	33		1 x sternal rib end	?Copper staining
F49	33		Small number of additional fragments	
F102	171		1 x intermediate foot phalanx	Adult
F102	171		1 x sesamoid bone	
F102	171		1 x fragment of ?proximal tibia	
F102	171		Small number of additional fragments	
F142	177		Small number of cranial fragments	
F142	177		1 x sesamoid	
F142	177		1 x unidentified fragment	
F54	59		1 x fragment of temporal	

SubUrbia: evidence for suburban activity in the medieval town of Trim

MANDY STEPHENS

This paper assesses evidence for suburban activity outside the walls of the medieval town of Trim. Excavations in 2006 revealed the remains of two medieval houses and their associated burgage plots. The discussion assesses the physical remains excavated, evidence for domestic life and economy within the suburb, and the interdependence of town and suburb.

INTRODUCTION

The archaeological excavations were conducted by CRDS Ltd, on behalf of Trim Town Council, in advance of a scheme of infrastructural works described

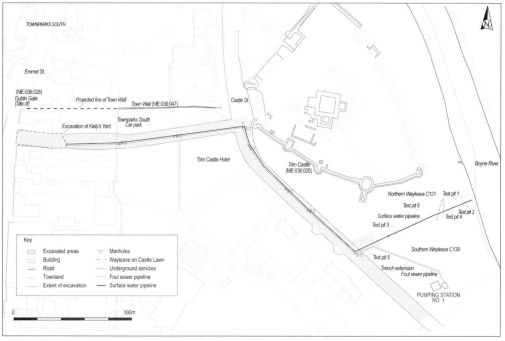

6.1 Location map and plan of development (base-map courtesy of Ordnance Survey Ireland, Permit 8565 © Ordnance Survey Ireland/Government of Ireland)

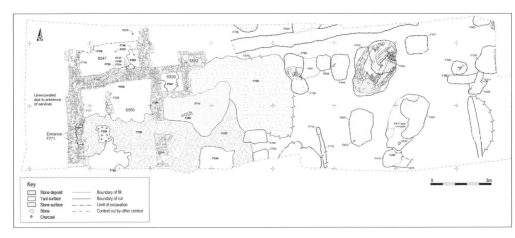

6.2 Post-excavation plan of Kiely's Yard

in a separate paper in this volume (O'Carroll). These works included upgrading the mains drainage system and the construction of a new road, Finnegan's Way, to link Emmet Street with Castle Street. Construction of the link-road necessitated advance excavation of a wider corridor between the public car-park and Emmet Street (in the former yard and beer garden of Kiely's Bar, referred to here as Kiely's Yard; fig. 6.1). The most significant remains, which are the subject of this paper, were a post-medieval structure, associated with a mill, and two medieval houses and their burgage plots.

EXCAVATIONS AT EMMET STREET/KIELY'S YARD

Excavations at the west side of Emmet Street took place in a corridor *c*.40 by 12m on the south side of an eighteenth-/nineteenth-century mill in the former yard of Kiely's Bar. The site is *c*.20m south of the assumed locations of the Dublin Gate, the town wall and the course of the Leper River (fig. 6.1). The site sloped from south to north, as a spine of bedrock naturally fell away in this direction. An annexe or extension to the post-medieval mill building on the northeast side of the site was represented by wall-footings and a series of post-holes. These were excavated, and the building was found to truncate features associated with two medieval houses and their burgage plots. The houses, in turn, disturbed earlier remains. Three main phases of activity were identified: Phase 1 was the earliest occupation; Phase 2 comprised the medieval houses and the yards; and Phase 3 consisted of post-medieval activity. Each of these phases is discussed, in turn, below.

Phase 1: earliest occupation, c.AD1027–1290
The earliest phase of occupation at the western end of the site was represented by a series of quarry-pits, a cess-pit, post-holes, stake-holes and a hearth

(fig. 6.2). The quarry-pits and the cess-pit (F825) measured up to 2.45m wide and 1.8m deep. All were excavated through the bedrock. The quarry-pits were characterized by longitudinal splitting or clefting of the bedrock and the back-fill deposits, which contained mixed deposits of shattered stone and boulder clay, with fragments of organic material, were interpreted as quarry waste.

These pits were truncated by a large cess-pit F825. A stone wall (F830) constructed with cut limestone blocks, was built into the west side of the pit to retain this side where it cut into an earlier quarry-pit (fig. 6.5). The pit was filled with a series of organic clays from which four leather shoes, a leather strap and other leather fragments were recovered. Analysis of the animal bone from this pit suggests that it contained butchery waste (Beglane, 'Meat and craft', this volume). Pomoideae charcoal from the fill of the cess-pit has been radiocarbon-dated to 1045–1252 cal. AD (2 Sigma).

A series of post-holes, pits and stake-holes (some of which contained in situ stakes and post-butts) beneath the stone houses might represent an earlier structure at the site. The plan of a structure could not be identified, however, due to the degree of truncation by later activity. A hearth (F790) is likely to date to this phase of activity also; charcoal from the lowest deposit has returned a date of 1030–1220 cal. AD (Table 6.1).

Further east on the site, early occupation evidence included a linear gully. Charcoal from the gully (F743) returned a date of 1027–1185 cal. AD (2 Sigma). The gully was deliberately sealed with a stone deposit related to surfacing of yards during later occupation. This gully is likely to be contemporary with the Phase 1 activity described above.

Table 6.1 Earliest occupation at Kiely's Yard and historic records time-line

Date	Feature	Description	Phase	Notes
1027–1185 cal. AD	F743	Gully	1	Function unclear
1030–1220 cal. AD	F790	Hearth material	1	Subsequently sealed with stone flags
1045–1252 cal. AD	F825	Cess-pit	1	Contained leather shoes, horn-cores and butchery waste
1040–1270 cal. AD	F766	Cess-pit	1	Wooden lid or seat over the pit; Food waste & straw fragments recovered
Pre-dated F766	F738	Cess-pit	1	Contained a wooden bowl; Food waste & flax seeds recovered
AD1167–1216	ME:036:025	Ringwork at Trim Castle site	1	Radiocarbon date
AD1175±9	ME:036:025	Ringwork at Trim Castle site	1	Dendrochronology date
AD1290 Murage grant	ME:036:047	Trim Town Wall	2	See also Seaver 2008

These dates are particularly interesting as they suggest that the site was occupied quite early in the development of Trim, and very likely before the construction of the town wall. The ringwork beneath Trim Castle has been dated to AD1167–1216

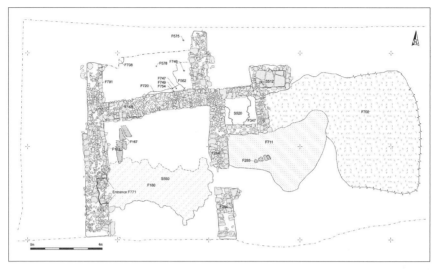

6.3 Plan of houses and ancillary structures S550, S547, S513 and S520, showing hearths (F302 & F708), stone floors (F160, F167 & F564) and yard surfaces (F702 & F711)

6.4 Remains of medieval houses

(radiocarbon) and AD1175±9 (dendrochronology) (Potterton 2005). The Phase 1 activity at Kiely's Yard is broadly contemporary with these dates.

Phase 2

The medieval houses Phase 2 activity on the site was represented by the construction of two houses at the Emmet Street (west) end of the site and the excavation of associated rubbish, cess and semi-industrial pits in the yard area. The structures fronted onto Emmet Street and comprised a dividing wall, oriented east-west, and front and rear walls. The return or gable walls lay outside the limit of excavation and it is assumed that they are beneath adjacent properties either side of the development corridor (figs 6.3 & 6.4). The southern and larger house, S550, measured *c*.7 by 6m, while the northern structure, S547, measured *c*.5 by 3m. Two ancillary structures were recorded to the rear of the properties. The foundations of the houses were stone-built and laid over a series of mixed deposits of silt, stone and clay, interpreted as ground-levelling or consolidation material to compensate for the natural slope of the site.

The rear wall of the southern house was constructed over a timber raft foundation (fig. 6.5) laid over the sealed Phase 1 cess-pit (F825). The walls reached a maximum of five courses in height on the north side of the site, where the ground naturally fell away. Only one course survived on the higher,

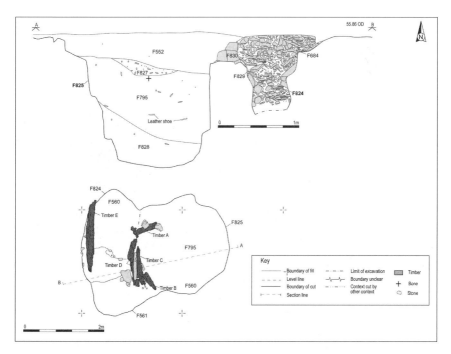

6.5 Section of cess-pit (F825) and quarry-pit (F824)

southern side. The walls of the structures had an average width of 1m, and it is suggested that the houses were originally two or possibly three storeys in height. While little evidence was found for timber partitions, it is possible that upper floors were constructed primarily of timber above low stone walls. Wooden 'jetties' may have been used to increase floor space at upper levels.

The Emmet Street houses are unlikely to represent a single dwelling with extensions and additions. Although only the lower courses of the structural walls survived, there was no evidence for a doorway or other access point between the two houses, suggesting that each property had its own separate access. While no evidence for a doorway was identified to the front or rear of the northern house, only a limited portion of that structure lay within the development corridor, and the access points may remain intact beneath the modern adjoining property (Kiely's Bar). Entrances were recorded in the front (F171) and rear (F284) walls of the larger southern structure, and these led to the street (Emmet Street) and the back yard respectively. The front entrance way stepped down into the house, suggesting that the medieval street level was higher than the floor of the house (fig. 6.3). The difference was not so great as to suggest that these were cellared buildings similar to that recorded at High Street in Waterford (Walsh 1987).

Associated floor surfaces, two hearths, two ancillary structures and a sequence of associated yard surfaces were also recorded (fig. 6.3). A hearth in the northern property returned a date of 1290–1420 cal. AD, suggesting continuity of occupation from Phase 1. Furthermore, a Phase 1 hearth appears to have been sealed with flag-stones and then re-used as a hearth during the lifespan of these houses.

Deposits of stone cobbling were found within the structures, and these were interpreted as stone floors (fig. 6.3). A single piece of a two-colour floor-tile was also recovered. Unfortunately, it came from a disturbed deposit to the front (west) of the northern structure, but it tentatively suggests the use here of ceramic tiles for flooring. The fabric of the roofs of the buildings is not known, but a single fragment of a glazed and decorated crested ridge-tile was recovered, suggesting that the roof might have been covered with thatch or shingle with a line of ceramic ridge-tiles.

The ancillary structures To the rear of each of the two houses were the remains of a small, stone-built structure (S520 was behind the southern house and S513 was behind the northern house (fig. 6.3)). These ancillary structures may have been used as garderobes. The southern one was built some time after the construction of the main house. Square in plan, it enclosed a space 1.6m by 1.6m. It was paved with a denuded layer of cobbling and overlay an infilled Phase 1 quarry-pit. The cobbled layer was fragmentary, but probably originally covered the entire area of the structure. It was composed of angular stones, tightly packed together to form a level surface.

6.6 Rectangular stone trough

The other ancillary structure (S513) is later in date. Its walls were a maximum of two courses in height, consisting of small, cut limestone blocks, bonded with mortar. A break in the northern wall measured 40cm. This break was too small to represent an entrance and may have functioned as a shovel hole. Rectangular in plan, the structure enclosed a space measuring 1.7m by 90cm. The enclosure was paved with eight large, irregularly-shaped, flat slabs of limestone (F512), which were cut to fit together to form an even surface (fig. 6.6). The slabs were set into a rectangular cut that in turn overlay a layer of yellow grey marl that was deliberately laid to set the slabs. It is likely that the marl would have made the structure water-tight. This trough-like structure was filled by a layer of lime. The function of this building is unclear. It is very similar in scale and morphology to stone-lined pits recorded on Market Street (Hayden, 'Market Street', this volume), and similar to a later medieval cess-pit recorded at Worcester (www.worcestershire.whub.org.uk). Two post-medieval stone-lined pits containing lime were recorded at Phillips Lane, Cork (O'Donnell 2003, 78–99), and these were interpreted as soak-pits for skins associated with the tanning process.

The second ancillary structure (S513) was initially interpreted as a bunker or storage container for holding lime, or alternatively as a trough for some semi-industrial process utilizing lime. Certainly, the presence of flax seeds and bolls and faunal remains associated with leather-working in a number of the pits further east in the yard suggests that flax and leather were being processed on site. Lime was also used as a disinfectant in the middle ages. The trough may have functioned as a bleach pit for linen or as a garderobe, regularly cleaned out into the pits in the yard and disinfected with lime. The other ancillary structure (S520), which was also paved, was a later addition to the rear of the southern house and might have functioned as a garderobe. It did not, however, contain any indicators, such as organic deposits, that might confirm that function.

Trim houses and wider comparisons A limited number of medieval houses have been excavated in Trim. Domestic activity has been recorded at Market Street and High Street (Hayden, 'Market Street', this volume; Hayden, 'High Street', this volume; Duffy, this volume). While discussions of urban tower houses and hall houses, their architecture and origins, are numerous, there are relatively few publications dealing with urban medieval domestic architecture in the corpus of Irish literature, in part due to the fact that only higher-status examples survive and are obvious in the archaeological record. Hurley (2003, 151–69) has suggested a chronology of medieval urban domestic architecture, which is outlined below in tabular form.

Table 6.2 **Chronology of medieval domestic architecture**

Date range	House-type	Description
Early 12th century	Wattle walled	Constructed with post-and-wattle
Mid 12th century	Sill beam, stave built	Earthfast staves supported by base stones
Mid to late 12th century	Sill beam	Foundation sill beams and earthfast timber uprights
Late 13th to 14th century	Stone houses	Hybrid constructions: timber and stone constructed on low stone wall-footings
15th century	Stone hall houses	Fortified town houses

Based on this chronology, the Emmet Street properties fall into the late-thirteenth- to fourteenth-century date-range. Discussions of house-types in Dublin's medieval suburb of Oxmantown suggest that housing in the suburb would have been of a lesser standard than in the walled town, perhaps reflecting the suburb's lesser status (Purcell 2005, 199). Building styles have not been tied in to a typological chronology, as a more fluid situation, with different house-styles co-existing over these time-spans and including mud-walled cottages, wood, stone and hybrid constructions, have all been evidenced (Cryerhall 2006, 38; Purcell 2005, 207). Purcell suggests that this reflects the diverse social stratification of the Oxmantown suburb and that this pattern is comparable to other medieval suburbs. Given the description of the range of burgage plot sizes along Emmet Street and Watergate Street (Potterton 2005, 198–200), the Emmet Street suburb is likely to reflect similar levels of diversity to that seen in Oxmantown.

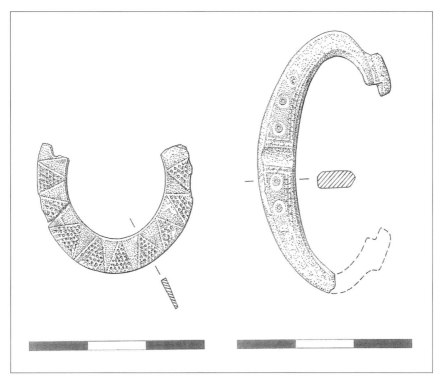

6.7 Artefacts recovered during excavations at Kiely's Yard (left: brooch fragment E2016:161:009; right: buckle E2016:673:001)

The medieval yards: AD1250–1400 The yards of the medieval properties were delimited by plot boundaries (F476, F200 & F153; fig. 6.2). They were truncated to varying degrees by later activity and were partial in some cases (fig. 6.2). Boundary F153 was recorded in the 40 by 12m area excavated to the east of the Kiely's Yard site; it would have had a total length of *c*.50m. The parallel (northern) boundary marker (F476) ran into the northern limit of excavation and a later stone kerb or wall-footing (F200) was identified on the south side of this boundary. This is likely to have been laid after the gully had silted up, to continue or revet the boundary marker. This development is interesting, as it shows a concern with maintaining the original land divisions over time and is paralleled in other urban centres (Simpson 2006, 113–50).

Comparison with Trim burgage plots The burgage plot boundaries in the Emmet Street suburb are well-defined on the west side of the street and they replicate the pattern identified within the walled town. The plot pattern on the east side of the street is less well-defined and is likely to have suffered from modern development. The evidence from the Kiely's Yard site certainly suggests that the foundation levels and plot boundaries of the medieval suburban properties may remain extant beneath the modern properties.

Potterton's analysis of the plot pattern on the west sides of Emmet Street and Watergate Street (2005, 198–200) suggests that the plots were laid out to a clearly-defined pattern based on a measurement equivalent to 9.1m, and that the regularity in the plots is a standard feature of medieval towns. Forty per cent of examined plots in Trim were 9.1m wide, 24% were 7.1m wide and the remainder measured between 3.9m and 18.2m. These figures suggest that a range of sizes was being used in the plots.

Simpson's assessment of burgage plot boundaries in Dublin (2006, 113–51) suggests that the plot boundaries on South Great Georges Street were relatively consistent, measuring *c*.5.5 to 6.6m in width and between 55m and 60m in length. The boundaries were remarkably similar to those identified in the course of this project. The full widths of the Emmet Street houses were never exposed, as they lay outside of the road corridor. The southern house had an exposed width of *c*.7m, while the exposed width of the northern structure was *c*.5m. Investigative sections excavated through the baulk at the southern limit of excavation did not reveal the return wall for the southern structure, and this is likely to lie below the gable end of the adjoining property, approximately 1m beyond the limit of the excavation. If the modern property has been built over the foundation level of the earlier house, then it appears likely that the medieval house falls into the 7.1m limit identified by Potterton. This suggests a high degree of control of space being exercised by the medieval authorities in the suburb as well as within the walled town itself.

The structural walls and plot boundaries identified on the Kiely's Yard site are slightly off-line with the adjacent modern properties, suggesting that the plots have changed slightly in orientation over time. The medieval properties do appear to front directly onto Emmet Street, although the presence of live services and associated disturbance at this end of the properties limited the archaeological investigations in this area. The location of the street may have been determined by the course of the Leper River and a pre-existing defensive ditch (Fallon 2003, also this volume) in this area.

An intense sequence of pit-cutting was recorded in the yards, indicating use of the site over a protracted period of time, as was common on medieval domestic sites (fig. 6.2). A large number of pits were recorded in the yards, including cess, refuse and quarry-pits. Some may have been multifunctional, being used periodically or seasonally for industrial processing.

Sequential layers of stone surfacing in the yards suggests attempts to keep the area directly to the rear of the houses clean and dry, but these would also have delimited space in the yards. The immediate area around the back door was likely to have been an extension to the living space, with the unsurfaced

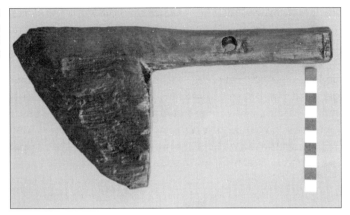

6.8 Wooden locking mechanism or latch recovered from rubbish pit

yard further east primarily dedicated to waste disposal, industrial activity and procurement of raw material from a series of quarry-pits. Where deposits of stone were recorded in the east end of the yards (F605), these appeared to be largely concerned with the sealing of pits rather than providing clean, dry work surfaces.

Wood- and stave-lined pits and stone-lined pits have been recorded on numerous medieval domestic sites. The evidence for these at Kiely's Yard, however, is limited to fragmented and decomposed pieces of wood along the sides and bases of a number of the pits in the main pit cluster. Two substantial sub-circular, inter-cut pits were recorded in the yards (F644, F447). These measured between 2.6m and 4.2m in diameter, while a maximum depth of 1.2m was recorded. These are likely to represent quarrying activity. The earlier pit in the sequence (F664) had been back-filled with quarry waste and was later re-cut and extended (F447).

Subsequent to quarrying, the later pit had been utilized for the disposal of rubbish, including a large quantity of poor-quality, worked wooden objects, wood-working waste and structural pieces, primarily pieces of stakes, boards and planks. Specialist analysis of these remains suggests that many of these were structural elements associated with timber-frame building technology (Moore 2008). The presence of dumped structural material suggests that a building was cleared from the site and it is tentatively suggested that these remains represent the Phase 1 building. A wooden locking mechanism recovered from the pit was the only intact object found (fig. 6.8). The specialist report points out a parallel with excavations at Coppergate in York and Christ Church in Dublin. A similar object was also recovered in the course of excavations at Skiddy's Castle in Cork (O'Donnell 2003). This is a rare artefact, most likely used as the latch for a door or window (Moore 2008).

Material from cess-pit F766 has been dated to 1040–1270 cal. AD. A collapsed wooden frame (possibly the toilet seat) or a lid supported by wooden stakes, was uncovered in the upper levels of this pit, which had been deliberately sealed with layers of thick yellow clay (fig. 6.9). Food waste and straw fragments were also recovered. This pit truncated an earlier one (F738), which was probably another cess-pit. A wooden bowl had been preserved in the organic material in this pit (fig. 6.13), as had food waste and flax seeds. Specialist analysis of the bowl (Moore 2008) indicates that it is of thirteenth-century date and would have been a common domestic vessel. Pottery sherds recovered from these pits have been identified as Dublin-type finewares and coarsewares and locally-produced Trim-type wares, suggesting a later thirteenth-century date (McCutcheon 2008). Radiocarbon dates for this phase of activity are outlined in tabular form below.

Table 6.3 Phase 2 time-line

Date	Feature	Description	Notes
1205–85 cal. AD	F407	Cess-pit	Radiocarbon
1040–1270 cal. AD	F766	Cess-pit	Radiocarbon
AD1224		Siege at Trim	Documentary reference
AD1228	ME036:024	Franciscan (Grey) Friary	Documentary reference
AD1263	ME036:021	Dominican (Black) Friary	Documentary reference
1290–1420 cal. AD	F708	Hearth	Radiocarbon
AD1290	ME:036:047	Trim town wall in existence by this date	Murage grant; See also Seaver, this volume
AD1315–18		Bruce invasion	Documentary reference
AD1330		Boyne flood	Documentary reference
AD1335		Leper hospital	Documentary reference
AD1348–9		Black Death, famine, fire and flood	Documentary reference

Phase 2a: the later medieval yards, AD1400–1640 The question of water sources for the houses is a mystery. A stone-walled pit (F601) was initially interpreted as a cistern, but it appears to occur late in the sequence of features in the main pit cluster (radiocarbon-dated to 1440–1640 cal. AD; 2 Sigma), begging the question of where water was drawn from prior to its construction. Furthermore, the pit truncated a cluster of refuse and cess-pits, and is therefore unlikely to have been used for storing potable water (fig. 6.2). It is possible that there was a well on Emmet Street, but there is no evidence for this. The likeliest source of water for the houses is the Leper River, the assumed course of which lies directly north of this development.

6.9 Possible wooden toilet seat from cess-pit F766

Table 6.4 Phase 2a time-line

Date	Feature	Description	Notes
AD1368		Much of Trim burned	Annalistic reference (Potterton 2005, 299)
1440–1640 cal. AD	F601	Stone-lined pit	Radiocarbon
AD1450s		Trim under increasing attack from Gaelic enemies	Documentary reference

Analysis of the palaeo-environmental samples from the pits indicates that the medieval diet on the site was similar to that recorded at other medieval urban centres (Beglane, 'Meat and craft', this volume). Cattle, sheep, goat and pig were represented, with cattle predominating. Domestic and wild fowl, fish, cereals, fruit and nuts were also represented, suggesting a varied diet consisting of beef, mutton, pork and goat meat, domestic fowl, dairy products, eggs, cereals for bread and porridge, fruit and nuts. In addition, some sea fish were also noted (Hamilton Dyer 2007; Lyons 2007). This pattern fits well with the overall picture from other medieval centres.

The faunal remains suggest that cattle and sheep were reared in the rural hinterland and that older animals and animals of lesser quality were sold for consumption in the urban area. Goats are likely to have been reared in the suburb, where they would have been exploited for meat, milk, hides and horn. Hides, horn and wool were important resources for industry. Urban dwellers had little control over farming and therefore over the quality and supply of meat and dairy products. Goats reared in the town may have supplemented the meat and dairy components of the diet. The majority of cattle pathologies identified suggest that cattle were also used as traction animals (Beglane, 'Meat and craft', this volume).

The murage grants for the town suggest a variety of foodstuffs were available in the market, including cereals, flour, sea and fresh fish, processed and unprocessed meats, vegetables, cheese and butter, honey, salt and wine (Potterton 2005, 145–7). Much of this produce would have been available locally, but trade through the port at Drogheda would have also contributed.

Craft-working Evidence for craft-working in medieval Trim suggests that bone-, wood- and leather-working, linen-processing and metal-production were all being carried out on or near the Kiely's Yard site. The inter-relationship of crafts and the seasonality of a domestic economy are important factors. The domestic economy would have relied on small-scale and often seasonal industrial processing (such as flax) for domestic needs, with surpluses used for trade. Workshops for craft might have occupied the lower floors of houses, and the yards might have been used for 'dirty' processing.

Bone-working was evidenced by the presence of craft off-cuts and horn-cores (Beglane, 'Meat and craft', this volume), and a range of tools and objects might have been produced in a workshop at Emmet Street or nearby. These objects were recovered from the pits to the rear of the properties and deposits in the yards.

Table 6.5 Features associated with bone-working and metalworking (Beglane, 'Meat and craft', this volume)

Artefact / object	Phase	Feature	Interpretation
Drilled cattle metatarsal	1	181	Partial artefact or 'anvil'
Drilled cattle metatarsal	2	340	Craft-work off-cut
Drilled horse metatarsal	2	271	Tool or sheath
Pierced rib (remains of button manufacturing)	2	340	Craft-work off-cut
Sawn longbone	2	251	Craft-work off-cut
Rib and vertebra fragments with metal splatter	2	506 = 161	Metalworking
Rib fragment with metal splatter	2	518	Metalworking
Horn-core fragment with possible glaze splatter	2	518	Horn-working for artefact production
Horn-cores	2	175 = 453	Horn-working for artefact production
Cattle horn-cores with chop-marks	2	427	Horn-working for artefact production

6.10 Pit (F468) possibly used for tanning

Evidence for the processing of hides, in the form of cattle and goat skull and horn fragments, came from pits in the yards. The presence of calf metatarsals suggests that vellum production might also have been carried out (Beglane, 'Meat and craft', this volume). The lime deposits, in particular those identified in pits, are interesting, as lime was an important raw material in the processing of hides.

Table 6.6　Phase 2 features and deposits associated with hide-processing

Artefact/object	Feature	Cut	Interpretation
Calf metatarsal	498	497	Hide-working, possible vellum production
Cattle and goat, skull, horn and foot fragments, calf metatarsal	410, 411	404	Hide-working, possible vellum production
Lime deposit	409	468	Waste from linen-processing, tanning or disinfectant
Lime deposit	486	Yard deposit	Waste from linen-processing, tanning or disinfectant

Tanning is usually associated with thick hides (cattle) and tawing with thinner hides (sheep, goat, pig, horse, deer, dog and other skins). Both trades utilized lime or ash for the initial processing of hides, followed by immersion in either an alkaline solution in the case of tanning, or alum and oil in the case of tawing.

6.11 Loom-weight recovered
from cess-pit

Tawing could be carried out in barrels, however, and as a result may have
required less space (Albarella 2003, 71–82). Hides would have been soaked
with horns and hooves attached, possibly for quality control. This process
would also have rendered hooves and horns into a more plastic and transparent
raw material. The horner very likely got his raw material from the tanner and
not from the butcher (Albarella 2003, 71–82). Tanning and horn-working were
closely-related trades. The majority of the evidence for tanning comes from
one feature (F404). This linear channel may have been a gully to collect water
for an adjacent pit (F468) used for tanning (Beglane, 'Meat and craft', this
volume) (figs 6.2 & 6.10). The content of this pit has been radiocarbon-dated
to AD1160–1280.

The flax bolls and seeds recorded from pit fills are indicative of the
processing of flax for linen production, although flax may also be used as a
foodstuff, for medicinal purposes and in the production of linseed oil (Lyons
2007). The removal of flax bolls from their woody stems involves a process
known as rippling, followed by retting to encourage bacteriological attack. The
retting process is dirty and polluting and was usually carried out in open
streams or ponds or by soaking in specially dug pits or ditches. After retting,
the flax was threshed, spun and woven into cloth and finally bleached. The
bleaching process consisted of boiling the cloth in either ashes or lime, after
which the cloth was laid out in the sun to whiten (www.nhm.ac.uk/
jdsml/nature-online/seeds-of-trade). Flax is harvested in late summer and
early autumn, and processing was a seasonal activity. Flax was considered to be
a garden crop and linen-making was typically a small-scale domestic activity
up until the nineteenth century (Geraghty 1996, 45–6).

6.12 Iron shears recovered from cess-pit

The flax seeds and bolls recovered from Phase 2 levels at Emmet Street were from deposits initially interpreted as cess-pits or refuse pits, based on their similarity to other features in the yards. Evidence from the Viking levels at Fishamble Street in Dublin, however, suggests that pits may have been seasonally used for flax-retting and intermittently as toilets (Geraghty 1996, 29–30). A stone loom-weight was recovered from the fill of a Phase 1 cess-pit at Trim (fig. 6.11) and while this does not directly relate to flax-processing on the site, it might indicate textile production. A pair of shears was also recovered and this may also be related to this craft (fig. 6.12).

The ancillary building (S513) to the rear of the northern house contained a thick layer of lime (figs 6.2 & 6.6). Initially interpreted as a possible trough or bunker, it may well have functioned as a bleaching trough for linen. A deposit of lime spread across the northwest portion of the yard might represent cleaning of material from the pits and may have been associated with either linen-bleaching, tanning or the disinfecting of cess-pits.

Wool was an important trade good for many of the coastal towns in the medieval period, and the port at Drogheda was an important point of export. The faunal remains from Trim, however, suggest that it was of lesser importance here (Beglane, 'Meat and craft', this volume). Nonetheless, the documentary sources suggest that the cloth trade was an important part of the economy of Trim (Potterton 2005, 145–60), and murage grants for the town mention silks, samite, linen web, wool and cloth.

Potterton (2005, 163–5) also uses place-name evidence to demonstrate the presence of cloth- and leather-working industries, but the exact location of 'Skinners Street' and 'Dyersland' are unknown. Possible locations include the area around High Street, where a pair of medieval craft scissors was recovered during excavations. Loman Street, on the north side of the town, was formerly known as Scarlet Street. The surname 'Scarlett' was originally an occupational name related to textile-trading or dying (www.askoxford.com).

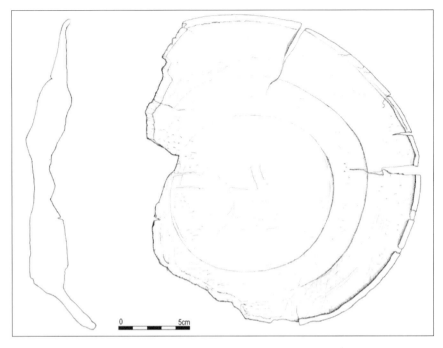

6.13 Thirteenth-century wooden bowl

Table 6.7 Features and deposits associated with flax-processing

Artefact/object	Phase	Feature	Cut	Interpretation
Flax bolls and seeds	2	436	318	Flax-processing, linen production
Flax bolls and seeds	2	637	634	Flax-processing, linen production
Flax bolls and seeds	2	742	738	Flax-processing, linen production
Lime deposit	2	509	S513	Linen bleaching, tanning, mortar production
Lime deposit	2a	486 deposit	Yard	Waste from linen bleaching, tanning or disinfectant
Stone loom-weight	1	795	825	Cloth production

Wood-working

Wood chips and wood-working waste recovered from the yards suggest that this craft may also have been carried out here (Moore 2008). Two wooden objects – a high quality, lathe-turned wooden bowl (fig. 6.13) and a composite wooden object, possibly part of a window fitting or a chest lid – were recovered from the cess-pits. The presence of structural timbers indicates that timber-frame building technology was also in use at Kiely's Yard.

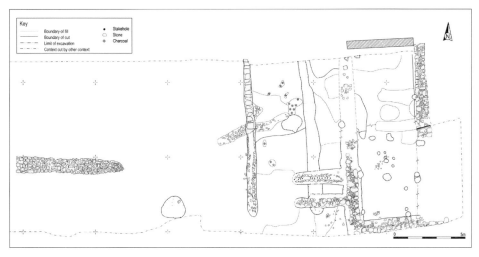

6.14 Post-medieval mill-buildings at Kiely's Yard

All of the above suggest that craft-working, possibly horn-working, seasonal flax-processing and linen production, leather-working and possibly vellum production were carried out. Horn-cores were a waste product from the processing of hides for leather, vellum production and bone-working. Given the times of year that vellum and flax are processed, it is quite possible that all of these inter-related crafts were being carried out seasonally, utilizing the same pits and space in the yards. These would have been dirty industries that town authorities are likely to have insisted were kept outside the walled town. This fits with evidence from other urban centres, where dirty industry was relegated to the suburbs for reasons of hygiene and safety.

The location of the site, in close proximity to the assumed course of the Leper River, would have provided a water source for industrial processing, and the long burgage plot would have provided ample space for all of these activities. The location of the site, just outside the Dublin Gate, was surely prime commercial space that capitalized on trade with the townspeople and visitors alike.

Phase 3

The post-medieval mill At the east end of the site, post-medieval activity was represented by an extension (S682) to the post-medieval building that forms the north-eastern boundary to the site (fig. 6.14). This building is depicted on the 1836 Ordnance Survey map (fig. 6.15). The excavated structure enclosed an area measuring 12m by 4m, and was orientated north-south. Eighteen post-holes within this area delimited an entrance passage, a larger northern room measuring 6 by 4m and a southern room or annexe

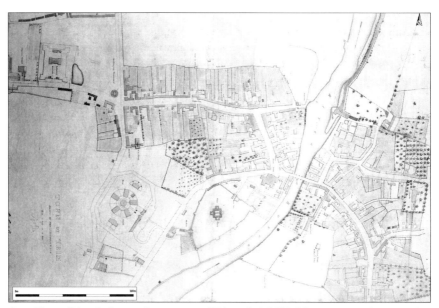

6.15 First edition Ordnance Survey map of Trim, 1836 (NAI OS140: manuscript town plan (1:1056), Trim (1836) © the National Archives of Ireland, courtesy of the Director of the National Archives of Ireland. Rectified version)

measuring 2.6 by 4m. A 2.4 by 4m internal passage or hallway, aligned east-west, divided the two rooms. Five post-holes arranged in a cluster centrally within the passage are interpreted as stair supports. An associated, contemporary wall-footing (F216), that was probably an external support or yard boundary, was recorded to the southwest of the structure.

The structure truncated a number of earlier features, including a group of medieval pits, post-pits and post-holes. Other post-medieval features investigated included pits, stone dumps and a French drain (fig. 6.14). Analysis of palaeo-environmental material recovered from the post-medieval features and from other published reports on the town and castle suggests increased economic specialization during that period. There is little evidence for animals being kept within the town (Beglane, 'Meat and craft', this volume).

CONCLUSION: DEVELOPMENT AND EXPANSION OF THE TOWN

The existence of a medieval suburb centred on Emmet Street has often been mooted, based on analysis of the property boundaries and the dimensions of yard plots (Hennessy 2004, 2; Potterton 2005, 199). The results of this project have confirmed the existence of the suburb. The suburbs of Dublin and Cork are referred to here for comparative purposes because of the wealth of published material on these towns.

Cork's north island was not walled until the late thirteenth century, and it continued to be known as the suburb of Dungarvan after it was enclosed (Hurley 2003, 151–69). The large number of urban hall houses and other large urban dwellings there suggests that the suburb was dominated by wealthy traders and merchants, whereas Dublin's suburbs, centred on Thomas Street and Oxmantown, appear to have had a mixed residential and industrial character. Industrial activities included milling, pottery production and iron-working, usually kept outside the town due to risk of fire and spatial considerations (O'Donovan 2003; Purcell 2005, 161–88). It seems likely that the Emmet Street properties functioned as residential units, with some commercial and/or industrial functions. The town and suburb would have been economically inter-dependant.

Evidence from other medieval urban centres, including Dublin (Purcell 2005, 161–88), suggests that a diverse range of social and economic activities co-existed and that sub-division of space within suburbs was based to a large extent on commercial occupation. Economic activities, such as craft-working and food production, are likely to have been located in different areas for hygiene purposes. It remains to be seen whether the Emmet Street suburb follows this pattern. Despite medieval suburbs being considered of secondary importance, a high degree of control would have been exercised over them by town administrations. The suburbs would have contributed to town coffers through rents as well as through enterprise, and their economic activities would have made the suburbs an integral part of the town.

The early thirteenth century was a period of dynamic urban growth related to the consolidation of Anglo-Norman power in Ireland. This is borne out in Trim with the expansion of the de Lacy castle, the construction of the town wall and the growth of the town in general. Rapid growth of an economically successful base, with consequent competition and pressure on space within the walled town, would have necessitated suburban development. Radiocarbon-dating suggests that this suburb pre-dates the earliest-documented town defences and is probably contemporary with the construction of the castle. This raises a number of possibilities: a) that the town expanded faster than previously thought; b) that a successful economic base (proto-town?) already existed; and/or c) that certain sections of the town were deliberately left outside the walls.

A large labour force would have been required during the consolidation of Anglo-Norman power in Trim. Constructing a ringwork and associated defences would have been a huge undertaking, requiring labour, tools, food and other provisions. It is possible that the properties at Kiely's Yard represent the dwellings and workshops of those serving or conducting the first wave of colonization. Construction of a stone replacement for the destroyed ringwork got underway at an early date and this would have necessitated an even larger work-force.

While there is no evidence for a pre–Anglo-Norman town at Trim, an Early Medieval ecclesiastical house (most likely at the site of St Patrick's Cathedral; see Kieran, this volume) may have operated as a proto-town, essentially as a market centre. Documentary sources suggest that St Mary's Abbey was already established by 1150 (Potterton 2005), and the Kiely's Yard properties may have served the abbey prior to the consolidation of Anglo-Norman power in the town.

The earliest historical record for a wall defending the town is a murage grant dating to 1290 (Potterton 2005). The actual construction date of the wall is unknown and the early town may have been defended by a palisaded bank and ditch or a branch of the Leper River prior to the construction of the wall. This begs the question as to why the site at Kiely's Yard was left outside the wall once it was built. Two possible answers are offered: a) that the limits of the town were largely defined by topography and/or existing defences; or b) that this side of the town was already being used for 'dirty' industry and was deliberately kept outside the wall. A north-south ditch identified to the north of the site at the Emmet Street/Market Street junction (Fallon, this volume) might well represent such an early town defence. It might have determined the location of the Dublin Gate, Emmet Street and the property pattern on this side of Trim. The Leper River is assumed to have flowed north of this site, along the outside of the town wall, and its course may have determined the siting of the wall.

During the later medieval or post-medieval period, the Emmet Street houses were destroyed and the site was subject to a change of use, represented by the extension to the mill building. According to local folklore, the story of the building of the extension contains a salutary and timely lesson for property speculators. There is no reference to the building ever having functioned as a mill in the Griffiths' Valuations and conversations with local people suggest that the extension was built when the Boyne Canal was being planned. The canal was never built, however, and the mill building is unlikely ever to have functioned as anything more than a grain store. After the mill fell out of use, the site was used as a forge, a market place and a car park for Kiely's Bar. Today it is a link road, Finnegan's Way, providing access to the proposed town centre to the west of the town wall.

ACKNOWLEDGMENTS

Trim Town Council funded all excavation works on the project. Finola O'Carroll provided project management and advice throughout the programme of works. I would like to thank the excavation team, particularly the supervisors Mark Kelly and Liam Chambers, who endured difficult conditions throughout the winter in Trim. I am grateful to Milica Rajic and Joanne Gaffrey for co-ordinating the post-excavation analysis.

BIBLIOGRAPHY

Albarella, U., 2003, 'Tawyers, tanners, horn trade and the mystery of the missing goat' in Murphy, P., & Wiltshire, P.E.J. (eds), *The environmental archaeology of industry*, 71–83. Oxford.

Barry, T.B., 1987, *The archaeology of medieval Ireland*. London.

Beglane, F., 2007, 'Report on the faunal material from Townparks South, Trim, Co. Meath'. Unpublished specialist report.

Bennett, I. (ed.), 2006, *Excavations 2003: summary accounts of archaeological excavations in Ireland*. Bray.

Bradley, J., 1984, 'Urban Archaeological Survey of Co. Meath'. Unpublished report.

Cryerhall, A., 2006, 'Excavations at Hammond Lane, Dublin: from hurdle-ford to iron-foundry' in Duffy, S. (ed.), *Medieval Dublin* 7, 9–50. Dublin.

Fallon, D., 2003, 'Pre-development testing report on the site of the proposed extension to Trim Credit Union, 18 Market St., Trim, Co. Meath'. Unpublished excavation report.

Geraghty, S., 1996, *Viking Dublin: botanical evidence from Fishamble Street*. Dublin.

Hamilton-Dyer, S., 2007, 'Bird and fish bones: Townparks South, Trim, Co. Meath: CRDS 494'. Unpublished specialist report.

Hayden, A., 2001b, '01E1146ext: Unpublished excavation report, High Street, Trim', Sites and Monuments Record, National Monuments Service.

Hayden, A., 2006, '01E0145 ext. unpublished excavation report', Sites and Monuments Record, National Monuments Service.

Hennessy, M., 2004, *Irish Historic Towns Atlas, No. 14: Trim*. Dublin.

Hurley, M.F., & Scully, O.M.B., 1997, *Late Viking-Age and medieval Waterford: excavations 1986–1992*. Waterford.

Hurley, M.F., 2003, 'A review of domestic architecture in Cork' in Cleary, R.M., & Hurley, M.F. (eds), *Cork City excavations, 1984–2000*, pp 151–70. Cork.

Lyons, S., 2007, 'Plant remains: assessment from the archaeological excavations at Trim, Co. Meath [E2016]'. Unpublished specialist report.

Lynch, A., & Manning, C., 1985–7, '15.4: Dublin Castle E296/E297/E298/E323/E324'. http://www.heritagecouncil.ie/archaeology/unpublished_excavations/section15.html.

McCutcheon, C., 2006, *Medieval pottery from Wood Quay, Dublin*. Dublin.

McCutcheon, C., 2008, 'The medieval pottery from Kiely's Yard, Town Parks, Trim, Co. Meath (E2016)'. Unpublished specialist report.

Meenan, R., 1996, '96E0175: unpublished excavation report'. www.excavations.ie.

Moore, C., 2008, 'E2016 Report on worked wooden remains from Townparks South, Trim, Co. Meath'. Unpublished specialist report.

Moore, M., 1997, *Archaeological inventory of County Meath*. Dublin.

O'Donovan, E., 2003, 'The growth and decline of a medieval suburb? Evidence from excavations at Thomas Street, Dublin' in Duffy, S. (ed.), *Medieval Dublin* 4, 127–71. Dublin.

O'Donnell, M., 2003, 'Skiddy's Lane' in Cleary, R.M., & Hurley, M.F. (eds), *Cork City Excavations, 1984–2000*, 99–111. Cork.

Potterton, M., 2005, *Medieval Trim: history and archaeology*. Dublin.

Purcell, E., 2005, 'The city and the suburb: medieval Dublin and Oxmantown' in Duffy, S. (ed.), *Medieval Dublin* 6, 188–223. Dublin.

Simpson, L., 2004, 'Excavation on the southern side of the medieval town at Ship Street Little, Dublin' in Duffy, S. (ed.), *Medieval Dublin* 5, 9–51. Dublin.

Simpson, L., 2006, 'John Rocque's map of Dublin (1756): a modern source for medieval property-boundaries' in Duffy, S. (ed.), *Medieval Dublin* 7, 113–51. Dublin.
Walsh, C., 1987, 'High Street/Peter Street, Waterford' in Bennett, I. (ed.), *Excavations 1987: summary accounts of archaeological excavations in Ireland*, no. 24, p. 42. Bray.
www.excavations.ie
www.museumoflondon.org.uk
www.worcestershire.whub.org.uk
www.nhm.ac.uk/jdsml/nature-on-line/seed-of-trade
www.askoxford.com

Towards the Rogues' Castle: excavations on Navan Gate Street, Trim

DENIS SHINE & MATTHEW SEAVER

with a contribution by SARAH COBAIN

INTRODUCTION

Trim was a walled town in the middle ages, with five major gates along the circuit of its walls. One of these was called 'Navan Gate', as it controlled access to the town on the road that linked Trim with Navan. Like most of the town's gates, it went out of use and was demolished at some unknown time in the past. Although no part of the gate survives above ground level, its former presence is attested by the fact that the name 'Navan Gate' is still used to describe the area in which it once stood. Investigations were carried out in order to locate the site of the 'Navan Gate' in advance of street reconstruction works by Trim Town Council (fig. 7.1). Excavations uncovered a substantial east-west ditch and traces of a further north-south ditch close to the place where the gate is thought to have stood. Further archaeological monitoring of road-works in the vicinity noted the presence of more areas of metalling, overlain by medieval organic deposits, beneath the modern street surface. These metalled deposits comprise small compacted stones laid down to form a road surface. Samples from these deposits were analyzed by a palaeo-environmentalist (Appendix 7.1). All of these archaeological works on Navan Gate Street were conducted under Ministerial Consent (reference C150:E2398).

THE NAVAN GATE

Navan Gate Street is an extension of High Street beyond Haggard Street, leading to the Navan Gate. There are no medieval references to the construction or maintenance of the gate, but a gate on this important road would have been necessary from the time the town's defences were first built. The Navan Gate is first mentioned in the 1655 Down Survey, and in 1682 orders were made for its repair (Potterton 2005, 170–1). It was still standing in the late eighteenth century (Hennessy 2004, 11). It was sometimes referred to as the Rogues' Gate or Rogues' Castle, the latter name suggesting that it was a well-fortified structure.

7.1 Location map showing Navan Gate and excavated features (base-map courtesy of Ordnance Survey Ireland, Permit 8565 © Ordnance Survey Ireland/Govenment of Ireland. Inset from *Irish Historic Town Atlas, no. 14: Trim*, by permission of the Royal Irish Academy © RIA)

The exact location of the gate is not clear. The town wall survives for 200m from the Sheep Gate northwards and then disappears for 80m. It is depicted on the Down Survey parish map of 1660 as a rectangular gate with a crenellated top. The exact site of the gate is not indicated on the first edition Ordnance Survey map of 1836, although the name is indicated within the street at the point where the wall is thought to have met it (fig. 7.2). The line of the wall here is thought to coincide with the Urban District Boundary. The site of the gate is indicated by a cross on the 1909 second edition Ordnance Survey map.

The area to the east of the site of the Navan Gate, and therefore outside the town walls, is known as Greek Park. In 1632 Archbishop Ussher mentioned a church at Trim known as the 'Greek church' and a fifteenth-century altar cross was found in this field in the early twentieth century (Potterton 2005, 200). Sources mention suburban housing to the east of the town, which may have been beyond the Navan Gate. Previous monitoring of a 229m-long service-trench identified traces of the medieval metalled street–surface, overlain by an organic deposit (Fallon 2006, 394–5).

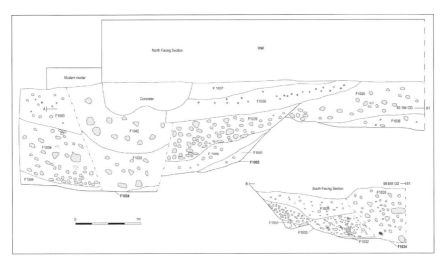

7.2 Section through excavated ditch

THE EXCAVATION

The excavation focused on the southern side of the street, at a point where the least amount of disturbance from services had taken place. The site is bounded to the north by St Mary's Villas and to the south by Greek Park. It is *c*.150m to the east of the junction of High Street and Haggard Street. In total, an area of 30.5m by 2m in width was opened.

Phase 1, medieval (fig. 7.2)
Four medieval features were encountered on the site. These comprised a ditch, two pits and the ephemeral remains of a small wall. There was also some evidence for a second ditch, although the trench was badly disturbed in this area and could not be extended to confirm its presence.

A substantial ditch ran broadly east-west. Only part of its northern edge and its western terminus were exposed within the trench. Most of the ditch was beneath the adjoining private residence. It seems to have been back-filled in two basic sequences. The lowest three layers appeared to be natural accumulations, while most of the upper deposits seemed to have been deliberately deposited.

A marked inconsistency was noted in the fills towards the western terminus of the ditch (F1041, F1042, F1043 & F1045). These deposits were very different to the others in the ditch and it is thought that they might belong to a second medieval ditch that forms a junction with the first at its western terminus. The basal shape of the ditch in this area also indicated a second north-south orientated feature. Unfortunately, this relationship was largely removed by the excavation of modern disturbance. The trench could not be extended further to the south to confirm this feature due to the presence of a private residence. A sample of animal bone from the lower deposits within the ditch has been radiocarbon-dated to 1270–1390 cal. AD. Pottery from the ditch suggests a thirteenth-/fourteenth-century date. A small ephemeral wall was built into the upper fill of the ditch at its western terminus and this was bonded by clay (F1002). At its eastern end, the ditch was cut by two small pits (F1009 & F1011) that were partially exposed as they continued under the southern section. They both appear to be sealed by a clay deposit (F1017), which contained medieval pottery.

A large limestone block forming the centre of a larger chunk of masonry consisting of rounded stone, pebble and mortar was uncovered in the centre of the modern broadband trench to the north of the cutting.

Phase 2: post-medieval/early modern
The early modern features consisted of the remains of a possible street frontage as well as a series of clay and rubble deposits. Two east-west walls (F1006 & F1022) were partially constructed on clay and rubble deposits (F1007 & F1023).

Metalling and medieval deposits on Navan Gate Street
During monitoring of pipe-laying, metalled deposits were encountered at a number of locations on High Street, Navan Gate Street and Mill Street. On Navan Gate Street, they were encountered 60cm below the ground surface. They were commonly overlain by deposits of organic silty loam. Two samples of these deposits were analyzed for palaeo-environmental evidence (Appendix 7.1). These are similar to sequences of metalling and organic deposits uncovered on Haggard Street (Mullins, this volume).

DISCUSSION

The excavation was intended to assess the remains of the Navan Gate. Although no definite remains of the gate were uncovered, the presence of medieval archaeology was confirmed. The western terminus of the ditch broadly corresponds to the supposed location of Navan Gate. The defences are known to have run roughly north-south, however, transecting Navan Gate Street, while the ditch that we exposed runs directly perpendicular to these. It may have been that the approach to the town gate had a ditch on either side, funnelling traffic towards the gate itself. This would explain the terminus of the ditch corresponding to the site of the gate. To fully explain its form and function, more of the ditch would have needed to be exposed, but this was not possible as it was under a private residence.

The variance in fills at the western terminus of the ditch may indicate a second north-south feature forming a junction with the ditch terminus. This evidence has largely been removed by a modern service-cut. Such a north-south linear feature would roughly follow the mapped line of the town defences.

The existence of a small stone wall over the western terminus of the ditch possibly indicates a structure in the same location as the Navan Gate. Although this is not thought to be in any way related to the Navan Gate, it does show medieval buildings broadly contemporary to the gate in the same general area.

Also of note are the remains thought to represent the old street frontage, marking the entrance to Greek Park. Artefacts recovered from deposits underlying both of these features date them to the seventeenth to nineteenth century. No features are marked in this area on the first edition Ordnance Survey map however.

The remains of the street surfaces exposed during these investigations along Navan Gate Street conform to the general characteristics noted on a range of investigations on Haggard Street, High Street, Mill Street and elsewhere on Navan Gate Street. All of the evidence indicates that the roads were re-paved periodically, and that domestic refuse and weeds accumulated on the street surfaces over time.

Monitoring of pipe-laying led to the identification of a metalled surface underlying the centre of Mill Street. This consisted of small angular stones bonded by a gritty yellow-grey mixed silty sand deposit that contained extensive animal bone and some medieval pottery sherds. This is likely to be another medieval road surface. A sample of this deposit is presented alongside the Navan Gate Street analysis for comparison (Cobain, Appendix 7.1).

ACKNOWLEDGMENTS

The authors would like to thank the excavation and monitoring team: Ludovic Beaumont, Gavin O'Reilly, Mark Kelly and Karen McCoy. Post-excavation was managed by Joanne Gaffrey and Milica Rajic. All illustrations were prepared for publication by Niall Lynch and Catherine Bishop. Trim Town Council funded all excavation and post-excavation works.

BIBLIOGRAPHY

Fallon, D., 2006, 'Navangate Street, Trim' in Bennett, I. (ed.), *Excavations 2003: summary accounts of archaeological excavations in Ireland*, no. 1477, 394–5, Bray.
Hennessy, M., 2004, *Irish Historic Towns Atlas, No. 14: Trim*. Dublin.
Potterton, M., 2005, *Medieval Trim: history and archaeology*. Dublin.

APPENDIX 7.1: THE PLANT AND CHARCOAL MACROFOSSIL REMAINS
FROM NAVAN GATE STREET AND MILL STREET

By Sarah Cobain

INTRODUCTION

The archaeology uncovered on the sites at Navan Gate Street and Mill Street included deposits thought to be domestic waste that had accumulated over time (Matthew Seaver, pers. comm.). Two samples, one from Navan Gate Street and one from Mill Street, were analyzed for both charcoal and plant macrofossils. No charcoal was retrieved from either sample. This report identifies the seed species recovered. The methodology followed was the same as in the Market Street analysis (Hayden, 'Market Street', this volume).

RESULTS

Navan Gate Street
Sample 3 (F2030) was from an organic deposit located above a mettled surface. It contained seeds of blackberry (three seeds), fat hen (two), common orache (one), nettle (two) and sedge (two) (Table 7.1). It also contained one charred barley grain and one charred oat grain, both of which had damage to their outer layers. This damage had exposed 'popcorn-like' starch from inside the grain, causing the loss of identifiable characteristics. Consequently, the grain could not be identified to species. No charcoal was recovered from this deposit.

Table 7.1 Macrofossil taxa from Navan Gate Street

Sample no.	Context	Flot volume	Context description	Taxon	Common name
3	(F2030)	6ml	Organic deposit above mettled surface	*Atriplex patula* (1)	Common orache
				cf *Avena* spp (1)	cf oat
				cf *Hordeum* (1)	cf barley
				Chenopodium album (2)	Fat hen
				cf *Carex* spp (2)	Sedge
				Rubus fruticosus (3)	Blackberry
				Urtica urens (1)	Nettle

Mill Street
Sample 1 (F2013) was recovered from a deposit associated with the old road through Trim. The deposit contained seeds of fat hen (three seeds), common chickweed (two), grass (one) and nettle (one) (Table 7.2). No charcoal was recovered.

Table 7.2 **Macrofossil taxa from Mill Street**

Sample no.	Context	Flot volume	Context description	Taxon	Common name
1	(F2013)	8ml	Deposit bonding and above stones	*Chenopodium album* (3) *Poaceae* (1) *Stellaria media* (2) *Urtica urens* (1)	Fat hen Grass (indeterminate species) Common chickweed Nettle

DISCUSSION

General

Navan Gate Street The deposit at Navan Gate Street (F2030) was organic in consistency and was located on top of a mettled surface believed to be a road leading into/out of Trim. The deposit contained common orache, fat hen, blackberry, nettle and sedge seeds. There were also charred barley and oat grains. The organic consistency of this material, together with the evidence of blackberry, charred barley and oat seeds, indicates that this deposit accumulated through the disposal of domestic waste from nearby houses. Herbaceous taxa, such as fat hen and nettles, are known to have been consumed during this period, so they too may have been part of the domestic waste. They may also (together with the common orache and sedge) have been weed species growing on the edge of the road.

Mill Street The plant macrofossil remains recovered from the fill at Mill Street do not provide any conclusive evidence for the function or origin of the deposit (F2013). The herbaceous taxa recovered included fat hen, common chickweed, grass and nettle seeds. Although some of these taxa (fat hen, common chickweed and nettles) were consumed in the medieval period, they are all present in this deposit in relatively small numbers. This suggests that, rather than being waste material disposed of from nearby houses on Mill Street, they are more likely to have been weed species growing adjacent to the road at Mill Street, and their seeds became incorporated into to the deposit as it was accumulating.

Diet, socio-economic and industrial activity

Navan Gate Street Oat and barley grains were recovered from this sample. A fuller discussion of the processing and use of grain is presented elsewhere in this volume (Cobain, in Seaver et al., 'Black Friary', this volume). It cannot be confirmed at which stage the grain from the fills (F2030) became burnt, but it is likely that the charred grain originated from rake-out waste from the stoking areas of a corn-drying kiln or from a domestic fire used to dry or process grain. The grain could have originated from accidental spillage while it was being placed into the drying bowl of the kiln or could have been swept up with waste accumulated during the threshing and winnowing stage and burnt on the fire.

Navan Gate Street and Mill Street Although the herbaceous taxa recovered from the fills at Mill Street and Navan Gate Street were few, it is worth mentioning that herbaceous plants were often used as salads, vegetables and for herbs in cooking. Common chickweed and nettle leaves would have been boiled down in the same was as spinach can be prepared, and common chickweed seeds are also known to have been used instead of cereal to make items such as bread (Defelice 2004, 195–6). Fat hen leaves were also used as a spinach substitute (Dennell 1970, 154). Blackberries are likely to have been harvested and eaten raw or processed into jams, tarts and sauces (Dennell 1970, 154). Studies such as that from a medieval garden in Hull (Crackles 1986), demonstrate that all of these species were being cultivated and harvested for food. As the climate in Britain and Ireland was similar during this period, there is no reason why these species were not being cultivated and used in Ireland in the same way. As all of these taxa were recorded in small numbers in Trim, however, it is also possible that they were weeds growing along the edge of the road.

Composition of local flora
Navan Gate Street and Mill Street The vegetation in the immediate area of the sites at Navan Gate Street and Mill Street appears to have been dominated by herbaceous species such as grass, fat hen, common chickweed, nettle, common orache and sedge. The development of Trim town would have meant that any vegetation in the area was kept to a minimum; therefore the only species that were likely to grow would be the pioneer herbaceous taxa that can establish themselves in marginal areas such as cracks in the road. The seeds for these would have been carried in and then dropped on the ground by the wind, birds or brought in from outside the town walls by carts delivering goods to Trim.

The blackberry, fat hen, common chickweed and nettle seeds recovered from the deposit on High Street (F2030) are species known to have been harvested for salads, fruits and vegetables. These could have been deliberately cultivated and processed within the local area or in nearby houses, which may be representative of vegetation on a wider scale – particularly in the case of the blackberry seeds, which may have been growing in hedgerows separating houses or at the rear of houses. A larger assemblage of seeds would be required to arrive at any firm conclusions however.

BIBLIOGRAPHY

Aitkinson, E., & Aitkinson, M.D., 2002, '*Sambucus nigra L.*', *The Journal of Ecology* **90:5**, 895–923.
Anderberg, A.-L., 1994, *Atlas of seeds: part 4.* Uddevalla, Sweden.
Berggren, G., 1981, *Atlas of seeds: part 3.* Arlöv, Sweden.
Cappers, R.T.J., Bekker, R.M., & Gronigen, J.E.A, 2006, *Digital seed atlas of the Netherlands.* Eelde, The Netherlands. www.seedatlas.nl.
Crackles, F.E., 1986, 'Medieval gardens in Hull: archaeological evidence', *Garden History* **14:1**, 1–5.

Defelice, M.S., 2004, 'Common chickweed, *Stellaria media (L.) vill.*: "Mere chicken feed"', *Weed Technology* **18**:1, 193–200.

Dennell, R.W., 1970, 'Seeds from a medieval sewer in Woolster Street, Plymouth', *Economic Botany* **24**:2, 151–4.

Edwards, N., 2000, *The archaeology of Early Medieval Ireland*. London.

Edwards, N., 2005, 'The archaeology of Early Medieval Ireland, *c.*1400–1169: settlement and economy' in Ó Cróinín, D. (ed.), *A new history of Ireland I: prehistory and early Ireland*, 235–96. Oxford.

Gibson, A., 1989, 'Medieval corn-drying kilns at Capo, Kincardineshire and Abercairny, Perthshire', *Proceedings of the Society of Antiquaries of Scotland* **118**, 219–29.

McCutcheon, C., 2009, 'Pottery from Navan Gate, Trim'. Unpublished report for CRDS Ltd.

O'Keeffe, T., 2001, *Medieval Ireland: an archaeology*. Stroud, Gloucestershire.

Stevens, C., & Wilkinson, K., 2003, *Environmental archaeology: approaches, techniques and applications*. Stroud, Gloucestershire.

Porta Via: excavations at the Athboy Gate, Trim

MATTHEW SEAVER

with contributions by CAMILLA LOFQVIST, SUSAN LYONS &

CLARE McCUTCHEON

INTRODUCTION

Two substantial gates allowed entry to Trim from its northern side during the medieval period. Little is known about the dates of construction of the walled circuit on this side of the town, and the precise location, form and date of the Navan and Athboy Gates are matters of conjecture. In November 2006 excavations at the northern end of Haggard Street by the author uncovered a substantial ditch of thirteenth-century date, which contained the foundations of a large stone structure at its terminal. This is likely to be the location of the Athboy Gate. The present paper describes the background to and the results of this excavation.

THE NORTHERN WALLED CIRCUIT

Relatively little is known about the chronology of the walling of the northern side of the town, and much of the circuit has been removed above ground (fig. 8.1). While a range of murage grants are known, dating between 1290–7 and 1417–37 (Hennessy 2004, 11), it is not known when the northern part of the town was enclosed. Few of the gates are mentioned in the pre-seventeenth-century written sources. Stretches of wall survive on the eastern section of the northern circuit, and these are depicted in more detail on the 1836 first edition Ordnance Survey map, from the river to 55m south of Navan Gate Street. They also survived on the western side of the town for 188m, from close to the northern bank of the river to a point bordering the rectory orchard. They had been removed beyond this point on this side, perhaps for the construction of the rectory in the early eighteenth century. Beyond this point on both sides, the line of the wall is unclear. On the eastern side, it probably followed the plot boundaries and may be seen as part of an earthen bank to the east of the supermarket (Bradley 1984, 163). The earliest documentary mention of gates on the northern side refers to the Porchgate or Sheep Gate, and dates to 1476–7, although this gate was evidently in existence before that. Potterton suggests that an earlier line of town defences may have run across Loman Street, along

154

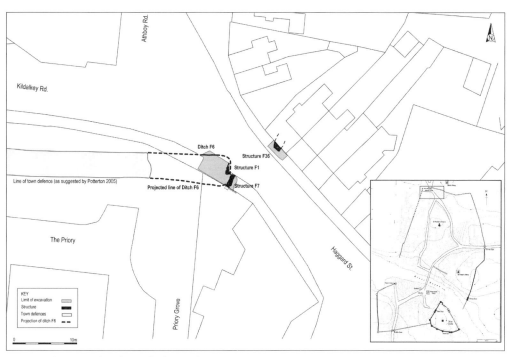

8.1 Map showing walled area of northern part of Trim and gate positions, with location of excavation (base-map courtesy of Ordnance Survey Ireland, Permit 8565 © Ordnance Survey Ireland/Govenment of Ireland. Inset from *Irish Historic Town Atlas, no. 14: Trim*, by permission of the Royal Irish Academy © RIA)

the line of the boundary of St Patrick's Cathedral (2005, 180). A wall was found during monitoring at this point, but its course could not be plotted from the limited area exposed. Such an arrangement would imply the need for two gates; one on Haggard Street and one on Loman Street. There is no mention of further gates in the area.

ATHBOY GATE

The exact location of the Athboy Gate was also unknown. Potterton suggests that it may even have been a suburban gate outside the walls, acting as a tolling point (2005, 183–4). It was first referred to in a property transaction as the *Bl'aac'zhat*, in 1532. In 1616 a property was mentioned as being near Blackgate, a name derived from the fact that it allowed access to the medieval Dominican friary, also known as the Black Friary (Potterton 2005, 183–4). Properties 'without the north gate' are mentioned in 1571 (ibid., 200). It is likely that the gate and walls were established prior to 1263, the date of the foundation of this religious house. These mendicant houses were frequently

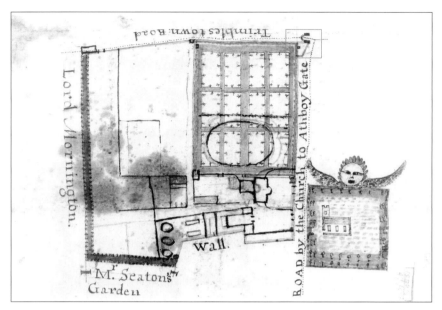

8.2 Detail of map of Mr Seaton's Garden, showing Athboy Gate in 1747 (© Representative Church Body; reproduced from *Irish Historic Towns Atlas, no. 14: Trim*, by permission of the Royal Irish Academy)

located outside the walls of towns, for example at Kilkenny and Kilmallock. The gate was to be repaired in 1682 and a drawbridge is mentioned in the corporation records (Thomas 1993, 196). It is clearly depicted on the map of 'Mr Seaton's Garden' in 1747, which indicates that the gate stood at the corner of the Trimblestown (Kildalkey) Road and Loman Street, attached to a stretch of wall that adjoined the parsonage or rectory garden wall (Hennessy 2004, Map 5). Loman Street is referred to on this map as the 'road by the church to Athboy Gate'. The gate was still standing in 1752 (ibid.), and it may well have been standing in 1796 (Potterton 2005, 184). The 1816 'Plan of the manor of Trim' still calls the junction Athboy Gate (Hennessy 2004, Map 8). The first edition Ordnance Survey map (1836) simply has the words 'Athboy Gate' close to the junction, with no indicator of its location. Loman Street (then called Church Street) splays widely at its junction with Haggard Street and is occupied by a number of buildings. A long east-west building is located along the eastern boundary wall of the rectory garden. Athboy Gate is indicated at the corner of this building. On the second edition Ordnance Survey six-inch map (1909), a cross in the centre of the junction of the Kells Road, Athboy Road and Kildalkey Road indicates the 'Site of Athboy Gate'. A boundary wall projected from the corner of the rectory garden across to the buildings within the Loman Street/Haggard Street junction (then called St Lomond Street). This wall was evidently built between 1836 and 1909, and is clearly the wall (F33) identified

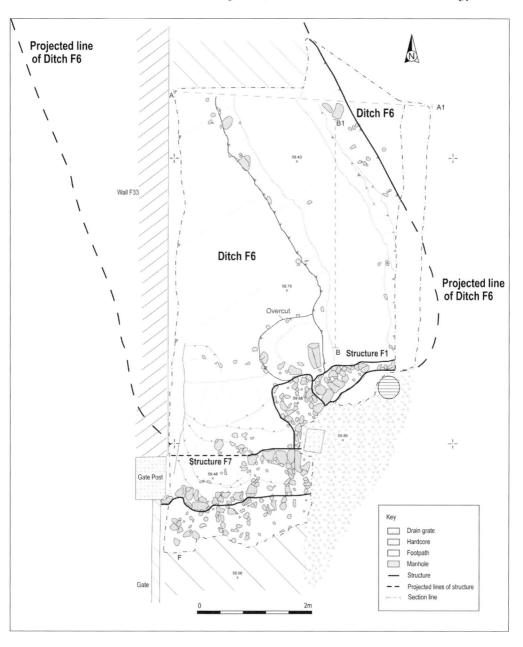

8.3 Plan of excavated features at Athboy Gate

during these excavations adjoining the rectory wall that formed the boundary of
the excavations. It contains an Edward VII post-box (1901–10).

Archaeological assessment undertaken by Mullins in 1999 included test-
trenches covering all aspects of this three-road junction (2000). No traces of
the gate or wall were identified, and the general picture was of cobbled surfaces
overlying natural boulder clay. Based on the results of this testing programme
and field observation, it was suggested that the gate would be located at the
narrowest point of this part of Haggard Street, rather than at the much larger
splayed junction. Even though the Kells and Kildalkey roads were probably
straightened prior to 1781 these routes were in existence in the medieval period
(Hennessy 2004, Map 7). A gate at the position indicated on the second edition
Ordnance Survey map would have to span a very large area and is unlikely to
have been at this location.

THE EXCAVATION

Following this cartographic analysis, it was decided to target the western side
of the street for test-trenching. This area of pavement had been laid prior to the
1950s and had not been subject to disturbance through the insertion of services
in recent years. A test-trench measuring 30m in length and up to 2m in width
was excavated using a JCB with a flat bucket. This trench ran along the western
side of Haggard Street from the Loman Street junction to the point at which
Haggard Street splays into the Kells Road, Athboy Road and Kildalkey Road.
The test-trench revealed that the tarmac was up to 10cm in depth. It overlay
deposits of road-fill up to 30cm in depth, in turn overlying boulder clay and
subsequently silty sandy gravel deposits with large stones. The only feature
encountered was a stone box-drain 4m to the south of the excavation site.

Immediately outside an entrance gate of 'The Priory' public house, north of
the 'Porta Via' restaurant, extensive archaeological deposits were uncovered.
An area measuring 11m north-south by 4.5m east-west was excavated. The
main archaeological remains were partially under the concrete footpath and
partially beneath the road surface. They included a collapsed masonry structure cut on its eastern side by a recent concrete man-hole, which was part of
the water main constructed in 1999. A large east-west ditch under the Haggard
Street pavement was found to terminate at this masonry structure at the
narrowest point of the road.

The ditch
A section of a substantial ditch, measuring 6m east-west by 4.6m in width and
1.6m in depth, ran from the stone structure. It ran under the pavement on the
western side of Haggard Street. It had a stepped profile, with a 2m-wide
channel in the centre. The western edge was not visible and clearly lay under

8.4 Excavated ditch and structure, from north

the eighteenth-century rectory wall. At its terminal, on the western side of the area excavated, this ditch had a sloping southern edge. The remainder of the terminal was not visible, as the structure was within the cut and it had been obscured or destroyed by the water main. On the north-eastern side, the edge of the ditch (the only clear edge within the excavated area) had a steep gradient. Given the trend of the gully at the base, it is likely that the ditch would assume an overall east-west direction as it ran under the rectory garden wall.

Stone structure F1 and Wall F7
A curving stone structure was built into the southern terminal of the ditch. It consisted of an un-mortared stone footing, with random coursing surviving up to 1.2m in height and 1m in thickness. It had been substantially damaged by the construction of a large water main man-hole in 1999, and the southern end of the structure was not visible. The upper surviving section was bonded by a yellow-brown sandy mortar. It had been further damaged at the junction of the road and pavement by the insertion of a shore-box in the last five years. It was composed of a northeast-southwest section of wall built from un-mortared rough, random limestone. A northwest-southeast section had collapsed south-wards, probably through pressure from the man-hole. This section was built from larger blocks and was mortared. It appears that the original structure was D-shaped or rectangular.

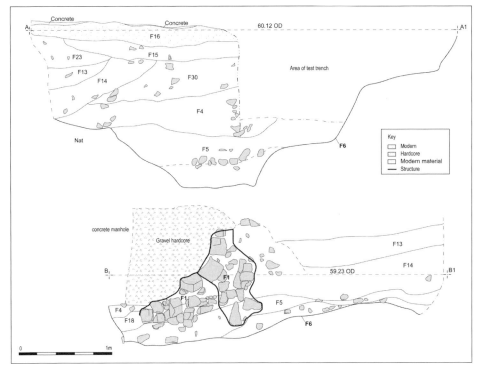

8.5 Sections through Ditch F6

A 1m-thick east-west stone wall was keyed into the stone structure. This wall was revetted against the natural yellow boulder clay for one course along the edge of the ditch. This was a well-built mortared wall of squared limestone blocks. It was cut by the concrete footing of the gate that accesses the beer garden of the public house. It survived to one course in height. It was composed of two faces with a rubble core, and was set into re-deposited yellow clay up to 30cm in depth (F26). This clay was also within the internal rubble core.

The filling of the ditch
For the purposes of description, the deposits filling the ditch can be divided into three episodes:

1. Organic deposits formed from rotting vegetation and refuse when the ditch was open;
2. A thick bank of deliberate clay and stone back-fill;
3. Deposits of silt and refuse that abutted and covered the bank on its western side, suggesting gradual silting.

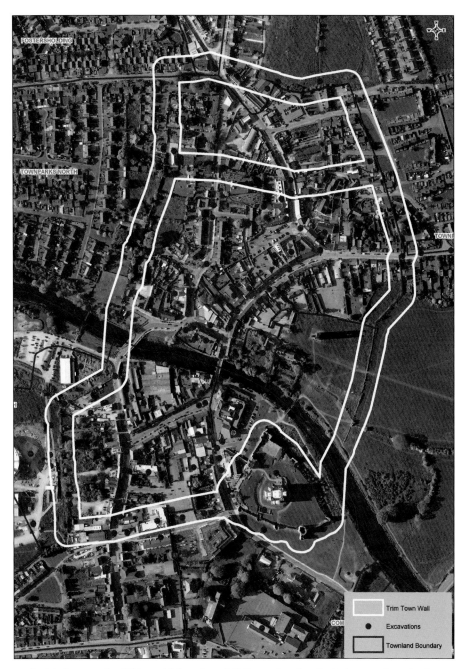

1 Aerial photograph of Trim, with location of all licensed archaeological excavations that have taken place within and around the town. The building being constructed to the west of the town is the new headquarters for the Office of Public Works. Map prepared by Rosanne Meenan, Amanda O'Brien, Irene D'Arcy and Michael Potterton (photograph courtesy of Ordnance Survey Ireland, permit 8565 © Ordnance Survey Ireland/Government of Ireland)

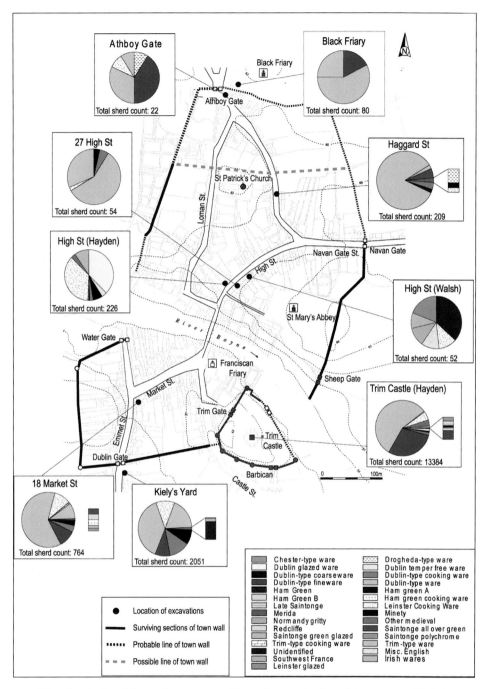

Athboy Gate
Total sherd count: 22

Black Friary
Total sherd count: 80

Black Friary

Athboy Gate

27 High St
Total sherd count: 54

Haggard St
Total sherd count: 209

St Patrick's Church

High St (Hayden)
Total sherd count: 226

Navan Gate St. Navan Gate

Loman St.

High St.

High St (Walsh)
Total sherd count: 52

River Boyne

St Mary's Abbey

Water Gate

Franciscan Friary

Sheep Gate

Trim Castle (Hayden)
Total sherd count: 13384

Market St.

Trim Gate

Emmet St.

Trim Castle

Dublin Gate

Barbican

Castle St.

0   100m

18 Market St
Total sherd count: 764

Kiely's Yard
Total sherd count: 2051

Chester-type ware	Drogheda-type ware
Dublin glazed ware	Dublin temper free ware
Dublin-type coarseware	Dublin-type cooking ware
Dublin-type fineware	Dublin-type ware
Ham Green	Ham green A
Ham Green B	Ham green cooking ware
Late Saintonge	Leinster Cooking Ware
Merida	Minety
Normandy gritty	Other medieval
Redcliffe	Saintonge all over green
Saintonge green glazed	Saintonge polychrome
Trim-type cooking ware	Trim-type ware
Unidentified	Misc. English
Southwest France	Irish wares
Leinster glazed	

● Location of excavations

—— Surviving sections of town wall

••••• Probable line of town wall

- - - Possible line of town wall

2 Map showing breakdown of pottery assemblages from a selection of sites excavated in Trim (map and graphs by Matthew Seaver, Ciara Travers and Catherine Bishop, based on published and unpublished pottery reports; base-map from *Irish Historic Towns Atlas, no. 14: Trim*, by permission of the Royal Irish Academy © RIA)

3 Geoffrey de Geneville, justiciar 1273–6 and lord of Trim 1252–1308 (from the Great
Charter Roll of Waterford; courtesy of Waterford Museum of Treasures)
4 Fragment of late sixteenth- or seventeenth-century Frechen jug found during excavations
on Castle Street, Trim (photograph by Mark Condren)
5 Fragment of line-impressed tile found during excavations on Castle Street, Trim
(photograph by Mark Condren)

6 Reconstruction of a Trim-type ware jug, found during excavations at Trim Castle in the 1970s (courtesy of David Sweetman, © Department of the Environment, Heritage and Local Government, Dublin)

7 Copper-alloy strap-end from a leather strap, found during excavations at 18 Market Street, Trim. Probably thirteenth-century (photograph by Richard Johnston)

8 Sherds of Ham Green A ware found during excavations at 18 Market Street, Trim
(photograph by Richard Johnston)
9 Sherds of Ham Green B ware found during excavations at 18 Market Street, Trim
(photograph by Richard Johnston)

10 Sherds of Dublin-type fineware found during excavations at 18 Market Street, Trim
(photograph by Richard Johnston)
11 Sherds of Dublin-type cooking ware found during excavations at 18 Market Street, Trim
(photograph by Richard Johnston)

12 Sherds of Trim-type cooking ware found during excavations at 18 Market Street, Trim
(photograph by Richard Johnston)
13 Sherds of Trim-type ware found during excavations at 18 Market Street, Trim
(photograph by Richard Johnston)

14 Sherds of Leinster Cooking Ware found during excavations at 18 Market Street, Trim
(photograph by Richard Johnston)
15 Human burial recovered within a well at the site of the Black Friary, Trim
(photograph courtesy of CRDS Ltd)

Lower deposits filling Ditch F6

The lowest deposits within this ditch were dark-brown clayey silts with a high organic content. These contained frequent large animal bones (particularly cattle), oyster shell fragments, large clumps of moss and occasional medieval pot-sherds. An unidentifiable animal bone from this context was radiocarbon-dated to 1280–1400 cal. AD (Wk–23891). This corresponds with the pottery, which is generally thought to be of thirteenth-/fourteenth-century date (McCutcheon 2007). These deposits also contained a roofing slate with a peg-hole, and fragments of wool cloth with a herring-bone weave. This deposit was largely confined to the central channel within the ditch, although it did overlap the sides. It abutted the stone structure. It thickened in depth from south to north, from 30cm to 50cm. It was clear that the same deposits had formed within the stone structure. Large quantities of un-mortared stone were found within it, and these may have originated from the structure or they may have been part of the upper stone dump deposit that had sunk into the soft mud. This stone spread extended 2.8m north of the stone structure. An isolated patch of red-brown clay was found on the western side of the ditch. It contained an iron pitchfork/trident (fig. 8.5). This object is likely to have been a garden fork, and three-pronged examples are listed among inventories of medieval garden equipment (Steane 1985, 215). The vast majority of the animal bone came from this context, including many horse bones, some of which were covered in mortar.

Table 8.1 Medieval pottery from ditch deposits (by Clare McCutcheon)

Context	Links	Fabric-type
3		Dublin-type fineware (x4), Trim-type ware (x1), Drogheda-type ware? (x1)
4	Sherd link F5	Leinster Cooking Ware (x1), Dublin-type ware (x1), Drogheda-type ware? (x1), Dublin-type fineware (x1), Floor tile (x1)
5	Sherd link F4	Dublin-type ware (x1), Drogheda-type ware? (x1)
13		Leinster Cooking Ware (x1), Dublin-type ware (x1), Dublin-type fineware (x4), Trim-type ware (x1)
14		Dublin-type ware (x1)
20		Dublin-type ware (x1)
25		Dublin-type ware (x1)

Bank deposits within the ditch

These organic deposits were overlain by very compact mid-reddish-brown silty clay with frequent stones of various sizes. Some were mortared. This was in

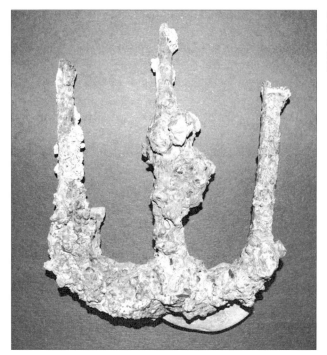

8.6 Iron trident (E2398:12:1) from clay on western side of ditch (photograph by Jane Hamill for CRDS Ltd)

turn overlain by compact grey-brown sandy-silt (F3). Together, these deposits formed a bank that was 80cm in depth, and which abutted and filled the ditch on its eastern edge and sloped downwards on the eastern side. It was interpreted as an episode of deliberate back-filling.

Deposits on the western side of ditch
The lowest of the deposits filling the ditch on the western side of the bank was gritty compacted clayey silt with mortar inclusions up to 18cm in thickness. It was overlain by the dark-brown organic layer that also filled the remainder of the ditch. This was overlain by grey-brown silty clay with infrequent stones and orange flecking. A deposit of grey-brown silty clay had formed above this (F25). This was up to 55cm in thickness and contained a human skull fragment. This was below a further deposit of grey-green silt (F35). They abutted the stone structure at their western limit. They were covered by soft grey-green silt (F14). This was overlain by a thin band of charcoal rich silt (F20) that was sealed in turn by light green-grey silt up to 20cm in depth (F13). All of these deposits were sealed by a band of mid-brown clayey silt that directly underlay the footing of the rectory wall. East of the rectory wall this deposit was overlain by a band of mid-brown clayey silt directly under the concrete footpath.

Post-medieval deposits

A series of localized post-medieval deposits associated with the top of the stone structure were uncovered. Two mortared bricks may have been part of a drain pre-dating a modern shore-box. It was surrounded by a number of gritty deposits (F8), which contained coal and glass.

Wall on the western side of the street

Monitoring work in September 2007 identified a substantial east-west wall on the western side of the street, immediately under the pavement. It had been heavily truncated by services, and the top of the wall had been covered in concrete. The wall measured 1m east-west by 1.6m in width by 70cm in depth. It was a maximum of four courses in depth and was built of large masonry limestone blocks bonded by yellow-brown mortar with a high sand content. It was placed within a wall foundation cut measuring 2.1m by 70cm. The wall continued under the garden of the 1930s houses on the western side of the street. No artefacts or dating evidence was associated with the wall, and a sample of the mortar was taken for analysis. Large quantities of masonry were found within the old service trenches, and these clearly came from the truncated wall.

DISCUSSION

Excavations uncovered a large ditch that clearly runs under the rectory garden wall at the location marked on cartographic sources as the Athboy Gate, and a substantial east-west wall on the western side of the junction. It is important to enter a caveat in any discussion of fragmentary traces of town defences. It is tempting, when excavating medieval towns, to uncritically interpret ditches and walls as being part of town defences. There are clearly a number of problems with automatically interpreting the medieval features uncovered as a gate and wall:

- If the masonry structure represents the base of a gate inserted into the ditch, why was a corresponding feature not found on the eastern side of the road? It may be that the corresponding arch lies under the footpath. This would make the gate entrance over 5m in width. The Sheep Gate archway only provides for a 3m gap.

- If wall F7 represents the town wall, why was it not battered? Stretches of wall excavated on the south side of the river are clearly very thick, and battered into the town ditch. It may equally be one of the buildings depicted on the 1747 and 1836 maps, which ran up to and abutted the wall.

Monitoring of the installation of the water main in 1999 and for the Trim Street Reconstruction Project in recent years has allowed a comprehensive view of what lies under the tarmac at Athboy Gate. This has suggested that natural boulder clay beneath metalled surfaces underlay all of the junction area except for the medieval ditch and the structure described within this report. This precludes any major ditch crossing the junction. The form of two of the town gates is known: the Sheep Gate, which survives, and the Water Gate, which was photographed in the nineteenth century (Potterton 2005, 186–7). Both of these were square in plan with a single-arched gateway. The Water Gate clearly had a chamber above it. It is likely that this was topped by a crenellated wall-walk. The 1747 image of the Athboy Gate, while figurative, shows a single arch supported by two piers.

The rectory garden was clearly an insertion into the pre-existing street plan, and its construction probably entailed the destruction of the town wall and perhaps the re-use of some of the stone for the boundary wall. This was clearly accomplished prior to 1747. Recent excavations at the rectory by IAC uncovered the remains of medieval pits and indications of structures, but no further traces of the town wall (Tim Coughlan, pers. comm.).

Despite the difficulties in interpreting the structure archaeologically, it represents the only large-scale medieval site to have been found on the upper section of Haggard Street. The combination of this with the cartographic evidence does suggest that this represents part of the town defences. The ditch is aligned with the suggested outline of the town defences as indicated by Potterton (2005, Plate 7).

The large wall (F36), which had been badly damaged by the digging of a water main, a sewer and telecom cabling, is likely to be the remains of the town wall. Unlike excavated sections to the south of the River Boyne, it was not battered and there was no evidence for a ditch on the western side of the street.

The basal deposits indicated a number of things about the surrounding environment. Two waterlogged samples of the basal fill and a sample of the upper deposits were examined by Susan Lyons (Appendix 8.2). The plant remains suggest that four different environments were represented: woodland and scrub; arable/cultivated land; waste places and disturbed ground; and finally heaths and wet ground (Lyons 2008). The variety in remains probably resulted from the wet nature of the ditch outside the town, where several environments lay in close proximity to each other. Woodland and scrub were represented by hazelnut, blackberry, bramble and elderberry. Alder and willow were also present. The presence of relatively infrequent charred oat, wheat and, to a lesser extent, barley, is typical of Irish urban medieval sites, such as Drogheda. Weeds associated with crop cultivation were also identified from the ditch, namely corn marigold, lesser stitchwort, chickweed and hemp nettle. The infrequency of carbonized arable weed seeds, together with little or no incidence of cereal chaff and arable weeds from urban medieval deposits, suggests that their processing and distribution was a commercial rather than a domestic activity. Processed cereal grain would have arrived at the site as clean grain void of any impurities and contaminants. A range of weeds associated with waste ground are indicated in the appendix below. Heather and bracken were also noted, and this hints at the exploitation of heaths, perhaps for building material, latrine sealants and toilet paper.

The thirteen fragments of textile indicate woollen cloth, and these were examined by Maria Fitzgerald (2008). The fragmentary nature of the textile makes it difficult to ascertain its original function. The cloth has a relatively coarse and loose weave, with a thread count of only nine to seven threads per centimetre. One fragment has a finished edge and another appears to have had a hemmed edge, indicating that the cloth was modified or tailored for use. Coarse woollen cloths were used for horse-blankets and for packing goods, as well as for surcoats and mantles during the fourteenth century (Dunlevy 1989). The evidence for some tailoring (hemmed edges) suggests that the cloth represent the remains of an outer garment. Ultimately, the cloth ended up at the base of the ditch near the town gate and it may have been lost or discarded by a passer-by. While the evidence from animal bone assemblages within the town indicates that the rearing of sheep for wool was not a priority, it is likely that large quantities of wool were brought into the town for sale. Wool-fells, sacks of wool, Irish cloth, linen are all listed in the murage charter of 1290, while there was a weaver's house in the town in the sixteenth century (Potterton 2005, 164, 147). The animal bone remains (Appendix 8.1) indicate that horses were over-represented compared to the norm for medieval urban sites, and that there may have been an industry in dealing with transport and the rendering of horses close to the gate. The discovery of a human skull fragment is notable, despite the absence of pathologies indicating the cause of death. Human skull fragments with trauma were uncovered at the excavations at Kiely's Yard (Stephens, 'SubUrbia', this volume) and indicate the violent nature of society at this time. The display of human remains, particularly skulls, took place at gates and on the walls and the Athboy Gate example may be linked to this practice. The exhibition of severed heads at Trim Castle was documented in the fifteenth century (Potterton 2005, 136).

In summary, the remains uncovered during this assessment are likely to be the only surviving remains of the Athboy Gate and the town wall in this area. The ditch may have acted to funnel traffic approaching the gate. All masonry and the excavated ditch were preserved in situ.

ACKNOWLEDGMENTS

I would like to thank Trim Town Council, particularly Paul Donlon, for initiating and providing the funding for the project. Thanks to the excavation team from CRDS: Greg Flanagan and Colum O'Brien and to Niall Lynch and Catherine Bishop for preparing excavation drawings for publication. I would also like to thank Milica Rajic and Joanne Gaffrey, who managed all aspects of post-excavation analysis. I am very grateful to the specialists who allowed me to publish and use extracts from their reports.

BIBLIOGRAPHY

Bradley, J., 1984, 'Urban Archaeological Survey of Trim, County Meath'. Unpublished report for the Office of Public Works.
Fitzgerald, M., 2008, 'Appendix 9: excavation C150/E2398: textile remains' in Seaver, M., 'Final report on excavations at the Athboy Gate E2398'. Unpublished report for National Monuments Service.
Hennessy, M., 2004, *Irish Historic Towns Atlas, No. 14: Trim*. Dublin.
Lyons, S., 2007, 'Analysis of the plant remains from Athboy Gate, Trim, Co. Meath [E2398]' in Seaver, M., 'Final report on excavations at the Athboy Gate E2398'. Unpublished report for National Monuments Service.
Potterton, M., 2005, *Medieval Trim: history and archaeology*. Dublin.
McCutcheon, C., 2007, 'Medieval pottery' in Seaver, M., 'Final report on excavations at the Athboy Gate E2398'. Unpublished report for National Monuments Service.
Mullins, C., 2000, 'Kildalkey Road/Athboy Road/Haggard Street, Trim' in Bennett, I. (ed.), *Excavations 1999: summary accounts of archaeological excavations in Ireland*, no. 717, pp 247–8. Bray.
Steane, J., 1985, *The archaeology of medieval England and Wales*. Beckenham, Croom Helm.
White, N.B., 1943, *Extents of Irish monastic possessions 1540–41*. Dublin.

APPENDIX 8.1: ANIMAL BONE ANALYSIS

By Camilla Lofqvist

GENERAL RESULTS

A total of 527 bone fragments with a total weight of 14,603.1g were submitted for examination. These were assessed and identified to species when possible. From these, a total of 161 fragments (30.6%) were not possible to identify to species as the bones were too fragmented. The remaining 366 fragments (c.69.4%) from 204 anatomical units (for instance, two fragments of the same femur were counted as an MNE of one) were identified and divided into species (Table 8.2).

Table 8.2 Total number of identified specimens present (NISP), minimum
number of anatomical elements (MNE), minimum number of individuals
(MNI) and total weight, identified to species

Group	Number of fragments	% of fragments	MNE	Weight in g.	Weight in %
Fragments identified					
to species	366	69.4	204	14011.8	95.8
Unidentified	161	30.6	161	618.3	4.2
Total	**527**	100	**365**	14,630.1	100

Table 8.3 NISP, MNE, MNI and total weight, for all species present

Species	NISP	NISP in %	MNE	MNE in %	MNI	MNI in %	Weight	Weight %
Horse	161	44	79	38.7	4	17	9346.6	66.7
Cattle	83	22.7	47	23	2	8	3489.8	24.9
Pig	52	14.2	36	17.6	4	17	620.9	4.4
Caprinae	43	11.7	21	10.3	6	25	375.8	2.7
Dog	12	3.3	11	5.4	2	8	129.1	0.9
Cat	9	2.5	5	2.5	3	13	39.1	0.3
Bird	6	1.6	5	2.5	3	13	10.5	0.1
Grand Total	**366**	100	**204**	100	**24**	100	14,011.8	100

The quality of the bones was generally fairly good. The average weight per fragment of
the 366 fragments identified to species was 38.3g. The average weight of the unidentified
fragments was only 3.8g per fragment. This illustrates the high fragmentation of the
unidentified pieces.

A total of thirty-six fragments displayed cut-marks, while only four exhibited traces of
gnawing, mainly by dog but also by a rodent. Thirteen fragments displayed pathological
changes (Table 8.4). None of the bone fragments had been exposed to burning.

Table 8.4 Number of fragments with cut-/gnaw-marks or pathology

Species	Cut	Cut in %	Gnaw	Gnaw in %	Path	Path in %	Total
Cattle	11	30.6	0	0	1	7.7	12
Horse	8	22.2	0	0	8	61.5	16
Caprinae	6	16.7	0	0	0	0	6
Pig	2	5.6	3	75	1	7.7	6
Dog	0	0	0	0	2	15.4	2
Unidentified	9	25	1	25	1	7.7	11
Grand Total	**36**	100	**4**	100	**13**	100	53

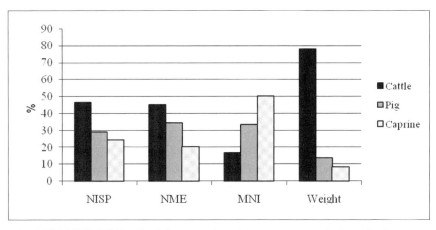

8.7 NISP, MNE, MNI and weight comparisons between meat-producing animal groups

Cattle (bos)

Cattle were the second most common species in the bone assemblage from Athboy Gate, in terms of weight of the bone, number of bone fragments (NISP) and MNE. In total, 83 bone fragments from 47 bone elements were retrieved. The total weight of the cattle bone was 3,489.8g (24.9% of the bones identified to species) and the MNI was 2: one juvenile and one adult (Table 8.3).

The age at which the cattle were slaughtered was estimated from fusion data and on the basis of the tooth eruption and wear of the teeth in the mandible. The data indicated that one individual was a juvenile younger than two years at the time of death, while the second individual was an adult of *c.*7–9 years. Animals reaching the highest age were in general the milk cows. A few bulls were also kept for breeding, however, along with a few draft animals. The general medieval pattern is that oxen were usually taken into work at four years of age and were used for an average of four years before being fattened and slaughtered (Trow-Smith 1957, 70; Vretemark 1997, 175). In the rural economy it was milk production that was of primary importance and, conse-quently, the majority of animals kept were milk cows. The older cows yielded the most and the best milk, which was then used to make products like butter. Meat-production was only of secondary importance, as it was the result of replacing older animals with younger individuals, removing juveniles which were not needed as draught-oxen or when young milk cows were not producing enough milk. In bone assemblages from rural sites, therefore, there is a tendency towards cattle being more evenly divided between the different age categories, while in urban material there is a predominance of older animals. The reason for this is that it was more profitable for outside producers to send mature or semi-mature animals to the market in town.

The bone sample from Athboy Gate was limited but it seems to indicate that both the meat and the milk were of importance, as one of the animals was a juvenile, while the other was an adult. A coxa, metacarpal and skull were used to determine the older individual was a cow. This suggests that milk-production may have been of importance and that cows were kept, but also that occasional young (possibly male) animals were slaughtered for meat and by-products. For example, bone combs, bone pins, needles, drinking goblets and spoons were made from the bone and horns of cattle. Hides were retrieved and used to make leather and vellum for manuscripts, while bovine tallow was used to produce candles (Kelly 1998, 52–7). It has been shown that the change to dairy farming at the expense of meat-production led to an increase in productivity, resulting in a general improvement in people's health.

Several bone elements retrieved from Athboy Gate were measured, but only two were complete enough to be used in an estimation of stature (Table 8.6). One of the estimated withers height was 100.7cm, and this was based on a metacarpal from a cow (from F14). The second estimated withers height was 111.7cm, but the sex of this individual was not known. It is possible that this was a second adult individual. The distal metatarsals fuse at 2–2.5 years of age, indicating that this bone element was not from the juvenile. The estimated withers height, however, as indicated by the metacarpal from the cow, is 11cm shorter than the metatarsal, so these two metapodiale might have been from two different individuals. As there is a lack of obvious duplication of the bone elements, the MNI can still only be estimated as two. It also has to be taken into consideration that the metacarpal displayed pathological changes, possibly resulting in a lower estimated withers height. The metatarsal came from F5, which was the lowest deposit within a ditch (F6). F5 was dark-brown clayey silt containing frequent animal bones, oyster shell and occasional medieval pottery. The average withers height in twelfth- to fourteenth-century Dublin was between 106.2 and 111.8cm (McCormick 1997, 212, Table 50).

Table 8.5 Estimation of stature of cattle

Sample no.	Context	Bone	Part of bone	Side	GLI	GL	Bp	Bd	CF	ESH	Comment
25	14	Mc	Complete	Dx	–	167	48.83	49.24	6.03	100.7	Cow
17	5	Mt	Fairly complete	Sin	–	205	38.66	45.88	5.45	111.7	–

The distribution of anatomical units indicates a fairly even division between the elements, indicating that all parts of the animals were present on the site. This suggests that this site may have been used as a rubbish deposit, where mixed refuse of butchery and food waste was dumped.

A total of eleven fragments (13.3% of the total number of cattle bones) displayed cut-marks. The large majority of these were chopped up diaphyses fragments of long-bones, but there were also coxae, mandibles and scapulae. These chop–marks were most likely associated with the slaughter process and the chopped up diaphyses suggest that the marrow may have been extracted. One coxa fragment from a cow also displayed finer cut-marks (fig. 8.8).

None of the fragments displayed any traces of gnawing, which suggests that the bones were deposited in a location where scavengers, like dogs and rats, had limited access. One fragment, a cow metacarpal, displayed pathological changes (discussed above). The diaphysis had a swollen appearance, suggesting that it might have had a

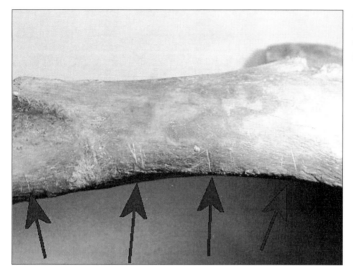

8.8 Ilium from cow, with fine cut-marks indicated

green-stick fracture that had healed, or an ossified haematoma. An ossified haematoma is a smooth bone swelling resulting from a contused wound caused by a blunt impact, leading to bleeding at sub-periosteal level (fig. 8.9). It is possible that this condition resulted in the relatively low estimated withers height (100.7cm). The cattle bone came from six fills: 007; 3; 4; 5; 14; and 25. The majority (55.4%) of these came from F5.

Pig (sus)

The total number of bone fragments identified as pig was 52, from 36 anatomical units. The MNI was 4: two juveniles, one semi-adult and one adult. The total weight of the pig bone was 620.9g or 4.4% of the total weight of all bones identified to species (Table 8.3). The age at which the pigs were slaughtered was estimated on fusion data and on the basis of the tooth eruption and wear of the teeth in the mandible. This data indicated that the bones were from two juvenile animals younger than 1.5 years, one of which was probably younger than six months at the time of death. There was one semi-adult of *c*.3–3.5 years, along with one older adult of 6+ years.

Most of the pigs were culled when they were young, as they were only a source of meat, fat and skin (slaughter products) and it was not beneficial to keep them any longer (Davis 1995, 181). The medieval pig was sexually mature at 2–3 years and would have yielded *c*.40kg of pork at this age. As a comparison, today young pigs are sexually mature at six months and yield *c*.75kg of pork (Sten 1992, 207).

None of the pig elements retrieved from Athboy Gate could be used in sex estimation. Many of the long bones were in bad condition and, as a result, only one of the bone elements could be used in stature estimation. This measurement, along with the proximal width of a radius and measurements from a scapula, are presented in Table 8.7. The estimated withers height indicated a stature of 68.1cm. This tibia came from a juvenile, however, which was not yet fully grown.

8.9 Metacarpal with area of possible ossified haematoma indicated. To the right is a normal metacarpal, for comparison

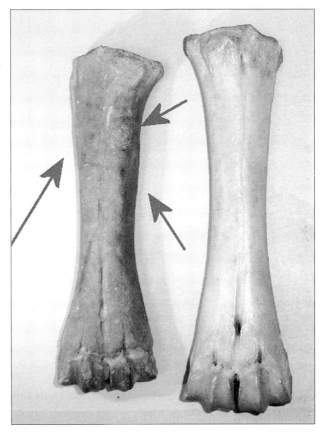

Table 8.6 Pig measurements

Sample no.	Fill	Bone	Part of bone	Side	GLl	GL	Bp	CF	ESH	Juv.	Comment
9	5	Tibia	Distal dia. + epi.	Sin	–	171	–	3.92 + 11	68.10	Juv.	From juv. prox. epi. missing
18	4	Radius	Fairly complete	Dx	–	–	22.31	–	–		Juv.	Fused at 3.5yrs
					GLP	**BG**	**SLC**				
17	5	Scapula	Fairly complete	Dx	2.84	28.95	19.42	19.82			

The distribution of anatomical units indicates a fairly even division between the elements, indicating that all parts of the animals were present on the site. The most frequently present anatomical unit was the tibia. The flesh of pig was highly

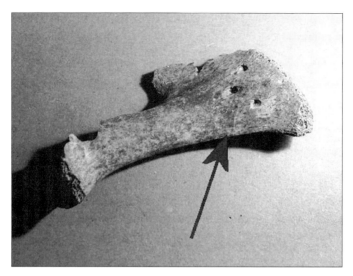

8.10 Pig coxa
with evidence for
gnawing

appreciated and it could provide a feast for visiting high-ranking guests. The pig was often chopped up into shoulder joints and hams which were the most appreciated cuts, but even the head of a pig, mainly boar, was a cherished dish. A perforation in the pig's shoulder blades usually indicates that these parts were being hung up and cured, either by smoking or by salting.

Two fragments (3.8% of the total number of pig bones) showed traces of cuts, while three (5.8%) displayed traces of gnawing (Table 8.4). Of the two fragments with cuts, one frontal fragment displayed finer cut-marks, while the remaining bone element was a perforated shoulder blade, indicating that this had been hung up and cured. The elements with gnawing were a long bone fragment of a femur, a skull fragment and a coxa. The coxa and the femur displayed pointed tooth imprints, probably caused by a dog (fig. 8.10), while the skull fragment had most likely been gnawed by a rodent.

One complete tibia with an unfused proximal diaphysis (which normally fuses at 3.5 years) exhibited pathological changes associated with osteoperiostitis and ossified haematoma. Osteoperiostitis is an inflammation of the membrane (periosteum) that surrounds and envelops a bone. This inflammation was most likely active at the time of death (fig. 8.11). The pig bones came from six fills: 003; 3; 4; 5; 14; and 25. The majority (48%) of the fragments came from F5.

Caprinae (sheep/goat, ovis/capra)
Sheep and goat are difficult to distinguish from each other and are therefore grouped as 'caprinae'. Female sheep are ewes while a female goat is called a doe. Intact male sheep and goats are referred to as rams and buck respectively, while castrated males are wethers. Lambs/kids are immature individuals of less than a year, while the term 'mutton' is used for the meat of semi-adult/adult sheep of at least two years of age. At Athboy Gate, the total number of bone fragments identified as sheep/goat was 43, from 21 anatomical units. The MNI was 6: two juveniles, three semi-adults and one adult. The total weight of caprinae bone was 375.8g or 2.7% of the total weight of all

8.11 Tibia with ossified haematoma highlighted (right arrow) and active osteoperiostitis (left arrow)

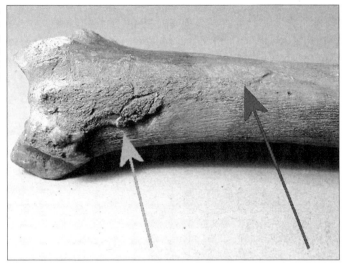

bones identified to species (Table 8.3). None of the fragments could be used for an estimate of sex.

The average life expectancy of a sheep is 10–12 years, but a normal and slow decline starts from 4 years and onwards. While present day females generally reach sexual maturity at 6–8 months of age, it is thought that in early Irish farming a ewe was expected to lamb for the first time at around three years of age. Modern rams generally reach sexual maturity at 4–6 months. In early Irish farming, most male lambs were castrated after weaning and these wethers were then normally slaughtered in their first summer or autumn (Kelly 1998, 69). The dressing-out weight of a lamb during the fourteenth century was 7kg. Today, lambs are slaughtered at 4–6 months and they have a dressing-out weight of 15kg (Sten 1992, 207). The dressed weight of an adult was *c.*55–60kg (Luff 1984, 25; Murray 2000, 6, table 2).

The age at which the caprinae were slaughtered was estimated on the basis of fusion data, tooth eruption and wear of the teeth in the mandible. This data indicated that two of the individuals were between 6 and 24 months. Three animals were semi-adults of between 2 and 4 years, and one individual was an adult of 6+ years at the time of death.

A higher percentage of older animals on a given site suggests that the sheep were being kept for their wool and not for their meat, as the wool was of poor quality until the animal passed its second winter. A high percentage of juveniles being slaughtered suggests that the animals were mainly kept for meat and not for wool, as the meat on an animal gets less tasty and fattier with the rising age of the animal. The few animals reaching a higher age were most likely used for breeding and for small-scale wool-production. The Athboy Gate bone sample contained two individuals younger than 2 years of age, while four were semi-adults of between 2 and 4 years, and one adult of 6+ years. This suggests that on this site *c.*33% of the young caprinae including lambs/kids were slaughtered, while the majority (67%) of the animals reached higher ages. Only one individual reached an older age of 6+ years. This bone sample is limited, but it suggests that the animals were kept for the meat, milk and hides and less for their wool.

This does not totally exclude the retrieval and usage of the wool, however. For example, wool fabric was recovered from F51 during the excavation at Athboy Gate. Previous excavations in Trim, however, suggest that the town was not an important centre for wool products (Beglane 2007; Murray 2000). It is likely that the majority of the animals reaching higher ages were females and that they were kept for their milk, which is ideal for cheese-making, and for their wool.

During the medieval period, sheep milk was regarded as nutritional and invigorating. The common presence of loom weights and spindle-whorls also shows that the wool was highly appreciated. Sheepskin was used for making clothes and footwear along with other products. Sheep carcasses yielded by-products like tallow, which was used in candle- and soap-making, while bone and cartilage was used to carve items like buttons and dice.

The anatomical units from caprinae seem to indicate a distribution of cuts with a lower meat contents. Skull and phalanges seem to be less frequent however. This indicates that animals may have been butchered but that cuts with higher meat content were removed from the site to be cooked and consumed somewhere else. Furthermore, it suggests that the skins, probably with the skull and lower extremities still attached, were also removed from the site, possibly to be turned into clothes, footwear or other products.

Five bone elements were measured, but only one of these could be used in a calculation of estimated withers height (ESH) (Table 8.8). This metacarpal was most likely from a sheep.

Table 8.7 Estimated withers height of sheep and goat

Sample no.	Fill	Bone	Part of bone	Side	GLI	GL	Bp	Bd	CF	ESH	Juv.	Comment
25	14	Mc	Complete	Sin	–	114.1	19.86	22.56	4.89	55.77	–	Poss. sheep
24	5	Mc	Prox. epi. + dia.	Sin	–	–	22.99	–	–	–	Juv.	Fuse at 20–24 months
17	5	Radius	Dist. epi. + dia.	Sin	–	–	–	24.77	–	–	–	Sheep/goat
22	4	Tibia	Dist. epi. + dia.	Dx	–	–	–	21.31	–	–	–	Sheep/goat
17	5	Tibia	Dist. epi. + dia.	Sin	–	–	–	23.86	–	–	–	Sheep/goat

The total withers height estimated from the single metacarpal of a possible sheep came to 55.77cm. This metacarpal came from F14. Analysis of sheep metapodia from different urban sites, for example in Dublin, shows an increase in size from the tenth/eleventh century to the twelfth/fourteenth century – a metacarpal in the tenth/eleventh century was an average length of 114.3mm (estimated height of 55.9cm), but by the twelfth/fourteenth century this had increased to 122mm (estimated height of 59.6cm) (McCormick 1997, 203, table 42). The average withers height in Early Medieval Lund, Sweden was between 63cm (ewes) and 68.5cm (rams/wethers) (Ekman 1973, 94, table 21). The mean GL (greatest length) of sheep metatarsals in twelfth- to fourteenth-century Patrick Street, Dublin was 13.02cm, which would give a mean withers height of 59.11cm (McCormick 1997, 203, table 42). Stature estimations from a number of post-medieval sites around Ireland show a general increase in sheep size.

A total of six bone fragments (13.9% of the total number of caprinae bones) showed traces of cuts. The large majority (83%) of these elements consisted of chopped up diaphyses, but a scapula fragment may have had a perforation through the shoulder blade. It is possible that this bone had been hung up and cured. Legs of lamb were often cured, preserving the meat and making it an ideal food to bring on long trips as provisions (Sten 1992, 205).

The caprinae bones came from seven fills: 007; 3; 4; 5; 13; 14; and 25. The majority of these came from F4 and F5.

Horse (equus)

Horse was the most common species in the assemblage in terms of the weight of the bone (66.7% of bone identified to species), the number of bone fragments (NISP) and the MNE. A total of 161 bone fragments from 79 anatomical units were retrieved and the total weight of the horse bone was 9,346.6g. The MNI was 4: one juvenile/semi-adult, one 4–5 year old and two adults.

The age of the individuals was estimated from fusion data and on the basis of the tooth eruption and wear of the teeth in the mandible. This data indicated that one of the individuals was younger than 3–3.5 years at the time of death, while one fusing vertebra suggests the presence of a young adult individual of c.4–5 years of age. The remaining individuals were two adults: one of c.10–15 years, and the other an older adult of c.20+ years at the time of death.

Most anatomical units of horse were present. The sex of the horses was estimated from coxae and the canine in the lower jaw. This estimation concluded that there were at least three males, of which two were older individuals. A total of 19 bone elements were complete enough to be measured, and seven of these could be used in a calculation of estimated withers height (Table 8.9).

Table 8.8 Estimated withers height of horse

Sample no.	Fill	Bone	Part of bone	Side	GLI/GL	Bp	Bd	CF	ESH	Comment
8	5	Mc3	Complete	Dx	209	43.01	43.46	6.41	133.9	Path
9	5	Mc3	Complete	Dx	225	47.86	47	6.41	144.2	–
11	5	Mc3	Complete but in frags	Sin	216	46.13	45.03	6.41	138.5	Broken
18	4	Mt3	Complete	Dx	264	48.24	47.85	5.33	140.7	–
7	5	Mt3	Complete	Dx	262.5	46.01	44.49	5.33	139.9	Covered in mortar
18	4	Mt3	Fairly complete	Dx	351.5	88.68	72.50	4.36	153.3	–
18	4	Tibia	Complete	Sin	267.5	–	46.17	5.33	142.6	–

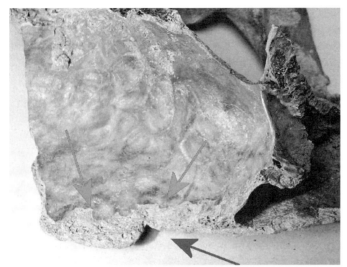

8.12 Interior of horse skull with (lower) arrow highlighting location of blow and (upper) arrows showing interior flaking, which is usually the result of breakage of fresh bone

The estimated withers height varied between 133.9cm and 153.3cm, giving an average height of 141.9cm. Today, an animal of 14.2 hands (*c*.144.3cm) or over is usually considered to be a horse, while one less than 14.2h is considered to be a pony. Some smaller horse breeds, pony breeds and light riding horses are exceptions to this rule. One (14.5%) of the seven bone elements from which an estimated withers height was calculated, came from fill F4. Together with F3, these fills form a bank deposit within the ditch (F6; possibly of medieval date) and this has been interpreted as the result of a period of deliberate back-filling. This tibia gave an estimated withers height of 153.3, which was the largest within the sample and would be considered a horse rather than a pony. The remaining six bone elements came from F5 (57%) and F4 (28.5%), and the estimated withers height of these elements indicate that these came from a pony/ponies. The fill (F5) was the lowest deposit in the ditch (F6).

Eight fragments (*c*.5% of the total number of horse bones) displayed traces of cuts, with a majority being consistent with chopped up diaphyses, while one fragment displayed finer cuts and one skull fragment exhibited traces suggesting a blow to the forehead. The chopped up diaphysis fragments suggest that the bones had been broken to retrieve the marrow, while the finer cuts across the proximal diaphysis of a radius suggest that this animal had been skinned and the hide retrieved (fig. 8.13). A partial horse skull with a fracture to the forehead is from an animal that was probably killed by a blow to the head (fig. 8.12).

Eight fragments displayed pathological changes. A fairly complete lumbar vertebra exhibited bone-growths or a callus formation on one of the processes and the articulating surfaces. This pathology might have been caused by trauma on the left side of the lower back or by repeated stress to the vertebra. It is possible that this individual was an older working horse, used as a draught-horse or for carrying loads, which caused stress to the spine or resulted in an injury to it. Five anatomical units of horse exhibited osteoperiostitis, of which three had healed while two were still active at the time of death (figs 8.13 & 8.14).

8.13 Proximal radius with fine cuts across diaphysis (left arrows) and a healed osteoperiostitis (right arrow)

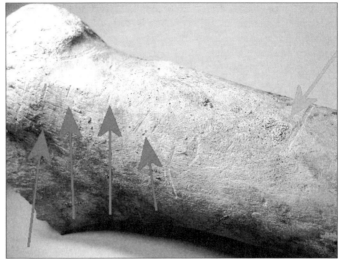

8.14 Metacarpals 2 & 3 with active osteoperiostitis

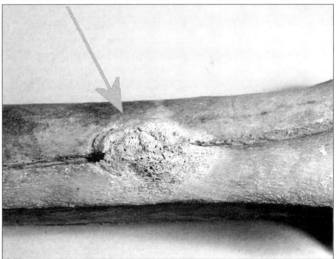

The legs and feet of a horse are especially sensitive to blows, sprains and overwork, especially if the horse is young or is worked on hard surfaces. Lameness may be caused by bony growths such as splints, spavins or ringbones. An equine hock from Athboy Gate displayed what might be a case of spavin, which had resulted in two fused tarsals (fig. 8.15). This is a disease of the tarsus bones of the horse, but cattle and camels can also be affected. The disease affects the smaller bones in the joint and produces extensive exostosis, which limits its movement. The cause of the disease is undetermined, but it has been suggested that it might be:

- hereditary;
- caused by an inflammation of some of the soft tissues, which has spread to the periosteum, stimulating new bone formation or;
- caused by severe concussion due, for example, to faulty shoeing or heavy work.

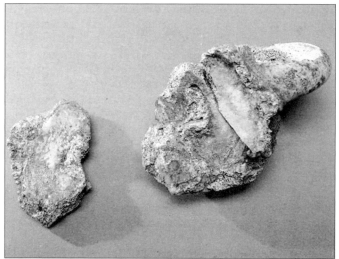

8.15 Fused tarsals with exostoses from an equine hock, likely symptomatic of spavin

One horse tooth exhibited a dental pathology. This third lower molar displayed deposits of calculus, which is closely linked with the health and functioning of the teeth. The formation of calculus can be caused by a number of variables. In dogs, for example, it may be due to a lack of friction from food during chewing. Dental trauma is relatively common in mammal dentition (Baker & Brothwell, 1980).

The fragments were retrieved from seven fills: 003; 3; 4; 5; 14; 18; and 25, but the majority came from fills F003 and F3 (35%) along with fill C5 (34%). The bone assemblage from Athboy Gate is slightly unusual due the high frequency of horse bone. On the large majority of sites, the most frequent species is usually one of the meat-producing domesticated animals – cattle, caprinae or pig.

The average withers height of the horses at Athboy Gate was 141.9cm, indicating that most of these individuals were ponies. The high frequency of horse bone suggests that working horses/packing animals were either kept at the vicinity of the site or brought to this location to be slaughtered after getting too old to carry out heavy work.

Dog (canis)
There were 12 fragments of dog bone from 11 anatomical units. The total weight came to 129.6g (which is 0.9% of the total number of animal bone) and the MNI was 2: two adults (Table 8.3). The age of the dogs was only estimated on fusion data and indicated that one of the individuals was younger than 20–24 months at time of death. The other individual was an adult. The anatomical units present were humeri, thoracic vertebrae, coxae, femora, tibiae and metatarsi. None of the dog bones could be used in sex estimation. Four fragments were measured and two of these could be used in an estimation of stature (Table 8.10). The measurements were taken from a humerus and a femur, revealing an average withers height of 52.5cm. This dog was of a medium- to large-sized breed, comparable in size to a modern sheep dog.

Table 8.9 Dog bone measurements

Sample no.	Fill	Bone	Part of bone	Side	GLI	GL	Dp	Bd	CF	ESH	Juv.	Comment
17	5	Humerus	Complete	Sin	–	164	37.71	30.05	3.37	55.30	–	Medium size
9	5	Femur	Complete	Dx	–	165	33.15	29.44	3.01	49.70	–	Medium size

Two bone elements (including the above humerus) displayed traces of possible patholo-gies. The humerus displayed pathological changes associated with osteoarthritis, probably associated with the ageing process. This 'lipping' is associated with wear and tear in older adult mammals, resulting in new bone formation. The second element with pathology was a diaphysis of an ulna. This bone had once been fractured but had healed (fig. 8.16). The dog bones came from four fills: 3; 5; 14; and 25. The majority of the dog bones (41.6%) came from F5.

8.16 Ulna with a healed fracture highlighted. To the right is a normal ulna for comparison

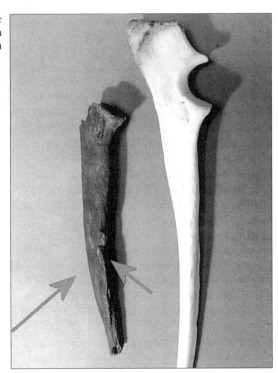

Cat (felis)

The bone assemblage contained nine bone fragments identified as cat, from five anatomical units. The total weight of the cat bones came to 39.1g. The MNI was 3. The age of the cats was estimated on the basis of fusion data and on the wear on teeth. This indicated that two of the individuals were younger: one being 8.5 months and the other being 11.5 months at the time of death. One fragmented skull with much-worn teeth was from an old cat.

The anatomical units present from cats were skull, femur, tibia and fibula. Apart from the skull these were in a fairly good condition. It was not possible to estimate sex from any of the bones, but three complete bone elements could be measured (Table 8.11). Two of these elements came from individuals that were still growing, so it is likely that the greatest length (GL) would be slightly higher.

Table 8.10 Cat bone measurements (1: Calculation Factor; 2: Estimated Shoulder Height)

Sample no.	Fill	Bone of bone	Part	Side	GL	Bp	Bd	CF	ESH	Juv.	Comment
17	5	Femur	Complete	Sin	91.1	17.45	15.51	–	–	Juv.	*c.*8.5 months
17	5	Tibia	Complete	Sin	99.11	11.96	11.96	–	–	–	11.5 months+
17	5	Tibia	Complete	Dx	100.3	12.89	12.89	–	–	Juv.	*c.*11.5 months

None of the bones displayed any cuts, gnawing or pathologies. The cat bones came from two fills: 5 and 13. The two younger individuals were represented by the femur, tibiae and fibula, and all come from F5. The deteriorated cat skull from the old adult came from F13.

Bird (aves)
The bone assemblage contained six bone fragments from five anatomical units of bird, and the total weight came to 10.5g. The MNI was 3. The anatomical units were radius, carpo-metacarpus, femur and tibia-tarsus, and they were retrieved from three fills: 3, 4 and 5. The two bone elements that came from F3 were probably domestic fowl, pheasant or bantam, which belong to the order of Galliformes. The tibio-tarsus from F5 most likely came from a mallard, while one of the two bone elements from F4 could be determined as a possible domestic goose. This species is from the order of Anseriformes.

From the sex fragments identified as bird, 50% were Galliformes. This is an order of birds containing turkeys, grouse, chickens, quails and pheasants, and about 256 species are found worldwide. Some Galliformes are adapted to grassland habitats. They are vegetarian and slightly omnivorous species, adapted for foraging on the ground for rootlets or the consumption of other plant material such as heather shoots. Other breeds of the Galliformes order prefer to capture live insects in leaf-litter, in sand and in shallow pools or along stream banks, and they tend to frequent seasonally wet habitats to forage, especially during chick-rearing. The pheasant was an Anglo-Norman introduction to Ireland (Kelly 1997, 300).

About 33% of the bird bones were identified as Anseriformes. The order Anseriformes contains about 150 living species in three families: the Anhimidae (the screamers), Anseranatidae (the magpie-goose) and the Anatidae. The latter includes over 140 species of waterfowl, among them ducks, geese and swans. All species in the order are highly adapted to aquatic conditions. All are web-footed for efficient swimming, although some have subsequently become mainly terrestrial. None of the fragments from Athboy Gate displayed any traces suggesting that they had been cut up or gnawed. There were no evident pathologies.

BIBLIOGRAPHY

Baker, J., & Brothwell, D., 1980, *Animal diseases in archaeology*. London.

Beglane, F., 2007, 'Report on faunal material from Townparks South, Trim, Co. Meath: licence no. E2016'. Unpublished report for CRDS Ltd.

Clutton-Brock, J., 1999, *A natural history of domesticated mammals*. Cambridge.

Cohen, A., & Serjeantson, D., 1996, *A manual for the identification of bird bone from archaeological sites*. London.

Davis, S.J.M., 1987, *The archaeology of animals*. London.

Driesch, A. von den, 1976, *A guide to measurement of animal bones from archaeological sites*. Harvard.

During, E., 1997, 'Bildkompendium i animalosteologi'. Unpublished document.

Ekman, J., 1973, *Early Mediaeval Lund: the fauna and the landscape*. Lund.

Getty, R., 1975, *Sisson and Grossman's The anatomy of the domestic animals*. 2 vols. Philadelphia, London & Toronto.

Habermehl, K.H., 1961, *Die Altersbestimmung bei Haustieren, Pelztieren und beim jagdbaren Wild*. Hamburg & Berlin.

Hayden, T., & Harrington, R., 2001, *Exploring Irish mammals*. Dublin.

Hillson, S., 1996, *Teeth*. Cambridge.

Higham, C., & Message, M., 1969, 'An assessment of prehistoric techniques of bovine husbandry' in Brothwell, D.R., Higgs, E. (eds), *Science in archaeology*, 315–30 (2nd ed.), London.

Kelly, F., 1998, *Early Irish farming: a study based mainly on the law-texts of the 7th and 8th centuries AD*. Dublin.

Lisle, L., 1957, *Observations on husbandry*. 2 vols, London.

Luff, R.M., 1984, *Animal remains in archaeology*. Aylesbury.

McCormick, F., 1988, 'The domesticated cat in Early Christian and medieval Ireland' in Mac Niocaill, G., & Wallace, P.F. (eds), *Keimelia: studies in medieval archaeology and history in memory of Tom Delaney*, 218–28. Galway.

McCormick, F., 1995, 'Cows, ringforts and the origins of Early Christian Ireland', *Emania* **13**, 33–7.

McCormick, F., & Murphy, E., 1997, 'Mammal Bones' in Walsh, C. (ed.), *Archaeological excavations at Patrick, Nicholas and Winetavern Streets, Dublin*, 199–218. Dublin.

McCormick, F., & Murray, E.V., 2007, *Knowth and the zooarchaeology of Early Christian Ireland*. Dublin.

Murray, E.V., 2000, 'Maynooth Castle, Co. Kildare: animal bone report, QUB, Belfast'. Unpublished report.

O'Connor, T., 2000, *The archaeology of animal bones*. Gloucestershire.

O'Conor, K.D., 1998, *The archaeology of medieval rural settlement in Ireland*. Dublin.

Ó Cróinín, D., 1998, *Early Medieval Ireland, 400–1200*. London & New York.

O'Sullivan, T., 1997, 'Report on the bird bones from Site C' in Walsh, C. (ed.), *Archaeological excavations at Patrick, Nicholas and Winetavern Streets, Dublin*, 219. Dublin.

Schmid, E., 1972, *Atlas of animal bones, for prehistorians, archaeologists and quaternary geologists*. Amsterdam.

Silver, I.A., 1969, *The aging of domestic animals*. Science in Archaeology, 283–309. London.

Sten, S., 1992, *Borgar fran forntid och medeltid I Vastsverige*. Goteborg.

Teichert, M., 1966/9, *Osteometrische Untersuchungen zur Berechnung derWiederisthöhe bei vor- und frühgechichtlichen Schweinen*. Halle.

Troy-Smith, R., 1957, *A history of British livestock husbandry to 1700*. London.

Vretemark, M., 1997, *Fran ben till boskap: Kosthall och djur hallning med utgangspunkt I medeltida benmateral fran Skara, Del 1*. Skaraborgs.

Wagner, K., 1929, *Rezente Hunderassen*. Oslo.

Walsh, C., 1997, *Archaeological excavations at Patrick, Nicholas and Winetavern Streets, Dublin*. Dublin.

Warner, D., Linnane, K., & Brown, P.R., 1980, *Fishing in Ireland: the complete guide*. Belfast.

Wiseman, J., 2000, *The pig: a British history*. London.

APPENDIX 8.2: PLANT REMAINS

By Susan Lyons

SAMPLING STRATEGY

An on-site soil sampling strategy was implemented and deposits deemed archaeologically significant were sampled. A total of three potentially waterlogged samples were selected for specialist analysis. Two of the samples were associated with F5 (lower fill of ditch F6) and one with F25 (uppermost fill of ditch F6). Two unprocessed samples (F5) and one processed sample (F25) were submitted to the author by CRDS Ltd in October 2008 in order to carry out identifications and analysis of the plant remains assemblage associated with the aforementioned samples.

PRESERVATION BY WATERLOGGING

The soil samples were deemed to be 'waterlogged', since an array of organic material was recorded. Waterlogged remains are found where organic material has been kept cool, damp and stagnant and where oxygen is at a minimum (anaerobic conditions). On many archaeological sites, this type of preservation occurs where the material has remained under a permanent water-table, such as in bogs/fens or in medieval towns and cities, where layers of organic material have accumulated over many centuries, slowing down the rate of degradation. These waterlogged plant remains differ from fresh material in that the cellulose and starch have degraded, leaving only the lignified (woodier) structure of the plant behind. Some seeds are provided with tough outer layers, which are lignified to protect the starchy material (endosperm) and embryo. These seed remains are preserved, while the cellulose and starchy endosperm rarely survive. It must be noted also that many plant species have very thin lignified layers (Fabaceae species for example) and may not survive and therefore may be under-represented in the archaeo-botanical record of a site. Similarly, bran fragments, or thin plant fibres can go unrecognized in an assemblage, and these too can alter archaeo-botanical interpretations.

METHODOLOGY

Plant macrofossil remains
In the case of Athboy Gate, where just two samples were analyzed, the entire ten litres from F5 were processed and assessed. The moist sample was broken down by gentle hand pressure, then soaked in warm water and washed through a bank of Endecott brass sieves (2mm, 1mm, 0.5mm & 0.25mm). This method allows for the separation of larger seeds and plant remains from the much smaller plant particles, which can often go unnoticed. The residual material from the sieve fractions (2mm, 1mm, 0.5mm) was then separately stored in water, placed in polythene bags (double bagged) and labelled accordingly. Each of the fractions was subsequently scanned wet, using a binocular microscope (magnification x0.8 to x8), and the plant remains were recorded and identified to genus/species level where possible. It is recommended that residual material remain in a wet state during storage and the identification process, as fragile plant remains and smaller plant components can be more visible. The plant remains were recorded using an abundance key to highlight the concentrations/quantities of material identified from each sample; + = rare (1–5), ++ = occasional (6–10), +++ = common (11–50) and ++++ = abundant (>50). The identifications were made using reference to the author's seed collection and standard seed atlases and references (Clapham et al., 1957; Beijerinck 1976; Stace 1997; Cappers et al., 2006).

Waterlogged wood identification
Fragments of waterlogged wood remains were recovered from F5 and, in cases where the fragments were thin enough, a non-destructive preliminary identification of the wood was undertaken. The fragments were mounted onto a glass slide with a temporary water medium and sealed with a cover slip. Identifications were conducted under a transcident light microscope at magnifications of x40 to x400 where applicable. Wood species identifications were made using wood keys devised by Franklin and Brazier (1961), Schweingruber (1978) and the International Association of Wood Anatomists (IAWA) wood identification manuals by Wheeler et al. (1989).

RESULTS

The results of the plant remains are summarized in Table 8.12. The samples analyzed were dominated by waterlogged plant remains. Species associated with disturbed ground and nitrogenous areas of the town were frequently encountered, as were occasional species reflecting damp environments close by. A variety of arable weed seeds were regularly recorded, along with cultivated cereal grains that were recovered in carbonized form.

Carbonized plant remains
Wood charcoal Fragmented wood charcoal was recorded in relatively low concentrations in both samples. The material was very fragmented and while it denotes a degree of burning, no in situ deposits were recorded from these features and the charcoal may represent the discarded remains of fuel debris or kindling.

Carbonized cereal remains Carbonized cereal grains were identified from both F5 (lower fill of ditch F6) and F25 (uppermost fill of ditch F6). The majority of the carbonized cereal remains were in a poor state of preservation and hindered identification to species level in most cases. These vesicular and eroded grains appear in the tables as indeterminate grain. Cereal grains can become eroded and abraded as a result of charring at high temperatures, of being damp when burnt or due to re-deposition and/or exposure. Where grains were identified, wheat (*Triticum* sp.) and oat (*Avena* sp.) were recorded in relatively moderate concentrations, with just a small number of barley (*Hordeum* sp.) grains identified. The poor preservation of these grains and the absence of wheat and oat chaff did not allow for further species identification.

Carbonized wild taxa The remains of carbonized weed seeds were identified from F5. Fragments of knotgrass (*Polygonum* sp.), goosefoot (*Chenopodium* sp.), corn marigold (*Chrysanthemum segetum)* and corn spurrey (*Spergula arvensis)* were all recorded.

Waterlogged plant remains
A high concentration of waterlogged plant remains was recorded from both F5 and F25, which suggests that these deposits were waterlogged. The majority of the material survived in seed form, with the exception of bracken fronds and heather florets. Fragments of waterlogged wood remains were also recorded from F5 and identified to genus/species level where possible. The wild taxa can be divided into five broadly-named habitats. It is worth noting that there may be overlapping between the groups, where some species are common to more than one of the following habitats:

- Woodland and scrub;
- Arable/cultivated land;
- Waste places and disturbed ground;
- Heaths;
- Wet ground.

Woodland and scrub Fragments of *Corylus avellana* (hazelnut) shell were recovered from F5 in relatively low concentrations. A high incidence of blackberry (*Rubus fruticosus*), bramble (*Rubus* sp.) and elderberry (*Sambucus nigra*) were noted from both F5 and F25. Traces of bracken fronds (*Pteridium aquilinum*) were also recorded from F5. Elements of waterlogged wood fragments in the form of large heartwood fragments and small twigs (<5mm diameter) were recorded from F5. A preliminary identification of the wood species confirmed that many of the larger woody components were made up of alder (*Alnus* sp.) and willow (*Salix* sp.), while many of the twigs were identified as hazel (*Corylus avellana*) and willow (*Salix* sp.).

Arable/cultivated land The arable and cultivated weed assemblage was dominated by seeds of corn marigold (*Chrysanthemum segetum*), lesser stitchwort (*Stellaria graminea*), chickweed (*Stellaria media*) and hemp nettle (*Galeopsis* sp.).

Waste places and disturbed ground A wide range of weeds associated with waste ground and disturbed areas were recovered from both samples, with the majority recorded from F5. These species included fat hen (*Chenopodium album*), goosefoot (*Chenopodium* spp), black bindweed (*Polygonum convolvulus*), knotgrass (*Polygonum* spp), sheep's sorrel (*Rumex acetosella*), dock (*Rumex* spp), mouse-ears (*Cerastium* sp.), field penny-cress (*Thlaspi arvense*), cinquefoil (*Potentilla* sp.) charlock (*Sinapsis* sp.), stinging nettle (*Urtica dioca*), nipplewort (*Lapsana communis*) and varieties of buttercup (*Ranunculus* sp.).

Heaths A relatively high incidence of sedge (*Carex* spp) nutlets was noted from both F5 and F25, with occasional fragments of heather florets (*Calluna vulgaris*) identified from F5.

Wet ground Species associated with wet or marshy land, notably hawk's beard (*Crepis* sp.) were recovered in a fragmentary state from F5. These generally indicate an area of increased wetness.

DISCUSSION

The botanical material contained an array of plant remains reflecting domestic debris, gathered foodstuffs, plants potentially brought to the site for building materials, and flora from a variety of habitats that may have grown near the site or have been brought from another source. The plant assemblage, albeit relatively small for waterlogged samples, is typical of the species encountered on urban medieval sites, where dense living conditions inevitably resulted in an accumulation of domestic rubbish mixed with cess material and locally growing species.

Site economy
The cereal assemblage of oat, wheat and, to a lesser extent, barley is typical of crops recovered from other Irish urban medieval sites such as Drogheda (Mitchell & Dickson 1985), Dublin (Mitchell 1987), Waterford (Tierney & Hannon 1997), Cork (McClatchie 2003), Cashel, Co. Tipperary (Lyons 2004) and Trim (Lyons 2007). These cereals would have been cultivated and consumed by all social classes during the medieval period and into modern times, with oat also being used as animal fodder. Carbonized cereal grains found in archaeological deposits are the charred remains from crop-drying accidents. Crop-drying was an essential yet hazardous domestic and industrial procedure during the medieval period. Drying kilns were an integral part of the crop-drying practice and were used to dry bulk volumes of grain for a number of reasons, as discussed by Scott (1951) and Monk (1983):

- To dry the un-threshed crop prior to threshing;
- To allow for the de-husking and removal of awns from hulled grain;
- To harden the grain for grinding;
- To kill the germinating grain after malting;
- To improve the storage properties of the grain (killing pests and driving off excess moisture).

The regular use of fire as part of the cereal-processing would have increased the risk of accidental burning in these structures (Fenton 1978; Evans 1957, 123). For this reason these features are likely to have been located in controlled areas.

While the crop remains from Athboy Gate are likely to be a mix of domestic and industrial crop-drying debris that found its way into the ditch (F6), an interesting feature is the lack of chaff elements and the low occurrence of charred arable weed seeds present. Such crop-processing debris would be common-place in areas where cereal-drying was taking place. The infrequency of carbonized grain, together with little or no incidences of cereal chaff and arable weeds from urban medieval deposits, suggest that their processing and distribution was a commercial rather than a domestic activity (Geraghty 1996, 49). Processed cereal grain would therefore have arrived at the site as clean grain void of any impurities and contaminants.

Crops of cultivation were also identified from the ditch (F6). These were corn marigold, lesser stitchwort, chickweed and hemp nettle, all of which were common and troublesome weeds during the medieval period, only becoming marginalized after the introduction of herbicides. These taxa are likely to have arrived at the site as natural building materials or with gathered foodstuffs or cultivated crops. Such wild plants are documented in many medieval and post-medieval texts as being used in the production of medicines and dyes and as flavourings in food.

The presence of heather and bracken indicates that heaths and acidic environments were also being exploited. They are also likely to have been used as general building materials and insulation as well as sealants for cess-pits and latrines. The high volume of moss fragments in the medieval deposits at Winetavern Street and Fishamble Street, Dublin, has been interpreted as evidence for 'toilet paper' that may even have been sold commercially in the larger town centres (Geraghty 1996, 34).

Hazelnuts are a common natural foodstuff and would have been gathered for consumption or brought to the site with wood for fuel or building. Wood was one of the most utilized natural resources in all construction and utensil manufacturing during the medieval period in Ireland, and so the fragments of wood recorded from the Athboy Gate samples (alder and willow) are likely to represent the remains of wooden structures and products that would have been common-place. The hazel and willow twigs recorded from F5 could represent a natural deposit or a selection of material for use as fuel or in construction. Willow and hazel both have flexible properties suitable for wattle construction and rope manufacture.

Site environment

The majority of species present are common elements on disturbed, nitrogen-rich ground with some, such as alder and willow, preferring damp stream sides. Elder, brambles and alder would be typical of a scrub environment, whereas others suggest a more open environment (fat hen, docks, buttercup and chickweed). The presence of sedge, nettle and hawk's beard are all species indicative of much waterlogged acidic conditions and, together, these suggest that parts of the site were becoming more waterlogged. All of these species are likely to have thrived in these conditions, and may even have become part of the local urban vegetation (Greig 1991, 318).

Table 8.11 Plant remains from Athboy Gate (Key: + = rare, ++ = occasional, +++ = common, ++++ = abundant)

Latin name	Plant part	Common name	F5/S34 1450ml	F25/S36 120ml
Cereals: carbonized			Waterlogged	Poss. waterlogged
Triticum sp.	caryopsis	wheat	++	+++
Avena sp.	caryopsis	oat	+	++
Hordeum sp.	caryopsis	barley	+	+
Cereal indet.	caryopsis	indeterminate	++	++
Carbonized wild taxa				
Polygonum sp.	seed	knotgrass	+++	+
Chenopodium sp.	seed	goosefoot		
Chrysanthemum cf segetum	seed	corn marigold	+	+
Spergula arvensis	seed	corn spurrey	++	
Wild taxa: waterlogged				
Pteridium auilinum	fronds	bracken	++	
Ranunculus sp.	seed	buttercup	+	++
Urtica dioica	seed	common nettle	+	+
Corylus avellana	nutshell	hazel	+	
Chenopodiaceae spp	fragments	goosefoot	++	+
Chenopodium sp.	seed	goosefoot	++	++
Chenopodium album	seed	fat hen	+	++
Cerastium sp.	seed	mouse-ear chickweed	++	
Stellaria graminea	seed	lesser stitchwort	+	
Stellaria media	seed	chickweed	++	++
Polygonaceae spp	fragments	knotgrasses	+	
Polygonum sp.	seed	knotgrass	+++	+
Polygonum convolvulus	seed	black bindweed	++	+
Rumex sp.	seed	dock	++	+
Rumex acetosella	seed	sheep's sorrel	+	+
Sinapis sp.	fragment	mustard	+	
Thlaspi arvense	seed	field penny-cress	+	
Calluna vulgaris	florets	heather	+	
Rubus sp.	fragments	bramble	+++	++
Rubus fruticosus	seed	blackberry	++	+++
Potentilla sp.	seed	cinquefoil	+	+
Sambucus sp.	fragments	elder	++	+
Sambucus nigra	seed	elderberry	++	++
Chrysanthemum segetum	seed	corn marigold	+	
Galeopsis sp.	seed	hemp nettle	+	
Lapsana communis	seed	nipplewort	+	
Crepis sp.	fragments	hawk's beard	++	+
Carex sp.	fragments	sedge	+++	+++
Waterlogged wood: uncarbonized				
Corylus avellana	twigs	hazel	+++	
Salix sp.	twigs/fragments	willow	++	
Alnus sp.	fragments/fibres	alder	+	
Waterlogged wood	fragments/fibres	indeterminate wood spp	+++	
Other plant remains: carbonized				
Charcoal			++	+
Other material				
Oyster shell	fragments			+

CONCLUSIONS

The plant remains assemblage, along with the on-site recovery of animal bone, medieval pottery, oyster shell, moss, roof-tiles and textile from F5 (lower fill of ditch F6), support the interpretation that this feature was left open for quite some time (Seaver 2008). The use of local watercourses and drainage channels was common-place in medieval and post-medieval urban centres and these would have provided the perfect medium for natural components and all manners of domestic and industrial debris and rubbish to travel and enter any open feature, such as ditch F6. As such, a diverse assemblage is generated of plant remains reminiscent of many habitats and environments, proving difficult to fully interpret.

While the only botanical evidence for domestic activity is the presence of carbonized cereal grain, it is not enough to understand the importance of crops to the economy of the site or the use of crop-processing practices. There was no botanical evidence for any imported foodstuffs such as grape or fig or any species pertaining to the use of orchards or garden plots, which are common from many of Ireland's medieval urban cities, such as Drogheda (Mitchell & Dickson 1985), Dublin (Mitchell 1987), Waterford (Tierney & Hannon 1997) and Cork (McClatchie 2003). It must be remembered, however, that just three samples were analyzed from Athboy Gate and that the plant remains discussed as part of this report do not reflect the area at large.

BIBLIOGRAPHY

Beijerinck, W., 1976, *Zadenatlas der Nederlandsche Flora*. Amsterdam.
Brazier, J.D., & Franklin, G.L., 1961, *Identification of hardwoods: a microscopic key*. London.
Cappers, R.T.J., Bekker, R.M., & Jans, J.E.A., 2006, *Digital seed atlas of the Netherlands*. Groningen.
Clapham, A.R., Tutin, T.G., & Warburg, E.F., 1957, *Flora of the British Isles*. Cambridge.
Evans, E., 1957, *Irish folkways*. London.
Fenton, A., 1978, *The Northern Isles: Orkneys and Shetland*. Edinburgh.
Geraghty, S., 1996, *Viking Dublin: botanical evidence from Fishamble Street*. Dublin.
Greig, J., 1991, 'The British Isles' in Van Zeist, W., Wasylikowa, K., & Behre, K.E. (eds), *Progress in Old World palaeoethnobotany*, 299–334. Rotterdam.
Kenward, H.K., Hall, A.R., & Jones, A.K.J., 1986, 'A tested set of techniques for the extraction of plant and animal macrofossils from waterlogged archaeological deposits', *Science & Archaeology* 22, 3–15.
Lyons, S., 2004, 'The waterlogged and carbonised plant remains' in Moloney, C., & Gleeson, C., 'Chapel Lane, Cashel, Co. Tipperary: a final report on the archaeological rescue excavation (licence no. 03E0396)'. Unpublished technical report.
Lyons, S., 2007, 'Plant remains assessment from the archaeological excavations at Trim, Co. Meath E2016'. Unpublished technical report.
McClatchie, M., 2003, 'The plant remains' in Cleary, R.M., & Hurley, M.F., *Cork City excavations, 1984–2000*, 391–413. Cork.
Mitchell, G.F., 1987, *Archaeology and environment in Early Medieval Dublin*. Dublin.
Mitchell, G.F., & Dickson, C.A., 1985, 'Plant remains and other items from medieval Drogheda', *Circaea* 3:1, 31–7.
Monk, M., 1983, 'Post-Roman drying-kilns and the problems of function: a preliminary statement' in Ó Corráin, D. (ed.), *Irish antiquity: essays and studies presented to Professor M.J. O'Kelly*, 216–30. Cork.

Scott, L., 1951, 'Corn-drying kilns', *Antiquity* **20**, 196–208.

Seaver, M., 2007, 'Archaeological excavation results from Athboy Gate, Trim, Co. Meath E2398: preliminary archaeological report'. *CRDS* Ltd unpublished report.

Stace, C., 1997, *New flora of the British Isles* (2nd ed.), Cambridge.

Tierney, J., & Hannon, M., 1997, 'Plant remains' in Hurley, M.F. & Scully, O.M.B., *Late Viking Age and medieval Waterford: excavations, 1986–1992*, 854–93. Waterford.

Schweingruber, F.H., 1978, *Microscopic wood anatomy*, Birmensdorf.

Wheeler, E.A, Bass, P., & Gasson, P.E., 1989, 'IAWA list of microscopic features for hardwood identification', *IAWA Bulletin* **10:3**, 219–332.

Excavations on Haggard Street, Trim

CLARE MULLINS

INTRODUCTION

Archaeological excavations in Haggard Street in 1999 revealed deep and relatively complex stratigraphy in the form of four consecutive cobbled surfaces, intervening deposits, and other structural features including one wall-base, one probable wall-base, gullies and pits. The excavations followed the identification of archaeological stratigraphy at the southern end of Haggard Street during monitoring of ground-works for the laying of a water-pipe that ran through Mill Street, High Street and Haggard Street, and along a short distance of the western end of Navan Gate Street. The extent of the required excavation in Haggard Street was determined by testing the route of the proposed pipeline (fig. 9.1).

THE EXCAVATION

The excavation trench measured 90m in length and, because its purpose was the removal of archaeological layers in advance of the laying of a new water pipe, it was limited to 1m in width (fig. 9.1). The deepest stratigraphy was located at the southern end of the excavation, where the combined depth of the individual cobbled surfaces and their intervening layers was almost 2m (figs 9.2, 9.3). The intervening layers were interpreted as representing the deliberate heightening of the ground level, prior to each following episode of resurfacing; a process that was most visible within the southern part of the excavation trench, where there was evidence for a cobbled surface pre-dating the one that was the earliest in other parts of the street. The second earliest cobbled surface found in Haggard Street (that is, the earliest in most parts of the street) appeared to correspond to a surface identified during monitoring in Mill Street and High Street. Unfortunately, feature sequences within the excavation were sometimes impossible to determine as a result of disturbance from earlier groundworks, primarily an old gas-pipe that ran parallel to the excavation trench and had removed deposits along its eastern side. It is suggested on the basis of the pottery analysis that the general stratigraphy, particularly the most extensive layer of cobbling and its associated features, dates to the thirteenth to fourteenth centuries.

The cobbled surfaces, with the possible exception of the earliest one, which was confined to the southern end of the excavation, were interpreted as repre-

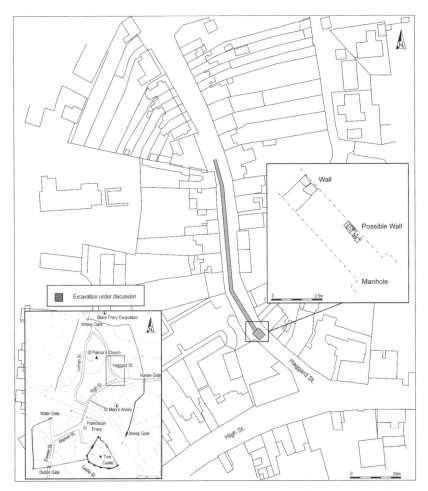

9.1 Plan showing location of excavation trench and main features (based on original drawing by Clare Mullins, redrawn by Catherine Bishop (CRDS). Base-map courtesy of Ordnance Survey Ireland, Permit 8565 © Ordnance Survey Ireland/Government of Ireland. Inset from *Irish Historic Towns Atlas, no. 14: Trim*, by permission of the Royal Irish Academy © RIA)

senting formal street surfaces. As well as being a major focus of the excavation, they served as the main anchors of the overall stratigraphic framework. As such, they are similarly used in this report as stratigraphic reference points. For clarity, they are referred to as CS1 to CS4, with numerical order corresponding to stratigraphic sequence, and CS1 representing the earliest. A manhole that had been dug to the immediate south of the southern end of the excavation trench, and which was of considerable help in creating an overall perspective of the stratigraphy, is also occasionally referred to in this report.

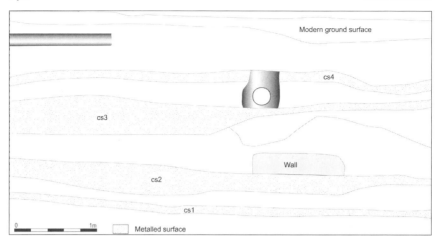

9.2 Layers within southern area of excavation trench, north of man-hole

9.3 Trench profile at southern end of excavation, showing build-up of street surfaces

Cobbled layers

Along Mill Street, High Street and lower Navan Gate Street, the cobbles appeared in section as a compact stony layer. They lay directly upon the subsoil, approximately 50cm beneath the existing road surface. In these areas, they were at all times overlain by a black/brown silty layer, with organic inclusions. Medieval pot-sherds of thirteenth- to fourteenth-century date were

9.4 Second earliest cobbled surface (CS2)

frequently associated with both the cobbled layer and the overlying dark silty layer. Although the cobbled layer was somewhat intermittent, the various stretches were interpreted as representing the same episode of street surfacing because of their compositional similarity, consistent depth beneath the modern ground surface, and association with the black silty layer. A well was cut through the cobbled layer near the northern end of High Street. That this well was back-filled in relatively recent times was indicated by fragments of modern plate glass in the fill.

Although a direct link between the cobbled surface identified in High Street and Mill Street and any of those found on Haggard Street could not be made, it is postulated that the cobbling on Haggard Street identified as the second earliest layer (CS2) was the structural equivalent and contemporary of that uncovered in the other areas. This conclusion is supported by the presence of a black/brown silty layer, similar to that on top of the cobbling in the other streets, overlying the Haggard Street cobbling too, as well as by the fact that it is also the earliest formal surface along most of Haggard Street. In Haggard Street, this surface continued unbroken from just north of the junction with High Street to the northern end of Haggard Street. Along most of the 90m of the excavation trench, this cobbled layer was uncovered in plan, and this showed it to be remarkably consistent in composition and appearance. It was composed of angular stones of varying sizes, generally 10–20cm in diameter, set firmly into a sandy matrix. It was extremely compact and could be removed only with great difficulty. The cobble-stones, though roughly hewn, had clearly been prepared for this purpose, as the embedded under-surface was generally more angular and sharper than the exposed upper surface. In areas where this layer was particularly well-preserved, the arrangement of the stones was most striking (fig. 9.4). Several horseshoes, horseshoe fragments and a rowel from a spur (fig. 9.5) were recovered from within this cobbled layer. It also produced a complete leather shoe, a key from a barrel padlock (fig. 9.16) and a copper-alloy crutch-headed stick pin (originally a ring pin; fig. 9.6). Some distance beyond the northern end of the excavation trench, this cobbled layer degenerated into a thin gravel layer, though it was still clearly visible in section and overlain by the dark silty layer. At the southern end of the excavation trench and south of the excavation trench, this cobbled layer occurred at a depth of *c*.1.8m beneath the present ground surface, rising to 1.3m beneath the surface at the northern end of the trench, and to 1.1m just north of the northern end of the excavation

9.5 Rowel spur from main cobbled layer (CS2), near southern end of trench

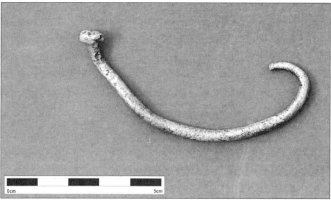

9.6 Crutch-headed copper-alloy stick-pin from main cobbled layer (CS2), near northern end of trench. The pin appears to have been re-worked from a ring pin

9.7 Third cobbled surface (CS3)

trench. Where it petered out, near the northern end of Haggard Street, it was recorded at a depth of 75cm beneath the ground surface.

Both at the southern end of the excavation trench and for several metres south of it, a later cobbled layer (CS3) was also identified (fig. 9.7). These cobbles were also visible intermittently in section further to the north within the excavation trench on the western side. This layer of cobbling was generally very similar to that which preceded it, in terms of stone-size and setting. The cobbles were set into a layer of what appeared to be random dumps of material, interpreted as an episode of level-heightening, which was partly composed of the black silty material that lay over the earlier cobbles. These cobbles lay at a depth of *c*.80cm beneath the present ground surface at the southern end of the excavation trench.

A final street surface (CS4), which existed immediately prior to the creation of the modern surface, was also encountered. This was visible at the extreme southern end of the excavation and was the only surface visible on the east face of the large man-hole that had been dug immediately south of the excavation trench (it had presumably also existed on the west side of this man-hole, but had been removed by an earlier service pipe). It was also visible in the pipeline trench to the north of the excavation. Where this cobbled layer was visible at the southern end of the excavation trench, it rested upon *c*.40cm of fill

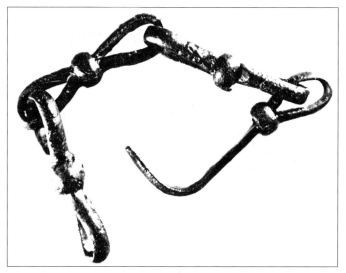

9.8 Iron chain links from earliest level-heightening layer. Each link is *c*.4.5cm in length

overlying CS3. It seems likely that this is the same episode of cobbling as that identified under the modern pavement during the archaeological monitoring of foundations for a development at the southwest end of Haggard Street (Mossop 2001).

It was within the southern area of the excavation trench that the very earliest phase of cobbling was encountered (CS1). This was confined to the southern 15m of the trench, but it also continued south of here for several metres further, being identifiable on the western side of the large man-hole, lying directly upon the subsoil, approximately 30cm beneath the later cobbles. This cobbled layer measured 10cm in depth and was compositionally quite distinct from the later cobbles, being composed of smaller stones and thus forming a comparatively smooth surface. It is unfortunate that the northern limit of this earliest surface could not be examined as the area had been disturbed by earlier works. It could be established, however, that this cobble layer sloped upwards towards the north, with a gradient of 30cm over a distance of approximately 15m, converging with the subsequent cobbling around the entrance to the car park on Haggard Street. Its precise southern limit was not identified, but it lay somewhere south of the man-hole.

Level-heightening episodes
The layers which separated these various cobbled surfaces were interpreted as level-heightening deposits, as each appeared to have been deposited in a single event. At the southern end of the trench, it was obvious that the earliest of these deposits had been lain in preparation for the overlying cobbled layer, as it and the underlying cobbles had the same northern terminus, while the level-heightening layer also corrected the slope in the underlying cobbling. Thus,

9.9 Iron hook recovered from level-heightening layer above cobbles CS2 (length from tip to tip: 5.5cm)

this level-heightening layer decreased gradually in depth from 35cm at the southern end of the trench until finally petering out some 15–20m further to the north. Indeed, this layer appeared to have had an even greater depth in the man-hole to the south of the excavation trench, suggesting that the surface gradient of the earliest cobbling continued further south. This earliest level-heightening deposit was composed of loose sandy silt, with frequent stone inclusions, and it contained a large volume of bone and wood. It produced a number of metal finds, including an iron chain (fig. 9.8), an arrowhead and two iron horseshoes (fig. 9.15). It also produced a fragment of a leather shoe sole and a number of medieval pot-sherds.

The level-heightening layer that overlay the second cobbled layer was of varied composition and measured approximately 60cm in thickness. It was largely composed of the black/brown organic silt already mentioned, but it also contained layers and lenses of light brown/orange stony clay and of compact grey silty clay. Generally, the black organic material was overlain by a brown/orange soil, but some interleaving was also evident. This layer, particularly the black organic component of it, was the most productive in terms of artefacts, producing a large volume of pot-sherds and a number of metal finds, including several horseshoe nails and an unusual iron hook (fig. 9.9). It also produced fragments of leather shoes, two fragments of roof ridge-tile and a perforated roof-slate. A perforated roof-slate was also found in a basal layer of a ditch at the north end of Haggard Street in 2007. This feature was radiocarbon-dated to the thirteenth or fourteenth century (Seaver 2007, 13, 14, Appendix 7; Seaver, this volume). This level-heightening layer is inter-preted as the stratigraphic counterpart of the dark silty layer that was observed to overlie the layer of cobbling in High Street and Mill Street, where it also produced pot-sherds similar to those found in this excavation. This layer also continued northwards beyond the excavation trench, at all times overlying the cobbles, though its depth appeared to diminish as it progressed northwards. In

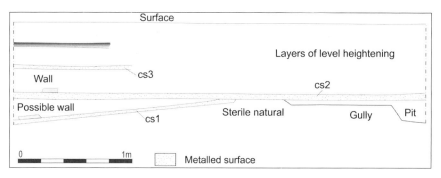

9.10 Schematic representation of stratigraphy along length of excavation trench

the southern end of the trench, a more detailed examination of this layer was possible, and this seemed to reveal a number of distinctive tip-lines, supporting the interpretation of this layer as an episode of deliberate level-heightening. A layer of black, organic silt containing medieval pottery sherds was also identified during monitoring of foundations at the southwest end of Haggard Street (Mossop 2001). It is possible that this is a continuation of the black organic layer found during this excavation.

Other features

As well as the various cobbled surfaces and intervening layers, a number of other features were found. These included one wall-base, another probable wall-base and a number of pits and gullies (fig. 9.10). Where stratigraphic relationships could be established, these features either pre-dated or were contemporary with the second earliest cobbling.

The lower course of a linear stone feature, interpreted as a possible wall, was identified at the southern end of the excavation trench, resting on the earliest cobbled layer (fig. 9.11). It was aligned approximately parallel with the excavation trench, running north-south. The exposed extent of this feature was 97cm in length. That it may have continued some distance further south beyond the end of the excavation trench is suggested by the presence of a worked block of stone in the western face of the man-hole, resting on the southern continuation of this layer of cobbles, and by a number of large stones that were disturbed by machine at the same stratigraphic level within this man-hole. Although the exposed feature survived to only one course, a second course is suggested by the presence of a cut stone at a higher level within the baulk. The interpretation of this feature as a wall is somewhat problematic, as there was no mortar present on or around its stones, though this could have been weathered away. There was no foundation cut for this feature and the layer of cobbling on which it rested continued uninterrupted beneath it. Whatever this feature represented, it was clearly contemporary with the cobbles on which it rested.

9.11 Possible wall lying on earliest cobbled surface

9.12 Mortared wall resting on cobbled surface 2

Another wall-base was uncovered, again near the southern end of the
trench, though this time in association with the next layer of cobbles (fig. 9.12).
This wall was aligned approximately east-west – at a right angle to the line of
the excavation trench – and it continued beneath the east and west baulks. The
wall was mortared and survived to only one course, measuring 1m in width.
Three large rectangular masonry blocks lined its southern side, and another
was present on the north-east corner of the exposed part, suggesting that its
original width is represented by the remaining stones (fig. 9.13). The core of
this wall and much of its northern side was constructed of smaller irregular
stones. It was constructed without a foundation trench, resting directly upon
the cobbled surface. It was covered by the level-heightening material which
also lay over the cobbles that it rested upon and its upper courses may have
been deliberately demolished prior to the deposition of this layer. There was no
return for this wall, either to its north or south, although other associated walls
could presumably have been more effectively demolished after going out of
use. A linear arrangement of stones that were larger than the surrounding
cobbles in which they were embedded occurred some 2m south of this wall (fig.
9.14). This deviation from the otherwise random arrangement of the cobbles
possibly represents a feature connected in some way with the wall.

What was interpreted as a linear gully was found near the northern end of
the excavation trench beneath CS2. The eastern edge of this gully ran parallel
to the western side of the excavation trench for the final 20m, extending across
50cm of the trench from the baulk; its western edge was not exposed, as it lay
beneath this baulk. The gully was cut into the subsoil to a depth of just over
20cm for most of its length, but at 5m from the northern limit of the
excavation trench its base began to descend steeply, converging with the
southern edge of a deep pit that was identified in the service trench just
beyond the northern end of the excavations trench. This pit measured 15m
north-south, but neither its eastern nor western edges were uncovered. It was
excavated to a depth of 60cm beneath CS2, which sealed it, but its base was not
exposed. It seemed probable that the centre of this pit lay on the west side of
the service trench, as the subsoil could be seen at the base of the trench on the
east side, suggesting the presence of a rising pit-base. The gully contained a
single fill throughout most of its length – brown/grey silty clay with frequent
pebbles and small stones. From the point at which the level of the gully base
began to descend, however, a distinctly more organic deposit became evident
beneath the silty clay, and by the extreme northern end of the excavation
trench, three distinct layers were present. These layers corresponded in
number, approximate depth and constituency with the layers of the pit
uncovered in the service trench to the north. The gully and pit were clearly
functionally related. A wide, U-shaped cut, which ran across the trench at a
right angle, transected the gully. Like the gully, this feature was sealed by the

9.13 Close-up of wall, showing large masonry blocks

9.14 Linear arrangement of stones within cobbled surface 2. Wall is just to right of photograph

cobbled layer. This cut was tentatively interpreted as a drain and, interestingly, it lay directly beneath and in line with an eighteenth-century stone culvert that continued westwards beneath the floor of the domestic dwelling adjacent to the excavation trench (local information). This feature had a maximum depth of 50cm and was filled with mid-brown sandy clay with inclusions of stone and large quantities of bone.

Archaeological stratigraphy was also identified to the south of the excavation trench, principally within the large man-hole. There was a striking contrast in the nature of the material on the east and west sides of this man-hole. Although a stratigraphy of consecutive cobbled layers comparable to that observed at the southern end of the excavation trench occurred on the western face of this man-hole, the only cobbling in evidence on its east face was that which immediately preceded the modern street surface. A 40cm-deep layer of stony silt with animal bone inclusions directly underlay these cobbles and this, in turn, overlay a black/brown organic layer that was 80cm in depth and contained small pieces of bone, straw, timber and shell. This overlay what appeared to be a shallow pit, which showed in the section face as a bowl-shaped cut that had been dug into the natural subsoil. It was filled with brown silt. The pit had a small stake inserted in its southern edge. While these two very different stratigraphic sequences were also visible in the south face of this man-hole, the crucial point that marked the juncture between them had unfortunately been destroyed by earlier ground-work. Evidence of a large pit, measuring at least 3m north-south and with a minimum depth of 2m, was also discovered to the south of the man-hole. It was not possible to determine the relationship between this pit and the more extensive layer of cobbling (CS2), which was also identified in the immediate vicinity.

DISCUSSION

The results of the excavation in Haggard Street suggest activity in the area prior to the laying out of the medieval street pattern, as well as later alterations to that pattern. Although informative, the excavation raises many questions that could only be answered through further excavation in the area. It is tempting to interpret the presence of the earliest cobbled surface at the southern end of Haggard Street and the northwards expansion of its replacement as evidence of an expanding street infrastructure within the medieval town. If this were the case, however, it is curious that there is no evidence of an earlier surface beneath what is interpreted as the continuation of CS2, further to the south. The earliest surface (CS1) may therefore have been an isolated phenomenon, confined to a restricted area of southern Haggard Street, and this may further suggest that this surface represents a localized feature rather than an actual route-way. An alternative suggestion is that CS1, and not CS2 as previously assumed, is the continuation of the street surface identified in High Street, but all other pointers combine to make this unlikely. The existence of a possible wall upon this earliest surface supports the suggestion that it does not represent a street surface.

The existence of the wall upon the second cobbled surface (CS2), which almost definitely represents a formal street surface, is particularly difficult to explain. Its position and especially its alignment seem to contradict its location on a street line. Indeed, if this wall extended much further eastwards, it would have blocked access through the street. Despite this, it appears that the wall did not serve as a major boundary demarcation. This is suggested by the extension of the same layer of cobbles on both sides of it. It is tempting to suggest that either the central axis of the street has shifted westwards since medieval times and that this wall was originally positioned to the west of the original street line, or that the street has been widened to incorporate the area that abutted its original western edge. The evidence from the man-hole to the south of the excavation may be of some relevance in the explanation of this wall. The stratigraphy in the man-hole indicates expansion eastwards of the latest cobbling to include an area not previously surfaced, suggesting some alteration of the street pattern since its original inception, at least in this area.

That the area near the centre of the modern street lay outside the formal street-line until the creation of a later cobbled layer is an interesting possibility. Such an event appears to have occurred sometime between the laying of CS3 and CS4. This suggests, however, that the central axis of the original street in this area was located to the west of the present street line – implying an eastwards shift, and such a suggestion would be in conflict with the presence of the wall, which would certainly have interrupted the line of such a street. Because the opportunity to examine stratigraphy in the central area of the street arose only at the location of the large man-hole, it is impossible to say whether or not evidence for an eastwards expansion of the later cobbling also exists in other areas of the street.

Other features which seem to attest to the use of the area before its conversion to a street include the linear gully, the drain which transected it and the large pit into which the gully connected. All of these pre-dated CS2, which clearly sealed them, suggesting that this area was only incorporated into the formal street network after these features had gone out of use. Although another large pit was identified south of the man-hole, it was not possible to determine its stratigraphic relationship with CS2.

Regarding the date for the above events, Dublin-type ware, which was first manufactured in the mid-thirteenth century (McCutcheon 2003, 122), occurred within all contexts that produced pottery sherds, and also represented by far the largest single group of ceramics found, both in the

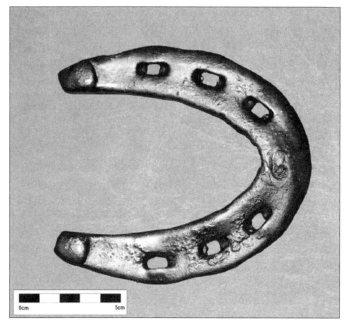

9.15 One of two horseshoes from first episode of level-heightening, at southern end of trench. Seven other horseshoes or fragments were recovered from main cobbled layer (CS2)

0cm   5cm

excavation and during monitoring. Other smaller ceramic groups identified within the pottery assemblage mainly dated to the late twelfth to fourteenth century. Within the excavation, the surface of CS2 and the layers of level-heightening material overlying it were the most productive in terms of pottery. Other features which produced pottery were the layer of level-heightening underneath CS2, and CS3, but the overall quantities from these features were small. The vast majority of sherds retrieved during monitoring on High Street also came from the layer immediately overlying what is being proposed as the continuation of CS2, thereby strengthening the suggestion that the cobbled surface evident elsewhere in the town was indeed the counterpart of CS2 in Haggard Street. The pottery analysis suggests that little time elapsed between the deposition of the various pottery-yielding contexts, however, indicating that much of the stratigraphy centres on the thirteenth century. It may therefore be impossible to temporally distinguish some features on the basis of ceramic assemblage alone.

Other finds from the excavation that may be pertinent to its date include the horseshoes (fig. 9.15) and the copper-alloy pin (fig. 9.6). It is thought that the widespread shoeing of horses was an innovation of the Norman period in Britain, with relatively few horseshoes dating from the pre-Norman period (Ottaway 1992, 707–9). The horseshoe presumably became more common in Ireland after the Anglo-Norman invasion, and the presence of a total of nine examples within the excavated material, with two coming from the level-heightening layer overlying CS1, accords with the ceramic evidence. The pin is

9.16 Barrel
padlock key from
main cobbled
layer (CS2)

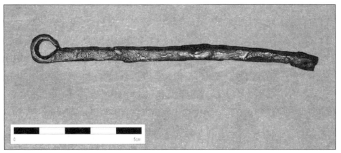

more problematic, as it is of a type that is predominantly dated to the eleventh
century on the basis of the Dublin excavations, though it may still have been in
use in the early twelfth century (Fanning 1994, 43–4). This find could be
explained, however, as a residual item from earlier activities in the area. Among
the artefacts recovered from the main cobbled layer (CS2) was a key from a
barrel padlock (fig. 9.16).

It is clear that the history of Haggard Street is more complex than a simple
sequence of episodes of street resurfacing, but the restricted scope of the
investigation hampered the construction of a clearer picture of the topographical
development of the area. Many of the features and sequences uncovered
suggest a complex development of the area, including a possible phased,
northwards expansion of the street, activity that pre-dates the use of the area
as a route-way, and an eastwards expansion of the street some time after its
first formal surface had been lain. Evidence of a wall that would have blocked
access across part of what is being interpreted as the first definite formal street
surface complicates the picture further. While the most complex stratigraphy
and the greatest number of apparent anomalies were found in the same area, it
is impossible to know whether this reflects a more complex biography for this
part of the street or whether it is a mere coincidence of discovery, arising from
the nature of the ground-works in the area. In spite of the number of episodes
of cobbling that are represented and the depth of stratigraphy, however, the
ceramic evidence still allows for the possibility that a relatively short time-span
is represented by most of the activity. The ceramic types from the level-
heightening material that overlay the earliest cobbling at the southern end of
the excavation trench are much the same as those retrieved from the material
overlying the second phase of cobbling and from the third phases of cobbling,
suggesting that all of these events occurred within a limited time period.
Nonetheless, comparatively few ceramic sherds came from the earliest level-
heightening layer, which overlay CS1, while no sherds were found within or
beneath this earliest cobbled layer. Ceramics were also conspicuously absent
from the gully, drain and pit at the northern end of the excavation trench.

It is clear that a conscious effort was made to correct the surface gradient of
the earliest cobbling during the laying of the later cobbles. Although no direct

connection could be made between this earliest phase of cobbling and the pit and drains that also pre-dated CS2, it is tempting to speculate that the slope of CS1 may have been associated with a more generalized drainage problem that had ceased to exist by the time CS2 was laid.

Given the evidence from this excavation for the possible realignment and expansion of Haggard Street, the uncertainty surrounding the historical line of the town wall and the location of the mural gates on the north side of Trim is of interest. Both Potterton and Thomas discuss this issue and postulate a later extension of the northern circuit wall, or the existence of a twin walled area (Potterton 2005, 180–1; Thomas 1992, 196–9). Hennessy also draws attention to the unusual street pattern on the north side of the river and suggests that the area north of the Boyne may have been developed in two stages, both during the medieval period, although the earlier urban area according to this theory would not have reached as far as Haggard Street (Hennessy 2004, 2–3). Such a secondary extension of the medieval town may have a bearing on the meaning of both the northern expansion of CS2 beyond the limit of CS1 and the apparent eastward shift in the street axis some time after that. Both of these events appear to have occurred in the thirteenth or fourteenth century, on the basis of the ceramic assemblage. It is unfortunate that no dating evidence was found for the activity that pre-dated CS2 at the northern end of the excavation. A medieval date for this would considerably bolster the evidence for a phased development of the town on the north bank of the Boyne. It is tempting to draw an analogy between the cobbling that was identified during this excavation as CS2, which is regarded as the structural counterpart of that identified during monitoring in High Street, Mill Street and the western end of Navan Gate Street, and that observed during a separate monitoring project in Market Street (Meenan 1997), particularly as both were overlain by a dark organic deposit containing medieval ceramics. It is also probable that the cobbling identified by CRDS Ltd further east along Navan Gate Street is the continuation of that found during this project at the western end of Navan Gate Street (Shine & Seaver, this volume). Definite evidence of either continuity or breaks in this cobbling throughout the town may go some way towards clarifying the issue of the layout and growth of the medieval town.

The possibility that the very earliest phases of activity are aceramic is of particular interest, given the speculation on the location of the Early Medieval ecclesiastical foundation. The exact location of this site cannot be determined from historical sources (Gwynn & Hadcock 1988, 97, 195), and it was originally thought that the curving line of Castle Street, High Street and Navan Gate Street may preserve the boundary line of the monastic enclosure (Bradley 1984, 155, 164, 170). A more recent study, however, argued that the Early Medieval church was almost certainly located on, or close to, the site of the present-day St Patrick's Church of Ireland Cathedral (Hennessy 2004, 1), a suggestion that has since been strongly supported by the discovery of burials, one of which was dated to the eighth to early eleventh century, at the rear of St Patrick's Cathedral (Kieran, this volume). Hennessy proposes two possible outlines for the enclosure, based on an examination of plot boundaries and street alignments in the vicinity of St Patrick's Cathedral. One of these outlines abuts the location of the Haggard Street excavation, while the other encompasses it (Hennessy 2004, fig. 1). The possibility that the earliest cobbling at the southern end of the excavation trench and the activity in the northern area of the trench that pre-dated the more extensive phase of cobbling might be associated with the Early Medieval origins of the town is one that should be considered, pending more definite dating evidence for this phase of activity.

This excavation demonstrated the amount of information that can emerge from even limited investigation. As a corollary, however, it also demonstrated the numbers of questions that arise from the fragmentary information that is the inevitable consequence of such small-scale projects. Yet, in time, and with collaboration between researchers and between disciplines, it is to be hoped that the information that has been gleaned from such small excavations will combine with that derived from other sources to help create a clearer picture of the medieval foundations and development of Trim town.

ACKNOWLEDGMENTS

I would like to express my sincere thanks to all those who worked with me during the excavation: Helen Bermingham, Rob Browne, Pádraig Clancy, Agnes Kerrigan, Sarah Meehan and Tori McMorran. I would also like to thank Rosanne Meenan, who carried out the ceramic analysis, and David Jennings, Department of Archaeology, UCD, who photographed the artefacts. The excavation and post-excavation were funded by Meath County Council.

BIBLIOGRAPHY

Bradley, J., 1984, 'Urban Archaeological Survey, Part 2: Co. Meath'. Unpublished report prepared for the Office of Public Works.
Fanning, T., 1994, *Viking-Age ringed pins from Dublin*. Dublin.
Gwynn, A., & Hadcock, R.N., 1988, *Medieval religious houses: Ireland*. Repr. Blackrock, Co. Dublin.
Hennessy, M., 2004, *Irish Historic Towns Atlas No. 14: Trim*. Dublin.
McCutcheon, C., 2003, 'Pottery' in O'Donovan, E., 'The growth and decline of a medieval suburb? Evidence from excavations at Thomas Street, Dublin' in Duffy, S. (ed.), *Medieval Dublin* 4, 127–71. Dublin.
Meenan, R., 1997, 'Monitoring of a sewage and water supply scheme for Trim' in Bennett, I. (ed.), *Excavations 1996: summary accounts of archaeological excavations in Ireland*, no. 315, p. 89. Bray.

Mossop, M., 2003, 'Haggard Street, Trim' in Bennett, I. (ed.), *Excavations 2001: summary accounts of archaeological excavations in Ireland*, no. 1064, p. 339. Bray.

Ottaway, P., 1992, *Anglo-Scandinavian ironwork from Coppergate.* London.

Potterton, M., 2005, *Medieval Trim: history and archaeology.* Dublin.

Seaver, M., 2007, 'Trim street reconstruction project, TRSP 1: excavations at Athboy Gate'. Unpublished report.

Thomas, A., 1992, *The walled towns of Ireland.* Blackrock, Co. Dublin.

Excavations at 18 Market Street, Trim

DONAL FALLON

with contributions by SARAH COBAIN & CLARE McCUTCHEON

INTRODUCTION

Excavations at the Credit Union site, 18 Market Street, Trim, uncovered the remains of a previously unidentified substantial defensive ditch from the earliest phase of the town, as well as archaeological material relating to the occupation and development of the site from the late twelfth century to the twentieth century. The following paper gives a brief overview of the results of these excavations, focusing on the evidence for the medieval town defences and occupation of the site. The site has significant implications for the overall

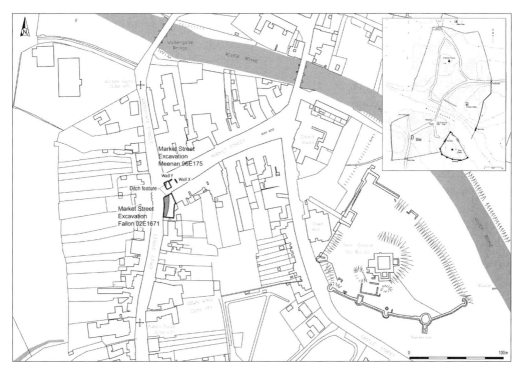

10.1 Location of site, possible town ditch and ditch identified by Rosanne Meenan (base-map courtesy of Ordnance Survey Ireland, Permit 8565 © Ordnance Survey Ireland/Government of Ireland. Inset from *Irish Historic Towns Atlas, no. 14: Trim* by permission of the Royal Irish Academy © RIA)

understanding of the extent and development of the early Anglo-Norman town. The works were carried out on behalf of St Loman's Credit Union.

The site is located on the junction of Market Street and Emmet Street. The area of excavation was sub-rectangular, extending south for *c.*28m from the Market Street façade to the rear boundary wall. The width of the area excavated broadened from 10m at the northern end of the site to 17.5m to the south (fig. 10.1). Excavations uncovered a range of significant medieval features. A metalled surface encompassing the full extent of the site appears to pre-date the layout of the medieval borough. A substantial north–south ditch extending along the Emmet Street frontage has been tentatively interpreted as an early town boundary, providing new evidence for the early extent and development of the medieval borough. A metalled surface and stone wall-base adjoining Market Street may represent the remains of a sill-beam structure. A series of features characteristic of the 'backsides' of burgage plots, including refuse pits, a cess-pit, a substantial dry-stone well and a lime pit were exposed in the southern half of the site. A substantial stone structure of early modern date was exposed at the rear of the site.

Before the commencement of excavation, two phases of pre-development testing were carried out by Carmel Duffy and the author. These identified significant late medieval features (Duffy 2003; Fallon 2003). The subsequent excavation, directed by the author, took place in July 2003. Prior to the excavation, a two-storey building of late nineteenth-century date occupied the Market Street frontage. The original building façade, extending for 10m along Market Street and *c.*6m along Emmet Street, was retained. The interior of the building and a number of small modern outbuildings abutting the rear boundary wall and the Emmet Street frontage were demolished to ground-floor level, leaving the foundations at the front of the site intact. The southeast area of the site had been a garden, while the northern half of the site was covered by a shallow layer of demolition rubble.

EXCAVATION RESULTS

Earliest features: metalled surface
The earliest feature exposed was a metalled surface (F147; fig. 10.2) covering the entire excavation area and extending beyond the site limits. Its extent to the west had been truncated by a later ditch (F132; fig. 10.2). The surface consisted of a shallow, very compact layer of pebble and small stone, *c.*5cm thick, directly overlying natural boulder clay, with no intervening organic deposits or fossilized sod layer, suggesting that the site was deliberately scarped or cleared prior to the surface being laid. No finds were recovered in the surface. It was sealed by a patchy, shallow layer of dark-brown organic sediment (F40), which was up to 15cm thick. Although this contained no finds, it did yield a quantity of animal bone, including nineteen cattle horn-cores and four goat horn-cores.

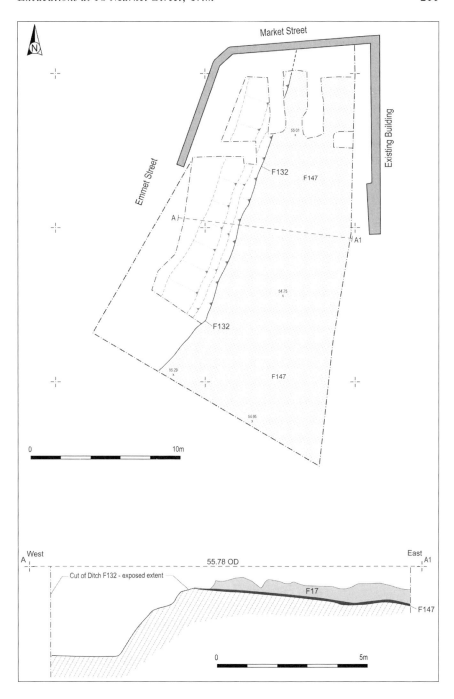

10.2 Early metalled surface and possible town ditch

Beglane has interpreted the assemblage as a likely indication both that slaughter and primary butchery were taking place on-site and that a tanner or horn-worker was based there. The age of the animals at death also suggests that horn was being imported onto the site from elsewhere. This may be in keeping with the location of the site, adjacent to the early town boundary. Dog, horse and red deer bone were also recovered from this phase (Beglane, 'Meat and craft', this volume). A horn-core provided a radiocarbon date of 1020–1180 cal. AD (Wk-25660; Table 1.1). The evidence suggested a brief phase of use for the surface. This surface and its overlying deposits were sealed by a substantial twelfth-century ditch and its up-cast, and appear to pre-date the layout of burgage plots.

Possible enclosure ditch
A substantial north-south ditch (F132) was exposed along the entire western edge of the site parallel to Emmett Street, continuing beyond the excavation limits. Excavations exposed the ditch for a length of 24m; it was at least 2.2m deep and at least 5m wide (its full width was not exposed; fig. 10.2). The profile of the ditch was regular: it had a steep east side and a flat base. Assuming that its western profile mirrored the excavated eastern side, the ditch would have been at least 6m wide. It appears to be a continuation of a ditch discovered in 1996 by Rosanne Meenan during archaeological monitoring of a pipeline excavation on Market Street; Meenan discovered a substantial ditch extending north-south across the northern end of Market Street (Meenan 1996, 6–8). Its position and orientation suggest that it was a continuation of the current feature, which then extended along the eastern side of Emmet Street and across the western end of Market Street, cutting directly across the established topography of the medieval town.

A stepped section 4m wide was excavated through the ditch fills, within the area to be impacted upon by the construction of foundations. An estimated 18–20 tons of material were excavated by hand. It was not possible to excavate up to the western boundary of the site. The remainder of the ditch, lying below the building's finished floor level, was planned and left in situ.

The early metalled surface and the organic deposit were sealed by a substantial deposit of sterile dark green clay, 60cm–1m in depth. This deposit was assumed to be outcast from the excavation of the adjacent ditch (F132). Though level at the time of excavation, it may originally have formed an adjacent bank (fig. 10.2). A small number of animal bone fragments recovered within it were assumed to have been disturbed from the underlying deposit (F40).

The lowest three fills of the ditch (F213, F212 & F211) consisted of natural silts with no finds. Above these, a series of four shallow layers containing organic material appeared to represent both natural silting and dumped organic deposits (F183, F210, F180, F129 & F171). These layers did contain finds: Dublin-type ware; Dublin-type cooking ware (pl. 11); Ham Green A ware (pl. 8); and Leinster Cooking Ware (Appendix 10.2; pl. 14). A bovine

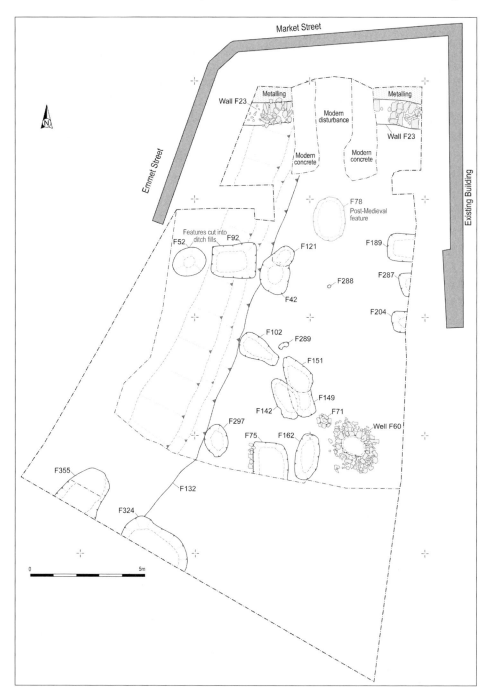

10.3 Features dating from the medieval period within the burgage plot

tibia provided a radiocarbon date of 1030–1220 cal.AD (Wk-25661; Table 1.1). By contrast, the upper fills (F209, F208 & F118) contained far less organic material and were more homogeneous, suggesting a phase of deliberate back-filling, most likely to reclaim the Emmet Street frontage. As the position of the ditch appears to cut across the topography of the later medieval town, this presumably took place at an early date. It is likely that the ditch became redundant with the expansion of the town to the west. The pottery suggests that the ditch was still open in the thirteenth century however.

Two medieval pits (F49 & F92) were identified cutting through the later back-fills of the ditch (fig. 10.3). The recovery of Trim-type ware (pl. 13), Dublin-type fineware (pl. 10) and a ceramic roof-tile from within their fills suggests that they were inserted in the late thirteenth or fourteenth century, providing a terminus post quem for the ditch and also, it would appear, for the creation of Emmet Street and the expansion of Trim town (Appendix 10.2).

The Market Street frontage: structural evidence and surfaces
Archaeological deposits at the northern end of the site had been disturbed and truncated by the insertion of the nineteenth-century structure, with deep foundation trenches cutting through all deposits down to the level of natural soils. The absence of pit-cuts or external features at the Market Street frontage, however, suggests that this area of the site was occupied by structures. Medieval burgage plots were laid out with the houses fronting onto the street and out-houses and external features in the yards to the rear.

The direct evidence for medieval structures was limited to a few features adjacent to Market Street. After the ditch was back-filled, this area of the site appears to have been deliberately raised with a series of shallow bedding deposits (F198, F153 & F110); this provided a level area for a compact stone surface (F105). This surface extends beyond the limits of excavation; the southern extent appeared to have been truncated by later disturbance. Fragments of a Dublin-type coarseware vessel were recovered from these deposits, while sherds of Dublin-type coarseware, Dublin-type ware, Dublin-type fineware (pl. 10) and Trim-type cooking ware (pl. 12) were found within the surface, suggesting a late thirteenth- to fourteenth-century date (Appendix 10.2). Although organic material was compacted into the surface, it is unclear if it originally functioned as an internal feature or a yard surface, or whether it represented the original southern extent of Market Street.

A crude stone wall-base (F23) was set directly atop this surface, extending parallel to the street frontage and beyond the excavation limits to east and west (fig. 10.3). The exposed portion measured 8m long, 80cm wide and 40cm deep. It consisted of a single course of relatively flat, angular, undressed stone with no clay or mortar bonding. Dublin-type ware and Trim-type ware fragments were recovered within (Appendix 10.2, pl. 13). Comparative evidence suggests that it supported a timber-frame or sill-beam building fronting onto Market Street, rather than a stone-walled structure; comparative evidence is discussed in more detail below.

A succession of three cobbled or metalled surfaces (F316, F313 & F312) divided by two layers of shale, mudstone and inorganic clay (F315 & F314) extended from the northern face of the wall to beyond the northern excavation limit. Only small portions of these features were exposed in key-hole trenches adjoining the Market Street façade. These were interpreted as the remains of a number of successive street surfaces. The uppermost surface (F312) consisted of relatively modern cobbles sealed by modern building foundations. This indicates that the width of Market Street has narrowed in the last one-hundred-and-fifty years, following the construction of modern buildings. No finds were recovered.

The medieval structural remains, which appear to date to the later thirteenth to fourteenth century, were in turn sealed by a series of deposits that appear to date to the later medieval period. These consisted of alternating layers of burnt clays, ash and organic dumps, interspersed with layers of re-deposited natural clays (F140, F127, F126, F125, F109, F135 & F81). A small quantity of medieval pottery recovered from these deposits suggested a late medieval date; they may represent an abandonment phase (Appendix 10.2). The final layer (F13), directly beneath the demolished nineteenth-century building, contained a quernstone or whetstone fragment, a clay pipe and post-medieval pottery.

The 'backside' of the burgage plot: pits, well and lime pit
Twelve medieval pit-cuts (F42, F102, F142, F150, F162, F189, F196, F204, F287, F297, F311 & F324) cut into the deposit of ditch outcast, which was presumably levelled after the ditch passed out of use (fig. 10.3). Nearly all of these were located in the centre or southern half of the site. No pits were present along the Market Street frontage, presumably because it was occupied by structures. All pits were well-defined with steeply-cut sides; varying from 80cm to 2.2m in diameter and 35cm to 1.2m in depth. The majority were deep relative to their width. The upper portion of many of the cut features and deposits across the site had been removed by the insertion of eighteenth- and nineteenth-century buildings, hindering a relative chronology for the pits. A single steep-sided pit at the eastern limit of excavation contained small loose stones with a large timber fragment at the base, suggesting that it may have functioned as a post-setting. It yielded ceramic roof-tiles and a line-impressed floor-tile fragment. A pit (F121) cutting across the edge of the ditch, contained a homogeneous deposit of lime, suggesting the remains of a lime-slaking pit; the pit was 2m wide and 75cm deep (fig. 10.3). No corresponding kiln was exposed.

The primary fills of the pits largely consisted of organic sediment, suggesting that they were used to dump refuse. One feature (F162) was clearly identifiable as a cess-pit, with a possible stone-lining. A range of pottery was recovered from the pits, including Dublin-type ware, Dublin-type cooking ware (pl. 11), Trim-type ware (pl. 13), Dublin-type fineware (pl. 10) and Leinster Cooking Ware (pl. 14), dating to the thirteenth to fourteenth centuries (Appendix 10.2). Plant remains from the fills of four pits were assessed by Sarah Cobain (Appendix 10.1). Three of the four pits sampled contained occasional wood-chippings in the primary and secondary fills. Edible plants, which presumably formed part of the diet of the medieval occupants, included oats, barley, figs, elderberry, blackberry, white goosefoot, common chickweed, dock, fennel and cabbage. A number of medicinal plants, including opium cannabis, poppy and drug fumitory were identified.

A medieval dry-stone well was exposed at the southeast extent of the site. This consisted of a sub-circular cut, 2.5m in diameter, lined with undressed regular stones that were un-bonded and randomly coursed. The well appeared to have collapsed and been repaired at some point. Dublin-type fineware, Dublin-type ware and Leinster Cooking Ware recovered from the stonework suggest a late thirteenth- to fourteenth-century date for its construction. A small stone post-setting adjacent to the well may have contained a support for the upper structure or drawing mechanism. The well was excavated to a depth of 1.5m; its full depth was not exposed for safety reasons and it remains in situ beneath the developed site. It had been back-filled with a single deposit of organic refuse containing large amounts of animal bone, including a number of cattle horn fragments, a single sherd of Dublin-type ware and a quartz sandstone window mullion.

North of the well, a number of ill-defined layers and deposits with a high organic content (F160, F197 & F218) were revealed. These appear to represent loose backyard garden deposits. Fragments of a single Dublin-type ware jug were found here (fig. 16.1). A range of animal bone was recovered from across the medieval features, including cattle, sheep/goat, pig, horse, dog, cat, bird, whelk, cockle-shell and fish. In addition, a human humerus was recovered from the fill of a cess-pit (F162). Some of these animals may have been slaughtered for consumption and others maintained as pets. The recovery of additional horn fragments suggests that tanning or horn-working activity may have continued on-site (Beglane, 'Meat and craft', this volume).

The southern extent of the site: later structural evidence
The southwest corner contained the remains of a structure of possible early modern date. Assuming that this area of the site functioned as a separate burgage plot, any associated medieval structures would have been located along the western edge of the area – fronting onto Emmet Street.

In the southern half of the site fronting onto Emmet Street, a number of ill-defined and disturbed stone deposits were exposed overlying the back-fill of the medieval ditch. Some of these appear to have been structural and may have functioned as wall-bases or stone settings. Two possible wall-bases (F339 & F348) broadly match the orientation of a post-medieval structure exposed at a higher level, suggesting successive phases of rebuilding. Unfortunately the foundations of later modern buildings heavily disturbed these remains.

A single deposit (F220) sealed these features and extended over the entire southwest corner of the site. This consisted of alternating lenses of soils rich in burnt clay, ash, charcoal and organic garden soils; these appear to represent a phase of disuse of the Emmett Street side of the site. A substantial amount of pottery was recovered from this layer; mostly medieval Dublin-type ware,

10.4 Post-medieval structure

Leinster Cooking Ware (pl. 14), Ham Green ware (pls 8 & 9), Dublin-type
cooking ware (pl. 11) and Trim-type ware (pl. 13). A small amount of post-
medieval pottery from these layers suggests that the disuse dates to the
sixteenth or seventeenth centuries.

A substantial stone structure (fig. 10.4) was built on this deposit, fronting
onto Emmet Street. The southern extent of the structure was not exposed and
it had been heavily disturbed to the east and north. The surviving portion
consisted of three adjoining walls (F70, F320 & F321) and a possible mortar
floor surface (F333). A number of disturbed stone deposits (F64–66) extending to
the north appeared to form part of the structure. The walls were constructed
of large, randomly-coursed un-worked stone; the eastern wall (F320) was
mortar-bonded and more solidly constructed, with a regular outer face. The
remaining walls were clay-bonded; the outer mortar wall may represent the
original extent, with the mortar surface representing the final extent of the
structure. Fragments of post-medieval pottery were recovered from the layers
immediately underneath this structure: two fragments of red-glazed earthen-
wares and a clay pipe suggest a terminus ante quem of *c*.1600 for it.

DISCUSSION

The earlier features exposed may have considerable significance for our understanding of the topography and development of Trim town. The metalled surface is the earliest feature, and its extent and the absence of ceramic finds and
occupational debris suggest that it functioned as an external surface, extending
over a broad area. This surface appears to have been cut by a large enclosure
ditch; the outcast of the ditch lay directly atop this surface in places, suggesting
that the surface cannot have been in use for long before the creation of the
ditch. Whether the surface represents a feature pre-dating the Anglo-Norman
period, or – more likely – dates from the earliest period of the town, is unclear.
The radiocarbon date places it within the eleventh or twelfth century. It has been
suggested that the surface may have been used during butchery of livestock
and that tanning and/or horn-working may have taken place on the site
(Beglane, 'Meat and craft', this volume). 'Since both horners and tanners used
by-products of butchery in their crafts these two industries were often to be
found in close proximity' in medieval towns (ibid.; Schofield & Vince 2003, 133).

The presence of a substantial medieval ditch running along Emmet Street,
its early position in the site stratigraphy and the evidence that it extended
across Market Street, contradict the previously recognized topography of the
mature medieval town. This suggests that this ditch – and the possible bank –
pre-date both the creation of Emmet Street and the western circuit of the town
walls. The minimum dimensions of the ditch – 2.2m in depth and 5–6m in

width – indicate a substantial investment in labour and suggest that the ditch and bank formed a major defensive or enclosing feature for the early Anglo-Norman town. The dimensions of the ditch compare well with excavated sections of other Irish town ditches: the ditch at Athenry was 5.5m wide and 1.7m deep (Rynne 1986, 24); at Carrickfergus, the thirteenth-century ditch was 4m wide and the later ditch was 5m to 5.5m wide and 1m deep (Simpson & Delaney 1979, 82, 85); in Kilkenny the ditch was 5.5m wide and 1.6m deep (King 1991, 40). The radiocarbon date confirms the early date of the ditch (Table 1.1).

Hennessy's representation of the development of medieval Trim town suggests that this entire area, including the excavation site, as far west as the town wall, was developed in one phase between 1180 and 1220 (Hennessy 2003, map 10). The substantial ditch excavated at the Credit Union site, however, which was also identified by Meenan in the middle of Market Street, appears to have formed an earlier western boundary to the town. In the twelfth to thirteenth century, the western boundary of Trim town ran along the eastern side of Emmet Street (fig. 10.1). The range of pottery recovered from the later fills of the ditch suggests that it remained open in the thirteenth century. Most of what survives of Trim's circuit of walls dates from the late fourteenth and early fifteenth century, and appears to have been built after the expansion of the town west of Emmet Street. This expansion may also be apparent in the smaller size of the properties on the west side of Emmet Street: by comparison with the older properties on Market Street, perhaps the result of deliberate town planning or the higher value of property near the market during a fourteenth-century phase of expansion westward (see Bradley 1985; Dargan 1998; and O'Keeffe 2000, 95, for further analysis of medieval town planning in Ireland). The earliest recorded murage grants from Trim date to 1290 and 1316. The next murage grant dates to 1393 (Potterton 2005, 168), *after* the ditch on the Credit Union site was back-filled. Another possible implication of this newly identified town boundary is the potential presence of a gate or crossing point at the end of Market Street in the twelfth and thirteenth century, pre-dating Trim's western Dublin Gate and Water Gate. The identification of a possible stone wall extending north-south across the western end of Market Street by Meenan (1996) may be the remains of such a structure (fig. 10.1).

When the town boundary ditch identified in the Credit Union site went out of use it appears to have been deliberately back-filled, possibly with the remains of the internal defensive bank. The site appears then to have been converted to burgage plots. No archaeological features were identified during the excavation to confirm that the site was divided into two separate burgage plots, as suggested in the Urban Archaeological Survey, although it is possible that any such boundary may have not have survived.

Nearly all of the pottery recovered during the excavation of the Credit Union site was of domestic origin, in keeping with assemblages recovered elsewhere in Trim. Only six stray sherds of Ham Green ware and Saintonge ware were recovered. All of the pottery dates from the late twelfth to fourteenth century, with the exception of some sherds of Ham Green A ware of mid-twelfth-century date (pl. 8), recovered as stray finds in obviously later contexts (Appendix 10.2). Curved ceramic roof-tiles from the site were similar to those found elsewhere on Market Street by Hayden and by the same director in twelfth-century contexts at Trim Castle (Hayden, 'Market Street', this volume). A fragment of line-impressed floor-tile recovered from the Credit Union site could not be matched with known examples (Eames & Fanning 1988), although it is likely to be of fourteenth-century date. The roof- and floor-tiles suggest the possible demolition or refurbishment of a substantial building elsewhere in the town in the fourteenth century.

While the structural evidence recorded was limited, it suggests a sill-beam structure that fronted onto Market Street. It is often difficult in an urban context to distinguish the base of a wooden structure from that of a structure of stone or cob (Munby 1987, 156). Hayden's excavations on High Street, however, identified dry-stone wall-bases interpreted as having supported a sill-beam structure of thirteenth-century date (Hayden, 'High Street', this volume). In Cork, the majority of street-fronting houses of the thirteenth and fourteenth century were assumed to be 'timber-framed houses constructed above low stone walls or sills', gradually replaced by stone houses throughout the fourteenth century, though timber houses may still have predominated in the seventeenth century. The Cork excavations suggested that 'stone footings for timber structures are positively identifiable when they are represented by a single row of stones or two abutting rows with opposing faces' (Hurley 2003, 160). In Waterford, the evidence suggests that low stone walls supporting fully-framed wooden super-structures were predominant by the early thirteenth century, with stone-built houses following from the mid thirteenth century (Scully 1997, 39). Limited evidence for sill-beam structures resting on a foundation 'of a single line of flat stones' has also been identified in urban contexts in Scotland (Murray 1982, 226). At Trim, the wall-base may have supported the front wall of a structure facing onto Market Street. The surfaces and levelling deposits exposed at the northern extent of the excavation, in particular the latest phase of cobbling, appear to be street surfaces, suggesting that Market Street was broader, extending further to the south prior to the modern period. Evidence for substantial later medieval stone structures was absent from the Credit Union site, unlike the sites excavated by Hayden on Market Street and High Street (Hayden, 'High Street', this volume). Wood-framed buildings may have continued in use, or later medieval structures may have been entirely removed. While the presence of a lime-pit suggests the use of lime for mortar, it may have been used to render the exterior of wooden buildings. Tanners also used slaked lime to remove fat and hair from fresh hides (Schofield & Vince 2003, 140).

A stray window mullion and a decorated floor-tile represent stray material from a demolished building – probably ecclesiastical – elsewhere in the town. Curved ceramic roof-tiles were recovered. They were similar to those found on Hayden's excavations on Market Street and High Street and to those used on the twelfth-century roof of Trim Castle (Hayden, 'Market Street', this volume; Hayden, 'High Street', this volume).

The concentration of pits and external features at the centre and rear of the site, and their absence to the front of the site, suggests the typical layout of a medieval burgage plot with a structure facing onto the Market Street frontage. Pits are largely absent from the western front, which may indicate the continued use of the ditch into the thirteenth century and, after this ditch was back-filled, the presence of structures.

Plant remains and animal bone recovered from the site provide information on the diet and economy of medieval Trim (Appendix 10.1; Beglane, 'Meat and craft', this volume). Figs are likely to have been imported and their presence may indicate higher social status, as would be expected with dwellings in the market area of a medieval town (McClatchie 2003, 401; Tierney & Hannon 1997, 893). On the other hand, British evidence suggests that figs were relatively common imports in the medieval period (Fraser & Dixon 1982, 244). As in the majority of medieval urban sites, the proportion of grain was relatively small (McClatchie 2003, 398) and there is no evidence for grain-processing on-site, although barley and wheat was consumed. Of speculative interest are a number of plants with potential medicinal uses, such as chickweed, opium cannabis, poppy and drug fumitory (Appendix 10.1). Cattle, sheep, goat, pig, red deer, bird, fish and marine molluscs all appear to have formed part of the diet of the inhabitants. Sheep are likely to have been used for meat rather than wool (Beglane, 'Meat and craft', this volume).

Limited evidence was recovered for Trim's medieval craft and industries. Flax seeds from the refuse pits may derive from the production of linen. The presence of fairy flax remains suggests that dying also took place, if not on-site, then within the town (Appendix 10.1). Evidence for flax-cultivation was also uncovered from Kiely's Yard, to the south of the Credit Union site (Stephens, 'SubUrbia', this volume). Potterton identified later references to an area known as 'Dyersland' in the fifteenth and sixteenth centuries and the establishment in Trim town of 'broad looms and a dyehouse' in 1538, and this may be relevant (Potterton 2005, 165). Cultivated flax was identified from medieval urban contexts in Cork; the seeds may also have been used for oil (McClatchie 2003, 399). The presence of wood-chippings suggests that carpentry took place on the Credit Union site, possibly in relation to the construction of the houses. Horn-cores were recovered from atop the early metalled surface and from within the later well. Beglane has suggested that horn-processing and possibly tanning were carried out during the pre-burgage

10.5 Aerial photograph of site, mid-excavation

phase, and that these activities, particularly tanning, may have continued when the site was in use as a burgage plot. Horn was used for a variety of purposes in medieval towns, including the manufacture of combs, lanterns and windows, although actual horn artefacts or off-cuts rarely survive (Schofield & Vince 2003, 133). Excavations in the medieval Scottish town of Perth yielded a range of animal horn indicating horn-working within the 'backlands' of burgage plots. Cox suggested from historical evidence that if horn-working was an artisan craft it may have been of relatively low status (Cox 1996, 787, 813).

CONCLUSIONS

Archaeological excavations at the Credit Union site provided an opportunity to investigate the very earliest phase of Trim town. The discovery of a substantial enclosing ditch dating from the late twelfth to the fourteenth century substantially alters our understanding of the development of the town and its morphology, as well as suggesting the presence of a previously unidentified town gate or entrance at the west end of Market Street. Although evidence for medieval structures on the site was slight, the artefactual, plant and animal remains, particularly from the securely stratified pits, provide a valuable addition to our understanding of the economy and diet of medieval Trim.

ACKNOWLEDGMENTS

A debt of gratitude is due to St Loman's Credit Union, who financed the excavation, to Aaron Johnston, Marta Muñiz Pérez, Alexander William Sotheran,

Denis Shine, Laura Gildea and John Swift, who worked tirelessly on the excavation, to Richard Clutterbuck for editing and comment, to Clare McCutcheon, Fiona Beglane and Sarah Cobain for their work on the pottery, animal bone and plant remains, and in particular to Matthew Seaver and Michael Potterton, who took on this publication, arranged much of the post-excavation works required and provided much needed editing and comment. Any errors or omissions are the author's own.

BIBLIOGRAPHY

Bradley, J., 1985, 'Planned Anglo-Norman towns in Ireland' in Clarke, H.B., & Simms, A. (eds), *The comparative history of urban origins in non-Roman Europe: Ireland, Wales, Denmark, Germany, Poland and Russia, from the ninth to the thirteenth century*. 2 vols, vol. 2, 411–67. Oxford.

Cox, A., 1996, 'Backland activities in medieval Perth', *Proceedings of the Royal Society of Scottish Antiquaries* **126**, 733–821.

Dargan, P., 1998, 'Nobber: an Anglo-Norman village', *Ríocht na Mídhe* **9:4**, 28–39.

Eames, E.S., & Fanning, T., 1988, *Irish medieval tiles*. Dublin.

Duffy, C., 2003, 'Archaeological assessment of a site at Market Street and Emmet Street, Trim, Co. Meath'. Unpublished excavation report.

Fallon, D., 2003, 'Pre-development testing report on the site of the proposed extension to Trim Credit Union, 18 Market St, Trim, Co. Meath'. Unpublished excavation report.

Fraser, M., & Dixon, J.H., 1982, 'Plant remains' in Murray, H. (ed.), *Excavations in the medieval burgh of Aberdeen, 1973–1981*, 239–44. Edinburgh.

Hennessy, M., 2004, *Irish Historic Towns Atlas No. 14: Trim*. Dublin.

Hurley, M.F., 2003, 'A review of domestic architecture in Cork' in Cleary, R.M., & Hurley, M. (eds), *Cork city excavations, 1984–2000*, 151–70. Cork.

King, H.A., 1991, 'Pennyfeather Lane/Pudding Lane, St Mary's/St Patrick's Ward, Kilkenny' in Bennett, I. (ed.), *Excavations 1990: summary accounts of archaeological excavations in Ireland*, no. 78, p. 40. Bray.

McClatchie, M., 2003, 'The plant remains' in Cleary, R.M., & Hurley, M. (eds), *Cork city excavations, 1984–2000*, 391–413. Cork.

Meenan, R., 1996, 'Archaeological monitoring of excavations for Trim Water and Sewerage Scheme: licence no. 96E0175'. Unpublished excavation report.

Meenan, R., 1997, 'Trim' in Bennett, I. (ed.), *Excavations 1996: summary accounts of archaeological excavation in Ireland*, no. 315, p. 89. Bray.

Munby, J., 1987, 'Medieval domestic buildings' in Schofield, J., & Leech, H. (eds), *Urban archaeology in Britain*, 156–66. CBA Research Report **61**.

Murray, H.K., 1982, 'The excavated secular buildings' in Murray, J.C. (ed.), *Excavations in the medieval burgh of Aberdeen, 1973–1981*, 224–8. Edinburgh.

O'Keeffe, T., 2000, *Medieval Ireland: an archaeology*. Stroud, Gloucestershire.

Potterton, M., 2005, *Medieval Trim: history and archaeology*. Dublin.

Rynne, E., 1986, 'Athenry' in Bennett, I. (ed.), *Excavations 1985: summary accounts of archaeological excavations in Ireland*, no. 28, p. 24. Bray.

Simpson, M.L., & Dickson, A., 1981, 'Excavations in Carrickfergus, Co. Antrim, 1972–9: summary report on the excavations directed by the late T.G. Delaney', *Medieval Archaeology* **25**, 78–89.

Tierney, J., & Hannon, M., 1997, 'Plant remains' in Hurley, M., & Scully, O.M.B., *Late Viking Age and medieval Waterford: excavations, 1986–1992*, 854–93. Waterford.

Schofield, J., & Vince, A.G., 2003, *Medieval towns: the archaeology of British towns in their European setting*. London.

Scully, O.M.B., 1997, 'Domestic architecture: houses in Waterford from the eleventh century to post-medieval times' in Hurley, M., & Scully, O.M.B., *Late Viking Age and medieval Waterford: excavations, 1986–1992*, 34–44. Waterford.

APPENDIX 10.1: PLANT REMAINS

By Sarah Cobain

INTRODUCTION

The survival of seed and wood macrofossils from dry-land archaeological sites is usually dependant on the water-table being high enough to keep the archaeological features in damp/wet and anoxic conditions. This does not usually occur on archaeological sites in Ireland, but the location of this site, adjacent to the River Boyne floodplain, meant that the water-table was high enough to allow the macrofossil remains within the archaeological features to be preserved in anoxic conditions, preventing decay. As plant remains are fundamentally linked to human activity in the past, it is the aim of this report to identify the macrofossil species recovered from the features at Market Street and to use this information to:

1.   Determine the function of features sampled;
2.   Interpret the diet and living conditions of the occupants at Market Street;
3.   Interpret socio-economic and industrial activities on the site;
4.   Infer the composition of the local flora and woodland.

METHODOLOGY

There were five samples to be analyzed for plant macrofossil remains, all of which originated from the medieval phases. These samples were retrieved from two domestic rubbish pits (F196 & F297), one cess-pit (F162) and one possible cess-pit/domestic rubbish pit (F92) (Fallon 2003, 15–16; Fallon, above). The following methodology was used to identify the plant macrofossil remains:

Plant macrofossils
The plant macrofossil remains were wet-sieved by CRDS Ltd, using 500-micron and 250-micron sieves, keeping the wet-sieved material damp. The seeds were sorted by extracting a small amount of wet-sieved material and disaggregating it with water in a petri-dish. The seeds could then be identified using a low-power microscope (Brunel MX1) at magnifications of x4 to x40. This process was repeated until all of the wet-sieved material had been sorted. Identifications were made with reference to Cappers et al. (2006), Berggren (1981) and Anderberg (1994). Nomenclature follows Stace (1997).

Results

Sample 94 (from F305) was retrieved from the tertiary fill of domestic rubbish pit (F297). It contained herbaceous taxa consisting of white goosefoot/fat hen, stinking camomile, cabbage/mustard, common corn-cockle, common chickweed, bog stitchwort, remote sedge, common fumitory, long-headed poppy, opium poppy, sheep's sorrel, curled dock, marsh dock, broadleaf pond-weed and dwarf nettle. The sample also contained uncharred naked/free-threshing wheat and straw from cereal crops with culm nodes (indeterminate species). Elderberry seeds were also recovered.

F193 (sample 48) was the tertiary fill of a domestic rubbish pit (F196). The herbaceous taxa within this sample consisted of common orache, white goosefoot/fat hen, fennel, stinking camomile, cabbage/mustard, spurrey, common chickweed, bog stitchwort, remote sedge, everlasting pea, fairy flax, common flax, bog bean, long-headed poppy, opium poppy, false oat grass, smart-/pink-weeds, water pepper, common/spinach dock, sheep's sorrel, curled dock, great water dock, dooryard dock, willow dock, cinquefoils, stinging nettle and dwarf nettle. Charred oat, barley (hulled) and two charred cereal grains were recovered from the sample as well as eleven uncharred cereal straw fragments with culm nodes (indeterminate species).

The primary fill (F91) of a possible domestic rubbish pit/cess-pit (F92) was retrieved as Sample 2. It contained herbaceous taxa, charred material, tree seeds and fruit seeds. The herbaceous taxa consisted of white goosefoot/fat hen, fool's parsley, fennel, stinking camomile, touch-me-not balsam, mustard/cabbage, hemp, spurrey, common chickweed, bog stitchwort, sedge spp, dioecious sedge, glaucous sedge, greater tussock sedge, drooping sedge, remote sedge, thin-spiked wood sedge, everlasting pea, hop trefoil, vetch, fairy flax, common flax, bog bean, long prickly-headed poppy, long-headed poppy, opium poppy, false oat grass, small water-pepper, common dock, curled sock, great water dock, dooryard dock, broadleaf pondweed, buttercup spp, stinging nettle and dwarf nettle. The charred material consisted of charred oat and charred naked/free-threshing wheat. There were also occasional inclusions of uncharred cereal straw with culm nodes (indeterminate species), and common/black alder tree seeds and elderberry, fig and blackberry fruit seeds.

Sample 16 (from F166) was retrieved from the primary fill of a cess-pit (F162). It contained herbaceous taxa consisting of white goosefoot/fat hen, fool's parsley, fennel, stinking camomile, lettuce, hawkbits, mustard/cabbage, common corn-cockle, bog stitchwort, hop trefoil, bulbous rush, fairy flax, common flax, bog bean, long-headed poppy, rough meadow grass, common dock, sheep's sorrel, curled dock, slender-leaved pondweed, buttercup spp, stinging nettle and dwarf nettle. The sample also included uncharred cereal straw with culm nodes (indeterminate species).

Table 10.1 Macrofossil taxa from 18 Market Street, Trim

Sample number			2	16	48	94
Feature number			*(F91)*	*(F166)*	*(F193)*	*(F305)*
			[F92]	*[F162]*	*[F196]*	*[F297]*
Feature description			*Primary fill of cess-pit/ domestic rubbish pit*	*Primary fill of cess-pit*	*Tertiary fill of domestic rubbish pit*	*Tertiary fill of domestic rubbish pit*
Flot volume			*300ml*	*200ml*	*200ml*	*100ml*
Family	*Species*	*Common name*				
	Wood chippings	Sharp edges/ possibly worked	Occasional		Occasional	Moderate
Adoxaceae	Sambucus nigra	Common elder	5		1	1
Amaranthaceae	Atriplex patula	Common/spreading orache			2	
	Chenopodium album	White goosefoot /fat hen	19	17	47	7
Apiaceae	Aethusa cynapium	Fools parsley/poison parsley	1	2		
	Foeniculum vulgare	Fennel	3	14	5	
Asteraceae	Anthemis cotula	Stinking chamomile	2	10	7	3
	Lactuca spp	Lettuce spp		12		
	Leontodon hispidus	Hawkbits	14			
Balsaminaceae	Impatiens noli-tangere	Touch-me-not balsam	27			
Betulaceae	Alnus glutinosa	Black/common alder	2			
Brassicaceae	Brassica spp	Mustard	2	1	5	1
Cannabaceae	Cannabis sativa	Hemp	1			
Caryophyllaceae	Agrostemma githago	Common corn-cockle		1		2
	Spergula arvensis	Spurrey	1		2	
	Stellaria media	Common chickweed	41	7	20	26
	Stellaria uliginosa	Bog stitchwort	2	6	2	
Cyperaceae	Carex spp	Sedge	7	13		
	Carex acuta	Slender tufted sedge	1			
	Carex dioica	Dioecious sedge	8			
	Carex flacca	Glaucous/blue sedge	4			
	Carex cf paniculata	Greater tussock sedge	2			
	Carex cf pendula	Drooping/weeping sedge	15			
	Carex remota	Remote sedge	2		3	2
	Carex strigosa	Thin spiked wood sedge	1			

			2	16	48	94
Sample number						
Feature number			(F91)	(F166)	(F193)	(F305)
			[F92]	[F162]	[F196]	[F297]
Feature description			Primary fill of cess-pit / domestic rubbish pit	Primary fill of cess-pit	Tertiary fill of domestic rubbish pit	Tertiary fill of domestic rubbish pit
Flot volume			300ml	200ml	200ml	100ml
Family	Species	Common name				
Fabaceae	Lathyrus latifolis	Everlasting pea	1		1	
	Trifolium campestre	Hop trefoil/Low hop clover	2	5		
	Vicia spp	Vetch	2			
Juncaceae	Juncus spp cf bulbosus	Bulbous rush		7		
Linaceae	Linum catharticum	Fairy flax	3	2	2	
	Linum usitatissimum	Common flax	2	1	2	
Menyanthaceae	Menyanthes trifoliate	Bog bean/buck bean	2	4	1	
Moraceae	cf Ficus carica	Common fig	2			
Papaveraceae	Fumaria officinalis	Common/drug fumitory				1
	Papaver argemone	Long pricklyhead poppy	1			
	Papaver dubium	Long headed poppy, blindeyes	34	4	19	12
	Papaver somniferum	Opium poppy	3		2	1
Poaceae	Arrhenatherum elatius	False oak grass	2		4	
	Avena spp	Charred oat	1		1	
	Hordeum vulgare	Charred barley – hulled			2	
	Poa cf trivialis	Rough meadow grass		11		
	Triticum aestivum/durum	Charred wheat – naked/free threshing	1			
	Triticum aestivum/durum	Uncharred wheat – naked/free threshing				1
	Culm node (uncharred)	Straw	2	22	11	5
	Indeterminate charred grain	Indeterminate charred grain			2	

			2	16	48	94
Sample number						
Feature number			(F91)	(F166)	(F193)	(F305)
			[F92]	[F162]	[F196]	[F297]
Feature description			Primary fill of cess-pit / domestic rubbish pit	Primary fill of cess-pit	Tertiary fill of domestic rubbish pit	Tertiary fill of domestic rubbish pit
Flot volume			300ml	200ml	200ml	100ml
Family	Species	Common name				
Polygonaceae	Perscaria spp	Smart/pink weeds			3	
	Perscaria hydropiper	Water-pepper			1	
	Perscaria minor	Small water-pepper	4			
	Rumex acetosa	Common/garden sorrel/spinach dock	19	3	8	
	Rumex acetosella	Sheep's/field sorrel		3	2	1
	Rumex crispus (seed)	Curled/sour dock	25	10	45	11
	Rumex crispus (perianth)	Curled/sour dock		2	18	1
	Rumex hydrolapathum	Great water dock	2		3	
	Rumex longifolius	Dooryard dock	3		5	
	Rumex palustris	Marsh dock				2
	Rumex salicifolius	Willow dock			6	
Potamogetona-ceae	Potamogeton filiformis	Slender leaved pondweed	1			
	Potamogeton natans	Broadleaf/floating pondweed	1	2		
Ranunculaceae	Ranunculus spp	Buttercups/spearworts	1	1		
Rosaceae	Rubus fruticosus	Blackberry	1			
	Potentilla spp	Cinquefoils			5	
Urticaceae	Urtica dioica	Stinging nettle	7	2	6	
	Urtica urens	Dwarf/annual nettle	1	10	3	1

DISCUSSION

Function of features/diet and socio-economic activity at Market Street

As asserted by Fallon, above, the site at 18 Market Street was a burgage plot, and the cess-pits and waste-pits would have been associated with domestic and industrial activity. The pits contained macrofossil remains reflective of domestic waste, and also species from within the local environment. These pits would have served to contain day-to-day waste material (foodstuffs, medieval pottery, wood and bone) and, together with the high water-table in this area, this meant that the organic material was quickly inundated and preserved in anoxic conditions, preventing decay. This has allowed a relatively large assemblage of macrofossils to be preserved. The pits also contained some small fragments of wood-chippings, distinguished by their sharp edges, and these could have been waste from wood-working on the site. Together with the woodland/scrub, herbaceous taxa and cereals identified from the cess-pits/domestic rubbish pits, this gives an interesting insight into the diet and industry of – and possible medications used by – the inhabitants of the burgage plot at 18 Market Street.

Diet/food

There was limited evidence for cereal use and cultivation in the macrofossil assemblage (two charred oat grains, two charred barley grains and one charred and one uncharred naked/free-threshing wheat grains). The small number of grains together with the lack of cereal chaff (other than straw fragments) suggests that the drying and processing/cleaning of the grain (threshing – to break the ears of grain from the straw; winnowing – throwing grain into the air to allow the breeze to blow away lighter chaff (paleas, lemmas, awns) and coarse-, medium-, fine-sieving and final hand-picking of the grain (Stevens & Wilkinson 2003, 196–7)) was taking place elsewhere. This was also found at Kiely's Yard (Lyons 2007, 7; Stephens, 'SubUrbia', this volume) and suggests that cereal-processing may have been taking place at a central location in Trim.

The grain, once dried and processed, would have been used in a domestic environment to make a variety of foods. The wheat and oats would have been used to produce porridges, bread and cakes. Barley would also have been used to brew beer. Dyer (1983) suggests that up to one gallon (3.79 litres) of beer would have been consumed per person per day. A reason for this is because of poor water-sanitation during the medieval period, which meant that beer was consumed in preference to water to avoid contracting water-borne diseases (for example, cholera and dysentery). It would also have been an added source of vitamins and calories. The by-products of grains were also put to use; for example, wheat straw was often used for thatching, and barley straw was used as a winter-feed and bedding for livestock (Pearson 1997, 3). The frequent straw recovered from the domestic waste pits and cess-pits suggests that it may have been used to cover waste material and to reduce the smell.

Herbaceous plants were often exploited to be used as herbs in cooking, as vegetables or to be eaten raw in salads, all of which would have helped to add flavour to food and to provide vitamins, minerals and additional fibre. Many were also used for medicinal or industrial purposes. Common chickweed, dock/sorrel, common orache, white goosefoot/fat hen, cabbage/mustard and lettuce leaves were eaten raw as salad, boiled down and used as pottage in stews and soups and as vegetables similar to spinach

(Defelice 2004, 195–6; Harvey 1984, 91–2; Pearson 1997, 11; Williams 1963, 716; Behre 2008, 67–8). Common chickweed and spurrey seeds have also been recovered in Danish and other Scandinavian granaries (respectively), and are known to have been used as a substitute to grain at times of poor harvest (Defelice 2004, 195–6; New 1961, 214).

Water-pepper has a very acrid taste and, for this reason, its seeds have been used for spices in food (Timson 1966, 817). Fennel seeds have also been used as a herb/spice to flavour food, and the bulb at the base has been eaten raw or boiled as a vegetable (Harvey 1984, 92). Poppy and flax seeds were used to produce oil that would have been used to cook food with (Dickson 1996, 26; Duke 1973, 390). Poppy seeds were ground down and used to make porridges and glazes for bread/cakes (Duke 1973, 390).

There were fruit seeds (elderberries, blackberry and fig) from a cess-pit (F92) and domestic waste pits (F196 & F197). Elderberries and blackberries would have provided additional Vitamin C and they could be eaten raw or added into tarts/cakes (Pearson 1997, 14). Elderberries were also boiled down and used to make mousses and jams/jellies, as well as being used in juices and to make wine (Dennell 1970, 154). Figs may have been imported into Ireland from mainland Europe. They have high levels of calcium and iron and would have been a valuable addition to the diet (Dickson 1996, 26).

All of these species are known to have been used as food, through documentary sources, analysis of archaeological ecofacts and information based on the foods we eat today. There is also direct evidence of herbaceous taxa being consumed (including species found at the Market Street site). Macrofossil analyses of the stomach contents of bog bodies such as Kayhausen (Oldenburg, Germany), the Grauballe man (Jutland, Denmark), the Tollund man (Jutland, Denmark) and the Lindow man (Lindow Moss, Cheshire, Britain) have identified the presence of species such as dock (*Rumex crispus and Rumex acetosella*), white goosefoot/fat hen, common chickweed, spurrey, cabbage/mustard, flax and cereals (barley and wheat) – all of which were found within the Market Street assemblage. This suggests that these species were selected for consumption (Behre 2008, 67–8). Although the bog bodies were from various countries (Germany, Denmark, Britain), these taxa were all found in Ireland during the medieval period, and it can be assumed that they would have been selected and consumed (or processed to use in/or with cooking food) in Ireland too.

Industry

Both flax and cannabis can be used to produce linen. The stems of the plants are soaked in water in a process called 'retting', which breaks down the stems into fine fibres that can then be spun to produce cloth (Tanner 1922, 174–6; Ash 1948, 160). Fairy flax is also known to have been used to make a yellow dye, which may have been used to dye clothing (Crackles 1986, 84). As only small quantities of flax seeds and a single cannabis seed were retrieved, however, it cannot be determined whether these industrial processes were being carried out at this site. The presence of these seeds does suggest that it was being carried out *somewhere* within the town, even if not at the site itself.

There were several small fragments of wood from within the waste pits (F162, F196 & F297). These had sharp edges and relatively straight sides, which suggests that they had been cut with a knife, rather than breaking off branches naturally. This may indicate wood-working activity at the site.

Medication and drugs

During the medieval period, herbs were frequently experimented with to produce medication and treatments for all kinds of ailments and as drugs for recreational enjoyment. Elder flowers, leaves and berries had herbal medicinal uses and were used to treat inflammation, bruises and wounds (Atkinson & Atkinson 2002, 916–17).

Fennel has been used as a drug for regulating fertility, in particular as a potion used to induce/cause abortions (Newman 1979, 227). The opium poppy seeds within the Market Street assemblage indicate the possible use of opium to cure headaches, back pain, toothache and other ailments causing pain. This would have been done by extracting the 'milky' latex from the seed head and allowing it to dry (Grover 1965, 100–1). Cannabis leaves were also smoked and used as a drug to alleviate pain, although less reliably, as they caused the user to lose perception of time and the ability to control his/her body. For this reason, it was replaced by more reliable drugs for pain relief and became more popular as a recreational drug (Grover 1965, 103–4).

Drug fumitory is reported to have had several uses in the medieval period (Mitich 1997, 843). Its leaves have been distilled and juices used to make potions/cures for arthritis, liver disorders and gallstones. The juices have also been used to make laxatives and diuretics and have been made into lotions to treat eczema and scabies. From the Anglo-Saxon period onwards, it has also been associated with witchcraft and superstition, and the leaves have been burnt so that the smoke could expel and protect against evil spirits and spells (ibid., 844). Although all of the seeds within this assemblage were recovered in relatively small quantities, the use of herbalism was an important part of society during the medieval period. It is therefore possible that any or all of these were being used to 'treat' the local community.

The method of collection of these herbaceous taxa is less conclusive, however, as all of these species were recovered in relatively low numbers, and it cannot be concluded whether they were obtained by trade, deliberately cultivated or hand-picked. Many of these species are likely to have been hand-picked from the local environment, which would have been a cheap way of obtaining the raw materials required for industry and medicine and also for additional dietary supplements. Excavations of medieval gardens in Hull, England (at Sewer Lane and Scale Lane) have provided evidence that some species, such as white goosefoot/fat hen, cabbage/mustard, orache, fennel, opium poppy, flax, elder and blackberry, were being deliberately cultivated and harvested for food and other industrial and medicinal processes (Crackles 1986, 2–5). As the climate in Britain and Ireland was similar during this period, there is no reason why at least some of these species were not being cultivated and used here. Another method to obtain these species was through trade. As asserted by Comber (2001, 73–4), trade networks had hugely increased by the Early Medieval period. Evidence for the presence of fig, a species that would have been imported from Britain/mainland Europe, indicates that foreign trade occurred in Trim, and it is likely that some of these species were exchanged or brought by traders. It is possible that some of the seeds which have been recovered were brought in inadvertently with other foodstuffs. Without specific documentary evidence as to how all of these taxa were obtained, it is reasonable to assume that the woodland/scrub, herbaceous taxa and cereals found at the Market Street site were obtained by a mixture of these three methods.

Composition of local flora
Based on the geographical location of Trim, in the floodplain of the River Boyne, the vegetation would have been dominated by species tolerant of damp or waterlogged conditions. Further from the river bank, the soil begins to dry out and, through the process of vegetation, succession species tolerant of damp, marshy environments start to establish. As the soil dries out further, succession continues into climax community vegetation (in Ireland this was oak woodland) (Cox & Moore 2005). The site was located within relatively close proximity to the River Boyne, and it would be expected that the vegetation was dominated by species tolerant of damp or waterlogged soils. It is important that any reconstructions of the local environment are interpreted with caution, as it cannot be confirmed how many of the species identified at the site were brought in deliberately or inadvertently through trade or hand-collection from areas further outside the town.

   The woodland, submerged, opportunistic and dry-land species recovered from the assemblage at Market Street could represent flora growing in the vicinity of the site. They are discussed in more detail below.

Woodland species
The woodland macrofossil species consisted of elder and alder seeds. These trees are part of alder carr scrub that grows on waterlogged/damp soils (Aitkinson & Aitkinson 2002, 897, 900; McVean 1953, 450) and are species that would have grown in the floodplain of the River Boyne. Elder, in particular, grows well on nitrate-/phosphate-rich soils (Aitkinson & Aitkinson 2002, 899), and the domestic waste from Trim that would have flowed into the river would have caused increases in these nutrients, giving the elder optimum growing conditions. This is likely to have led to a relative abundance of elder trees, which may have been another reason that Trim was given its name *Áth Truimm*, which means 'the ford of the elder tree' (Herity 2001, 67). There was no other fossil evidence for any other woodland species, but trees such as willow, buckthorn and poplar, which also tolerate damp soils, are likely to have been present.

Submerged water plants
Bog bean, slender-leaved and broadleaf pondweeds and bulbous rush are species that grow submerged or partially submerged in water and would have grown in slow-flowing stretches of the River Boyne, or in sheltered small pools close to the banks of the river (Hewett 1964, 727; Haynes & Holm-Nielson 2003, 5; Balslev 1996, 1–2). These could have been inadvertently collected while harvesting other species, and discarded with other waste in the rubbish pits/cess-pits.

Marsh/fen species
Fools parsley, touch-me-not balsam, water-pepper, sedge species (slender tufted, glaucous, greater tussock, drooping, remote) are all species that grow on marshy/fen areas of, for example, rivers or lakes (M.R. 1870, 12; Hatcher 2003, 149–50; Timson 1966, 816; Inglis & Simpson 2001, 268, 274). Species such as the water-pepper would possibly have been hand-selected to use in foods (as discussed above) and the other seeds may have accumulated in the waste/cess-pits through being accidentally gathered with other resources or transported by birds or other small animals and dropped/disposed of on the site.

Opportunistic/ruderal species

The common orache, white goosefoot/fat hen, fennel, cabbage/mustard, hemp, common chickweed, bog stitchwort, drug fumitory, prickly-headed/long-headed/opium poppy, dock/sorrel (spinach, curled, great water, dooryard, marsh, willow dock and sheep's sorrel), blackberry and stinging/dwarf nettle are all opportunistic species that grow well on cleared/waste ground and tolerate damp soils (Williams 1963, 713; Haney & Kutscheid 1974, 93; Mitich 1997, 844; Harper & McNaughton 1964, 787; Cavers & Harper 1964, 758; Greig-Smith 1948, 352, 388). These species all could have grown easily within Trim town, taking advantage of cleared areas and waste ground on the sides of roads and verges, between cracks in the roads, around houses/out-houses and in gardens. White goosefoot/fat hen, common orache, common chickweed and nettles all grow abundantly on soils with high nitrate and phosphate levels (Williams 1963, 713; Defelice 2004, 194–5; Greig-Smith 1948, 352, 388). This could be a reason for their high abundance within the cess- and waste-pits, as the soil surrounding these features would have been polluted by domestic waste. It cannot be disregarded that these were all common food sources during this time, however, so their abundance among the archaeological features could have been a mixture of both their consumption and their presence growing within the burgage plots.

Dryland species

Stinking camomile, lettuce, hawkbits, common corn-cockle, spurrey, false oat grass, buttercups, cinquefoils, hop trefoil, vetch and flax are all species that would have grown in dry areas or in cultivated arable areas (Kay 1971, 623; Firbank 1988, 1234; New 1961, 206–8; Pfitzenmeyer 1962, 236–7; Burdon 1983, 308; Grover 1965, 100–1). It is possible that some of these arable weed species (stinking camomile, common corn-cockle, spurrey, false oat grass) would have been inadvertently brought into the town with cereal crops from outside the town centre and disposed of with hay and other waste into the rubbish pits and cess-pits. The flax is likely to have been deliberately harvested or brought into the town from outside, where it could have been cultivated or gathered from larger sources, as the plant itself has many uses. Some of these seeds may also have been dropped by birds or small animals or may have established themselves in drier areas around the site, and hence accumulated with waste within the rubbish/cess-pits.

Imported species

Fig is the only species obtained from the Market Street assemblage that would have been imported, as it was not grown in Ireland during this period.

CONCLUSION

The domestic waste pits and cess-pit at the Market Street site provided a relatively rich waterlogged assemblage of macrofossil material that has allowed an interesting insight into the diet and socio-economic and industrial activity of the occupants of Market Street, as well an idea of the local vegetation. The material from the cess- and waste pits has identified species that were consumed, such as oat and barley cereals, elderberry, blackberry, white goosefoot/fat hen, common chickweed, poppies, fennel, docks and cabbage. This has shown the effort that the occupants went to in order to obtain a varied diet to include various vitamins and minerals. Many of these species, such as opium, cannabis, poppy, fennel, flax and drug fumitory were also known to have been used in medieval herbalism to make pain-killing drugs and cures for other ailments (cuts, bruises, liver disorders, eczema), and in the case of drug fumitory, also to ward off evil spirits as a result of witchcraft and superstition. Although there were not sufficient numbers of seeds to come to a firm conclusion, the evidence of hemp and flax may indicate the production of linen within the town, and fairy flax is also used to make a yellow dye. The evidence of fragments of possibly worked wood within the waste pits may indicate wood-working activity on the site. Although these species would not have been used for all of these functions, as the gathering of resources took large amounts of time and effort, every part of the plants would have been used to its full potential before being discarded. The collection methods for these species cannot be confirmed, as without direct documentary evidence it is not possible to conclude whether the materials were obtained by trade, deliberately cultivated or hand-picked, although it is likely that it was a mixture of all three.

The local vegetation appears to have consisted of wetland and water-tolerant species, such as elder, alder, rushes, pondweed, fools parsley, touch-me-not balsam, water-pepper and sedge species that would be expected due to the location of the site next to the River Boyne floodplain. There is evidence of opportunistic species, such as common orache, white goosefoot/fat hen, fennel, cabbage/mustard, hemp, common chickweed, bog stitchwort, drug fumitory, prickly-headed/long-headed/opium poppy, dock/sorrel (spinach, curled, great water, dooryard, marsh, willow dock and sheep's sorrel), blackberry and stinging/dwarf nettle, which are typical in towns and would grow on disturbed ground around roads, houses and in ditches. There were also some species that prefer drier, undisturbed ground or cultivated fields, such as stinking camomile, lettuce, hawkbits, common corn-cockle, spurrey, false oat grass, buttercups, cinquefoils, hop trefoil, vetch and flax. These are more likely to have come into Trim directly by trade or inadvertently with other foodstuffs being brought into the town. Taken together, this macrofossil assemblage provides a view of the everyday lives of the occupants of Market Street and the socio-economic activities that took place within Trim town.

BIBLIOGRAPHY

Aitkinson, E., & Aitkinson, M.D., 2002, 'Sambucus nigra L.', *The Journal of Ecology* **90:5**, 895–923.
Anderberg, A.-L., 1994, *Atlas of seeds: part 4*. Uddevalla, Sweden.
Ash, A.L., 1948, 'Hemp: production and utilization', *Economic Botany* **2:2**, 158–69.
Balslev, H., 1996, '*Juncaceae*', *Flora Neotropica* **68**, 1–167.
Berggren, G., 1981, *Atlas of seeds: part 3*. Arlöv, Sweden.
Behre, K.-E., 2008, 'Collected seeds and fruits from herbs as prehistoric food', *Vegetation History and Archaeobotany* **17**, 65–73.
Burdon, J.J., 1983, '*Trifolium repens* L.', *The Journal of Ecology* **71:1**, 307–30.

Cappers, R.T.J., Bekker, R.M., & Gronigen, J.E.A., 2006, *Digital seed atlas of the Netherlands*. Eelde, The Netherlands. www.seedatlas.nl.

Cavers, P.B., & Harper, J.L., 1964, '*Rumex obtusifolius* L. and *R. crispus* L.', *The Journal of Ecology* **52**:3, 737–66.

Comber, M., 2001, 'Trade and communication networks in early historic Ireland', *The Journal of Irish Archaeology* **10**, 73–92.

Cox, C.B., & Moore, P.D., 2005, *Biogeography*. Oxford.

Crackles, F.E., 1986, 'Medieval gardens in Hull: archaeological evidence', *Garden History* **14**:1, 1–5.

Defelice, M.S., 2004, 'Common chickweed, *Stellaria media* (L.) Vill.: "mere chicken feed"', *Weed Technology* **18**:1, 193–200.

Dennell, R.W., 1970, 'Seeds from a medieval sewer in Woolster Street, Plymouth', *Economic Botany* **24**:2, 151–4.

Dickson, C., 1996, 'Food, medicinal and other plants from the 15th-century drains of Paisley Abbey, Scotland', *Vegetation History and Archaeobotany* **5**, 25–31.

Duke, J.A., 1973, 'Utilization of papaver', *Economic Botany* **27**:4, 390–400.

Dyer, C., 1983, 'English diet in the later Middle Ages' in Aston, T.H., Coss, P.R., Dyer, C., & Thirsk, J. (eds), *Social relations and ideas: essays in honour of R.H. Hilton*, 191–216. Cambridge.

Fallon, D., 2003, 'Pre-development testing report on the site of the proposed extension to Trim Credit Union, 18 Market St, Trim, Co. Meath'. Unpublished excavation report.

Firbank, L.G., 1988, 'Biological flora of the British Isles: *Agrostemma githago* L.', *Journal of Ecology* **76**, 1232–46.

Greig-Smith, P., 1948, '*Urtica* L.', *The Journal of Ecology* **36**:2, 339–55.

Grover, N., 1965, 'Man and plants against pain', *Economic Botany* **19**:2, 99–112.

Haney, A., & Kutscheid, B.B., 1975, 'An ecological study of naturalised hemp (*Cannabis sativa* L.) in East-Central Illinois', *American Midland Naturalist* **93**:1, 1–24.

Harper, J.L., & McNaughton, I.H., 1964, '*Papaver* L.', *The Journal of Ecology* **52**:3, 767–93.

Harvey, J.H., 1984, 'Vegetables in the middle ages', *Garden History* **12**:2, 89–99.

Hatcher, P.E., 2003, '*Impatiens noli-tangere* L.', *The Journal of Ecology* **91**:1, 147–67.

Haynes, R.R., & Holm-Nielsen, L.B., 2003, '*Potamogetonaceae*', *Flora Neotropica* **85**, 1–52.

Hewett, D.G., 1964, '*Menyanthes trifoliata* L.', *The Journal of Ecology* **52**:3, 723–35.

Inglis, C.A., & Simpsons, D.A., 2001, 'Cyperaceae of economic, ethnobotanical and horticultural importance: a checklist', *Kew Bulletin* **56**:2, 257–360.

Kay, Q.O.N., 1971, '*Anthemis cotula* L.', *The Journal of Ecology* **59**:2, 623–36.

Lyons, S., 2007, 'Plant remains assessment from the archaeological excavations at Trim, Co. Meath [E2016]'. CRDS Ltd unpublished report.

McVean, D.N., 1953, '*Alnus glutinosa* (L.) Gaertn.', *The Journal of Ecology* **41**:2, 447–66.

Mitich, L.W., 1997, 'Intriguing world of weeds: fumitory (*Fumaria officinalis* L.)', *Weed Technology* **11**, 843–5.

M.R., 1870, '*Aethusa Cynapium* L.', *Bulletin of the Torrey Botanical Club* **1**:3, 12.

New, K.J., 1961, '*Spergula arvensis* L.', *The Journal of Ecology* **49**:1, 205–15.

Newman, L.F., 1979, 'Ophelia's herbal', *Economic Botany* **33**:2, 227–32.

O'Keeffe, T., 2001, *Medieval Ireland: an archaeology*. Stroud, Gloucestershire.

Pearson, K.L., 1997, 'Nutrition and the Early Medieval diet', *Speculum* **72**:1, 1–32.

Pfitzenmeyer, C.D.C., 1962, 'Arrhenatherum elatius (L.) J. &. C. Presl (A. Avenaceum Beauv.)', *Journal of Ecology* **50**:1, 235–45.

Stace, C., 1997, *A new British flora*. Cambridge.

Stevens, C., & Wilkinson, K., 2003, *Environmental archaeology: approaches, techniques and applications*. Stroud, Gloucestershire.

Tanner, F.W., 1922, 'Microbiology of flax-retting', *Botanical Gazette* **74**:2, 174–85.

Timson, J., 1966, '*Polygonum hydropiper* L.', *The Journal of Ecology* **54**:3, 815–21.

Williams, J.T., 1963, '*Chenopodium album* L.', *The Journal of Ecology* **51**:3, 711–25.

APPENDIX 10.2: MEDIEVAL POTTERY FROM 18 MARKET STREET

By Clare McCutcheon

Key

HGA	Ham Green A ware	DTCW	Dublin-type cooking ware
HGB	Ham Green B ware	DTW	Dublin-type ware
HGCW	Ham Green cooking ware	DTF	Dublin-type fineware
SP	Saintonge polychrome	LCW	Leinster Cooking Ware
SGG	Saintonge green-glazed	TTW	Trim-type ware
DTC	Dublin-type coarseware	TTCW	Trim-type cooking ware

Note: Counts based on recovered sherds, before reassembly.

Cut	Fill	Context information	HGA	HGB	HGCW	SP	SGG	DTC	DTCW	DTW	DTF	LCW	TTW	TTCW	Total Sherds
	14	Hearth dump NW quarter								1					1
	23	Medieval wall foundation						2		3		1			6
	31	Metalled surface (FF12, 16, 24, 32, 105)								1	1				2
	35	Medieval garden soil								2					2
42	43	Organic fill of refuse pit								6					6
49	48	Clayey silt within pit						3		3	4		5		15
	51	Deposit overlying F134 medieval pit						1		44			5		50
92	57	Medieval refuse pit cutting ditch F132								1	2	4		1	8
60	62	Medieval back-fill of well								1					1
	67	Clean-back around well					1	1		19	27	2	2		52
151	68	Medieval fill of pit F151								5	6	4			16
	70	Early Med. clay-bonded wall SW quarter										6			6
71	72	Medieval stone-lined socket near well						1							1
196	74	Stone lining of cess-pit								1					1
196	75	Medieval cess-pit								10	2	6	4		22
142	76	Medieval organic fill of pit						1		15					16
83	83	Med. deposit NW quarter, cut by F78						1							1
94	84	Medieval hearth/dump									1				1
96	86	Medieval deposit in shallow cut								1	1				2
92	91	Medieval organic deposit								7	2				10
132	93	Fill of large medieval ditch								1					1
	105	Same as F16/12/24/32/141						2		13	2	1	2	4	24
132	118	Fill of large medieval ditch						4		6					10
	126	Medieval re-deposited clay						1		1					2
	128	Medieval deposit overlying F132 ditch (Sherd link F116)						2		26				1	29
132	129	Fill of large medieval ditch						1		5					6
132	130	Fill of large medieval ditch				1									1
189	134	Medieval fill of pit (Sherd link F10)										1	4	1	6
	137	Dump of ash and charcoal NW quarter								4					4
	139	Med. gritty deposit abutting wall F23								2					2
	145	Med. mottled grey-green clay NE quarter								1					1
149	150	Medieval fill of refuse pit								9					9
151	151	Cut of refuse pit								2					2
	153	Med. natural clay overlying ditch F132						8	1						9
69	156	Medieval organic silting near well								1					1
	157	In situ burning in SE quarter								2					2
159	158	Possible medieval foundation trench					1	1		4					6
	160	Medieval deposit in SE quarter						1	1	17				3	22

Cut	Fill	Context information	HGA	HGB	HGCW	SP	SGG	DTC	DTCW	DTW	DTF	LCW	TTW	TTCW	Total Sherds
	161	Medieval deposit in SE quarter	I						3	8	I	I	I		15
162	163	Fill of cess-pit								11			2		13
162	164	Medieval organic deposit in cesspit								13			3		16
162	165	Medieval organic deposit in cess-pit								10	I		2		13
162	166	Medieval organic deposit in cess-pit								2					2
102	167	Medieval fill within pit								I		I			2
	170	Medieval lens of burning within F174							2	I					3
132	171	Fill of large medieval ditch						I		I		I			3
	173	Lining of hearth associated with F157							I	2	I				4
132	180	Fill of large medieval ditch								I					I
132	183	Fill of large medieval ditch	I						5	6					12
204	188	Fill of medieval pit								6					7
189	190	Packing for large posthole?								6			I		9
196	192	Medieval pit – secondary fill											I		I
196	193	Medieval pit – primary fill								2		3			5
	197	Deposit in SE quarter truncated by F60						I		34	I	I	2		39
189	201	Medieval pit – organic primary fill										I			I
204	207	Medieval pit fill								2					2
60	221	Medieval packing of well F61								9	8	3			21
287	292	Medieval organic pit fill								I					I
297	296	Medieval organic refuse pit											2		2
324	325	Medieval – fill of refuse pit								3					3
	337	Same as F128								2	2				4
340	341	Fill in foundation trench for wall F320								7					7
	348	Medieval wall base								3			6		9
	353	Same as F353/324 – fill of med. pit								2					2
	64	Early post-medieval structure											2		2
	89	Post-medieval						I							I
	124	Post-medieval structure											I		I
	220	Post-med. clay associated with structure	I	I				I	I	46		II	2		63
285	286	Fill associated with post-med. structure								5			I		6
	320	Post-medieval wall								3					3
	334	Late med. – early post-med. SW quarter										5			5
	335	Early post-medieval deposit SW quarter								6	4	4	3		17
	336	Early post-med. stone and mortar deposit								I		2			3
	338	Portion of post-med. surface SW quarter											I		I
	342	Post-med. deposit in SW quarter						I				I			2
	343	Early post-med. dep. between F320+F70								7		3	I		12
	347	Early post-med. re-deposited clay overlying upper ditch fill F128								5					5
356	349	Late med. – early post-med. burnt clay								4		I			5
18	19	Nineteenth-century drain								I					I
36	37	Nineteenth-century building foundation						I							I
	10	Disturbance from testing (Sherd link F134)						2	I	37	II	9	9		72
	11	Modern structural deposit											I		I
53	54	Mod. building foundation										I			I
133	56	Mod. building foundation						I					I		2
120	116	Modern sump (Sherd link F128)								2					2
	182	Unstratified											5		5
	17?									9					9
Totals			2	2	I	I	I	23	31	472	74	76	73	7	766

Excavation of a small site at Market Street, Trim

ALAN R. HAYDEN

INTRODUCTION

The proposed development of a small site on the south side of Market Street, Trim (fig. 1), necessitated advance archaeological excavation as archaeological test-trenching (licence no. 01E1202) had demonstrated the survival of archaeological deposits on the site. The small excavation was undertaken in early 2002. The building standing at the street-front end of the site was retained and refurbished, so the archaeological excavation was confined to the small yards to the rear.

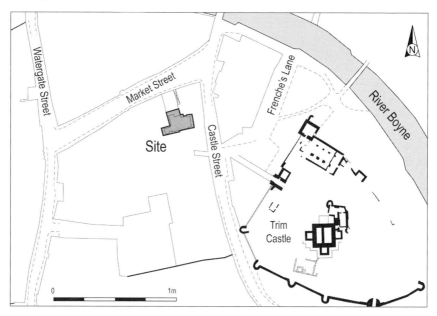

11.1 Location of site and excavated area

EARLY OCCUPATION

The subsoil lay between 0.45 and 1.15m below the modern ground level. The earliest feature uncovered was a substantial north-south aligned ditch at the east side of the site (figs 11.2 & 11.3). The ditch partly underlay adjacent

238

buildings and walls, so it was only possible to excavate a limited part of it. The ditch measured a minimum of 3m in width and may have been in excess of 5m in width at the southern end of the site. It was cut down into the underlying bedrock and measured up to 2m in depth. Its basal fill consisted of structured organic material that contained sherds of Dublin hand-built wares and Ham Green wares. These finds suggest that the ditch was open during the twelfth to earlier thirteenth centuries. Thick layers of re-deposited subsoil filled the majority of the ditch and were suggestive of a returned bank. If such a bank existed, it must have stood on the east side of the ditch as no traces of it were uncovered on the site. A small, unlined hearth lay on top of the infilled ditch, but there were no associated features.

A number of small and shallow pits dating from the later twelfth/early thirteenth to fourteenth centuries were cut into the subsoil on the remainder of the site (fig. 11.2). None measured more than 60cm in depth and all were featureless. The infilled ditch, the pits and most of the site were covered by a layer of medieval cultivated soil which measured up to 30cm in thickness.

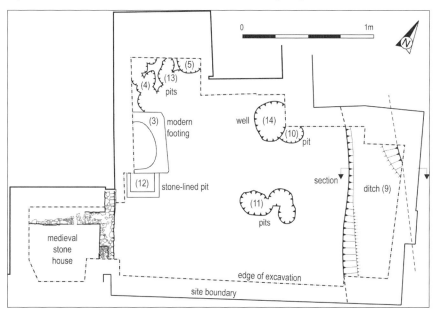

11.2 Features uncovered (see fig. 11.1 for cross-section of ditch (9))

LATE MEDIEVAL STONE BUILDING

A substantial stone-walled medieval building was built in foundation trenches cut into the layer of cultivated soil at the west end of the site (figs 11.2 & 11.4).

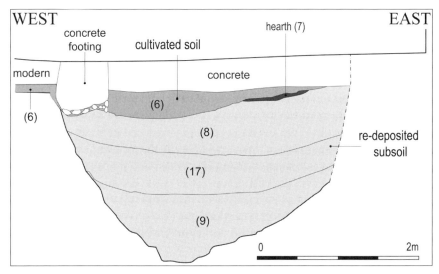

11.3 Section across ditch (see fig. 11.2 for location)

Only part of the building lay within the excavated area. A band of very soft and wet sand (an old glacial melt-water channel) ran north–south in the subsoil under the building and rendered the interior of the structure wet, soft and uneven. The north wall (24) of the building consisted of mortared stone pier and arch footings – a typical medieval response to building on soft ground (fig. 11.5). The north side of the wall was partly removed by later disturbance. The wall measured 72cm in width and survived to a maximum height of 70cm. The surviving masonry probably represents only the footings of the wall.

The east wall (21) of the building consisted of conventionally laid, mortared masonry. This wall measured 90cm in width and survived to a height of 50cm. Part of a fireplace, which survived only as a shallow, rectangular alcove measuring 54cm in depth and at least 70cm in width, remained in this wall of the building. The stones in its base and sides were all fire-reddened and cracked.

A series of clay floors and occupation levels, separated by deposits likely to represent phases of abandonment, survived in the building. A patchy floor of yellow clay covered in a thin layer of burnt material (28) survived on the harder subsoil; it did not survive over the softer sand-filled channel. There was a small, unlined hearth on the floor at the west end of the site. The floor beneath it was heavily oxidized. The fireplace in the east wall was also in use at this time and was covered by a thin layer of ash. The floor adjacent to the fireplace was also heavily oxidized. A post-hole and a large flat stone laid in a pit (a post-pad) set on the central axis of the building may represent an attempt to prop up a sagging timber first floor. A thick layer of stony silt and ash (27) sealed the floor and hearths.

The building may then have been refurbished, as a 2–3cm-thick layer of mortar (25) survived over much of its interior. This had a thin layer of yellow clay flooring (26) that spread into the fireplace where it was covered in ash, attesting to the continued use of the fireplace. A second phase of abandonment is represented by a thick layer of grey silty clay (22) that contained many stones that overlay the clay floor.

The ground floor of the building was then re-occupied again when a thin yellow clay floor (23) was laid down within the building. This floor survived very poorly, but also extended into the area of the fireplace. Burnt material again overlay the floor within the fireplace, showing that it was re-used. It was overlain by a thick layer of loose stony loamy soil (20) that represents another phase of abandonment. This deposit included a spread of charcoal (19).

The final occupation level consisted of a very poorly-preserved yellow clay floor (16). This survived only down the centre of the building and had no physical links with the walls and so could even post-date the demolition of the structure.

A mortar-bonded stone wall (30) extended north from the northeast corner of the stone building (figs 11.2 & 11.4). The wall was narrower than the walls of the building and had a clearly projecting footing, on its east side at least; it was not possible to excavate the base of the west side of the wall. This wall, in an altered and rebuilt state, forms the western boundary of the main part of the site.

A thick accumulation of late- and post-medieval soft, brown cultivation soil (2) built up over the underlying medieval cultivation soil (1) outside the east side of the medieval stone building and the stone wall running north from it. This material survived only in a narrow band less than 2m in width along this part of the site. It contained late medieval pottery and roof-tiles.

A mortared, stone-lined pit (12) with a stone-flagged base was built in the late medieval cultivation soil to the east of the wall running west from the medieval house (fig. 11.2). The pit had inclined sides and could have been a cess-pit connected with the later phases of the building. It was filled with the same soft soil (2) into which it was cut. Its west side was cut away by a modern mass concrete footing (3).

There was a deep pit (14) cut through the early cultivation soil (1) at the centre of the north side of the site (fig. 11.2). The pit was cut into bedrock and was at least 2m in depth. It was filled with soft, wet organic material, ash, charcoal and silt. It was not possible to fully excavate it as it extended beyond the edge of the site and its soft and very wet fill was highly unstable. The fact that it was rock-cut and held water suggests that it may have been a well.

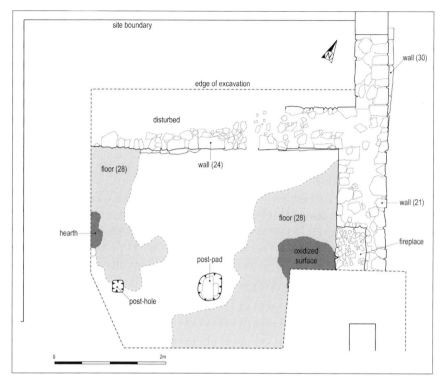

11.4 Late medieval stone building

ARTEFACTS

The small assemblage of finds uncovered included 299 sherds of medieval and post-medieval pottery, a small number of fragments of twelfth-century curved roof-tile (identical to those used on the roof of the first phases of the keep of the Trim Castle), several sherds of later medieval flat roof-tiles and a single fragment of an unclassifiable line-impressed floor-tile.

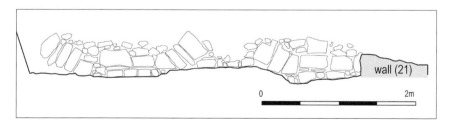

11.5 Elevation of internal face of north wall of medieval building

DISCUSSION

The presence of the medieval stone building on the site is echoed in a number of other sites excavated in Trim (for example on High Street; see paper in present volume). The fireplace in the building shows that it was intended as a habitation. It probably stood at the rear end of a courtyard behind the main street-front building on Market Street. It was not possible to date the building more precisely than to the fourteenth or fifteenth century, due to the lack of closely datable finds. It certainly went out of use, however, and was demolished by the seventeenth century. The town of Trim (along with its castle) went into serious decline at the end of the sixteenth century, from which it did not recover until the late twentieth century. The demise of the excavated building appears to relate to this decline.

A medieval stone building and other deposits at 27 High Street, Trim

CARMEL DUFFY

with contributions by CLARE McCUTCHEON, PATRICIA LYNCH
& SUSAN LYONS

INTRODUCTION

Archaeological monitoring and limited excavation (06E0418) at 27 High Street, Trim, revealed medieval deposits, pits and the corner of a stone medieval house with the remaining deposits preserved in situ. Specialist examination of artefacts and soil samples was carried out, providing interesting insights into the use of the site.

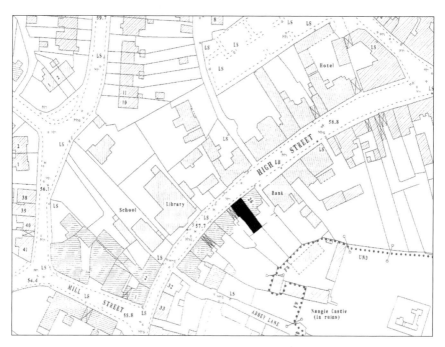

12.1 Site location on High Street (base-map courtesy of Ordnance Survey Ireland, Permit 8565 © Ordnance Survey Ireland/Government of Ireland)

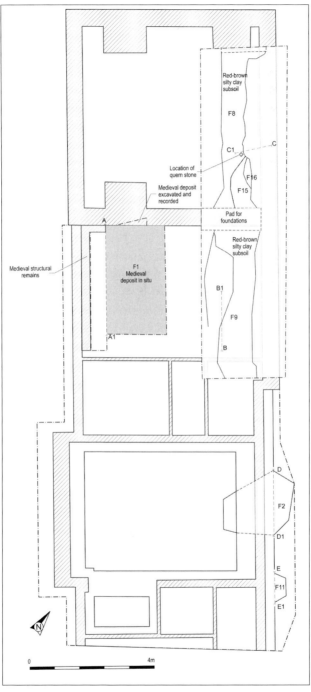

12.2 Location of excavated features at 27 High Street (based on original plan by Carmel Duffy, redrawn by Niall Lynch (CRDS))

High Street is located on the northern side of the River Boyne and continues the curve of Castle Street around the space enclosing St Mary's Augustinian priory, 70m to the southeast of the site. An urban tower house known as Nangle's Castle survives to first floor level, just to the west of the Yellow Steeple, and this may have been part of the monastic complex. It lies 20m to the southeast of the site. Excavations by Claire Walsh on the site of the new library on High Street uncovered the remains of a probable thirteenth-century house, clay floors and yards (Walsh 1990/1; Potterton 2005, 202). Testing carried out in 2001 by Linda Clarke at Abbey Lane revealed property boundary walls, most likely from a burgage plot, and a medieval occupation layer 1.1m below existing ground level (Clarke 2003). Extensive excavations by Alan Hayden also located medieval stone buildings on High Street (Hayden, 'High Street', this volume).

The archaeological features encountered are described here from the front (northwest) to the rear (southeast). Along the north-eastern edge of the site, a series of medieval deposits were exposed, but these were below the level for excavation. A series of dark silty clays were exposed (F15 & F16). The latter overlay a quernstone, which ran beneath the wall of the adjoining property. Two localized medieval deposits containing animal bone were also uncovered in the northeast corner of the site (F7 & F10).

Medieval building and deposits
On the western side of the building, excavations uncovered large, loose stones overlying a black, silty clay containing animal bone, shell, Dublin-type ware and Trim-type ware (F1). The clay also contained animal bone and a single fragment of human bone. It was up to 1.4m in depth and overlay the corner of a medieval building, which projected obliquely into the west foundation trench (F18). This wall was excavated in a narrow area to a depth of 70cm. The exposed corner measured 60cm east-west by 1.6m northwest-southeast. It was built of rectangular limestone blocks. Medieval pottery and a quantity of roof-slate fragments were recovered from the base of the wall. The wall was abutted to the east from the basal level upward by dark brown, silty peat-like clay, yellow-brown, gritty clay, and mid-brown, silty clay, all of which contained Dublin-type and Trim-type ware (F6, F5, F4 & F1).

Further to the east, excavations uncovered a series of dark brown, silty clays, which contained animal bone, Dublin-type coarseware and Dublin-type ware (F9 & F12). They overlay grey, sandy clay, which also had the same inclusions. These were contained within a substantial hollow (F17).

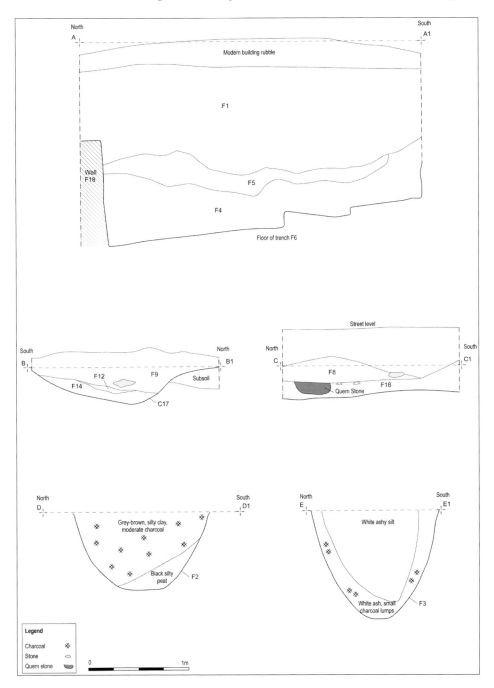

12.3 Sections through excavated features at 27 High Street (based on original section drawings by Carmel Duffy, redrawn by Niall Lynch (CRDS))

Medieval pits

Three refuse pits were uncovered within foundation trenches. F2 and F11 were located on the south-eastern edge of the site. F3 was located on the south-western edge, 16m south of High Street.

Table 12.1 Refuse pits at western and eastern edges of site

Pit	Width x depth	Deposits	Inclusions
F3	1.1m x 0.9m	White, ashy silt/charcoal	None
F11	1.2m x 1m	Dark, brown silty clay	Animal bone and charcoal
F2	2.1m x 1.1m	Grey brown, silty clay over black, silty peat	Moderate charcoal pieces and bone fragments. Medieval pottery – Dublin-type, Leinster Cooking Ware, Dublin-type cooking ware

Garden soil deposits

There was a large amount of garden soil forming a ramp 1m deep and 4m north-south by 9m east-west towards the back of the site. It was composed of loose, black, silty clay, with inclusions of post-medieval pottery, medieval and post-medieval roof-tiles and animal bone. There were also twenty-seven fragments of human bone.

12.4 Photograph of corner of medieval building (wall highlighted), looking northeast

CONCLUSIONS

The archaeological monitoring and limited excavation at 27 High Street uncovered part of a stone building on the south side of the street. A series of deposits built up within this building and contained thirteenth- fourteenth-century pottery. Roof-slates in direct contact with the lowest part of the wall suggest that, at some stage, the building had a slate roof. Fragments of medieval curved roof-tiles indicate another roof-form. The lowest deposits within the building contained cereal and chaff, suggesting that primary cereal-processing was carried out here. This would include winnowing and threshing of the crop. The quernstone, which remains in situ, may have been re-used as the base of a hearth, with the stone used as a baking slab, given the overlying charcoal rich deposits. To the southeast, a series of pits may have been used for refuse, with further evidence of grain and chaff within the hollow to the east. The presence of chaff is unusual considering its absence from samples at Market Street, Kiely's Yard and Athboy Gate (Appendices 8.2, 10.1). On these sites the cereal may have arrived as a dried crop ready for grinding.

Much of the evidence for diet and economy came from deposits which post-date the stone building, but still appear to be thirteenth- / fourteenth-century in date. The osteological assemblage is indicative of a society producing its own food by raising animals for milk and meat. The shell content may indicate a fish element in the diet, while a grape seed indicates an exotic element. This can be compared with Market Street, where excavations uncovered a fig within a pit (Fallon, this volume).

The garden soil deposits to the rear of the pits indicate cultivation in the post-medieval period. Human bone was present in a series of the later and post-medieval deposits, and this is likely to have come from the adjacent graveyard of St Mary's Abbey.

ACKNOWLEDGMENT

The author would like to thank Aidan Heffernan, for providing funding for the works.

BIBLIOGRAPHY

Clarke, L., 2003, 'Friar's Park, Abbey Lane, Trim' in Bennett, I. (ed.), *Excavations 2001: summary accounts of archaeological excavations in Ireland*, no. 1060, pp 337–8. Bray.
Potterton, M., 2005, *Medieval Trim: history and archaeology*. Dublin.
Walsh, C., 1990/1, 'An excavation at the library site, High Street, Trim', *Ríocht na Midhe* 8, 41–67.

APPENDIX 12.1: SUMMARY OF MEDIEVAL POTTERY REPORT
By Clare McCutcheon

The bulk of the medieval ceramics identified are further discussed elsewhere in this volume (McCutcheon & Meenan). The minimum number of vessels recorded was quite small, with a total of eight possibles (cooking jars and jugs) represented by fifty-seven sherds. Analysis of the stratification of these types did not refine the dating, as pottery of thirteenth-/fourteenth-century date was present in the lowest levels.

Table 12.2 High Street pottery, by context

Feature	Feature description	Fabric type
1	Medieval material base of F1	Dublin-type ware (x1), Trim-type ware (x1)
1	Upper fill of medieval pit/deposit	Dublin-type ware (x3), Trim-type ware (x6)
1	Pad 5	Trim-type ware (x4)
2	Eastern foundation	Dublin-type ware (x1), Brick (x1)
2	Western section of eastern trench	Leinster Cooking Ware (x1), Dublin-type cooking ware (x1), Dublin-type ware (x1)
2	Medieval pit, eastern section	Dublin-type ware (x1)
4	Yellow soil abutting medieval wall	Dublin-type ware (x3), Trim-type ware (x4)
5	Purple clay (Sherd link F9)	Dublin-type ware (x2)
5	Peat-like clayey silt abutting medieval wall	Dublin-type ware (x1)
9	East wall trench, north of second back wall of old house	Dublin-type ware (x1)
9	(Sherd link F5)	Dublin-type cooking ware (x2), Dublin-type coarseware (x2), Dublin-type ware (x18), Brick (x1)
15	Post-medieval deposit at north-western edge of site	Dublin-type ware (x1), Trim-type ware (x1), Glazed red earthenware (x1)
TS	Garden soil to rear (south) of where building stood	Porcelain (x1), Spongeware (x1), Transfer printed ware (x2), Over-painted pearlware (x1), Unglazed red earthenware (x3), Chinaware (x1), Stoneware (x4), Clay pipe (x1 Honest John Martin), Glass (moulded bottle), Glass (window)
TS	Ramp	Black glazed ware (x3), Mochaware (x1), Chinaware (x1), Pantile (x1)
TS	Topsoil: from western foundation	GRE: slip coated (x1), Brick (x1)
TS	Sewer trench	Black glazed ware (x4), Unglazed red earthenware (x2), Transfer printed ware (x4), Lustreware (x1), Spongeware (x2), Stoneware (x1), Curved roof-tile (medieval) (x3), Pantile (x4)
TS	Disturbed contexts	Trim-type ware (x1), Unglazed red earthenware roof-tile edge (x1)

APPENDIX 12.2: SUMMARY OF OSTEOLOGICAL ANALYSIS

By Patricia Lynch

Osteoarchaeological analysis of the bone recovered from the site at 27 High Street was carried out by Patricia Lynch. In total, 611 human and animal bones, one horn and fifty-eight tooth fragments were examined. The bone from the site was largely animal, with horse (*equus*), cow (*bos*), pig (*sus*), deer (*cervid*), goat (*capra*), sheep/goat (caprine), dog (*canis*), cat (*felis*), common hare (*lepus Europeaus*) and domestic fowl all represented. The age of the adult and sub-adult animals was estimated on the basis of dental eruption, epiphyseal union and tooth wear. The age structure of the bones suggests an organized society in which animals were used as a food source.

The remains of four humans were identified: one child aged between 8 and 10 years at death, one female aged between 17 and 25 (No. 5), and two adults of undetermined sex (Nos 2 & 18). Table 12.3 summarizes the results of the analysis of the High Street bone assemblage.

Table 12.3 Animal and human bones recovered from 27 High Street ('~' symbol denotes presence of pathology on bone; '*' symbol indicates evidence for post-mortem trauma. Bold Capra indicates identified goat

Feature & find #	Human	Equus	Bos	Sus	Capra/Caprine	Cervid	Canis	Felis	Fowl	Lepus	Unid?	S.a?	S.a. Bos	S.a. Sus	S.a. Caprine
F1, find # 18, 27, 31	1	1	2~*	1	2							2	1	1	
F2, find # 10, 12, 13	1~	1													
F4, find # 14, 16, 25	1	1~	2	1	1	1									
F4/5, find # 30	1	1													
F5, find # 22	1~														
F7, find # 24	2	1													
F8, find # 29	2~	1*	1	2	1	1									
F9, find # 26	1	1	1	1	1										
F14, find # 12	1	1	1												
F15, find # 33	1	1~	1	1											
Find # 2	1	1	1	1											
Find # 5	2~	1	1	1											
Find # 7	1														
Find # 9	1														
Find # 11	1~	1	1~*												
Find # 23	1														
Find # 34			2	1	1~									1	1
Total	4	3	18	4	1, 12	1	1	1	2	1	3	6	5	3	2

APPENDIX 12.3: PLANT REMAINS

By Susan Lyons

BACKGROUND

The excavation at 27 High Street identified a series of deposits containing evidence for medieval domestic debris. Five soil samples, totalling approximately twelve litres, were taken from each deposit recorded (Features 001, 004, 005, 006 & 012) and these were submitted to Headland Archaeology Ltd to assess their archaeological potential.

METHODOLOGY FOR SAMPLE ASSESSMENT

The soil samples were subjected to a system of flotation in a Siraf-style flotation tank. The floating debris (flot) was collected in a 250µm sieve and, once dry, this was scanned using a binocular microscope. Any remaining material in the flotation tank (retent) was wet-sieved through a 1mm mesh, and then air-dried. This was then sorted by eye and any material of archaeological significance was collected. The botanical remains recorded were preserved by charring. The results are presented in Tables 12.4 and 12.5.

Table 12.4 Composition of retents from flotation of samples from 27 High Street, Trim (key: + = rare; ++ = occasional; +++ = common; and ++++ = abundant; * = sufficient for AMS [Accelerator Mass Spectrometry] dating)

Context No.	Retent vol. (l.)	Context/sample description	Wood charcoal		Carbonized hazelnut shell	Carbonized cereal grain	Mammal bone		Mollusca	Metallic debris
			Qty	AMS			Burnt	Unburnt		
001	1	Deposit abutting wall; silty clay including charcoal, bone and medieval pottery; associated with F001	+++	*				+++		
005	2	Peat-like, clayey silt at north end of foundation trench; associated with F001	+++	*			++	+++		
004	1	Yellow-brown, gritty, stony sand with iron inclusions		*		*		+	+	
006	0.3	Dark brown, silty clay associated with F001	+++	*	+		+	++	+	+
012	1	Black, fibrous, peat-like deposit; fill of F009	++	*	+			++	++	

Table 12.5 Composition of flots from flotation of samples from 27 High Street, Trim (key: + = rare; ++ = occasional; +++ = common; and ++++ = abundant; * = sufficient for AMS [Accelerator Mass Spectrometry] dating)

Context no.	Flot vol. (ml)	Context/ sample description	Wood charcoal Qty AMS	Carbonized cereal grain	Carbonized cereal chaff	Carbonized/economic species wild taxa	Comments
001	10	Deposit abutting wall; silty clay including charcoal, bone and medieval pottery; associated with F001	+	+			Cereal indet. + *Vitis vinifera* +
005	10	Peat-like clayey silt at north end of foundation trench; associated with F001	+	++			Oat ++ Wheat +
004	10	Yellow-brown, gritty, stony sand with iron inclusions	+				
006	10	Dark brown, silty clay associated with F001	+	+++	++		Oat ++ Wheat + Cereal indet. + Oat palae & lemma + Cereal chaff (culm nodes ++)
012	20	Black, fibrous, peat-like deposit; fill of F009	+++	+++	+	+	Oat ++ Wheat + Barley + Rye + Cereal chaff (culm nodes ++) *Raphanus raphanistrum* +

RESULTS

Carbonized plant remains

Wood charcoal Charcoal was recovered from all five samples. The highest concentrations were recovered from Features 001, 005 and 006. The charcoal material was very fragmented, but in a good state of preservation.

Carbonized hazelnut shell Fragments of carbonized hazelnut shell were recovered from Features 006 and 012.

Cereal grain Evidence for cereal grain was identified from all samples with the exception of Feature 004. A relatively high concentration of carbonized cereal grain was identified from Features 006 and 012. Oat (*Avena* sp.), wheat (tentatively identified as bread wheat (*Triticum aestivo-compactum*)), barley (*Hordeum vulgare*) and a single rye (*Secale cereale*) grain were all present, but the preservation in all samples was generally poor, the grain being very vesicular and eroded. The vesicular character could be indicative of the grain having been charred at high temperatures, if the grain was damp when burnt or open to exposure. Oat and wheat were by far the most common crops present. Barley and rye grains were recorded in much lower numbers.

Cereal chaff With the presence of oat chaff in the form of palae and lemma, it was possible to further identify the oat to the cultivated or common type (*Avena sativa*) in some cases. Larger elements of cereal chaff and straw (culm nodes) were also recorded. Based on the fragmented nature of the material, however, it was difficult to identify further.

Wild taxa/economic species A solitary siliqua of wild radish (*Raphanus raphanistrum*) was identified from Feature 012.

Uncarbonized plant remains
A single grape (*Vitis vinifera*) seed was recorded from Feature 001. It was uncarbonized, suggesting that the deposit in which it was found was potentially partially waterlogged, which would have offered suitable preservation conditions for such material to survive.

Animal bone
Burnt bone Three features (005, 006 & 012) contained fragments of burnt bone of medium- to larger-sized mammals (Tourunen, pers. comm.).

Unburnt bone Fragments of unburnt bone were recorded from all samples. Medium-sized and larger mammals, such as rabbit, sheep, goat and cow were identified (Tourunen, pers. comm.) from Features 001, 004, 005 and 012, while Feature 006 contained fish bones.

Mollusca
Features 004 and 005 contained low concentrations of shell fragments. Mollusc shell assemblages can often be found in sediments associated with standing water. With such a small assemblage, however, it is difficult to ascertain whether these represent terrestrial or marine species and how they came to be in these deposits.

Metallic debris
A fragment of a corroded metal (copper) object was recovered from Feature 006.

DISCUSSION

The soil samples from 27 High Street contained an array of archaeo-botanical material and archaeological remains indicative of medieval domestic debris. Charcoal was frequently present, which is a common result of occupational activity, reflecting the use of hearths on and around the site. The lack of any conflagration deposits suggests that this material was secondary or tertiary deposition, re-distributed across the site and dumped into open features. The carbonized hazelnut shell may have been the waste debris of gathered foodstuffs, the remnants of drying or parching hazelnuts near or over a fire and/or material collected with hazel wood for fuel or kindling. Since the shell was recorded in such low concentrations, however, its origins here are uncertain.

The presence of oat, barley, wheat and rye collectively reflects a typical medieval crop assemblage, similar to those recorded from Drogheda (Mitchell & Dickson 1985), Waterford (Tierney & Hannon 1997), Cork (McClatchie 2003) and Cashel (Lyons 2003), to name but a few. All four cereals would have been processed for human consumption, as well as being used for animal fodder (oat) and possibly thatch (rye). While oat and wheat were identified as the dominant grain types, oat was recorded in slightly higher frequencies than the latter. High incidences of oat are also noted from drying kilns at Kilferagh, Co. Kilkenny (Monk 1987a), Ballyveelish, Co. Tipperary (Monk 1987b) and James Street, Drogheda, Co. Louth (Monk 1988). This could be due to the simple fact that oat and wheat were the primary crop-types processed in this area or at this period in time.

Many of the grains were abraded, which implies that the material may have been left exposed prior to deposition. It is likely, therefore, that it entered the deposits inadvertently during back-filling or levelling of the site.

The cereal chaff elements in the assemblage are undoubtedly the remains of crop preparation, in the form of threshing or raking or winnowing the grain. Whether this activity was carried out in the vicinity is difficult to ascertain. The weed seed component of the samples is generally low and is likely to have been brought to the site with the gathered crop. *Raphanus raphanistrum* (wild radish) was a common and troublesome weed of cultivation, particularly during the medieval period, only becoming marginalized after the introduction of herbicides. It is also possible that the chaff and weeds were brought to the site to be dried and used for animal fodder, or perhaps as fuel.

The presence of an uncarbonized grape seed suggests that certain luxury foodstuffs were imported, probably in a dried form, from countries such as France or Spain (McClatchie 2003, 401). It is possible that the grape seed represents an element of cess material and that such waste material was incorporated into these deposits.

The botanical remains, together with the animal/fish bones and metal debris from the deposits at High Street, Trim, are likely to reflect the gradual accumulation and/or dumping of domestic rubbish and material associated with waste matter from cess-pits, latrines or drains, which would have been common features in urban medieval centres such as Trim.

ACKNOWLEDGMENT

The author would like to thank faunal remains specialist, Auli Tourunen MA, for her help with identifying the animal bone assemblage.

BIBLIOGRAPHY

Lyons, S., 2004, 'The waterlogged and carbonised plant remains' in C. Moloney & C. Gleeson, 'Chapel lane, Cashel, Co. Tipperary: a final report on the archaeological rescue excavation (licence no. 03E0396)'. Headland Archaeology unpublished report.
McClatchie, M., 2003, 'The plant remains' in Cleary, R.M. & Hurley, M.F., *Cork city excavations, 1984–2000*, 391–413. Cork.
Mitchell, G.F., & Dickson, C.A., 1985, 'Plant remains and other items from medieval Drogheda', *Circaea* 3:1, 31–7.
Monk, M.A., 1987a, 'Appendix II: Kilferagh, Co. Kilkenny, charred seeds and plant remains' in Cleary, R.C., Hurley, M.F. & Shee-Twohig, E. (eds), *Archaeological excavations on the Cork-Dublin gas pipeline (1981–1982)*, 98–9. Cork.
Monk, M.A., 1987b, 'Appendix IV: Ballyveelish, Co. Tipperary, charred plant remains' in Cleary, R.C., Hurley, M.F. & Shee-Twohig, E. (eds), *Archaeological excavations on the Cork-Dublin gas pipeline (1981–1982)*, 86–7. Cork.
Monk, M.A., 1988, 'Appendix 3: archaeobotanical study of samples from pipeline site' in Gowen, M., Condit, E. & Cooney, G. (eds), *Three Irish gas pipelines: new archaeological evidence in Munster*, 185–91. Dublin.
Tierney, J., & Hannon, M., 1997, 'Plant remains' in Hurley, M.F. & Scully, O.M.B., *Late Viking-Age and medieval Waterford: excavations 1986–1992*, 854–93. Waterford.

Excavation of a site at High Street, Trim

ALAN R. HAYDEN

INTRODUCTION

The archaeological assessment (licence no. 01E1146) of a proposed development site on the south side of High Street, Trim, revealed that substantial archaeological deposits survived (fig. 13.1). As the proposed development could not avoid disturbing the remains, the site was excavated in February

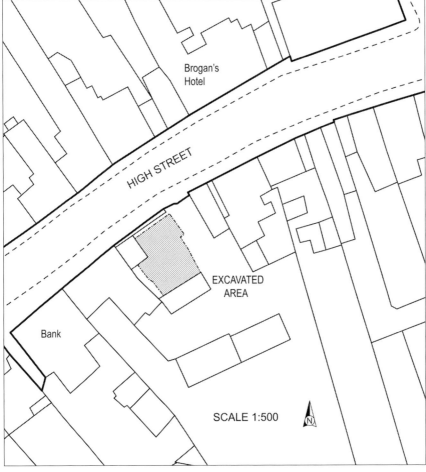

13.1 Location of excavated site

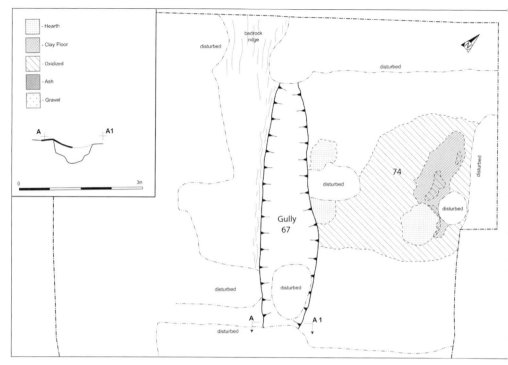

13.2 Phase 1: pre-Anglo-Norman features

2002. Bedrock lay less than a metre below the modern ground surface, which is typical of many areas in the town. The rear half of the site was completely disturbed by modern building, but a surprising number of levels of medieval activity survived on the front end of the site.

PHASE I: PRE-ANGLO-NORMAN (?)

The earliest human activity evidenced on the site consisted of a north-south aligned gully (67) and spreads of burnt material (74) emanating from a number of hearths (fig. 13.2). The gully (67) bisected the site, but its north and south ends were truncated by later activity. To its west the subsoil stood about 25cm higher than to its east, due to the presence of a slight bedrock ridge, the edge of which the gully followed. The gully measured up to 1.4m in width and 60cm in depth. It was infilled with grey stony soil that contained small fragments of carbonized material and a few sherds of Dublin hand-built ware and Leinster Cooking Ware.

East of the gully there were three small unlined hearths lying on the subsoil. They were surrounded by an area where the underlying subsoil was oxidized or

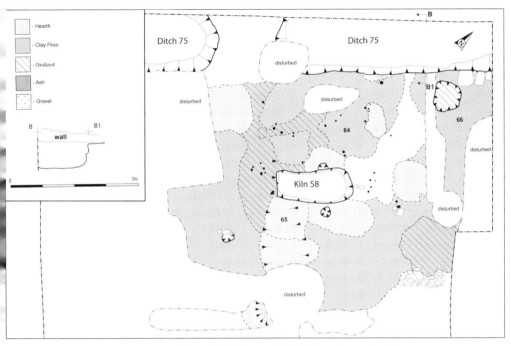

13.3 Phase 2, level 1a and 1b features: ditch, kiln and metalworking

covered by a very thin scattering of ash (74). There were no post- or stake-holes or other features. The burnt deposits were covered by a 2–30cm thick layer of decayed topsoil (68), which contained a few tiny sherds of Leinster Cooking Ware. The presence of the old topsoil layer over the features of this level suggests a period of abandonment when the site returned to grassland.

PHASE 2: ANGLO-NORMAN MEDIEVAL OCCUPATION

Level 1a (fig. 13.3)

After the phase of abandonment, a deep ditch (75) was excavated into bedrock along the northern edge of the site, parallel to High Street. A gap was left where the ditch crossed the higher bedrock ridge. The north side of the ditch lay outside the excavated area. The ditch measured at least 1.3m in width, had roughly vertical rock-cut sides, and measured up to 85cm in depth. It was back-filled with stone and gravel (70), which contained tiny fragments of broken shells, a few animal bones and one sherd of a rod handle from a thirteenth-century green-glazed vessel. The same type of gravel used to fill the ditch was also spread out on the ground to the south.

A yellow clay floor (64/66) was laid down over most of the site. Its north side, where it ran alongside the ditch, was revetted with stone and followed the

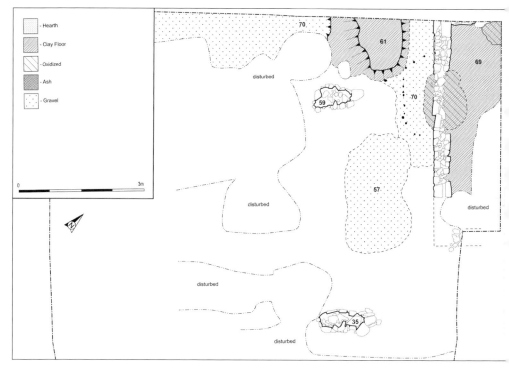

13.4 Phase 2, level 1c features: first medieval building and associated features

line of the ditch, suggesting that the latter was still open at the time. The bases of a number of unlined hearths survived on the floor and much of its surface was heavily oxidized, burnt and covered by layers of ash (65). There were a number of post- and stake-holes in the floor, but they did not conform to any recognizable pattern. Two shallow pits were cut into the east side of the floor. Both were filled with charcoal. The small hearths appear to have been used for metalworking and evidence suggests that similar activity continued on the site for a number of years.

Level 1b (fig. 13.3)
A rectangular pit (58), with a small rounded out-shot from the centre of its north side, was cut through the layers of ash and the hearths on the floor. The base and sides of the pit were heavily oxidized, and it was filled with loam that contained a lot of ash and charcoal. Its regular lines and the small out-shot suggest that this may have been the base of a kiln.

Level 1c (fig. 13.4)
The possible kiln was partly infilled with a layer of small, broken and fire-cracked stones in a matrix of gravely loam (57) and a mound of very

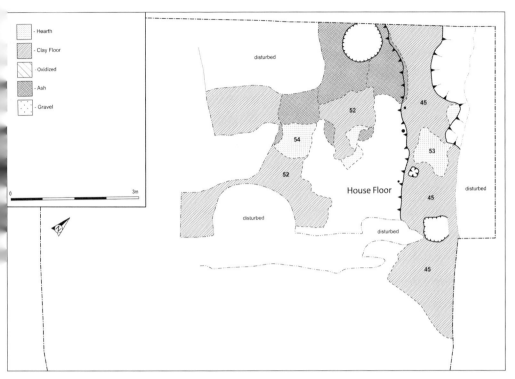

13.5 Phase 2, levels 2a and 2b: house floor and metalworking

compacted stony greenish clay (61) was spread over the burnt floor. A small stone-footed building (62) was then built at the northeast corner of the site. The dry-stone wall-footings were laid in a trench that was cut into the underlying clay floor and the infilled ditch at the north side of the site. The footing measured 40cm in width and survived to two stones in height. The full length of the west side of the structure survived, and it measured 4.75m in length internally. Part of its internal northwest corner also survived, but the north wall was largely removed by later disturbance. The line of the southern end wall partially survived but was also badly disturbed. The stone footing would have held large wooden sill-beams on which the walls of the building were constructed. Only a small part of the internal clay floor (69) survived, at the extreme north end of the building. There, its surface was heavily oxidized and burnt. The wall was partly removed at some stage, and an arc of stake-holes (63) defined an area 1.8m in length and 50cm across outside the line of the breach.

A pair of parallel east-west-aligned sub-rectangular pits (59 & 35), set 4.5m apart, were cut into the underlying burnt layers to the west of the house. Both were of similar size (1.4m in length, 50–60cm in width and 20cm–30cm in depth), and both were packed with stone. They form an obvious pair, and were probably the post-holes of a structure contemporary with the stone-footed building. The floored area to the west of the building was overlain by a thick layer of ash and burnt deposits (55/56).

The pottery from levels 1a and 1b consisted of Dublin wheel-thrown wares and Leinster Cooking Ware, which are not closely datable. It is likely, however, that these levels date from the thirteenth century. The presence of sherds of Saintonge green-glazed and Dublin temper-free ware in the deposits of level 1c suggest that it dated to the later thirteenth or earlier fourteenth century.

Level 2a (fig. 13.5)

Another building, this time with the wooden sill-beam walls (which left no traces) laid directly on the ground, was erected at the northeast corner of the site. The building had an internal grey clay floor (45) that covered an area measuring 7.2m in length north-south. It had a relatively straight west side, indicating the line of the side-wall of the building. A hearth (53), which measured a maximum of 1.2m across, lay on the centre of the west side of the floor. Apart from three stake-holes (which probably secured the sill-beam wall in place), no other structural elements survived.

After the building was demolished, a deposit of red ash covered the northwest corner of the clay floor and spread outwards to the west of the floor. It was in turn cut through by a 90cm diameter and 5–10cm deep pit. These features did not contain any finds.

Level 2b (fig. 13.5)

Another clay floor (52) – this time composed of yellow clay – was laid down at the centre of the north end of the site. This survived poorly due to later disturbance, but covered an area measuring at least 5.5m north-south by 3.7m east-west. The northwest corner of the floor was heavily oxidized, and covered by a layer of red ash. An unlined hearth (54) on the floor had a diameter of one metre. It consisted of a 10cm-thick layer of finely comminuted charcoal fragments that contained several large lumps of iron slag. Part of a second, smaller hearth survived to its east. The latter consisted of a thin deposit of red ash and again the clay floor beneath it was heavily oxidized. Spreads of carbonized material (44) and gravel (43) covered the floors. The clay floor at this level is unlikely to have lain inside a building, and the features simply represent continued metalworking on this part of the site.

Level 3 (fig. 13.6)

A large stone-walled building (25), with a stone-lined cess-pit (47) to its rear, was erected at the west side of the site. Only its rearmost 4.3m survived; the rest of the building was removed when a temporary bank premises was built on the site in modern times. The western side of the building lay beyond the area available for excavation; a maximum width of 3.4m of the building was revealed.

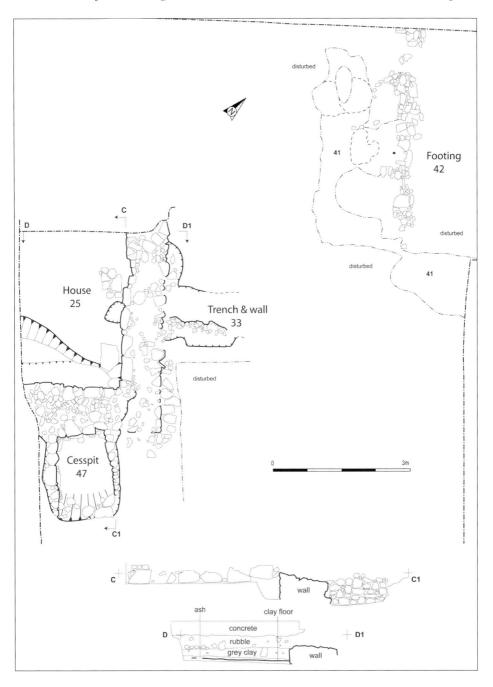

13.6 Phase 3, level 3: stone house and stone-footed timber house

The building was erected in a shallow pit cut about 30cm deep into the subsoil. Its walls survived only to the level of the top of the pit. They were faced internally with large, sub-rectangular, undressed limestone blocks. A possible off-set on the outer side of the footing survived at the southeast corner of the building and shows that the east wall (as opposed to the footings) originally measured about 90cm in width. The south wall measured 1m in width. The primary floor of the building consisted of the underlying gravely subsoil, which was covered by a thin occupation deposit consisting of burnt and organic material (73). A patchy yellow clay floor (71), with a stone-based hearth (72), was laid down over the primary occupation deposits at the east side of the building. There was a small charcoal-filled hollow to the south of the hearth. A thicker occupation deposit (27) overlay the secondary clay floor. It consisted of burnt and organic material and there was a thick layer of ash at the centre of the building.

There was a partly stone-lined cess-pit (47) outside the south end of the building. The pit measured 1.8m by 1.2m across, and up to 74cm in depth. It was built at the same time as the walls of the house, partly utilizing the pit (46). The cess-pit was walled on its east and west sides by rough dry-stone walling. The south wall of the house formed its north side, while its sloping south side, which was composed of bedrock, was unlined. A layer of light brown silt (60), which contained a number of large stones, filled the base of the pit. A 17cm-thick layer of black cess (51), containing occasional twigs, overlay the silt. This was in turn overlain by a thin layer of charcoal (50).

A 20cm deep and 80cm–1.2m-wide trench (33) extended for a distance of 2m eastwards from the east wall of the stone house. The southern side of the trench was retained by a rough dry-stone wall composed of small stones less than 15cm across. The wall was faced only on its north side.

A contemporary and smaller building was evidenced by a very poorly built, rough dry-stone footing (42) at the northeast side of the site, in the same location as the two earlier buildings. The footing measured 50cm in width and survived for a length of 4.9m. It stood to a maximum of two stones in height. A poorly-preserved grey clay floor (41) was laid down outside and to the west and south of the building. Its full original extent is not clear, as its west side was removed by later disturbance. There were three 70–80cm diameter unlined hearths on the floor. The floor under each was heavily oxidized, and all were covered by 5–10cm of lenses of red, orange and white ash, which inter-leaved with a general layer of burnt deposits (40) that covered the floor. Again, these burnt deposits indicate that metalworking was still being undertaken on the site.

Level 4a (fig. 13.7)

A patchy clay floor (39) survived at the northeast corner of the site overlying the Level 3 building and burnt floors. The floor only survived in small patches

13.7 Phase 2, levels 4a and 4b

and was featureless. A 20–30cm thick build up of ash, charcoal fragments and lumps of oxidized clay (37) overlay the floor and spread out to cover much of the northeast part of the site. The deposits ended abruptly on the line of the underlying building walls. This suggests that there was also some form of boundary on this line at this level. There were three orange ash-covered, 30–45cm diameter hearths within these layers. The hearths were unlined. One had a stake-hole in it, and there were several other isolated stake-holes not conforming to any pattern in and to the east of the burnt deposits. On top of the burnt deposits at the north end of the site was a hearth that measured 80cm in diameter. It was covered by up to 5mm of hard red ash.

At the extreme northeast corner of the site, where the burnt deposits (37) did not survive, there was a hard, oxidized clay floor, which included a small area of rough stone cobbling (48). The south end of the floor was more heavily oxidized, and was occupied by a 70cm diameter unlined hearth, which was covered by 5–60cm of red ash. These deposits support the view that metal-working continued to be undertaken on the site.

Level 4b (fig. 13.7)
Cut through the burnt deposits (37) was a pit (38) that measured 20cm in depth and had a diameter of 80cm. It was filled with loam and capped by rough stone flooring, which was heavily burnt and covered by red ash. There was another hearth just to the north at the same stratigraphic level. This one

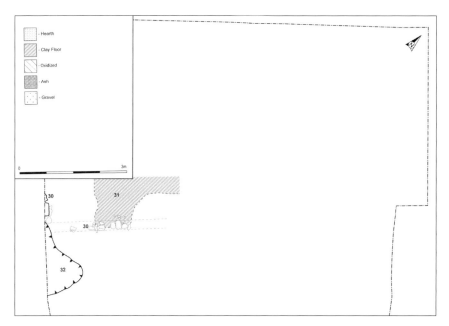

13.8 Phase 4, level 1: remains of late seventeenth-/early eighteenth-century building

measured up to one metre in diameter and consisted of a heavily oxidized clay
lining covered in ash. Further south, a 1.2m by 1m pit (36) was cut into the top
of the burnt deposits (37). It was filled with stone.

The large stone building (25) at the west side of the site continued in use
throughout the lifetime of Level 4. After the stone building and its cess-pit
(47) went out of use and were demolished, they were infilled with stone rubble
in a matrix of brown silty loam (49/26). These deposits contained fragments of
fourteenth-century line-impressed floor-tiles and thirteenth- to fifteenth-
century Irish pottery. While it is not possible to determine exactly when the
building was demolished, it is most likely that it was removed before the mid-
sixteenth century, as the demolition remains contained only medieval pottery.

PHASE 3: POST-MEDIEVAL

Level 1
A layer of cultivated soil (21) developed over much of the site after the
demolition of the large stone building. This deposit contained much burnt
material disturbed from the underlying deposits, and no doubt more levels of
metalworking on the site were removed. Over the southern third of the site, the
soil was stonier and contained fragments of broken roof-slates and mortar (20).

The soil built up gradually over a long time, probably beginning in the fifteenth or early sixteenth century and continuing until near the end of the seventeenth century. It evidences a long period when the site was simply used for agriculture or gardening.

PHASE 4: LATER SEVENTEENTH/EARLY EIGHTEENTH CENTURIES

Level 1 (fig. 13.8)
At least part of the site was again used for habitation or industry in the later seventeenth or early eighteenth century. The structures of this period only survived over a small area at the centre of the west side of the site. A small stone-walled building was erected there. Only parts of the southern and western walls (30) survived. These were of clay-bonded construction, and the interior of the building was floored with a thick deposit of stony yellow clay (31). The latter contained a sherd of Westerwald stoneware.

Level 2
After the building described above went out of use, it was replaced by another structure. A small area of stone cobbling (28), an unlined hearth and a small area of a mortared floor (29) were all that survived of the later building.

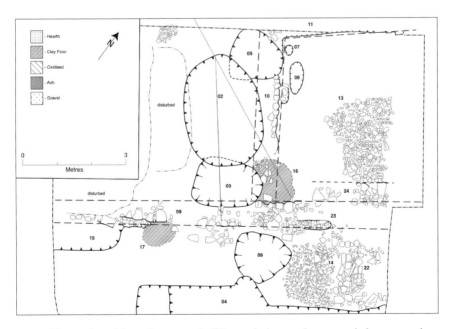

13.9 Phase 5: late eighteenth-century building and nineteenth- to twentieth-century pits

PHASE 5: LATER EIGHTEENTH AND EARLY NINETEENTH
CENTURIES

Level 1 (fig. 13.9)

The final phase of building activity on the site dates from the later eighteenth
to early nineteenth century. Again, only a very small part of these structures
survived modern truncation. It is not clear whether two separate buildings or a
single two-roomed building are represented. The walls (9, 10 & 11) of the
building consisted of clay-bonded masonry, while patches of cobbled floors
(12 & 13) survived in the interior. More extensive cobbling (14 & 22) survived
to the rear of the building. A dump of ash (17) abutted the outer side of the
rear wall. An east-west aligned, clay-bonded stone wall-footing (24) was later
built inside the eastern half of the building. A very disturbed layer of grey-
black stony loam (19), which contained a small patch of burnt limestone
fragments (18) – probably from a lime-kiln – lay on the cobbled flooring south
of the buildings.

Level 2 (fig. 13.9)

A number of pits (3, 5, 6, 7 & 8/34) were cut through the buildings after they
went out of use. These pits and the remains of the buildings directly underlay
modern deposits (1). The finds from the Phase 5 deposits consisted of
eighteenth- to early-nineteenth-century pottery, with some residual medieval
wares also present.

PHASE 6: MODERN

Two large holes (2 & 4) were dug on the site and back-filled with stone in
recent years. A temporary bank premises was built at the northwest corner of
the site in recent years, when the nearby bank was damaged by fire. The
construction of the foundations of this small building removed all deposits
within its footprint to well below the level of the subsoil.

ARTEFACTS

Only a very small assemblage of finds was uncovered during the excavation,
and none of the objects are worthy of illustration. The assemblage included
330 sherds of medieval and post-medieval pottery; the medieval pottery being
mainly Leinster Cooking Ware and Dublin pottery. Remains of buildings were
represented by three fragments of line-impressed floor-tiles (of Eames &
Fanning (1988) type L43, L44 or L45), flat, late medieval peg roof-tiles, a
single fragment of a green-glazed cockscomb ridge-tile, eight fragments of

curved roof-tiles (of the type used in the original late-twelfth-century roof of the keep of Trim Castle), and two diagonally-tooled brown sandstone blocks, each with a broad chamfer on one arris. None of these finds was uncovered from a primary position.

A few fragmentary, everyday medieval objects such as nails, horse-shoes, knives and a hinge pivot, as well as a late medieval spoon and a mid-seventeenth-century clay pipe bowl, were also uncovered. Not surprisingly, given the nature of the site, much iron and copper slag and fragments of copper alloy were also found.

CONCLUSIONS

The excavation revealed a surprising number of medieval features and structures, given the small size and shallowness of the site. The scarcity of finds, however, and the almost complete absence of closely datable material from the medieval levels rendered precise dating of the medieval structures and levels impossible.

The earliest features contained only a few sherds of twelfth-century pottery and, as they were followed by a period when the site was completely unused, they could represent pre-Anglo-Norman activity. Evidence of pre-Anglo-Norman activity on the High Street area was previously uncovered beneath the library, west of the site (Walsh 1991).

The abrupt change after the period of abandonment may reflect the alteration in status of the area after the establishment of the Anglo-Norman town. The line of the early gully, however, seems to have persisted intermittently as a property boundary right through the history of the site – the wall separating the two eighteenth-century buildings on the site roughly follows its line.

The deep ditch (75) of Phase 2 (Level 1a) appears to follow the line of High Street, suggesting that the street in this area was undeveloped at the time. The ditch was soon infilled, however, and a series of three superimposed sill-beam buildings were erected at the northeast corner of the site in the medieval period. Unfortunately, they lay right at the edge of the excavated area and, consequently, little was revealed. Over the rest of the site, bronze- and iron-working continued throughout the medieval period. The features uncovered (small hearths, burnt deposits and clay floors) are typical of medieval bloomeries and metalworking areas that have commonly been found in medieval towns. The fact that industrial activity was carried out on the street front (rather than at the rear of the property as was more usual), suggests that this area of High Street – one of the main streets of the town – must have been little developed.

The erection of the large stone medieval building and the two buildings to its east (probably in an adjacent property) in the fourteenth century marked a change in status for this area of the street. The remains of another medieval stone house were uncovered by the writer during an archaeological assessment behind Brogan's Hotel (fig. 13.1), almost directly opposite the site on the other side of High Street (licence no. 05E0149). These stone houses mark the high point of the development of Trim during the fourteenth and fifteenth centuries. In the sixteenth century, however, with the contraction of the Anglo-Norman colony, Trim became something of a frontier town, and clear evidence from the excavations in the castle and from historical references to the town (Hennessy 2004, 5), including the mention of 'waste messuages' on High Street itself, suggest a steep decline in its fortunes. This appears to be mirrored by the abandonment of the site for settlement until the later seventeenth century.

The later levels on the site were so badly disturbed by modern activity that little meaningful information was retrieved, save to say that the site was at least partly occupied by buildings during the seventeenth to twentieth centuries.

BIBLIOGRAPHY

Eames, E., & Fanning, T., 1988, *Irish medieval tiles*. Dublin.
Hennessy, M., 2004, *Irish Historic Towns Atlas No. 14: Trim*. Dublin.
Walsh, C., 1991, 'An excavation at the library site, High St., Trim', *Ríocht na Midhe* 8:3, 41–67.

What lies beneath: the development of Castle Street, Trim

FINOLA O'CARROLL

with a contribution by LINDA FIBIGER

INTRODUCTION

The origins of Castle Street in Trim are relatively recent. Within the walls of the town, it runs through a space previously occupied at the north end by the Franciscan friary or, more specifically, its cemetery, and to the south by the moat that ran outside the curtain wall of the castle. The Franciscan (or 'Grey') friary was located in an area now occupied by the courthouse. Archaeological testing and excavation to the south of the old courthouse indicated that the cemetery associated with the friary lay in this area. Burials were uncovered during sewerage works on Castle Street in 1951 but these were regarded as not being associated with the friary. Monitoring of mains drainage works on Castle Street from 2003 to 2004 uncovered more burials, however, and revealed them to be more extensive than previously thought. They were formally laid out in an east-west orientation and, while this does not automatically confirm that they were Christian, it nonetheless suggests that they represent burials from the friary cemetery. At the southern end of Castle Street, evidence for the moat around the castle was found beside the curtain wall. These findings raised questions about the extent of the cemetery, the layout of the streets in that area when the cemetery was in use, and the development of the street pattern of that part of the town in later years.

BACKGROUND TO THE EXCAVATIONS

In October 2003 Trim Town Council embarked on a programme of upgrading services in Castle Street (water, ducting for various services, and drainage). CRDS Ltd was asked to provide archaeological services for the project. The author and a small team of archaeologists spent time delving beneath the modern surface of Castle Street to find the hidden history of that part of the town. All archaeological work was carried out under licence from the Department of the Environment, Heritage and Local Government (03E1484).

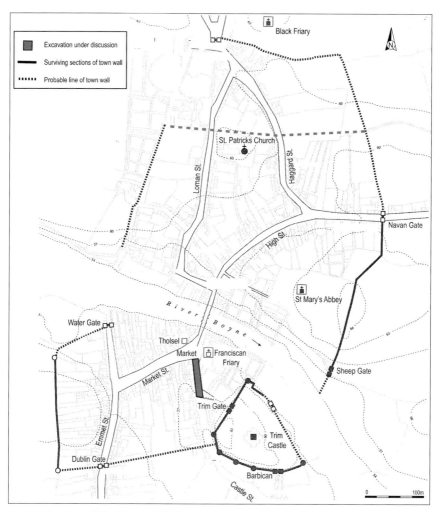

14.1 Location of development (base-map courtesy of Ordnance Survey Ireland, Permit
8565 © Ordnance Survey Ireland/Government of Ireland)

Castle Street extends northwest for approximately 300m from the roundabout at
the junction of the ring-road and the Dublin Road, then swings north by the
castle within the walls of the town for about 200m before it joins Market Street
(fig. 14.1). While part of the street within the walls is believed to be medieval in
origin, exactly how much is uncertain. It is described as forming part of the H-
plan layout of the streets south of the Boyne, regarded as one type of medieval
street pattern (Hennessy 2004, 2). But early maps indicate that it ran from
Market Street to join the causeway to the town gate of the castle and did not
extend south, as it now does, by the two towers of the curtain wall. The town
wall extended west to Emmet Street from the more southerly of those towers,

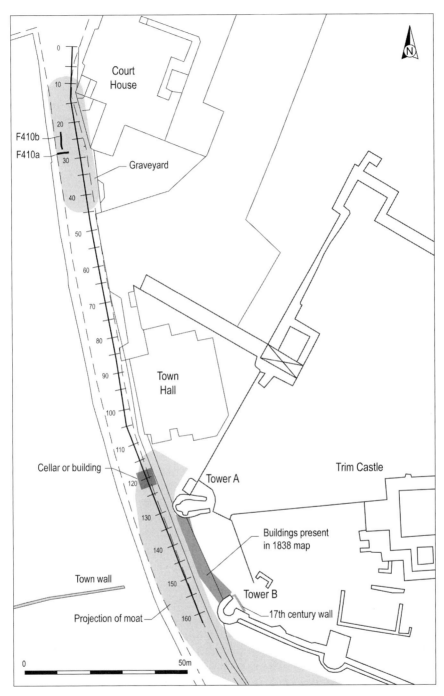

14.2 Projection of uncovered archaeological deposits over chainage scheme (base-map courtesy of Ordnance Survey Ireland, Permit 8565 © Ordnance Survey Ireland/Government of Ireland)

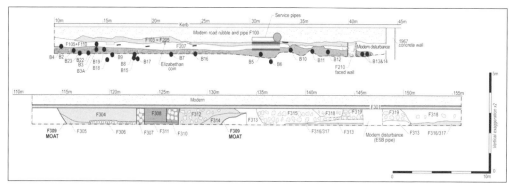

14.3 Sections along Castle Street, showing locations of burials (marked B-)

according to Bradley (1984; 1988, 37), though the known line suggests that the junction of the town wall and the curtain wall was between these two towers.

DESCRIPTION OF THE WORKS

Two machine-dug trenches were excavated. Each was about 170m long by 4.5m wide, which meant that the entire width of the street was dug up: first the eastern half, then the western half. The trenches were not of uniform depth as they had to take account of existing services and the different depth require-ments of the new services to be inserted. An asbestos pipe – an old water main – ran the length of the centre of the eastern trench to about 1m below the present pavement; between it and the pavement the trench was 1.5m deep, but it was only about 1m in width. The section of the trench west of the asbestos pipe was shallower, but all of that side had been severely disturbed by the insertion of the sewage pipe in the early 1950s. The sewerage and water mains trenches had been excavated to a depth of 2.6m and 1m respectively.

The western trench averaged 75cm in depth. It too had been disturbed by the insertion of the sewerage pipe in 1951. In general, the depth of the trench meant that most of the deposits exposed were post-medieval in date, though in places these had clearly disturbed earlier deposits. Human remains were identified towards the northern end of Castle Street, at 85cm to 1.8m below the existing street surface. Intact remains were found on the eastern side, and disturbed deposits were found in places on the western side. The burials were exposed from outside the southern corner of the old courthouse to the northern junction with Frenche's Lane. The remains of a medieval moat were detected towards the southern end of the trench and stone walls of possibly post-medieval date were noted at various locations (see fig. 14.2 for locations of features). The street slopes northwards down to the river, from OD56.6m at the town hall, to OD55m at the south side of the bridge. Where possible, the depths of the service trenches were reduced to avoid damage to surviving archaeological deposits. Where this was not feasible, the archaeological deposits were hand-excavated and preserved by record.

THE EXCAVATIONS

Burials from the graveyard of the Grey Friary

The burials in Castle Street were the uppermost of a series of unknown depth. Where possible, the remains were photographed and left in situ and their position noted; those at the impact level required for the pipe-works were fully excavated within the trench and recorded by an osteologist (Appendix 14.1). Nine articulated skeletons were recorded, of which two were preserved in situ and are not included in the osteoarchaeological report. At least three of the burials had stone-lined or simple grave-cuts. All were incomplete, and most had been disturbed by previous ground-works. Most of the retrieved human bone was disarticulated. The lowermost layer (F208) comprised compact grey silty gritty clay with frequent sub-angular stones, 20–30cm in exposed thickness. The majority of the burials were cut into this. The finds recovered from it were mainly medieval in date, with some early post-medieval material. This underlay a similar layer (F207) that contained noticeable amounts of mortar and appeared at a depth of 1m (all depths are given relative to street level). It was not continuous, and was interspersed with other deposits and cuts. Both layers contained a lot of disarticulated human and animal bone. A probable fragment of Cistercian-type ware, which dates from the sixteenth century, was recovered from the lower layer. No distinction could be seen between the soil inside the graves and layer F208, as the graves were dug and back-filled with the same soil, so the grave-cuts were not easily found. A fragment of a line-impressed tile (fig. 14.4, pl. 5) was recovered from within the upper layer F207, and a copper-alloy Elizabethan groat dated to 1556 came from the base of F207 at the interface with layer F208 (fig. 14.5).

14.4 Fragment of line-impressed tile, from F207

14.5 Copper-alloy Elizabethan groat
(1556), from base of F207

The burials (figs 14.2 & 14.3)

The remains were in a supine position, oriented east-west with the head to the
west, typical of the style of Christian burial. Burial 2, Burial 5 and Burial 7
were articulated skeletons buried in stone-lined graves. Burial 2 consisted of
the very fragmentary remains of a juvenile, encountered at a depth of 1.25m.
The grave-cut was visible to the south and west, but was disturbed on the north
side (fig. 14.6). It was lined with pieces of shale and slate, with an average
length of 10cm. Compacted clay and small fragments of slate were found at the
base of the grave. Four sherds of medieval pottery were also recovered.

Burial 5 (fig. 14.7), was uncovered at a depth of 1.3m, directly underneath
the asbestos pipe that disturbed the upper part of the grave. The burial had
been truncated on the western side by pipe-works in 1951, removing the skull
and cervical vertebrae. Apart from this, the preservation of the rest of the
skeleton was good, especially the spine, pelvis and upper legs. The lower limbs
were left in situ, as they were outside the limit of the excavation. The elbows
were flexed and the hands rested over the pelvis. The grave-cut was simple. A
concentration of medium-sized stones was found over the skeleton, suggesting
the remains of possible capping. Slab-like stones were detected along the
southern edge of the grave. One sherd of medieval pottery was recovered.

Burial 7 was an adult male found at a depth of 1.5m. Hand bones were
recovered from between the ribs, suggesting that the individual was buried
with his hands across his chest. The stone-lining of the grave-cut is evident to
its northern, western and southern sides. The eastern edge was beyond the
limit of excavation. Although Burials 1, 6, 8/15, 9, 22 and 23 contained
articulated skeletons, the grave-cuts were not discernible.

Burial 1 was at a depth of 1.2m. The remains belonged to an adult, probably
male. The bone was in poor condition and the remains were very fragmentary.
The right arm seemed to be extended along the body. One sherd of medieval

14.6 Burial 2, looking west. This juvenile had been buried in a grave
lined with shale and slate

14.7 Burial 5, looking south. This was a simple grave-cut containing the disturbed
remains of a male who had died in his twenties or thirties

14.8 Burial 8/15,
looking north. This was
the grave of a 36–45-
year-old individual

pottery was recovered. Burial 6 was found at a depth of 1.8m. The earlier
sewerage pipe had cut away the upper half of the body as far as the pelvis. Only
loose bone was collected, leaving the remaining skeleton in situ, as it was not
going to suffer further disturbance. The skeleton was that of an adult. The
pelvis was visible in the baulk, and bones from the right hand were lying over
the pelvis. One iron nail was recovered, which is the only artefact recovered
that could suggest the use of coffins.

Burial 8/15 (fig. 14.8), an adult, was uncovered at a depth of 1.7m. Some
stones were detected around the skeletal remains. These could be the disturbed
remains of a stone-lined grave-cut. The arms were disturbed, and the
disarticulated remains of other individuals were recovered. Five sherds of
medieval pottery and a lead shot (fig. 14.9), which could date from the fifteenth
or sixteenth century, were recovered.

Burial 9, the articulated remains of a juvenile, was located at a depth of
1.45m. It was outside the area of the new works, so only loose bone was
collected. One sherd of medieval pottery was retrieved. Burial 22 was at a

14.9 Lead shot found in association with Burial 8/15

depth of 1.5m and was left in situ. The pelvis, spine and arms of an adult were exposed (fig. 14.10). Some of the arm bones were collected as they were affected by the development. The remains of an infant were collected from the soil surrounding this burial.

Burial 23 consisted of the fragmentary remains of the skull of an infant. The skull was resting beneath the asbestos pipe to the west side of the trench, at a depth of 1.5m. Burial 4 was a fragmentary skull at a depth of 1.2m. It is uncertain if it represented disarticulated or articulated remains, as the remains were left unexcavated in the eastern baulk, which was outside the scope of the development.

The remaining recorded burials (3, 3A, 10, 11, 13/14 & 16–19) comprised disarticulated bone. Their positions were recorded. Further stray human remains were collected from the upper levels of both trenches. No further in situ burials were recorded during the excavation of the trench along the western side of Castle Street, but all bone was collected. Some disarticulated human and animal bone was recovered at a depth of 60cm below street level.

The majority of the burials contained bone belonging to a number of different individuals, as well as animal bone. This is due to the normal practice in cemeteries of digging graves through older grave-cuts, coupled with contamination from nearby settlement. Thus, the remains reflect the prolonged use of the cemetery during medieval and early post-medieval times.

Overlying the burials was layer F207, a mixture of deposits that included spreads of mortar-rich material at the northern end of the trench (F110, F201 & F202), and gritty clay deposits containing stones and some early post-medieval finds. A pit which disturbed Burial 19 was cut from this level. Partly overlying the pit was a possible path of flat slabs (F108), which was bedded into one of these mortar rich deposits and was truncated by the asbestos pipe (fig. 14.11).

14.10 Burial 22, looking west. The remains of this adult were left in situ as they were
unaffected by the development. The scattered and partial remains of an infant
surrounding the adult burial were collected

This comprised a single course of flat slabs laid in a line, running roughly east–
west. Medieval pottery was recovered from the path and underlying layer and
both contained frequent inclusions of pan-tile, grit, animal bone and shell.
Post-medieval floor- and roof-tiles were also retrieved, as was medieval pottery.
A fragment of a Frechen jug (late sixteenth/early seventeenth century) was
also recovered (fig. 14.12, pl. 4), as were disarticulated human remains.

These layers were sealed by a number of deposits of gritty soils that
contained varying proportions of mortar and stone (F30, F105 & F201), over
which was a thin layer (F110). These deposits appear to represent destruction
layers, probably from the time of the suppression of the friary. Medieval and
post-medieval pottery was recovered, including a single fragment of a post-
medieval floor-tile. A second small pit of uncertain function was detected
(F111). It contained animal bone in a matrix of sticky clay, above Burials 3, 3A,
18 and 9. All of the pits truncated F110. Disarticulated human remains were
identified in the deposits recovered from them. Later material overlying this
destruction level included deposits of sticky clays with stone and brick
(F105/30/201). These probably related to the construction of the 'old'
courthouse in the early nineteenth century.

Four courses of a partially-demolished, faced wall (F210) occurred at the
southern extent of the burials (fig. 14.3). Its stratigraphic position is uncertain
as it was disturbed by a modern pipe, the street kerb and a layer of concrete

14.11 Possible path of flat slabs (F108), truncated by the insertion of an asbestos pipe

14.12 Fragment of Frechen jug (late sixteenth/ seventeenth century)

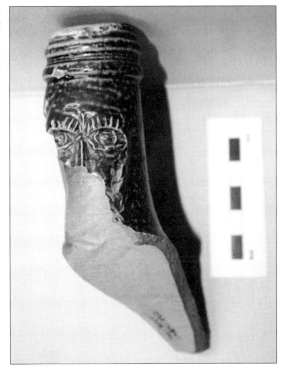

14.13 Remains of wall F210, at the southern extent of the burials. This whole area was heavily disturbed by the later insertion of pipes and cables (bottom right)

beneath. This wall may be related to an early construction phase of the courthouse, but it is unlikely to be part of the medieval Grey Friary, as it truncates the layer sealing the burials. No further archaeological deposits occurred along the stretch between Frenche's Lane and a point just beyond the town hall, a gap of 75m.

The castle moat (figs 14.2 & 14.3)
A large ditch was recorded cut through the natural subsoil, approximately 17.5m from the curtain wall. It followed the line of the wall and presumably extended towards the causeway to the gate of the castle. The ditch in the trench on the west side of the street seemed to extend under the footpath on that side. The moat swung to the north, then north-east from this point and was picked up close to the southern side of the town hall (fig. 14.14). Wet, peaty deposits (F316 & F317) appeared at a depth of 1.5m within this cut (see figs 14.2 & 14.3). These deposits were not excavated as they were not affected by the development. They contained medieval pottery, and have been interpreted as the medieval fills of the moat surrounding Trim Castle and/or the Leper River, which would have intercepted this section of the moat.

The moat of the castle thus appears to have been abandoned sometime after the sixteenth century as the deposits had to have built up sufficiently to justify the moat being back-filled by at least the eighteenth century. A series of post-medieval back-fills sealing the medieval fills of the ditch were revealed (F304, F305, F306, F312 & F314; see fig. 14.3). These included post-medieval pottery and glass and a mixture of rubble with fine-grained wet sediment. These fills are interpreted as the result of deliberate efforts to create a level surface. Further post-medieval deposits recorded at a depth of 1m are later than the post-medieval back-fills of the moat described above.

A hollow or small stream (F303) cut through bedrock was back-filled with sediment (F302) containing animal bone, shell, nineteenth-century glass, post-medieval pottery and building material. Two walls (F307 & F310) ran roughly parallel in an east-south-east/west-north-west direction, and were built through the earliest post-medieval deposits of the moat. They were poor-quality, thin walls (80cm), made of irregularly-shaped undressed stone (limestone and shale), with coarse bonding of sand and gravel. Eighteenth-century mottled ware was recovered from these walls. A deposit between these walls had frequent inclusions of eighteenth-century pottery, red brick, mortar and angular stones. This overlay a floor of sand, clay and mortar. These features were identified as the walls, floor surface and back-fill of an eighteenth- or nineteenth-century cellar.

Further north and west of the cellar a wall (F410) crossed the west side of Castle Street in an east-west direction. It may have been associated with a Victorian storm drain, although it could be earlier. The stone wall was thin (50cm) and poorly constructed. One fragment of medieval pottery, which was probably in a secondary position, was recovered from the vicinity. An arched wall ran perpendicular to the poorly constructed wall. A clay pipe stem-fragment and a large corroded metal object were recovered from the surrounding contexts. This wall is also about 50cm wide, and the two walls may be associated. They may relate to cellar structures, but their date is unknown.

An orangey brown layer containing charcoal, bone and shell (F422) was related to the wall F410. This is a disturbed soil layer with a low density of human bone found in a secondary position. A stem-fragment of a clay pipe was recovered, along with medieval pottery. Further rubble deposits overlying those sealing the back-filled moat were recorded (F313, F315, F318 & F319). These may have been deposited to raise the ground to lay out the new street. Finds of seventeenth- to nineteenth-century date were recovered. Alternatively, the deposits may be rubble from the demolition of buildings attached to the curtain wall as shown on the 1838 Ordnance Survey map and an antiquarian drawing of 1859 (Potterton 2005, 252–3, fig. 6.25).

Modern deposits
A series of deposits of modern date are responsible for the high degree of disturbance of the archaeological strata, especially those associated with the graveyard. These include the sewerage pipe, inserted to a depth of 2.6m in

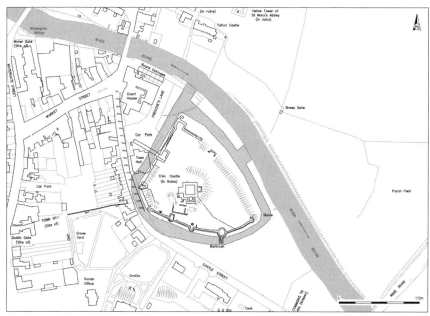

14.14 Projection of moat (base-map courtesy of Ordnance Survey Ireland, Permit 8565 ©
Ordnance Survey Ireland/Government of Ireland)

1951, an asbestos water pipe, which ran the length of the street, and various
service pipes. A layer of smooth, sticky clay (F103/205) containing charcoal
and red brick, was visible under the road bed. It may relate to the nineteenth-
century construction of the courthouse.

DISCUSSION

Archaeological monitoring and excavation of the two service trenches in Castle
Street produced a surprising amount of information leading, inevitably, to a
number of questions. The remains of a medieval graveyard associated with the
Franciscan friary were identified and partially excavated where necessary. What
was the extent of the friary cemetery?

The outer edge of the moat at the western side of the curtain wall of the
castle has been traced for some distance (see also Stephens, 'Empty space', this
volume). The town wall, which should have abutted the moat, was not in
evidence. While the line of the town wall is known as it extends towards Castle
Street from Emmet Street, it was not picked up at any point during these
works. What effect did the moat have on the later street pattern?

Masonry structures which may be post-medieval or earlier in date, and
other post-medieval structures, were uncovered and partly excavated in the

course of the work on Castle Street. Several post-medieval rubble deposits were also exposed. What was their relationship to the creation of Castle Street?

The cemetery

The excavations described in this paper, along with previous investigations, indicate that the area under two shops at the rear of the courthouse, the modern extension to the courthouse, and the part of Castle Street from the northern corner of Frenche's Lane northwards for 34m constituted part at of the cemetery of the Franciscan friary. Previous investigations in the area have revealed significant information that now makes more sense in the light of the excavations described above. Of particular importance are:

- The works associated with laying a sewage pipe down the centre of Castle Street in 1951. These uncovered skeletal remains that were regarded by Hartnett, who visited the site and observed the burials mostly in section, as not being associated with the friary, as they appeared to be laid haphazardly in a pit (Hartnett 1951). The burials recorded during the course of this work, however, were all laid east-west, where undisturbed, and the extent is greater than previously supposed;
- Two possible inhumations, displaced human bone and medieval and post-medieval pottery recorded by Delany at Trim Courthouse, Castle Street (96E247; Delany 1997, 437);
- Seven disturbed burials, as well as medieval pottery and floor-tile revealed by Purcell at Trim Courthouse. Remnants of walls were also encountered, and these were probably associated with the friary (96E247ext; Purcell 2000);
- Two human skeletons uncovered in situ, as well as medieval pottery and a fragment of a window mullion at Castle Street/Frenche's Lane (00E700; Byrne 2001).

The main buildings of the friary must have occupied the space where the old courthouse is, and possibly more ground to the rear of that. The church itself probably ran east-west from Market Street. The cloister is likely to have been to the north; indeed 'most friaries in Ireland have the cloister to the north of the church' (Greene 2005, 171). The cemetery would have been to the south and southwest of the church. The evidence from these excavations, and the description of the burials recorded during the sewerage works in 1951, suggest that there is a considerable density of burials there, at least in Castle Street. This is not surprising, as friaries quite rapidly became popular as places of burial. This in itself could be a source of tension with the secular church, as it meant that they received a greater share of legacies and donations (Platt 1996, 73). The densely-packed graveyards in places such as Northampton and Bristol testify to their popularity as places of burial (ibid.). This may be partly explained by the desire of the Franciscans particularly to share traditionally clerical spirituality

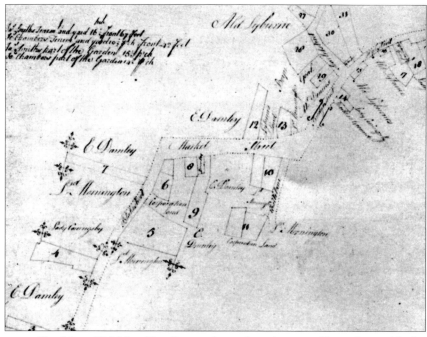

14.15 Detail from NLI Ms 21F70, 'A map of several tenniments and lotts of ground in the town & libertys of Trim in the county of Meath … 1770'. North is to the top. Market Street is clearly labelled and the bridge is also marked (this map is the property of the Board of the National Library of Ireland and is reproduced here with their permission)

with the laity. Thus, by the fourteenth century, funeral rites conducted in monasteries had found their way into parishes (Byrne 2006, 92). In Carmarthen, Wales, the fourteenth-century precinct around the friary was enlarged, 'perhaps to accommodate its increasing role as the premier burial place for the townspeople, as well as for many aristocratic families' (Williams 2003, 244).

The foundation date for the friary is not known, but Franciscan records suggest that it was established by 1260 (Moloney 1934). Its position, close to the castle, on church lands (as with the castle itself), coupled with the ministry of the Franciscans, may have ensured that the cemetery was in demand as a place of burial by the townsfolk. The inclusion of juveniles and infants suggests that the wider population group was represented. The extent of the cemetery is now known only to the south, and possibly to the north. The limits to the east and west are less clear, though the moat of the castle must have marked the limits of the friary precinct on the eastern side. We now know that burials extended right out into Castle Street, though the western limits of the graveyard here are not known. The graveyard continued in use up to the sixteenth century, and this is confirmed by finds from the burials. It is likely that it went out of use after the Reformation, when the friary was suppressed,

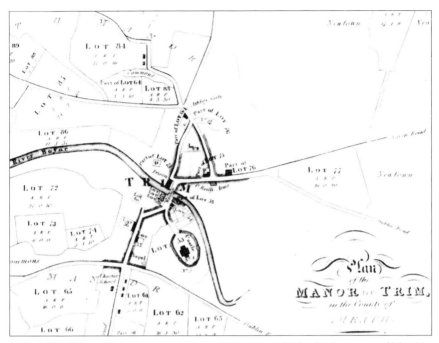

14.16 Detail from NLI Ms ILB336, 'Plan of the manor of Trim, in the county of Meath' (part of the 'Particulars and conditions of sale of the Wellesley/Mornington estate, 25–7 January 1816') (this map is the property of the Board of the National Library of Ireland and is reproduced here with their permission)

and the layers overlying the burials, which contained a lot of mortar and rubble (and one of which produced the Elizabethan groat), strongly suggest that this was the case.

The street pattern

Castle Street runs alongside the courthouse buildings, down to the junction with Market Street, and then to the bridge. There is an account of a market cross in Trim at this junction (Potterton 2005, 152), and it is almost certain that this area was the main focus of the market. The present line of Castle Street, extending south by the river, could not have existed in medieval times, as the friary precinct would have been in the way at the northern end and the moat and town wall would have blocked the southern end. The friary graveyard, the causeway to the castle gate and the line of the moat, which has been established in the course of this work, all pre-date the modern line of Castle Street.

Three maps, one late-eighteenth-century and two early-nineteenth-century, give some indication of the earlier street pattern (see figs 14.15–14.17). The earliest map, drawn by John O'Brien in 1770 (fig. 14.15), shows a property-line

14.17 Portion of William Larkin's map of Meath, 1812 (*A map of the County of Meath, 1812* by Williams Larkin. Courtesy of Meath County Council Library Service, Navan, Co. Meath)

running south from the east side of the bridge, which corresponds to the line of the front of the courthouse. It turns east, but no properties are shown along this part of Market Street. Instead, a lane (Castle Lane) is shown running alongside the easternmost property. A map dated to 1816 (fig. 14.16) shows a road or lane running directly from the town gate of the castle over the causeway, and curving to meet Market Street at the bridge end. The line taken by this road does not correspond with the present Castle Street, nor does it extend further south than the causeway. Larkin's map of Meath, however, published in 1817 but apparently surveyed in 1812 (Horner 2007), shows a road or lane pretty much on the line of the present Castle Street, extending south-eastwards to the Dublin Road (fig. 14.17).

The moat was recorded parallel to the east curtain wall of the castle. It is known that the Leper River ran along the external ditch of the town wall until it met the moat (Stephens, 'Empty space', this volume). The moat was neglected probably from the sixteenth century, and the resultant hollow had to be back-filled on several occasions in order to re-surface the road and erect buildings.

It was anticipated that the town wall would be detected during the course of the works, following projections made from the results of previous excavations. No remains were found. This may be due to the early destruction of the walls, or more probably because no wall existed at this location, as it may have terminated at the moat, whose 15–17m span may have been bridged or blocked by a wooden structure. The filling in of the moat and the probable dismantling of whatever structure may have spanned the gap from the town wall to the curtain wall would have allowed a route-way to develop directly alongside the curtain wall. The second gate to the castle, the heavily-defended barbican gate, faces south and leads out into the area which would probably have been a marshy area, with the Leper River running through it (see Stephens, 'Empty space', this volume). Some sort of causeway must have extended from the barbican to drier land, however, and this dry-land track must be the genesis for the southern part of the New Road, now also known as Castle Street.

The walls found at the northern end of Castle Street may be Victorian in date, but could be the remains of structures aligned with the east side of Castle Lane, near the junction with Market Street. Evidence that supports the suggestion that structures existed along the line of Castle Lane, as distinct from the later Castle Street, comes from two sources. The first is the map dated 1816 (fig. 14.16), which shows buildings at either side of the northern end of the lane running from the causeway to the castle to Market Street. The second comes from the excavations carried out by Hayden in Market Street (this volume). Here, excavations revealed a ditch running north-south on the eastern side of a plot to the rear of Market Street, and on the western side of the site there was a stone structure interpreted as a late medieval house. The location of this house and ditch relative to the position of Castle Lane on O'Brien's map (fig. 14.15) supports the tentative suggestion that this building fronted onto Castle Lane, which must have occupied some of the space to the east of the house. The ditch, approximately 20m to the east of the house, is believed by the author to have been back-filled in the early thirteenth century. Given that the Franciscans were established in Trim around that time, this infilling of the ditch may have been a re-ordering of space caused by their arrival. The buildings uncovered on Castle Street may have been related to the friary, or may have been later buildings, post-dating the Dissolution of the Monasteries, but pre-dating the re-alignment and transformation of Castle Lane into Castle Street.

The first edition Ordnance Survey map of Trim shows a laneway giving access to the rear of the buildings close to the eastern end of the south side of Market Street. It seems reasonable to suggest that this may preserve to some degree the line of Castle Lane, as the buildings to either side of this opening have slightly different orientations, and its position is close to that marked on O'Brien's map.

After the Dissolution, the cemetery must gradually have fallen out of use, and the open ground turned to other, secular purposes. It is known that the church was taken over as a courthouse by the corporation, and that assizes were held there up to the eighteenth century (Potterton 2005, 338–9). Thus, trans-forming the cemetery into a roadway, and opening up the southern part of the town, would have been a logical development. But the memory of the cemetery faded from the townspeople's minds, and the shape of the town as it is now was assumed to be the shape it had always had. The power of this assumption can be seen in the fact that a number of authorities have cited the curving line of Castle Street, Bridge Street and High Street as a possible contender for the Early Medieval monastic enclosure in Trim (Potterton 2005, pl. 1; Hennessy 2004, 2, fig. 1), although, as is now shown, the form of the southern part of that curve perhaps owes more to topography than to longevity of use.

ACKNOWLEDGMENTS

I would like to thank Trim Town Council, particularly the former town engineer David Keyes, and Aaron Smith for initiating and funding the project.

Thanks to the excavation team: supervisor Marta Muñiz Pérez, Denis Shine, Vera Power, Aisling Collins and Sorcha Grehan, and to all the crew from Trim Town Council who made working there such a pleasure.

BIBLIOGRAPHY

Bradley, J., 1984, 'Urban archaeological survey, County Meath'. Unpublished report.
Bradley, J., 1988–9, 'The medieval towns of County Meath', *Ríocht na Midhe* 8:2, 30–49.
Byrne, J.P., 2006, *Daily life during the Black Death*. Santa Barbara, CA.
Byrne, M., 2001, 'Castle Street/Frenche's Lane, Trim' in Bennett, I. (ed.), *Excavations 2000: summary accounts of archaeological excavations in Ireland*, no. 781, pp 265–6. Bray.
Delany, D., 1998, 'Trim courthouse, Castle Street, Trim' in Bennett, I. (ed.), *Excavations 1997: summary accounts of archaeological excavations in Ireland*, no. 437, pp 145–6. Bray.
Greene, J.P., 2005, *Medieval monasteries*. London & New York.
Hartnett, P.J., 1951, 'Burials in Castle Street, Trim, Co. Meath' (NMI files IA 189/51 & P 58/51).
Hennessy, M., 2004, *Irish Historic Towns Atlas, No. 14: Trim*. Dublin.
Horner, A., 2007, *Mapping Meath in the early nineteenth century*. Bray.
Moloney, J. (ed.), 1934, 'Brussels MS 3410: a chronological list of the foundations of the Irish Franciscan province', *Analecta Hibernica* 6, 192–202.
Platt, C., 1996, *Medieval England: a social history and archaeology from the Conquest to 1600AD*. London.
Potterton, M., 2005, *Medieval Trim: history and archaeology*. Dublin.
Purcell, A., 2000, 'Trim courthouse, Manorland, Trim' in Bennett, I. (ed.), *Excavations 1999: summary accounts of archaeological excavations in Ireland*, no. 721, pp 250–1. Bray.
Williams, H., 2003, 'Remembering and forgetting the medieval dead' in Williams, H. (ed.), *Archaeologies of remembrance: death and memory in past societies*, 227–54. New York.

APPENDIX 14.1: THE HUMAN SKELETAL REMAINS

By Linda Fibiger

The extent of the excavation at Castle Street was limited to a narrow trench (approximately 1m in maximum breadth and 1.5m in maximum depth), which was oriented north-south, whereas all human skeletal remains discovered were oriented east-west, according to the normative Christian burial custom of the period. As a result, only the section of each burial visible within the trench could be excavated and analyzed.

The osteological analysis confirmed the presence of a population group that included adults, children and infants, most likely inhabitants of the medieval town. The assemblage was small, consisting of seven articulated burials (Table 14.1) and a quantity of disarticulated bone representing a minimum of five individuals, including three adults, one child and one infant. Although overall preservation was incomplete and relatively poor, a number of conditions such as dental disease, degenerative joint disease, trauma, circulatory disorder and infection could be recorded, giving important information on health and lifestyle in medieval Trim.

Table 14.1 Overview of articulated burials

Burial number	Age at death	Sex
1	Adult	Male?
2	8–11 years	n.a.
5	26–35 years	Male
6	26–35 years	?
7	26–35 years	Male?
8/15	36–45 years	?
23	9–12 months	n.a.

The long bones of only one sexed adult individual (Burial 5; fig. 14.18) were complete enough for stature calculation. Using a regression formula for the femur, it was estimated that this individual's height was 169.40±3.27cm (Trotter 1970). This value lies within the normal range for adult males from medieval populations and slightly below most post-medieval values (Fibiger 2008).

14.18 Burial 5

Two adult burials, one child and one infant had complete or partially preserved dentitions, and in addition, two disarticulated mandibles and a quantity of isolated teeth from the disarticulated sample were available for analysis. Dental diseases noted include calculus, dental abscesses, ante-mortem tooth loss and enamel hypoplasia, all of which are common for the medieval period (Fibiger 2008).

Degenerative joint disease is another commonly observed condition in skeletal assemblages of all periods, and two articulated individuals (Burial 1 & Burial 5), both adult males, had suffered from osteoarthritis of the right shoulder joint. In addition, another adult male, Burial 1, also showed osteoarthritic changes of one of the neck vertebrae, with less severe degenerative joint changes also present on one other vertebral joint. In the disarticulated bone sample, degenerative changes were noted on only one thoracic vertebra.

One possible case of Legg-Calvé-Perthes disease was present in the assemblage, affecting the left femoral head of Burial 6. The condition results from disrupted blood supply to the hip joint during childhood, and is characterized by tissue death (necrosis) in part of this joint. Typically, the femoral head is mushroom-shaped with flared margins, and this distinct change was noted in the case of Burial 6 (Ortner 2003, 346).

Only one case of trauma was recorded. The fifth lumbar vertebra of Burial 5 had suffered a fracture of the right vertebral arch, which showed signs of healing. This type of fracture is called spondylolysis, and it usually affects the lower lumbar region of the spine. Although clinically it shows familial tendencies in its occurrence (Fredrickson et al., 1984), a high frequency among modern athletes highlights the role of habitual and strenuous movement, as well as body weight and muscle strength, in the development of spondylolytic defects (Fibiger & Knüsel 2005). An underlying development weakness of this part of the vertebra cannot be excluded as a contributing factor, however, and congenital defects noted on the eleventh and twelfth thoracic vertebrae of Burial 5 indicate that the occurrence of this case of spondylolysis could have had developmental origins.

The only evidence for infection (other than dental infection) occurred on the lower legs of Burial 8/15, where the presence of remodelled compact bone on the lateral and posterior shin bones indicated that a systemic infectious condition might have been present. As no other skeletal changes were noted, this diagnosis could not be further defined.

BIBLIOGRAPHY

Fibiger, L., 2008, 'Human skeletal remains' in Carlin, N., Walsh, F., & Clarke, L. (eds), *The archaeology of life and death in the Boyne floodplain*, 117–28. Dublin.
Fibiger, L., & Knüsel, C., 2005, 'Prevalence rates of spondylolysis in British skeletal populations', *International Journal of Osteoarchaeology* 15:3, 164–74.
Fredrickson, B.E., Baker, D., McHolick, W.J., Yuan, H.A., & Lubicky, J.P., 1984, 'The natural history of spondylolysis and spondylolisthesis', *Journal of Bone and Joint Surgery* 66A5, 699–707.
Ortner, D.J., 2003, *Identification of pathological conditions in human skeletal remains* (2nd ed.), San Diego.

Burials at the well: excavations at the Black Friary, Trim

MATTHEW SEAVER, MARK KELLY & CIARA TRAVERS

with contributions by SARAH COBAIN & CLARE McCUTCHEON

INTRODUCTION

Archaeological monitoring of resurfacing and drainage works at the southern end of the lane at the rear of the houses that front onto Haggard Street and the Kells Road in Trim uncovered human remains in November 2008. Site works were halted and a team of archaeologists, including Ciara Travers, osteologist, began excavation of the site. Human remains were only removed when it was clear that they were under threat, following exposure by machinery. The laneway at the Black Friary gives access to the backyards of houses constructed in the 1930s. This lane borders a large square area of two hectares, which is currently owned by the Office of Public Works and contains the bulk of the remains of the Black Friary (fig. 15.1). There are no unambiguous visible remains of the buildings within the heavily overgrown field, although much of the lower courses of the buildings are likely to survive under the earthworks which cover the area. The northern and eastern part of the site is bounded by houses built in the 1970s. The entire townland is known as Blackfriary, with the boundary formed by the backyards of the houses fronting onto Haggard Street and the rear of what is now a supermarket.

THE BLACK FRIARY: ARCHAEOLOGICAL AND HISTORICAL BACKGROUND

The Black or Dominican Friary at Trim was founded by Geoffrey de Geneville, Lord of Trim, in 1263 (Potterton 2005, 319). He had inherited the title by marrying Matilda, the granddaughter of Walter de Lacy, and controlled a wide area known as the Liberty of Trim. De Geneville spent his final years at the friary and was buried there in 1314. The Dominican order had arrived relatively late into Ireland (1224) and founded religious houses in and near many towns in the thirteenth century (Barry 1987, 159). Due to their relatively late arrival and the nature of their ministry, they were primarily granted sites outside urban centres.

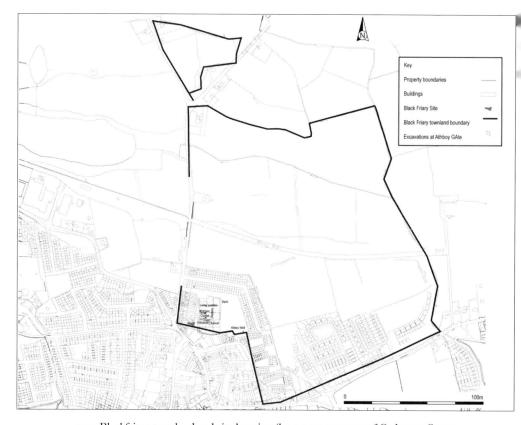

15.1 Blackfriary townland and site location (base-map courtesy of Ordnance Survey Ireland, Permit 8565 © Ordnance Survey Ireland/Government of Ireland)

The house was probably dedicated to St Mary of the Assumption. The friary was of considerable importance and was the venue for a meeting of Irish bishops that took place in 1291, indicating the status of the institution at that time. The archbishop of Armagh held a visitation in the guest-house in 1367, while the Black Friary was the location for parliamentary meetings in 1446 and 1491 (Hennessy 2004, 10). It had fallen into disrepair by 1540 and the hall, dormitory and kitchen were considered beyond repair. The friary was suppressed in 1540, with the church, cloister, chancel and other properties being sold to the bishop of Meath. It also had a four-acre orchard, a garden and a cemetery, as well as a three-acre close of pasture beside the wall of the house. Three houses and gardens were also located within its grounds. A belfry, a chapter house, a dormitory, a hall, three chambers, a kitchen, a pantry and a stable are mentioned in 1541. The community also held seventy-two acres of land. A friary was re-established in Trim in 1630, before being transferred to Donore in 1713 (Hennessy 2004, 11).

15.2 Location of excavations and geophysical survey of Black Friary (geophysics after Kennedy 1989; base-map courtesy of Ordnance Survey Ireland, Permit 8565 © Ordnance Survey Ireland/Government of Ireland)

Much of the building stone was sold during the eighteenth century. The site now consists of two hectares, with heavily overgrown areas of masonry. It is enclosed by a double bank and ditch at the south and east. The friary was situated outside the town walls, and the Athboy Gate was previously known as the Black Gate (Seaver, this volume).

In 1988, geophysical survey was carried out by Professor William Kennedy of Florida Atlantic University. The results of this research suggested a layout for the friary buildings (fig. 15.2). The team from Florida originally planned further work in the field, but due to logistical reasons this never took place. The potential plan of the buildings can be combined with the location of the cemetery to give an indication of the layout of the religious house.

THE EXCAVATION

Excavations uncovered a deep pit that has been interpreted as a well, and a series of burials at the southern end of the laneway (fig. 15.3).

Well
The earliest feature uncovered was a circular well (fig. 15.4). It was earth-cut and was 1.42m in width and 2.2m in depth. The well was abandoned and began to fill with soil. The basal deposits of the well comprised dark brown

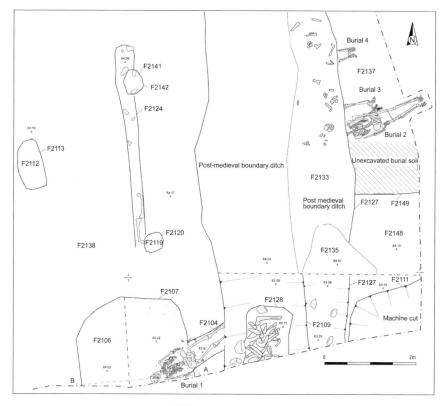

15.3 Mid-excavation plan of site

clayey silts, containing occasional animal bone and stone. A stony fill seemed
to have slumped into the well on its eastern side while it was partially open.
This was overlain by light greyish brown clayey silt. These soils were heavily
disturbed by root activity, which left cavities in the soil. Above this, on the
western side of the well, brown silt had slumped from the top of the well. This
was overlain by a deposit of light grey silt. The plant remains from the basal
fills indicate that a kiln may have existed in close proximity to the well
(Appendix 15.1).

Burial 1
A human burial was exposed cut into the natural boulder clay and the well (fig.
15.6). The extended supine burial was orientated east/northeast-west/
southwest. The feet of the burial were truncated by a post-medieval ditch,
while the upper torso of the skeletal remains had been covered by the silty clay,
with frequent stone chips and slate fragments covering the area of the well.

The torso of the skeleton had arched backwards into the well (pl. 15). This
is likely to have resulted from the decay of timber within the well, which

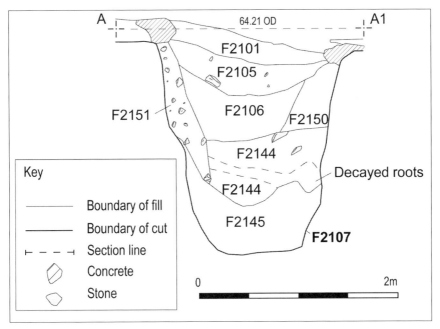

15.4 Section through well

15.5 Well, post-excavation, from north

15.6 Burial 1 within the well, from north

caused a collapse in the deposits within it, after the burial had taken place. This suggests that burial took place shortly after the well had been back-filled, as these deposits had not had time to settle. The upper stone fill of the well was then placed into the feature in an attempt to consolidate the ground-level at some period after the construction of the ditch and gully.

Burials 2, 3 and 4
A row of three further burials was identified to the southeast of the well and Burial 1, along the boundary between the lane and the land owned by the Office of Public Works. These burials directly underlay the surface of the lane. The burials were all orientated east-west and had been truncated at the west end by a north-south ditch. Burials 3 and 4 were represented by the lower legs and feet only, while Burial 2 was intact except for the skull, which had clearly been removed by the cutting of the ditch.

Post-medieval disturbance

The burials were heavily disturbed by a north-south ditch that formed a boundary feature running back from properties fronting onto Haggard Street/ Athboy Gate in the nineteenth century. This boundary contained large quantities of re-deposited disarticulated human bone. This was far greater than that created by the disturbance of the in situ articulated burials, suggesting that there was at least one more row of burials. Further post-medieval features included a gully and a number of post-holes, which are also likely to represent a boundary. A dog burial was also uncovered within a feature that is likely to date to this period. The whole area was covered in black silty soil, containing frequent coal fragments, animal bone and modern pottery.

DISCUSSION

Excavations have clearly established the position of the burial ground associated with the Black Friary. Monitoring of drain-laying on the laneway demonstrated that this cemetery did not extend to the west and northwest of the friary buildings. The burial ground was located to the southwest of the friary buildings, and must have extended as far as the town wall at the back of what is now Supervalu supermarket. Its eastern extent is unknown. The presence in this area of settlement-related features, such as the well, suggests that burial must have expanded into this area due to pressure for space. The earlier well was located close to an area in which cereal was being dried (Appendix 15.1). The wood gathered for use in cereal-drying and some of the seeds that were recovered came from a range of fruit-producing trees, which may have grown within the Black Friary landholding. The animal bone found within this feature is discussed elsewhere in this volume, but indicates that animal, fish and bird meat was being consumed at the friary during the time that the well was being back-filled (Beglane, 'Meat and craft', this volume). Bone from the well included waste from the butchery of cattle and sheep, with larger amounts of pig represented by a wider variety of body parts indicating food waste. They included the remains of a piglet. This feature also included two fragments of marine mollusc, possibly common whelk (*Buccinum undatum*), which would have had to be transported from the coast. It also contained three fragments of fish bone and two bird bones (Beglane 2009). The pottery from the well indicated a thirteenth- to fourteenth-century date (McCutcheon 2009).

The articulated skeletons, as well as the disarticulated bone, indicate that at least twelve burials took place in this restricted area (Appendix 15.2). The fifteenth- to sixteenth-century date for the burial may confirm that this was an expansion of the cemetery (Table 1.1). The violent nature of pathologies associated with two of the articulated burials indicates considerable conflict taking place during this period. It is likely that at least one of these young men was involved in fighting on more than one occasion. Political conflict and violent incidents within and outside the town were rife during this period (Potterton 2005, 113, 137). Indeed, in one of these incidents a man begged indulgence from the pope for striking in the head with a sword an individual who allegedly was plundering the town. Burials 2, 3 and 4 all appear to be within a single grave fill, possibly suggesting that they were buried at the same time.

Limited excavations have taken place at Dominican friaries elsewhere in Ireland. Excavations at the Black Abbey in Kilkenny revealed a large and densely-packed burial ground to the south of the church (Reid 1996). This religious house occupies a very similar position to that at Trim, close to the town wall and accessed through a postern gate. The cloister and abbey buildings are located to the north of the church. Extensive excavations at St Mary's of the Isle, Cork, also found the remains of a burial ground to the south of the friary (Hurley & Sheehan 1995). At this institution, a substantial number of burials were also found within the cloister. At both Kilkenny and Cork, the friaries were surrounded by walls that were exposed during excavation.

The limited evidence from the Black Friary in Trim, when combined with the limited geophysical survey, offers a tantalizing glimpse of the layout of this important religious house and provides important information for any future research programme.

ACKNOWLEDGMENTS

Thanks to Catherine Bishop for her work on the excavation and on the illustrations for this article. Thanks are also due to archaeologists Caoimhe Tuthill, Aaron Henry and John Clarke for their hard work on the site. We would also like to thank Professor William Kennedy for giving permission to use the geophysical survey results and Rosanne Meenan for liaising with him. The authors are indebted to Trim Town Council, particularly the Project Engineer, Martin Walsh, for co-operation and funding.

BIBLIOGRAPHY

Barry, T.B., 1987, *The archaeology of medieval Ireland*. Cambridge.
Beglane, F., 2009, 'Animal bone from Blackfriary, Trim' in Seaver, M., 'Final report on excavations at Blackfriary, Trim, County Meath, E2398'. Unpublished report.
Hennessy, M., 2004, *Irish Historic Towns Atlas No. 14: Trim*. Dublin.
Hurley, M.F., & Sheehan, C., 1995, *Excavations at the Dominican Priory, St Mary's of the Isle, Cork*. Cork.
Kennedy, W., 1989, 'An archaeological survey of the Blackfriary site, Trim, Ireland'. Unpublished report to the Office of Public Works.

McCutcheon, C., 2009, 'Medieval pottery from Blackfriary, Trim' in Seaver, M., 'Final report on excavations at Blackfriary, Trim, County Meath, E2398'. Unpublished report.

Potterton, M., 2005, *Medieval Trim: history and archaeology*. Dublin.

Reid, M., 1996, 'Abbey Street, Kilkenny' in Bennett, I. (ed.), *Excavations 1996: summary accounts of excavations in Ireland*, no. 204, p. 56. Bray.

APPENDIX 15.1: PLANT AND CHARCOAL MACROFOSSIL REMAINS

By Sarah Cobain

INTRODUCTION

This report provides information on the identification of the seed and charcoal species recovered during the Black Friary excavation, and uses that information to a) determine the function of features sampled; b) interpret the diet and living conditions of the occupants of the Black Friary; c) interpret socio-economic and industrial activities on the site; and d) infer the composition of the local flora and woodland.

METHODOLOGY

There were seven samples to be analyzed from The Black Friary. The samples from the medieval phase originated from two features – a well (F2107) and a pit (F2134). The post-medieval features consisted of a post-hole (F2142) and a gully (F2124). Plant macrofossil and charcoal remains were retrieved by standard flotation procedures by CRDS Ltd using 1mm and 250 micron sieves. The floated material was sorted and the seeds were identified using a low-power microscope (Brunel MX1) at magnifications of x4 to x40. Identifications were made with reference to Cappers et al. (2006), Berggren (1981) and Anderberg (1994). In order to identify the charcoal, each fragment was fractured by hand to reveal the wood anatomy on radial, tangential and transverse planes. The pieces were then supported in a sand-bath and identified under an epi-illuminating microscope (Brunel SP400) at magnifications from x40 to x400. As fragments less than 2mm in size cannot be accurately identified (it is not possible to get a wide enough field of vision to encompass the necessary anatomical features for identification), only fragments above this size were examined. During identification, any notable growth ring characteristics, evidence of thermal and biological degradation and any other unusual microscopic features were recorded. Identifications were carried out with reference to images and descriptions by Cutler and Gale (2000), Heller et al. (2004) and Wheeler et al. (1989). Nomenclature of species follows Stace (1997).

RESULTS

The results of the analysis are summarized in Tables 15.1 and 15.2 below. All cereal grains/fragments/chaff were carbonized unless otherwise specified.

Table 15.1 Macrofossil taxa from Black Friary site

Sample no.	Context	Flot volume	Context description	Taxon	Common name
4	(F2106) [F2107]	23ml	Upper fill of well [F2107]	*Poaceae* spp (3)	Charred grass seeds
				Lathyrus spp (1)	Pea
				Chenopodium album (1)	Fat hen
				Hordeum cf vulgare (1)	Naked 6 rowed barley
				Poaceae – spikelet fork	Cereal chaff
5	(F2141) [F2142]	11ml	Single fill of post-hole [F2142]	*Rubus idaeus* (2)	Raspberry
				Rubus fruticosus (2)	Blackberry
				Stellaria media (2)	Common chickweed
				Urtica urens (3)	Small nettle
				Avena spp (2)	
				cf *Hordeum* spp (2)	Oat
				Poaceae – Spikelet fork (1)	cf barley
					Cereal chaff – spikelet fork
				Poaceae – awn (1)	Cereal chaff – awn
6	(F2123) [F2124]	4ml	Single fill of narrow gully [F2124]	cf *Poaceae* (2)	Grass seeds (charred)
				cf *Polygomum aviculare* (1)	Common knotgrass
					Blackberry
				Rubus fruticosus (1)	Raspberry (fragment)
				Rubus cf idaeus (1)	Wheat – naked
				Triticum cf aestivum (1)	Wheat – spelt
				Triticum cf spelta (1)	
				Avena spp (33)	Oat
				cf *Avena* spp (25)	cf Oat
				cf *Hordeum* (4)	cf barley
				Carex cf acuta (1)	Sedge
				Hordeum vulgare (1) hulled	Barley (hulled)
					Barley (naked)
				Hordeum vulgare (9) naked	Charred grass seeds
					Charred cereal grains
				Poaceae spp (76)	Naked wheat
7	(F2144) [F2107]	35ml	Basal fill of well [F2107]	*Poaceae* (160)	Wheat – emmer
				Triticum aestivum (15)	Wheat – einkorn
				Triticum diococcum (1)	Wheat – spelt
				Triticum monococcum (1)	Possible almond
				Triticum spelta (3)	Sheep sorrel
				Charred nut	Curley dock
				Rumex acetosa / acetosella (1)	Dooryard dock
					Elder
				Rumex crispus (3)	Common chickweed
				Rumex longifolix (2)	Small nettle
				Sambucus nigra (2)	
				Stellaria media (2)	
				Urtica urens (2)	
				cf *Hordeum* (1)	cf barley
				Hordeum vulgare (1)	Hulled 6-rowed
				Poaceae (6)	barley

Sample no.	Context	Flot volume	Context description	Taxon	Common name
8	(F2143) [F2107]	11ml	Basal fill of well [F2107]	*Poaceae* (2) *Rumex spp cf palustris* *cf Triticum* (2) *Triticum aestivum* (2)	Charred cereal grain Charred grass seeds Dock cf marsh dock cf wheat Wheat – naked
11	(F2136) [F2134]	20ml	Single fill of semi-circular pit [F2134]	*Urtica urens* (2) *Avena* spp (6) *Cratygus monogyna* (1) cf *Hordeum* (3) *Poaceae* (24) *Lathyrus* spp (4)	Nettle Oat Hawthorn cf barley Charred cereal grains Pea
19	(F2145) [F2107]	117ml	Basal fill of well [F2107]	*Malus sylvestris* (2) *Sambucus nigra* (2) *Triticum cf dicoccum* (3) *Triticum cf spelta* (2) *Triticum spp* (7) *Vicia* spp (2)	Crab apple Elder Wheat – emmer Wheat – spelt Wheat Vetch

Table 15.2 Charcoal taxa from Black Friary site

Sample no.	Context	Flot volume	Context description	Taxon	Common name
4	(F2106) [F2107]	23ml	Upper fill of well [F2107]	Non ring porous charcoal (2)	
5	(F2141) [F2142]	11ml	Single fill of post-hole [F2142]	*Maloideae* spp – Crataegus monogyna/Sorbus spp/Malus Sylvestris (1)	*Maloideae* spp – hawthorn/rowan/crab apple
6	(F2123) [F2124]	4ml	Single fill of narrow gully [F2124]	*Fraxinus excelsior* (1) Indeterminate (5) *Alnus glutinosa/Corylus avellana* (5) *Prunus avium/spinosa* (8)	Ash Alder/Hazel Wild cherry Sessile/pedunculate
7	(F2144) [F2107]	35ml	Basal fill of well [F2107]	*Quercus robur/petraea* (1) *Salix/populus* (2) *Ilex aquifolium* (2) Indeterminate (22)	oak Willow/poplar Holly
8	(F2143) [F2107]	11ml	Basal fill of well [F2107]	*Alnus glutinosa* (3) *Quercus robur/petraea* (1)	Alder Pedunculate/sessile oak
11	(F2136) [F2134]	20ml	Single fill of semi-circular pit [F2134]	*Prunus avium/spinosa* (5) *Quercus robur/petraea* (22) Indeterminate (14) *Alnus glutinosa/Corylus avellana* (2)	Wild Cherry Sessile/pedunculate oak Alder/hazel Ash
19	(F2145) [F2107]	117ml	Basal fill of well [F2107]	*Fraxinus excelsior* (1) *Quercus robur/petraea* (9) Indeterminate (20)	Sessile/pedunculate oak

DISCUSSION

Diet, socio-economic and industrial activity: medieval
Macrofossils Wheat, oat and barley were recovered from the deposits in the well. Wheat is considered by Early Medieval sources to be a high-status food due to difficulties of cultivating it in wet weather (Edwards 2005, 267–8). The Black Friary assemblage does not show a higher percentage of wheat within the waste material. This may, however, be masked by the high number of unidentifiable grains. The prevailing damp climate during the medieval period meant that the grain would have been damp when harvested, so it needed to be dried before any further processing could take place. Drying halts any possible germination of the grain, prevents decay and makes the grain easier to mill (Gibson 1989, 219). The corn-drying kiln, therefore, would have been essential for arable farmers during this time and would have been indispensable at the Black Friary, where relatively large amounts of food would have been produced.

Once the grain was dried, several stages of processing had to be undertaken before it was ready to be used (Stevens & Wilkinson 2003, 196–7): a) threshing – to break the ears of grain from the straw; b) winnowing – throwing the grain into the air to allow the breeze to blow away lighter chaff (paleas, lemmas, awns); and c) coarse-, medium-, fine-sieving, and final hand picking of the grain.

It cannot be confirmed at which stage the grain from the fills (F2143, F2144 & F2145) became burnt, but it is tentatively assumed that the charred grain was deposited into the well from rake-out waste from the stoking areas of a corn-drying kiln. The grain could have originated from accidental spillage of grain while it was being placed into the drying bowl of the kiln, or it could have been swept up with waste accumulated during the threshing and winnowing stage, and burnt on the fire.

Once dried and processed, grain would be used to make a variety of foods, including porridges, bread and cakes. Barley would also have been used to brew beer. Dyer (1983) has suggested that up to one gallon (3.79 litres) of beer would have been consumed per person per day. A reason for this was the poor water sanitation during the medieval period, which meant that beer would have been consumed in preference to water to avoid contracting water-borne diseases (such as cholera and dysentery). Beer would also have been an added source of vitamins and calories. In addition, the by-products of grains were put to use. Wheat straw, for example, was often used for thatching, and barley straw was used as a winter feed and bedding for livestock (Pearson 1992, 3).

Herbaceous plants were often exploited to be used as herbs in cooking and vegetables for salads. Despite the low numbers of seeds obtained, studies such as that from a medieval garden in Hull (Crackles 1986), show all these species being cultivated and harvested for food. As the climate in Britain and Ireland was similar during this period there is no reason why these species could not have been cultivated and used here. Common chickweed leaves were used as vegetables and their seeds have also been recovered in Danish granaries. These were presumed to have been used as a substitute for grain at times of poor harvest. Nettle leaves would have been boiled down and used in a similar manner to spinach (Defelice 2004, 195–6). Docks were used as salad and for wrapping food before cooking to prevent it from being burnt. The charred dock remains in the well could be evidence for the use of dock on the site. This can only be done with certain species of dock, however, such as *Rumex acetosella* and *Rumex crispus* (both of which were identified at the Black Friary), as other species contain toxins that are harmful to health. Dock, common chickweed and crab apple seeds have been recorded in a study of the gut contents of a bog body from Kayhausen, Oldenburg, Germany. The high percentages and regular occurrence of these seeds in the stomach contents of this bog body suggest that these species were specially selected for consumption (Behre 2008, 67–8). Although this study is from Germany, it can be assumed that these species would also have been selected and consumed in Ireland.

Fruit seeds (crab apple, hawthorn berries and elder berry) were also found in the well. It is not possible to say whether these were from fruit that had been consumed or from fruits that had fallen into the well and decayed, but it can be assumed that if they were growing in close vicinity to the site, they are likely to have been harvested for food, providing supplements to the medieval diet. Hawthorn berries are a valuable source of vitamins and can be used to make jams and puddings, while the leaves can also be used as a salad or vegetable (Adamson 2004, 14, 97). Crab apples have been observed on numerous sites in Britain and Ireland, including in a medieval garden in Hull (Crackles 1986, 4), and in Paisley Abbey orchard in Scotland (Dickson 1995, 29). They would have been consumed raw as well as made into tarts and pies (Adamson 2004, 97). There was an orchard at the Black Friary, and it is likely that the crab apple seeds identified came from this orchard.

Elder berries were boiled down and used to make mousses and jams or jellies, and they were also used in juices and to make wine (Dennell 1970, 154). Elder flowers, leaves and berries also had herbal medicinal uses and were used to treat inflammation, bruises and wounds (Atkinson & Atkinson 2002, 916–17). Interestingly, the place-name 'Trim' derives from *Áth Truimm*, which means 'the ford of the elder tree' (Herity 2001, 67).

Charcoal

The oak and ash recovered from the rake-out waste from the base of the well are likely to represent the dominant fuels used in the corn-drying kiln. They did not display obvious curved growth rings and it is likely that the wood was derived from larger branches or stem wood. Ash and oak both have dense heartwood and, if dried properly, they are long-burning fuels. Together with the good ventilation that was necessary in a corn-drying kiln, this means that the fuel would have burned slowly and maintained an even temperature (Cutler & Gale 2000, 205). This is ideal for a corn-drying kiln, which requires constant heat for relatively long periods of time in order to dry out the grain.

Most of the wild cherry and alder charcoal fragments showed evidence of curved growth rings, which suggests that they derived from round-wood (lateral branches), rather than stem-wood. It is therefore likely that these branches were collected as deadwood and used as kindling for the fire. The alder also showed some evidence of fungal growth, suggesting that it was collected as deadwood. As fuels, alder and hazel are not as economical as ash and oak, because anatomically they are less dense and burn more quickly (particular alder) at relatively high temperatures (Cutler & Gale 2000, 205). This property does make them good to use as kindling, however, as the high temperatures produced by the hazel and alder would encourage the oak to start to burn. Medieval orchards grew apples and cherries (as, for example, at Paisley Abbey in Scotland – see Dickson 1995, 29) and it is not unlikely that the orchard at the Black Friary had both of these fruit trees. The wild cherry-wood would therefore have been a readily available source of fuel to use as kindling for the fire.

Diet, socio-economic and industrial activity: post-medieval
Macrofossils The charred grain (oat, barley and wheat) recovered from the gully and post-hole on the site at the Black Friary is likely to have been deposited as waste from a corn-drying kiln associated with the houses on Haggard Street/the Kells Road. The Corn Laws introduced in 1784 were put in place to reduce the food shortages by providing subsidies to produce grain and sell it abroad, thereby also increasing the availability of grain to the local population (Daly 1992). Corn-drying kilns were still in use across the country at this time, because although grain and flour could be bought, poorer members of society still processed grain themselves, into porridges, bread, cakes and beer (as discussed above; Stevens & Wilkenson 2003, 196–7). The herbaceous taxa (common knotgrass, blackberry, raspberry, common chickweed and fat hen) found at the Black Friary site are all likely to be weed species (or scrub hedgerows, in the case of raspberry and blackberry) growing in cleared areas at the rear of houses, although the raspberry and blackberry are likely to have been harvested and eaten raw or processed into jams, tarts and sauces.

Charcoal As only two identifiable fragments of charcoal were recovered, it is not possible to specify with any confidence the types of fuel being used. The presence of ash suggests the use of an effective, long-burning fuel (Stuijts 2005, 141), which was possibly used in the houses in the locality (in a fire or possibly a corn-drying kiln). A larger assemblage of charcoal would be required to provide any firm conclusions.

Composition of local flora
Medieval The vegetation in the immediate vicinity of the site at the Black Friary appears to have been dominated by cleared/open vegetation such as grasses and other herbaceous taxa (such as vetch, pea, dock, common chickweed, nettle and sedge). This is indicative of the clearance of land to make way for the building and use of the Black Friary and the clearance of land associated with the pasture and orchard. Some of these taxa (common chickweed, dock, nettles) are known to have been harvested as salads and vegetables. It is therefore possible that these could have been deliberately cultivated. A larger assemblage of seeds would be required to arrive at any firm conclusions however.

Despite the poor preservation of some of the charcoal, and the narrow range of species recovered, it was possible to gain some useful information about the local woodland at the Black Friary. As asserted by Scholtz (1986; cited in Prins & Shackleton 1992, 632), the 'Principle of least effort' suggests that communities in the past collected firewood from the closest available wooded area. The site is located within the area of Trim town, so access to specific woodland species would have required walking into woodland outside of the town. Following this theory, it suggests that the alder/hazel, oak, ash, wild cherry, willow and holly were growing in woodland close to the site. While this can be used as the basic theory, however, other variables affecting wood collection must be taken into account (Prins & Shackleton 1992, 632). These include: a) selection of particular species in favour of others within the woodland; b) local deliberately-cultivated species; c) differential preservation of charcoal/non-uniform survival of charcoal over time; and d) deforestation during the medieval period.

As discussed above, oak and ash are likely to have been selected for use in a corn-drying kiln as they are considered long-lasting and effective fuels (Stuijts 2005, 141,

143) so it is likely that they were searched for and harvested. Another variable is the presence of wild cherry-wood within the charcoal assemblage. If the orchard at the Black Friary did consist of wild cherry trees, this would have been a convenient source of material in close proximity to the Black Friary to collect for kindling for the fire. This corresponds with Scholtz's theory – as the orchard is an anthropogenic environment, it does not represent the local natural woodland. The kindling material originating from holly, willow and alder/hazel are more likely to have been collected locally as dead-wood, which was part of local natural woodland. Willow and alder are species that tolerate damp conditions (Mitchell & Wilkinson 1978, 36–7, 44) and with the River Boyne in close proximity, this may have been a convenient source of wood. Holly is an under-storey tree that can grow in oak woodland, as part of alder carr scrub vegetation, and is often found in marginal areas such as hedgerows and cleared scrubland (Lloyd & Peterken 1967, 847) so it is likely to have been collected in close proximity to the site.

The medieval period also saw a huge increase in the deforestation of natural woodland throughout Ireland. A pollen diagram from Derragh Bog, for example, shows a decrease in tree pollen from approximately 50% to 10% from AD1032 to AD1760 (Brown et al., 2005, 88). This occurred due to the intensification of both arable and pastoral agriculture and would have made wood for fuel harder to obtain. For these reasons, it is not possible to give a definitive depiction of the woodland surrounding the Black Friary site. As asserted by Comber (2001, 73–4), trade networks had hugely increased by the Early Medieval period, so that wood such as oak could easily have been brought in from elsewhere and purchased, while it could also have been available as waste-wood from wood-working in towns. It is likely, however, that the kindling wood was obtained close to the site, suggesting that alder carr scrub woodland was located nearby/within Trim (most likely by the River Boyne), and some of the kindling wood was obtained from the orchards next to the Black Friary.

Post-medieval The macrofossil data from the Black Friary suggest that the vegetation was dominated by weed species such as nettles, fat hen, common knotgrass and common chickweed. This is indicative of the maintained clearance of land for settlement in the area (for example, clearing of shrubs/trees). Raspberry and blackberry are shrubs which quickly colonize cleared land and, once established, are often maintained in hedgerows (possibly separating houses on Haggard Street/the Kells Road) in order for their fruits to be harvested.

As only two fragments of charcoal (ash and hawthorn/crab apple/rowan) were recovered, it is not possible to come to any firm conclusions about the woodland surrounding the Black Friary site. This charcoal could have originated from a local source or wood brought into the town for sale. Without a larger assemblage of charcoal, no conclusions can be drawn.

CONCLUSIONS

The macrofossil and charcoal evidence from the site at the Black Friary gives an interesting insight into vegetation composition, socio-economic activities and the diet of the community. The dates of the burials at the Black Friary site indicate activity occurring during the latter stages of the occupation of the Dominican friary. The macrofossil remains indicate the processing of grain, which would have been used to produce breads, porridges and beer for the occupants of the friary. There is also evidence for herbaceous taxa such as docks, common chickweed and nettles, which are likely to have been used as vegetables and salads. Fruit and berry seeds (apple, hawthorn and elder) were also identified and presumably had been harvested to use as additional vitamins in the diet. The woodland around the site appears to have consisted of alder carr scrub, possibly associated with the River Boyne floodplain. There is also evidence of an apple/cherry orchard associated with the friary, and this would have provided kindling material for the corn-drying kiln. There was evidence of oak and ash charcoal within the burning waste materials, but considering the increase in trade during the medieval period, it is not possible to confirm if these came from a local woodland source or from outside Trim.

During the post-medieval period the introduction of new Corn Laws in 1784 meant that more emphasis was placed on the growing of grain in order to increase food production. The cereal grains found in the post-hole and gully at the rear of houses on Haggard Street and the Kells Road suggest the processing of cereal within the local area. The herbaceous taxa recovered suggest a clear environment, which would be expected in an area of continuous settlement. As little charcoal was obtained from these features, it was not possible to extract any information about the local woodland.

BIBLIOGRAPHY

Adamson, M.W., 2004, *Food in medieval times*, Westport, CT.
Aitkinson, E., & Aitkinson, M.D., 2002, 'Sambucus nigra L.', *The Journal of Ecology* **90:5**, 895–923.
Anderberg, A.-L., 1994, *Atlas of seeds: part 4*, Uddevalla, Sweden.
Austin, P.J., 2005, 'Analysis of wood charcoal macro-remains from Glanworth Castle, Co. Cork: excavation no. E236'. Unpublished report.
Berggren, G., 1981, *Atlas of seeds: part 3*, Berlings, Arlöv, Sweden.
Behre, K.-E., 2008, 'Collected seeds and fruits from herbs as prehistoric food', *Vegetation History and Archaeobotany* **17**, 65–73.
Brown, A.G., Caseldine, C.J., Hatton, J., O'Brien, C.E., Langdon, P.G., Selby, K.A., & Stuijts, I., 2005, 'Vegetation, landscape and human activity in midland Ireland: mire and lake records from the Lough Kinale-Derragh Lough area, central Ireland', *Vegetation History and Archaeobotany* **14**, 81–98.
Cappers, R.T.J., Bekker, R.M., & Gronigen, J.E.A., 2006, *Digital seed atlas of the Netherlands*, Eelde, The Netherlands. www.seedatlas.nl (accessed 12 April 2009).
Comber, M., 2001, 'Trade and communication networks in early historic Ireland', *The Journal of Irish Archaeology* **10**, 73–92.
Cutler, D.F., & Gale, R., 2000, *Plants in archaeology: identification manual of artefacts of plant origin from Europe and the Mediterranean*, Kew.
Crackles, F.E., 1986, 'Medieval gardens in Hull: archaeological evidence', *Garden History* **14:1**, 1–5.
Defelice, M.S., 2004, 'Common chickweed, *Stellaria media (L.) Vill.*: "mere chicken feed"', *Weed Technology* **18:1**, 193–200.
Daly, S., 1992, 'Journal volume 2: the Old Corn Mill, Killincarrig', http://greystonesahs.org/web/j219 (accessed 18 February 2009).

Dyer, C., 1983, 'English diet in the later Middle Ages' in Aston, T.H., Coss, O.R., Dyer, C., & Thirsk, J. (eds), *Social relations and ideas: essay in honour of R.H. Hilton,* 191–216. Cambridge.

Dennell, R.W., 1970, 'Seeds from a medieval sewer in Woolster Street, Plymouth', *Economic Botany* **24**:2, 151–4.

Dickson, C., 1996, 'Food, medicinal and other plants from the 15th-century drains of Paisley Abbey, Scotland', *Vegetation History and Archaeobotany* **5**, 25–31.

Edwards, N., 2000, *The archaeology of Early Medieval Ireland.* London.

Edwards, N., 2005, 'The archaeology of Early Medieval Ireland *c.*1400–1169: settlement and economy' in Ó Cróinín, D. (ed.), *A new history of Ireland I: prehistory and early Ireland,* 235–96. Oxford.

Gibson, A., 1989, 'Medieval corn-drying kilns at Capo, Kincardineshire and Abercairny, Perthshire', *Proceedings of the Society of Antiquaries of Scotland* **118**, 219–29.

Heller, I., Kienast, F., Schoch, W., & Schweingruber, F.H., 2004, *Wood anatomy of Central European species.* Online version: www.woodanatomy.ch (accessed 12 April 2009).

Keepax, C.A., 1988, 'Charcoal analysis with particular reference to archaeological sites in Britain'. Unpublished PhD thesis, University of London.

Lloyd, P.S., & Peterken, G.F., 1967, '*Ilex Aquifolium L.*', *The Journal of Ecology* **55**:3, 841–58.

Mitchell, A., & Wilkinson, J., 1978, *A hand-guide to the trees of Britain and Northern Europe.* London.

O'Keeffe, T., 2001, *Medieval Ireland: an archaeology.* Stroud, Gloucestershire.

Pearson, K.L., 1997, 'Nutrition and the Early Medieval diet', *Speculum* **72**:1, 1–32.

Prins, F., & Shackleton, C.M., 1992, 'Charcoal analysis and the "Principle of least effort": a conceptual model', *Journal of Archaeological Science* **19**, 631–7.

Scholtz, A., 1986, 'Palynological and palaeobotanical studies in the Southern Cape', MA thesis, Stellenbosch, South Africa.

Stace, C., 1997, *A new British flora.* Cambridge.

Stevens, C., & Wilkinson, K., 2003, *Environmental archaeology: approaches, techniques and applications.* Stroud, Gloucestershire.

Stuijts, I., 2005, 'Wood and charcoal identification' in Gowen, M., Ó Néill, J., & Phillips, M., *The Lisheen Mine Archaeological Project, 1996–1998,* 137–86. Bray.

Wheeler, E.A., Baas, P., & Gasson, P.E. (eds), 1989, 'IAWA list of microscopic features for hardwood identification', *IAWA Bulletin* **10**, 219–332.

Seaver, M., 2009, 'Excavations in Trim town E2398'. Unpublished CRDS report.

APPENDIX 15.2: HUMAN BONE
By Ciara Travers

METHODOLOGY

Osteological analysis was carried out based on standards outlined by O'Sullivan et al. (2002) and BABAO/IFA (Brickley & McKinley 2004), and documented on standardized recording forms, devised by the IAPO (Irish Association of Professional Osteoarchaeologists), in order to ensure that the data is comparable for future research.

Preservation and completeness
Preservation refers to the condition of the bone with respect to post-depositional taphonomy and weathering processes. Preservation of the remains at the Black Friary

was recorded as poor, moderate or good. Completeness refers to the bones present and takes into account depositional practices as well as post-depositional truncation by later activity. This is recorded as a percentage of the total number of bones expected from a full adult inhumation. An inventory of all bones and teeth present was carried out, as well as visual recording. Generally, the human bone from the Black Friary was well-preserved, although all inhumations suffered from disturbance by the later cutting of a north-south running ditch across the burial ground. This resulted in a large amount of disarticulated bone.

Burial position
All four inhumations were oriented east/northeast-west/southwest and they were all extended and supine. Burials 2, 3 and 4 were placed within the same grave-cut, suggesting that their interment occurred at the same time. Unusually, Burial 1, originally within its own grave-cut, had slumped considerably into an infilled well (fig. 15.6). The position of surviving left hand bones suggests that this slumping may have occurred shortly after burial, while some soft tissue remained. As the left arm slumped with the torso into the well-cut, it brought with it carpals and metacarpals, leaving behind

Table 15.3 Minimum number of adults at Black Friary site
(R = right; L = left; U = unsided/side unknown)

	Male/?male			Female/?female			Unsexed adult		
	R	L	U	R	L	U	R	L	U
Frontal	0	0	0	0	0	0	2	1	0
Occipital	1	1	0	0	0	0	0	0	2
Petrous Temporal	1	1	0	0	0	0	2	1	1
Maxilla	1	1	0	0	0	0	2	2	0
Mandible	1	1	0	0	0	0	3	2	3
Medial Clavicle	2	1	0	0	0	0	0	2	0
Lateral Clavicle	1	1	0	0	0	0	1	2	0
Glenoid	1	2	0	0	0	0	1	5	0
Proximal Humerus	1	2	0	0	0	0	0	0	0
Distal Humerus	2	2	0	0	0	0	0	4	0
Proximal Radius	2	2	0	0	0	0	4	0	0
Distal Radius	1	2	0	0	0	0	0	2	0
Proximal Ulna	2	2	0	0	0	0	0	3	0
Distal Ulna	1	1	0	0	0	0	1	1	0
Proximal Femur	2	2	0	0	0	0	7	9	1
Distal Femur	2	2	0	0	0	0	6	3	0
Proximal Tibia	2	2	0	0	0	0	1	3	0
Distal Tibia	1	2	0	0	0	0	3	5	0
Proximal Fibula	0	1	0	0	0	0	0	1	0
Distal Fibula	1	2	0	0	0	0	2	3	0
Calcaneus	1	1	0	0	0	0	4	3	0
Talus	1	1	0	0	0	0	3	3	0

phalanges. It is tempting to suggest that if the soft tissues were completely absent, all hand bones would have remained intact beside the left pelvis. This would have taken place during the skeletonization process, when ligaments were still attached to bone. This stage occurs some months after death, depending on variables such as temperature and soil conditions (Clark et al., 1997).

Minimum number of individuals

To calculate the minimum number of individuals (MNI) represented by the articulated and disarticulated skeletal remains, an inventory of the main bones and joints of the body was carried out. The greatest number of any single bone part present represents the MNI of the assemblage. These are then correlated with age and sex in order to reach a more conclusive MNI. As can be seen in Table 15.3, the MNI of adults is two males and nine unsexed individuals. Only four juvenile bones were recovered (a deciduous mandibular right first molar, a fragment of left proximal fibula, a fragment of right distal tibia and a phalanx), giving a juvenile MNI of one. This brings the MNI to twelve (two adult males, nine unsexed adults and one juvenile).

Sex

Sex assessment of adult skeletal remains is based on differences in morphology between males and females, which are most pronounced in the pelvis due to changes made to the female pelvis for childbirth. The sex of adult individuals from the Black Friary was assessed by examining morphological traits, firstly from the bones of the pelvis and secondly from the skull (after Buikstra & Ubelaker 1994; Schwartz 1995). In addition, measurements of articular surfaces of long bones were used. This relies on the assumption that males are larger and more robust than females, and in order to determine sex, measurements are compared to standard measurements of known-sex individuals. Estimated sex of individuals was scored as indeterminate, possible female (?female), female, possible male (?male), and male.

Age

The assessment of the age-at-death of adult individuals is based primarily on the degeneration of skeletal elements. These include morphological changes in the pubic symphysis (after Brooks & Suchey 1990) and changes in the auricular surface of the ilium (after Lovejoy et al., 1985). Where possible, rates of dental attrition (or tooth-wear) were scored according to Brothwell (1981). Rate of epiphyseal union was also used for those individuals who died in early adulthood (Scheuer & Black 2000; Baker et al., 2005). Adults from the Black Friary were classified into the following broad age categories:

> 17–25 years: Young Adult
> 26–35 years: Early Middle Adult
> 36–45 years: Late Middle Adult
> >46: Older Adult

Stature

All complete long bones were measured in order to provide information on stature. The equations of Trotter and Gleser (1958) for white males and females were used in this regard. Only bones that gave the equation with the smallest standard deviation were used.

Non-metric variation
Analysis of a number of cranial and post-cranial non-metric traits was undertaken on adult skeletons. Non-metric traits are variations of the skeleton that are generally minor in nature, are non-pathological and do not interfere with the normal functions of the body. They were marked as present, absent or unobservable (after Finnegan 1978; Berry & Berry 1967).

Pathologies
Descriptions and locations of visible pathological lesions and evidence of trauma were recorded, and photographed when possible. All teeth were individually recorded and any dental disease and caries were recorded according to Brothwell (1981). Rates of attrition were scored (Smith, cited in Buikstra & Ubelaker 1994). Caries was recorded as pin-point, small, medium or large.

RESULTS

Table 15.4 Inhumations at the Black Friary

Burial no.	Sex	Age category	Years
1	?Male	Young adult	20–25
2	Male	Early middle adult	30–39
3	–	Adult	–
4	–	Adult	–

Burial 1
Burial 1 was a relatively complete young adult ?male. Ageing was based on epiphyseal fusion, dental attrition and the pubic symphysis, all of which suggested that this individual was 20–25 years old at time of death. Sexing of the incomplete skull (nuchal crest, mental imminence and mastoid process) and pelvis (ramus ridge, sciatic notch and pre-auricular sulcus) gave a ?male estimation. Metrical data from long bones, as well as the general robusticity of the skeleton, also supports this. His stature is estimated at approximately 165.4cm (5'5"). The only non-metric traits visible were bilateral ossicles in the lambdoid suture.

The dentition of Burial 1 survived nearly complete, with only one tooth missing due to post-mortem loss (maxillary right first pre-molar). Small to medium levels of calculus were noted on twenty-six of the thirty-one teeth present. Calculus is one of the most commonly occurring pathological conditions in archaeological assemblages and is formed when bacterial plaque mineralizes and attaches to the surfaces of the teeth (Hillson 1996).

Eleven of the teeth exhibited dental enamel hypoplasia and presented Brothwell's (1981) grade 3–4 (slight-medium). Hypoplasia is the result of episodes of nutritional or

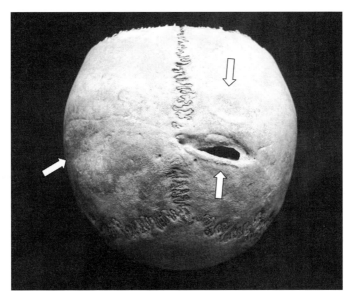

15.7 Burial 1: blunt force trauma to cranium (arrows)

pathological stress during youth, while the teeth are still forming. This leads to disturbance in the formation of enamel and defects in the teeth, observable as furrows or
planes on the surface of the enamel (Hillson 1996). An amount of disorganized new
bone formation was observed around the alveolar bone of the maxilla. While this may
be associated with periodontal disease, only slight signs of alveolar resorption were
present. Another dental anomaly present was the chipping of the occlusal (or biting)
surface of both the upper and lower incisors and canine teeth. This may have been
caused by activity, fights or accidents as well as pathological conditions which weaken
the tooth enamel.

This skeleton exhibited a number of traumatic lesions to the cranium (fig. 15.7).
The first was a depression fracture to the left parietal. It was roughly ovoid in shape,
with irregular edges which suggest that it was caused by blunt force trauma and was
also visible on the inner surface of the skull. The lesion showed signs of significant
healing, suggesting that it had occurred some time before the death of the individual.

The second traumatic lesion to the skull was on the right parietal bone, close to the
saggital suture. It was ovoid and shallow and was not visible on the endocranial surface.
While healed bone had obscured the borders of the wound, the edges were still well-
defined and sharp, suggesting a sharp force trauma, possibly a slicing injury from a
blade. The third and most conspicuous lesion was a large penetrating wound to the
right parietal. It was located just below the second lesion, slightly to the right of the
mid-line of the skull. It was ovoid/teardrop in shape and perforated the surface of the
skull completely. A large flake was visible on the inner table of the cranium. The lesion
showed considerable signs of healing and a bridge of new bone was present across the
right edge of the lesion. A radiating fracture was present from the saggital suture across
the dome of the skull to the parietomastoid suture. This fracture had healed, but

cracked again post-mortem. The level of healing indicated that the individual lived for several weeks or months after the wound occurred. The wound was most probably caused by a blade, the direction of which was from above and behind/to the right. The three cranial wounds show similar signs of healing, but they were most likely from three different weapons and may have been from different events.

A healed fracture was also visible on the distal shaft of the left ulna of Burial 1. While a large lesion of woven bone was present, the fracture was well-healed, with no misalignment, but possibly slight shortening to the affected bone in comparison to the radius. The good alignment of the healed bone may suggest splinting, although the radius was not affected and may have acted as a support for the healing bone. This fracture is a classic manifestation of a Parry fracture.

DJD (degenerative joint disease) is a non-inflammatory disease involving the degeneration of the articular cartilage of various joints. This degeneration can allow a variety of bony manifestations to develop, and these are frequently observed on skeletal remains. The disease is strongly related to age. A number of anomalies were present on the spine of this individual which may be associated with DJD. Pairs of Schmorl's node-like depressions were visible on the inferior bodies of a number of the thoracic and lumbar vertebrae. Schmorl's nodes are pressure defects in the superior or inferior margin of the vertebral disk. They are caused by a herniation of the inter-vertebral disk and are believed to result from falls or from lifting heavy objects incorrectly (Aufderheide & Rodriguez-Martin 1998). Two possible Schmorl's nodes were present on the anterior surface of the first body of the sacrum, and moderate amounts of osteophytes were visible on the second and third sacral bodies. This may be a developmental anomaly or may be related to activity. While these lesions could be related to DJD, the young age of this individual suggests that it may be a developmental anomaly or related to activity. The skeleton was generally very robust and the proximal head of the right ulna, along the site of attachment of the *M. Brachialis*, was particularly pronounced. This muscle flexes the elbow.

Burial 2

Burial 2 was an early middle adult male. The skeleton survived complete, except for the skull. A disarticulated and highly fragmented skull (DHB 8) was recovered close to Burial 2 and may belong to this individual. The skull displayed male characteristics. The pelvis of Burial 2 was incomplete and sexing was based on the ischiopubic ramus, sub-pubic concavity and angle, sciatic notch and pre-auricular sulcus. While these gave estimates of male, measurement of long bones was inconclusive. Age was based on the auricular surface and pubic symphysis which gave an estimate of 30 to 39 years. Only the radii were complete enough for stature estimation, which gave a result of 170cm (5'7"). The only non-metric trait visible was a slight third trochanter on the right femur.

Burial 2 also showed signs of significant trauma. Six right ribs were fractured on the body of the ribs, close to the angle. The lesions associated with the fractures indicate that healing was active at the time of death. Five of the fractures were slightly misaligned, with the sternal end of the rib displaced anteriorly. Their location near the angle of the ribs (on the back of the individual) suggests that they occurred due to direct trauma to the front of the chest.

Two of the left ribs also showed signs of trauma. The upper rib affected had a large lesion protruding from its inferior surface, towards the sternal end of the body of the rib. It was dense and smooth in character, and angled inferiorly-distally, towards the subsequent inferior rib, which contained another, smaller lesion on its superior edge, with which the superior lesion articulated. It is possible that these anomalies originate from a fracture to the upper rib, but the site of the break has fully healed. Trauma may have led to the ossification of the internal inter-costal muscles.

A healed fracture was present on the left radius. The anterior distal shaft was damaged post-mortem, and this is most likely the site of the fracture. A considerable amount of DJD was present on the distal head of the radius, and a number of the carpals of the left wrist, and this is most likely associated with the injury. This is a classic Colles fracture, which is associated with falls, when indirect trauma causes breaks to the hand and wrist.

A fracture to the left second metacarpal was also visible. It was well-healed and the fracture site was unclear. Boxer's fractures received their name from one of their most common causes – punching an object with a closed fist, such as during a fist-fight. Although these breaks usually occur when the hand is closed into a fist, they can also occur when the hand is not clenched and strikes a hard object such as in the case of a fall on a hard object. The degree of healing in all visible traumas on Burial 2 is similar, and this suggests that they all occurred at the same time. They may, however, have resulted from different events.

An amount of periosteal new bone formation was present on the left tibia. This occurred along the medial side of the shaft of the bone. New bone growth, including striation and moderate pitting, was visible and this indicates that the lesion was active at the time of death.

Burial 2 suffered from a moderate amount of degenerative disease. Slight to medium levels of osteophytes were present on the vertebral bodies. Additionally, the vertebral head and neck of a lower right rib fragment exhibited severe osteophytosis. T10 showed osteophytes on the superior surface of the right superior tubercle, and the site of insertion of the *M. levatores costarum*, which attaches the vertebrae to the rib immediately below it. Severe osteophytes were also present on the right inferior articular facets and costal facets of T11. It is assumed that these more severe proliferations are post-traumatic joint disease related to the trauma to the right ribs discussed above. As mentioned above, the bones of the left wrist showed signs of post-traumatic joint disease.

A possible instance of spina bifida occulta was observed on the fifth lumbar vertebra of this individual. The spinous processes, while joined, have not fully fused. The vertebral arches of the sacrum were unobservable. This anomaly is most likely congenital and is non-symptomatic.

Burial 3

Burial 3 was severely truncated by a ditch and survived only as the lower legs and feet. Incomplete preservation meant that sexing of this individual was impossible. The complete epiphyseal fusion of all bones present led to the age estimation of 'adult'. No non-metric traits or pathologies were visible.

Burial 4

Burial 4 was also truncated by the ditch and only the lower legs and feet survived intact. Again, a sex estimate of this individual could not be established, and all bones present were fused, suggesting the broad age category of 'adult'. No non-metric traits or pathologies were visible.

Disarticulated human bone (DHB)

A relatively large amount of disarticulated bone was recovered (see tables below). Most notable was the large collection from a pit at the base of the north-south running ditch that disturbed all of the inhumations excavated. The majority of bone from this context was large in size and reflects the collection of visible, recognizable human bone recovered during the digging of the ditch. No signs of weathering or gnawing activity were present on the bone. This indicates that the bone was not left in the open for a significant period of time and is consistent with the disturbance of already skeletonized remains by later human activity. Analysis of the bone showed moderate levels of DJD, and small numbers of dental caries, which is similar to the pattern found in the articulated bone assemblage. Apart from the single deciduous tooth, all bones were of adult individuals. Any bones available for sexing gave male or ?male estimates. A misaligned fracture was visible on the shaft of a portion of left humerus. The severity of misalignment indicates that no splinting occurred.

DISCUSSION

Unfortunately, the relatively small number of burials from the excavation means that no substantial and comparative demographic study can be carried out. Nonetheless, analysis has brought a number of interesting questions to light. It is clear that additional burials extend beyond the limits of excavation and, as such, these four burials represent a sub-set of a larger cemetery group. It may be that these skeletal remains represent a biased portion of the population. All of the individuals were adult, however, and all instances that could provide information on sex were male. It is possible that a single demographic group, primarily young adult males, was buried in this location.

The absence of recognizable sub-adult remains is notable. In medieval assemblages, juvenile remains can be expected to account for around 30–40% of all individuals interred in a cemetery population (Scott 1999; Grainger et al., 2008). Four disarticulated bones were the only evidence of juvenile individuals at the site.

In general, the individuals buried at the Black Friary were in relatively good health at the time of death. Linear enamel hypoplasia, present on the teeth of Burial 1, indicates periods of nutritional or metabolic stress during childhood. Traditionally, the periosteal reaction occurring on the left tibia of Burial 2 would be recorded as non-specific infection. This condition can be caused by trauma, however, or indeed 'anything that breaks, tears, stretches, or even touches the periostium (membrane of connective tissue that surrounds all bones)' (Weston 2008, 49). Periosteal reactions in tibiae are common, as these bones lie close to the surface and are therefore more prone to insult (Coughlan & Holst 2007). Prevalence of periosteal bone formation during the medieval period ranged from 5.9% to as high as 64% (Weston 2008).

The average stature in medieval Ireland was 170cm (5'7") (Buckley et al., 1998). The statures of Burials 1 and 2 were 165cm (5'5") and 170cm (5'7") respectively. While Burial 1 is slightly shorter than the average for the period, stature is dependant on heredity as well as environment and so is not necessarily related to the health of the individual (Coughlan & Holst 2007).

A number of indicators of strenuous activity were present on the skeletons from the Black Friary. Burial 1 was generally very robust and showed indication that the right elbow joint was exposed to mechanical stress during repeated muscular activity. Schmorl's nodes present on the spine of Burial 2, and possibly in Burial 1, also indicate heavy loading of the vertebral column.

The most distinctive aspect of this small assemblage is the large amount of trauma observed on the two near-complete inhumations (fig. 15.8). The injuries sustained from three instances of severe cranial trauma to Burial 1 would most likely have led to bleeding and brain injury due to acceleration forces, and later to mental incapacitation, brain damage, visions, headaches and behavioural changes (Boylston 2000). Healing that was evident around the lesions suggests that the individual lived for some weeks or months after the attack occurred (Lovell 1997). While many cases of cranial trauma have been associated with possible executions, the substantial healing to all wounds indicates that this individual survived for some time after the incident, and so the wounds were the result of an inter-personal attack. The location of the lesions on the cranium suggests that the assailant made the attack from the back and above, as if on horseback, or with the victim on his knees or on the ground.

The same individual also suffered from a broken distal ulna some time before his death. This type of fracture is often classed as a Parry fracture and is usually interpreted as resulting from the individual's attempt to ward off a blow directed at their head or upper body, or from blows hitting a shield with the forces being transmitted to the ulna. There is a strong likelihood that Parry fractures arise during conflict situations in certain settings (Larsen 1997).

Burial 2 also showed signs of significant trauma, most notably to the right ribs. The level of healing indicates that this individual survived for a considerable time after the injury occurred, presumably in some amount of pain. Due to pain associated with fractured ribs, it may be difficult for affected individuals to breathe deeply and to cough to clear the chest, and this may have implications for respiratory function (Brickley 2006). The fracture of even one rib can result in sufficient pain to prevent an individual from working, and can result in low quality of life until it heals. Soft tissue damage may have been more severe than inferred from damage to the bones themselves, particularly if the fractured bones are displaced inwards at the time of injury (Lovell 1997). Laceration of the soft tissues can result in serious complications such as pneumothorax or hemothorax and multiple rib fractures have a greater chance of sustaining injuries to the spleen or liver (Brickley 2006).

Rib fractures are usually due to blunt force trauma to the chest which, in the archaeological record, may be the result of a throw from an animal-drawn vehicle, a fall from a ladder or hayloft, an assault, or a work-related accident (Judd & Roberts 1999; Brickley 2006). Burial 2 also had a fracture to the distal radius. This lesion is a classic manifestation of a Colles fracture, which results when the individual attempts to break a forward fall by extending the arms forward (Aufderheide & Rodriguez-Martin 1998).

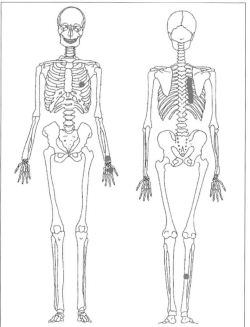 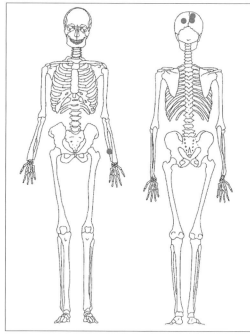

15.8 Distribution of traumatic injuries on Burial 1 (left) and Burial 2 (right)

Levels of healing indicate that this may have occurred at the same time as the other post-cranial injuries, suggesting a fall from a height.

Levels of healing observed on the trauma of Burials 1 and 2 indicate that while multiple lesions may have been inflicted at the same instance, not all occurred at the same time. This suggests that these individuals were particularly prone to trauma, whether through their profession or their lifestyle. It is not uncommon for fractures to occur in medieval assemblages. Fractures can be expected to affect from 10 to 17% of the population (Fibiger 2008; 2009), many of which may be inflicted during farming and associated activities (Judd & Roberts 1999). A comparable assemblage comes from Towton, Yorkshire. The individuals from this site were soldiers who had been interred in a mass grave after the Battle of Towton in 1461. The assemblage consisted of adult males, generally in a good state of health at the time of death. Similar to the Black Friary, the individuals at Towton suffered large numbers of severe cranial wounds and upper limb fractures, many of which showed different levels of healing. This led the authors to believe that these men were fighters involved in multiple battles/fights over the course of their lives (Knüsel & Boylston 2007).

While very few assumptions can be made about the small assemblage from the Black Friary, it is clear that the individuals uncovered had been exposed to trauma over the course of their lives.

ACKNOWLEDGMENT

Many thanks to Denise Keating for her advice and patience while supervising the analysis of this assemblage.

BIBLIOGRAPHY

Aufderheide, A., & Rodriguez-Martin, C., 1998, *The Cambridge encyclopaedia of human paleopathology*. Cambridge.

Baker, B., Dupras, T., & Tocheri, M., 2005, *The osteology of infants and children*. Texas.

Berry, A., & Berry, R., 1967, 'Epigenic variation in the human cranium', *Journal of Anatomy* **101**, 316–97.

Boylston, A., 2000, 'Evidence for weapon related trauma in British archaeological samples' in Cox, M., & Mays, S. (eds), *Human osteology in archaeology and forensic science*, 357–80. London.

Brickley, M., & McKinley, J. (eds), 2004, *Guidelines to the standards for recording human remains*. Southampton/Reading.

Brickley, M., 2006, 'Rib fractures in the archaeological record: a useful source of sociocultural information?', *International Journal of Osteoarchaeology* **16**, 61–75.

Brooks, S., & Suchey, J.M., 1990, 'Skeletal age determination based on the os pubis: a comparison of the Acsadi-Nemeskeri and Suchey-Brooks methods', *Human Evolution* **5**, 227–38.

Brothwell, D., 1981, *Digging up bones*. London.

Buckley, L.A., Ó Donnabháin, B., & Murphy, E., 1998, 'Decommissioning our dead', *Archaeology Ireland* **46:12:4**, 18–19.

Buikstra, J., & Ubelaker, D. (eds), 1994, *Standards for data collection from human skeletal remains: proceedings of a seminar at the Field Museum of Natural History*. Arkansas.

Clark, M., Worrell, M., & Pless, J., 1997, 'Post-mortem changes in soft tissues' in Haglund, W., & Sorg, M. (eds), *Forensic taphonomy: the post-mortem fate of human remains*, 151–60. Boca Raton, Florida.

Coughlan, J., & Holst, M., 2007, 'Health status' in Fiorato, V., Boylston, A., & Knüsel, C. (eds), *Blood red roses: the archaeology of a mass grave from the Battle of Towton AD1461*, 60–76. Oxford.

Fibiger, L., 2005, 'Minor ailments, furious fights and deadly diseases: investigating life in Johnstown, County Meath, AD400–1700' in O'Sullivan, J., & Stanley, M. (eds), *Recent archaeological discoveries on national road schemes 2004*, 99–110. Dublin.

Fibiger, L., 2009, 'The human skeletal remains from Raystown, Co. Meath' in Seaver, M., 'Final report on excavations at Site 21, Raystown, Co. Meath'. Unpublished report.

Finnegan, M., 1978, 'Non-metric variation of the infracranial skeleton', *Journal of Anatomy* **125**, 23–37.

Grainger, I., Hawkins, D., Cowal, L., & Mikulski, R., 2008, *The Black Death cemetery, East Smithfield, London*. London.

Hillson, S., 1996, *Dental anthropology*. Cambridge.

Judd, M., & Roberts, C., 1999, 'Fracture trauma in a medieval British farming village', *American Journal of Physical Anthropology* **10**, 229–43.

Knüsel, C., & Boylston, A., 2007, 'How has the Towton Project contributed to our knowledge of medieval warfare?' in Fiorato, V., Boylston, A., & Knüsel, C. (eds), *Blood red roses: the archaeology of a mass grave from the Battle of Towton AD1461*, 169–88. Oxford.

Larson, C.S., 1997, *Bioarchaeology: interpreting behaviour from the human skeleton.* Cambridge.

Lovejoy, C.O., Meindl, R.S., Pryzbeck, T.R., & Mensforth, R.P., 1985, 'Chronological metamorphosis of the auricular surface of the ilium: a new method for the determination of age at death', *American Journal of Physical Anthropology* **68**, 15–28.

Lovell, N., 1997, 'Trauma analysis in paleopathology', *Yearbook of Physical Anthropology* **40**, 139–70.

O'Sullivan, J., Hallissey, M., & Roberts, J., 2002, *Human remains in Irish archaeology: legal, scientific, planning and ethical implications.* Kilkenny.

Scheuer, L., & Black, S., 2000, *Developmental juvenile osteology.* London.

Schwartz, J.H., 1995, *Skeleton keys: an introduction to human skeletal morphology, development & analysis.* Oxford.

Scott, E., 1999, *The archaeology of infancy and infant death.* BAR International **819**. Oxford.

Trotter, M., & Gleser, G.C., 1958, 'A re-evaluation of estimation of stature based on measurements of stature taken during life and long bones after death', *American Journal of Physical Anthropology* **10**, 463–514.

Weston, D., 2008, 'Investigating the specificity of periosteal reactions in pathology museum specimens', *American Journal of Physical Anthropology* **137**, 48–59.

SKELETAL CATALOGUE

Abbreviations: general

–	unobservable	*OPS*	osteophytes
DHB	disarticulated human bone	*PO*	porosity
dist.	distal	*prox.*	proximal
DJD	degenerative joint disease	*R*	right
EMA	early middle adult	*sup.*	superior
inf.	inferior	*YA*	young adult
L	Left	*C3*	third cervical vertebra
LMA	Late middle adult	*T4*	fourth thoracic vertebra
OA	older adult	*L5*	fifth lumbar vertebra

Abbreviations: dental

–	tooth not present	*C*	caries
/	tooth lost post-mortem	*E*	erupting
X	tooth lost ante-mortem	*H*	dental enamel hypoplasia
- - -	alveolar bone missing	*P*	periodontitis
a	abscess	*Rb*	root broken
c	calculus	*U*	unerupted

Permanent dentition

Right maxilla   Left maxilla

| 18 | 17 | 16 | 15 | 14 | 13 | 12 | 11 | | 21 | 22 | 23 | 24 | 25 | 26 | 27 | 28 |
| 48 | 47 | 46 | 45 | 44 | 43 | 42 | 41 | | 31 | 32 | 33 | 34 | 35 | 36 | 37 | 38 |

Right mandible   Left mandible

Burial 1

Radiocarbon date	1390–1630 cal. AD δ13C: -19.38; δ15N: 13.34
Sex	?Male (pelvis & skull)
Age	20–25 years, Young adult
Stature	165cm (5'5) (femur & tibia)
Non-metrics	Ossicles in lambdoid present at R & L
Preservation	Good
Completeness	90%
DHB	DHB 1 (2 conjoins with sternal rib fragments; L clavicle most likely belongs to B1), DHB 2 (conjoin with distal L 1st metacarpal)

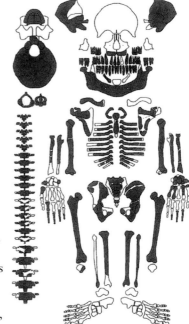

Trauma

Cranial Trauma

1) Depression fracture on L parietal, roughly ovoid in shape. Visible on endocranial surface. Signs of healing. Irregular edges of wound indicate blunt force trauma.

2) Traumatic lesion on R parietal, 17 mm from saggital suture.

Ovoid in shape, with ring of sclerotic bone around perimeter of lesion. Not visible on endocranial surface. Edges have defined, sharp feel which suggest sharp force trauma by blade, possible slicing injury.

3) Penetrating blade wound to R parietal, affecting saggital suture. Perforates endocranial surface. Sclerotic bone around edges of lesionith rounding of edges. Healed radiating fracture from saggital, across Wound 1 to L parietomastiod suture. Cracked post-mortem. Direction of blade in an inferior direction from posterior/right aspect.

Post-Cranial Trauma

1) Well-healed fracture to distal shaft of L ulna. No misalignment, but possible slight shortening of ulna in comparison to radius. Parry fracture.

Pathology

DJD

1) Osteophytes present only on T7 & L5. No PO or eburnation.

2) Schmorl's node-like depressions on inferior bodies of T2–T12, L3–5 (L1 unobservable). Present in pairs, on posterior of body. Lack of osteophytes on affected vertebrae, possible developmental anomaly?

3) 2 possible Schmorl's nodes present on R superior surface of body of S1. L side unobservable. Oval in shape, 10mm x 6mm and 10mm x 7mm. Also, moderate osteophytes on inferior body of S2 and superior body of S3. Skeleton very young for DJD – possible developmental anomaly or activity related.

Other   R ulna prox. head showed pronounced site of attachment of *M.
                             Brachialis*, which is involved in flexing of the elbow.

Dental pathology   Calculus: Slight to moderate (26/31). Buccal, lingual, mesial and distal
                             surfaces of tooth affected.
                             Attrition: Attrition was slight to moderate throughout (stage 1–4).
                             Enamel Hypoplasia: Slight lines on teeth 11–14, 21–24, 33, 41 & 43.
                             Periodontal Disease?: Disorganized new bone formation around
                             alveolar surfaces, on L & R maxilla, on lingual, buccal surfaces and
                             between teeth, and most pronounced on lingual side. Only slight signs
                             of alveolar resorption.
                             Teeth chipping: Maxilla: L canine, R 1st & 2nd incisor, R canine.
                             Mandible: R 1st & 2nd incisor, L 1st incisor. Chipping of enamel on
                             occlusal edges of buccal surfaces.

Dentition

		c	C		cH	cH	cH	cH		cH	cH	cH	cH	c	c	c	c
18	17	16	/	14	13	12	11		21	22	23	24	25	26	27	28
48	47	46	45	44	43	42	41		31	32	33	34	35	36	37	38
		c	c	cH	c	cH			c	c	cH	c	c	c	c	

Burial 2

Sex	Male
Age	Early middle adult
Stature	170cm (5'7) (L & R radius)
Non-metrics	Slight third trochanter on R femur
Preservation	Moderate
Completeness	70%
DHB	DHB 4, 8, 9, 10, 11
Trauma	1) Healed fractures present on 6 right ribs (3–10). All on body of rib, close to angle. 5/6 ribs displaced anteriorly. Extensive deposits of callus bone observed on all surfaces of the bone. They were particularly prolific on the superior and inferior surfaces of the ribs affected and may have involved the ossification of the surrounding inter-costal muscles. 2) Lesions on left ribs (3–10). Lesion protruding from inferior surface, smooth and dense, and angled infero-laterally. Articulates with lesion on superior edge of inferior rib affected. It is possible that it originates from

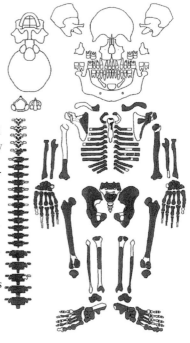

fracture, but site of fracture has fully healed. Angle of larger lesion suggests ossification of internal inter-costal muscles.

3) Healed Colles fracture to L radius. Severe osteophytes present on distal head.

4) Healed Boxers fracture to distal shaft of L 2nd metacarpal.

Pathology   DJD

1) Osteophytes present on all thoracic and lumbar vertebrae and S1. Schmorl's nodes observed on T4 & T9. Severity of osteophytes on T10 & T11 possibly related to trauma to R ribs. No PO or eburnation.

2) Osteophytes present on medial articular faced of R clavicle. No PO or eburnation.

3) Osteophytes present on distal L radius, L scaphoid, L hamate, L capitate, L triquitrum, L trapezoid, L trapezium. Post-traumatic DJD related to Colles fracture to L radius. No PO or eburnation.

4) Osteophytes visible on vertebral head of R rib affected by fracture. Post-traumatic.

Other   1) Periosteal bone formation present on L tibia. New bone growth, including striation and moderate pitting, was visible and indicates that the lesion was active at time of death. Visible on medial side of shaft, along anterior and interosseous crests. Proximal shaft missing.

2) Spina bifida occulta on L5. Vertebral arches of sacrum unobservable.

Dental   None
pathology
Dentition   None

Burial 3

Sex	–
Age	Adult
Stature	–
Non-metrics	None
Preservation	Good
Completeness	10%
DHB	DHB 4, 5, 6, 7, 9
Pathology	None
Dental pathology	None
Dentition	None

Burial 4

Sex	–
Age	Adult
Stature	–
Non-metrics	None
Preservation	Good
Completeness	10%
DHB	DHB 4, 9
Pathology	None
Dental pathology	None
Dentition	None

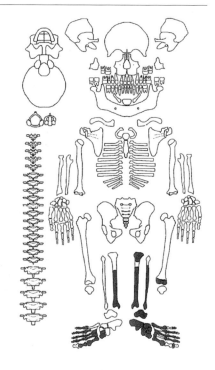

Disarticulated bone register

DHB 1	Description	Comments
Fill No: F2105 (Fill of well F2107) Possible Burial No.: B1 Preservation: Good	Upr L 2nd incisor (attrition stage 1, 0 caries, 0 calculus) L humerus, portion of distal shaft Fragment R scapula spine L clavicle	Adult. Not associated with B1 Adult Proximal epiphysis unfused. Most likely B1
	14 x unidentified shaft fragment 3 x R rib fragments, sternal end. 2 x L rib fragments, sternal end. 1 x unsided rib fragment Fragment L ischium 1 x L 5th metatarsal, fragment distal metatarsal	? Human 2 x conjoins with B1 Adult Adult

DHB 2	Description	Comments
Fill No: F2103 (Grave fill B1) Possible Burial No.: B1 Preservation: Moderate–Good	Distal half of L 1st metacarpal 4 x unidentified skull fragments Small ?R clavicle fragment 1 x L rib fragment, sternal end. 2 x R rib fragments, sternal end. 1 x R rib fragment, vertebral end. 4 x unsided rib fragment 3 x fragments L patella Large no. unidentified shaft fragments Deciduous mandibular 1st molar	Conjoin with B1: recorded with burial Adult. No direct osteological evidence to confirm relationship with B1. Juvenile: not B1

DHB 3	Description	Comments
Fill No: F2129 (Charnel pit within Ditch F2109) Possible Burial No.: - Preservation: Moderate–Good	11 x small cranial vault fragments. Portion of R frontal bone including part of R orbit. Portion occipital (?male, nuchal crest Fragment of R maxilla with R canine, 1st & 2nd premolars Adult (caries & periodontal disease present)	Adult
	1 x R humerus shaft portion. 1 x L distal epiphysis humerus with portion of distal shaft. R radius portion, with head and proximal half of shaft. 2 x distal portions of L radius with distal epiphysis and distal half of shaft. R ulna distal epiphysis. L ulna portion, with olecranon & proximal half of shaft. L ulna portion, with distal head and portion of shaft. 3 fragments unsided ulna shaft	Adult
	L lunate, R 2nd metacarpal, L 2nd metacarpal, R 5th metacarpal	Adult
	R clavicle, lateral 3/4. Portion of L scapula with small fragment of glenoid fossa and spine	Adult
	3 x sternal end L rib fragments. 2 x vertebral end L rib fragments. 3 x vertebral end R rib fragments. 1 x sternal end R rib fragment. 8 x unsided rib fragments. Small portion L sternal body	Adult
	1 x atlas, 2 x lumbar, 1 x partial lumbar, 5 x thoracic, 1 x thoracic spinous process	Adult
	1 x L ilium including iliac crest, sciatic notch, fragment of acetabulum. 1 x portion of unsided iliac crest. 1 x L portion of ischial tuberosity	Adult
	3 x R femur portions including head and proximal half of shaft. 1 x L femur portion including head, lesser & greater trochanter & proximal shaft. 1 x L femur portion including lesser & greate trochanter & proximal shaft. 1 x R femur distal shaft and distal epiphysis. 1 x unsided femoral head. L tibia distal epiphysis &portion of shaft. R tibia distal epiphysis. 2 x R tibia shaft. L tibia shaft. 5 x unsided fibula fragments	Adult
	R calcaneus, R talus, R 2nd cuneiform, L cuboid, 3 x R 1st metatarsal, L 1st metatarsal, 2 x R 3rd metatarsal, L 3rd metatarsal, L 4th metatarsal, 2 x L 5th metatarsals	Adult

DHB 4	Description	Comments
Fill No: F2133 (Fill of re-cut of gully F2127) Possible Burial No.: B2, B3, B4 Preservation: Moderate–Good	1 x portion of R parietal, including mastoid process, acoustic meatus, petrous portion. 1 x fragment of R sphenoid. 1 x portion of occipital including R & L occipital condyles, & pharyngeal tubercle. Portion of R mandible, including mental foramen, with 1st, 2nd & 3rd molars. Portion of L mandible, including mental foramen, mental protuberance, with 2nd incisor, 1st & 2nd premolars, 1st & 2nd molars. Portion of R mandible, including goneal angle and mandibular condyle, with 3rd molar. Portion of L mandible body, with M1. Portion of mandible, including mental protuberance and L mental foramen, no teeth present. R mandibular head. Large amount cranial vault fragments	All adult. No direct osteological evidence to confirm relationship of any bone from DHB 4 with B2, B3, or B4
	Mandibular teeth: 2 x L 2nd incisors, 1 x R canine, 1 x L canine, 2 x L 1st premolar, 1 x R 2nd premolar, 2 x L 2nd premolar, 1 x R premolar, 2 x R 1st premolar, 1 x R 1st molar, 2 x R 2nd molar.	Adult
	Maxillary teeth: 1 x R 1st incisor, 1 x L 3rd molar, 1 x L canine	Adult

DHB 4	Description	Comments
	Radius shaft fragment. R radius head including tuberosity & proximal shaft. 2 x R radius head. 2 x L ulna head including proximal shaft. Humerus shaft portion. L humerus distal shaft portion (healed fracture. Misaligned heal, with shaft distal of break rotated medially & posteriorly)	
	3 x metacarpal distal head fragments. L 2nd metacarpal. L 2nd metacarpal, proximal head and proximal shaft. L capitate. R hamate. Navicular fragment. Proximal phalanx fragment. 1 x distal hand phalanx. 4 x proximal hand phalanges. 3 x medial hand phalanges	Adult
	1 x L clavicle (proximal epiphysis fusing). R clavicle, shaft. 2 x fragments scapula blade. 2 x portions L scapula including glenoid, part of spine & axial border. 1 x fragment L scapula with part of blade & axial border. 2 x portion R scapula, axial border. 1 x R scapula, acromion	Adult
	23 x unsided rib body fragments. 5 x R rib fragments vertebral ends. I x R rib body fragment. 4 x L rib vertebral end fragments	Adult
	1 x lumbar vertebrae, missing R inferior process. 1 x lumbar vertebral body. 1 x lumbar fragment, including R superior articular surface, R inferior articular process. 2 x thoracic bodies. 1 x thoracic vertebrae. 1 x thoracic portion including body & R inferior process. 1 x thoracic portion including body & R superior process (Schmorl's node on superior centrum). 1 x thoracic including portion of body, R superior process, R & L inferior processes. Small number thoracic fragment including 2 x spinous processes, superior articular facets & transverse processes. Cervical body including L superior articular facet. Portion of atlas, including L sup articular facet, L inferior articular facet, L vertebral foramen & L spinous process. 2 x anterior tubercle of atlas	Adult
	Portion of R ilium, including part of auricular surface, acetabulum & sciatic notch, in 2 pieces (Male – sciatic notch). Fragment of R ischial tuberosity including portion of acetabulum. Fragment of L ischial tuberosity including portion of acetabulum. Fragment of R ischium. Fragment of L sacral auricular surface. S1 including R sacral auricular surface. 3 x sacral bodies. Portions of sacral crest	Adult
	R femur in 3 pieces, including distal epiphysis, shaft, greater and lesser trochanter. R femur in 2 pieces, including head & proximal shaft. R proximal femur including head, greater & lesser trochanters. R femur head. Fragment of femur shaft, including lesser trochanter. Distal half of R femur, in 2 pieces, including distal shaft & epiphysis. Distal epiphysis R femur. 2 x unsided fragments femur shaft. 2 x unsided fragments femur head. 2 x pieces L femur shaft. Distal L femur in 2 pieces including distal shaft & distal epiphysis. Medial epicondyle L femur. Proximal L femur including head, proximal half of shaft, in 3 pieces. Proximal L femur including head, greater trochanter, lesser trochanter proximal half of shaft, in 3 pieces. Proximal L femur including head, greater trochanter. Proximal L femur including greater trochanter & proximal shaft. 5 x L tibia shaft fragment. 2 x L tibia distal epiphysis. L tibia piece including proximal epiphysis and tuberosity. 1 x R patella	Adult

DHB 4	Description	Comments
	L tibia piece including proximal epiphysis, tuberosity & proximal half of shaft. R tibia piece including proximal epiphysis and tuberosity. L fibula fragment, proximal head. L fibula piece, lateral malleolus & portion of distal shaft. Fibula shaft portions	Adult
	1 x L calcaneus. 1 x R calcaneus. 1 x L talus. 1 x R talus. 1 x L 1st cuneiform. 1 x L 3rd cuneiform. 1 x R 1st metatarsal. 2 x R 3rd metatarsal. 2 x R 5th metatarsal. 1 x L 3rd metatarsal. 1 x R 4th metatarsal proximal head fragment. 2 x metatarsal distal fragment. 6 x proximal foot phalanges. 1 x sesamoid. 1 x medial foot phalanx Large quantity very small unidentifiable & shaft fragment	Adult

DHB 5	Description	Comments
Fill No: F2137 (Grave fill B2, B3, B4) Possible Burial No.: B3 Preservation: Poor	Sacrum, including body & R ala (very fragmented)	Adult. No direct osteological evidence to confirm relationship with B2, B3 or B4

DHB 6	Description	Comments
Fill No: F2137 (Grave fill B2, B3 B4) Possible Burial No.: B3 Preservation: Poor	Large amount femur shaft fragments including L femur head, fragmented distal epiphysis	Adult. No direct osteological evidence to confirm relationship with B2, B3 or B4

DHB 7	Description	Comments
Fill No: F2137 (Grave fill B2, B3 B4) Possible Burial No.: B3 Preservation: Good	R fibula, in 4 fragments, including distal 3/4 of shaft and distal epiphysis	Adult. No direct osteological evidence to confirm relationship with B2, B3 or B4

DHB 8	Description	Comments
Fill No: F2133 (Fill of re-cut of gully F2127) Possible Burial No.: B2 Preservation: Poor–Good	Large number of cranial fragments Frontal portion, including L orbit. Occipital portion including nuchal crest (?Male, nuchal crest). Basilar part of occipital. R. temporal portion including mastoid process, ext. auditory meatus, petrous portion (?Male, mastoid process). L temporal portion including external acoustic meatus & fragment of petrous portion. 1 x R zygomatic. 1 x L zygomatic. Portion R orbit 2 fragments of L maxilla including all teeth apart from 3rd molar (alveolar process resorbing, tooth lost pre-mortem). 1 x fragment R maxilla including 2nd premolar, 1st molar and 2nd molar (alveolar process for M3 resorbing, tooth lost pre-mortem). Loose teeth – R 1st incisor, 2nd incisor, canine & 1st premolar. 1 small shaft fragment	Adult. No direct osteological evidence to confirm relationship of any bone from DHB 8 with B2 All teeth from this DHB combine to make 1 full set of maxillary teeth. Calculus 14(14), AM tooth loss 2(14), Attrition 5–6

DHB 9	Description	Comments
Fill No: F2133 (Fill of re-cut of gully F2127) Possible Burial No.: B2, B3, B4 Preservation: Good	L femur in 5 pieces including head, shaft & distal epiphysis R femur in 2 pieces including shaft & distal epiphysis	Adult. No direct osteological evidence to confirm relationship with B2, B3 or B4

DHB 10	Description	Comments
Fill No: F2133 (Fill of re-cut of gully F2127) Possible Burial No.: B2 Preservation: Poor– Good	Cranial vault fragment, fragments of L & R zygomatic Portion R ilium Portion of C2 including L superior & inferior facets & transverse foramen Portion R scapula including glenoid Small no shaft fragments 1 x foot proximal phalanx 1 x R calcaneus. 1 x R 1st metatarsal Fragment of distal tibia (woven bone present on anterior side of bone)	Adult. No direct osteological evidence to confirm relationship with B2 Not part of B2 Juvenile: not part of B2

DHB 11	Description	Comments
Fill No: F2133 (Fill of re-cut of gully F2127) Possible Burial No.: B2 Preservation: Moderate	2 rib shaft fragments	No direct osteological evidence to confirm relationship with B3

DHB 12	Description	Comments
Fill No: F2138 (Post-medieval spread) Possible Burial No: - Preservation: Good	1 x small cranial vault fragment 3 x thoracic vertebrae fragments 8 x small shaft fragments 2 x unsided rib fragment 1 x L scapula including glenoid & spine. 1 x L scapula including glenoid Proximal fragment L 4th metatarsal, 1 x hand medial phalanx Fragment of L proximal fibula	Adult Adult Adult Adult Adult Juvenile

DHB 13	Description	Comments
Fill No: F2130 (Basal fill of ditch) Possible Burial No: - Preservation: Moderate	1 x small fragment occipital 5 x portions lumbar vertebrae 2 x unsided rib fragments 9 x fragments of pelvis, including L acetabulum & 2 x fragments L auricular surface (male – preauricular sulcus) 1 x distal metatarsal fragment	Adult Adult Adult Adult Adult

DHB 14	Description	Comments
Fill No: F2108	1 x R maxillary 1st incisor, 1 x L mandibular canine,	Adult
(Upper fill of ditch)	1 x mandibular R 2nd incisor (attrition stage 2,	
Possible Burial No: -	caries 0/3, calculus 0/3, hypoplasia 1/3)	Adult
Preservation: Good	Fragment L scapula spine	Adult
	1 x L discal humerus	Adult
	R 4th metacarpal, R 5th metacarpal	Adult
	1 x R femur shaft (in 3 fragments), 1 x R patella,	
	1 x fibula shaft fragment	
	8 x shaft fragments	

DHB 15	Description	Comments
Fill No: F2114	4 x cranial vault fragments, maxillary R 3rd molar,	Adult
(Secondary fill of	1 x maxillary	
ditch)	L canine	Adult
Possible Burial No: -	1 x L scapula spine fragment, 1 x cervical vertebrae	Adult
Preservation: Good	2 x L rib fragments, 1 x R rib fragment, 2 x unsided rib	Adult
	fragments	Adult
	1 x L proximal femur, 3 x femur fragments, 11 x shaft	Adult
	fragments	
	1 x L talus	
	1 x L 4th metacarpal, 1 x R 5th metacarpal, 1 x R 1st	
	metacarpal, 3 x 1st hand phalanxes, 1 x distal fragment	
	phalanx	

DHB 16	Description	Comments
Fill No: F2110	Fragment of R occipital including occipital condyle	Adult
(Fill of modern	Fragment R clavicle	Adult
refuse pit)	L distal humerus	Adult
Possible Burial No: -	Fragment thoracic vertebrae body	Adult
Preservation: Good	1 x R distal femur, 16 x shaft fragments	Adult
	L 1st metatarsal, 1 x L 3rd metatarsal, proximal foot	
	phalanx	Adult

Sample 7	Description	Comments
Fill No: F2144	4 very small bone fragments	Recovered from
(Secondary fill of		sieving (1mm
well)		mesh)
Preservation: Poor		

Sample 6	Description	Comments
Fill No F2123	4 small shaft fragments	Recovered from
(Fill of poss.		sieving (1mm
slot trench F2124)		mesh)
Preservation: Moderate		

Sample 19	Description	Comments
Fill No F2145	1 x phalanx fragment	Juvenile
(Basal fill of well)		Recovered from
Preservation:		sieving (1mm
Moderate		mesh)

Table 15.5 Adult craniometrics

	Burial 1 (mm)	Burial 2 (mm)	Burial 3 (mm)	Burial 4 (mm)
Max. cranial length	–	–	–	–
Max. cranial breadth	–	–	–	–
Basion–bregma height	–	–	–	–
Maxillo–alveolar breadth	–	–	–	–
Palate length	–	–	–	–
Biauricular breadth	–	–	–	–
Minimum frontal breadth	–	–	–	–
Minimum frontal breadth	–	–	–	–
Upper facial height	–	–	–	–
Upper facial breadth	–	–	–	–
Nasal height	–	–	–	–
Nasal breadth	–	–	–	–
Orbital height	–	–	–	–
Orbital breadth	–	–	–	–
Chin height	32.72	–	–	–
Bigonal width	–	–	–	–
Mandibular length	–	–	–	–
Min. ramus breadth	28.38 (L)	–	–	–

Table 15.6 Adult post-cranial metrics

	Burial 1 (mm)		Burial 2 (mm)		Burial 3 (mm)		Burial 4 (mm)	
	L	**R**	**L**	**R**	**L**	**R**	**L**	**R**
Clavicle length	–	–	157	–	–	–	–	–
Glenoid length	44	42	41	–	–	–	–	–
Glenoid breadth	–	31	–	–	–	–	–	–
Humerus length	330.5	331.5	–	–	–	–	–	–
Humerus head	53	52	47	–	–	–	–	–
Humerus epiphysis	–	66	58	57	–	–	–	–
Radius length	235	–	240	242.5	–	–	–	–
Radius head	25	25	–	22	–	–	–	–
Ulna length	–	–	–	–	–	–	–	–
Femur length	442	437	–	–	–	–	–	–
Femur head	50.5	51	47.5	46	–	–	–	–
Femur diaphysis (a–p)	29	27	–	30	–	–	–	–
Femur diaphysis (m–l)	34	36	–	31	–	–	–	–
Femur epiphysis	86	85.5	–	–	–	–	–	–
Tibia length	342	–	–	–	–	–	–	–
Tibia diaphysis (a–p)	33	31	33	–	–	–	–	–
Tibia diaphysis (m–l)	28	26	23	–	–	–	–	–
Tibia epiphysis	55	–	51.5	–	55.5	53	51.5	46.5
Fibula length	–	–	–	–	–	–	–	–

Table 15.7 Non-metric traits

	Burial 1	Burial 2	Burial 3	Burial 4
Ossicle at lambda	o	–	–	–
Ossicles in lambdoid	P	–	–	–
Ossicle at bregma	–	–	–	–
Ossicles in coronal	–	–	–	–
Metopic suture	–	–	–	–
Auditory torus	o	–	–	–
Palatine torus	–	–	–	–
Max/mand torus	–	–	–	–
Sternal foramen	o	–	–	–
Septal aperature	o	o	–	–
Supracondyloid process	o	o	–	–
Poirier's facet	o	o	–	–
Hypotrochanteric fossa	o	o	–	–
Third trochanter	o	P(R)	–	–
Vastus notch	–	o	–	–
Vastus fossa	–	o	–	–
Emarginate patella	–	o	–	–
Med. tibial squatting facet	o(L)	o	o	o
Lat. tibial squatting facet	o(L)	o	o	o

P = bilaterally present
o = bilaterally absent
– = bilaterally unobservable
o(R) = right absent, left unobservable
P(L) = left present, right unobservable
o(R); P(L) = right absent, left present

APPENDIX 15.3: MEDIEVAL POTTERY
By Clare McCutcheon

Table 15.8 Medieval pottery from Black Friary site

Context	Context description	Links	Fabric-type
2101	Topsoil	F2105	Dublin-type ware (x1), Trim-type ware (x1)
2105	Upper stony fill of well (2107)	F2101	Dublin-type ware (x14), Dublin-type fineware (x7), Trim-type ware (x13)
2106	Silty fill in well (2107)		Dublin-type ware (x10)
2125	Stony fill in drain (2126)		Dublin-type ware (x1)
2133	Upper fill of re-cut (2132)		Trim-type ware (x2)
2136	Single fill of semi-circular pit (2134)		Dublin-type ware (x1)
2138	Post-medieval deposit		Dublin-type ware(x2), Dublin-type fineware (x1), Glazed red earthenware (x1), GRE: slip decorated (x1)
2143	Basal fill of well (2107)		Dublin-type ware (x6)
2144	Basal fill of well (2107)		Dublin-type ware (x1)
2145	Basal fill of well (2107)		Dublin-type ware (x2)

Pottery in medieval Trim

CLARE McCUTCHEON & ROSANNE MEENAN

INTRODUCTION AND CONTEXT

Pottery was made locally in medieval Ireland, but local requirements influenced the quantity that was produced in any particular area. Given that pottery use was almost exclusive to the areas of Anglo-Norman influence (and even there it was neither a high-status item nor the most widely used medium for table-wares), its importance in the middle ages can often be over-rated. There seems to have been little effort to acquire exotic or imported pottery, and people used what was most readily available. The population of a large area of south Co. Dublin appears to have been content to use Leinster Cooking Ware, an unglazed pottery type, hand-built in a very coarse fabric. The potters who made this ware, however, were capable of producing a wide range of vessels, including the common medieval cooking jar with everted rim, sagging base and ovoid body. In addition, jugs, cisterns, small bowls, platters, shallow dishes and lamps appear regularly in the assemblages. Analysis of the pottery from a series of castle excavations at Carrickmines, Merrion, Dundrum and Nangor, all within a radius of approximately twenty-five kilometres, shows an over-whelming preponderance of Leinster Cooking Ware, ranging from 70% at Carrickmines to 99% at Merrion (McCutcheon, forthcoming a–d).

The most typical vessels present in excavated medieval assemblages, however, are unglazed jars used for cooking and glazed jugs used to contain all types of liquids. In general, this is what has been found in the pottery assemblages in Trim.

On the east coast of Ireland, the French wares from the Bordeaux area arrived primarily through the port of Dublin. Poor access to Dublin meant that very little French pottery arrived in the first place, and there was considerably less to distribute further inland. As a low-status item, pottery was rarely mentioned in customs dues, and so the already limited financial return was further lessened with double- or triple-handling. In contrast, easy access into the ports of Waterford and Cork allowed for the casual association of French pottery with the wine trade. Consequently, French wares may account for as much as 70% of the medieval pottery in Cork and as little as 20% in Dublin.

Within and around the greater Dublin area, the market appears to have been largely served by the local production associated with Crocker Street in

Dublin city, so-named as early as 1190 (Brooks 1936, 22). Excavations at Maynooth and Dunboyne Castles and on the Finglas to Ashbourne by-pass at Cookstown have certainly produced substantial quantities of pottery identifiable as being in the tradition of the Dublin-type glazed wares (McCutcheon, forthcoming e–g). Also, the countryside extending from Dublin and Kilkenny was much more firmly in the control of the Anglo-Normans than was Cork. For these reasons, it made good economic sense to be as self-sufficient as possible and, as the major centre of production, the evidence is mounting that the medieval pottery of Dublin had a wide range of distribution.

In addition to the more obvious role of the justiciar and his entourage travelling around the country to dispense justice, the abbey of St Thomas in Dublin appears to have played a major part in the systematic movement of goods, including pottery. This foundation in Dublin, dedicated to St Thomas the Martyr (Thomas Becket), was a very early dedication in 1177 as Becket had been murdered at Canterbury in late 1170 and canonized in 1173. Part of Henry II's penance was to build and dedicate churches in honour of the saint (Gwynn 1954, 12). St Thomas' was located outside the western gate of Dublin, and the canons set about developing the area with considerable vigour (Duddy 2003). 'St Thomas's was founded with ends in mind, that were advantageous to civil society, for example, the development of the suburb, but these ends were to be reached through the Christian ethic' (ibid., 82ff). It is well-documented that in the first years of the new Dublin community, most of the prominent Anglo-Norman adventurers in this country made more or less extensive grants to 'the canons who served God in the monastery of blessed Thomas the martyr near Dublin' (Gwynn 1954, 14).

The significance of the abbey of St Thomas in connection with the distribution of pottery lies in its location in the western suburbs. Clarke (1998, 50–1) describes Thomas Street as 'the great artery for food and other necessities entering the city', with an eight-day fair established in 1204, and lengthened to fifteen days by 1215. Down the hill and parallel to Thomas Street lay Crocker Street. As early as 1190 this street is named *vicus pottorum*, later reappearing as *vicus figulorum* and Crocker Street (Brooks 1936). No kilns or associated features such as workshops, clay-settling pits or waste-heaps have been uncovered on the street, although pottery wasters have been recovered at excavations in the Iveagh Markets to the south of the medieval wall (McCutcheon, in prep.), and waste material from ridge-tile production, in clay similar to Dublin-type coarseware, has been recovered at the Cornmarket (Wren, forthcoming). Nevertheless, the use of the imported word 'crocker' is substantial, if circumstantial, evidence for the association with the production of pottery. In addition, a number of leases between Thomas Street and Crocker Street (Brooks 1936) were held in the early thirteenth century by people whose names, such as Crocker and Figulus, clearly indicated that they were involved in the making of earthenware (McCutcheon 2006, 19). The vigorous development of the western suburbs by St Thomas' Abbey and the extensive properties that it held in Meath and Kildare in particular would have encouraged the lively production of familiar-looking pottery for the use of the new settlers in Dublin and beyond. The distribution of the Dublin-type wares is widespread and, in addition to Trim, extends at least to Dundrum and Carrickmines Castles, Co. Dublin and Maynooth Castle, Co. Kildare (McCutcheon, forthcoming a, c & e).

In Trim there is evidence of a different clay type (Trim-type ware), previously designated Trim ware (Sweetman 1978). This appears to be similar to, and contemporary with, the later-thirteenth- and fourteenth-century finewares found in Dublin and Kilkenny, both of which had a progression through three distinct groups – firstly, a hand-built coarseware, followed by a wheel-thrown ware with cleaner clay, and finally a fineware, also wheel-thrown but with very clean clay. In the case of both Trim and Cork, however, the only locally-made pottery appears to have been this single later-thirteenth-century wheel-thrown, clean clay and so the term fineware could be understood in both of these fabric types. The emergence of both these types, at a period when other wares were widely available, may simply reflect the market demand for more, rather than less, pottery.

METHODOLOGY

The pottery from each site was identified visually and the information was presented in tabular form. The number of sherds in each fabric type was listed with the probable vessel type represented and the date-range of the fabric. Accurate minimum numbers of vessels can only be given in the case of medieval jugs where the rim/handle junction is present, although several other vessels may be represented in the assemblage. This minimum number is based on the presence of rim/handle junctions, as this is the most accurate method of determining the presence of a jug. As jugs represent the majority of the forms produced, this method of quantification ensures at least that the glazed wares can be accurately quantified. It is safer and more useful for indicating overall use of pottery at any particular time if conservative and consistent numbers can be produced on a site-by-site basis, leading to greater use for researchers in the future. The minimum vessels represented (MVR) gives a more subjective indication of the possible number of jugs, taking the variety of handle, bases and spouts into account. The probable form and the date-range of the fabric types are also listed in the tables.

The identification of each sherd was entered on a database (Access format) as per the requirements of the National Museum of Ireland, the body responsible for the material remains from excavations within the state. The databases show the *licence, context* and *finds* number; the *links* of reassembled sherds within and between contexts; the *category* and *type* of material (that is, ceramic and pottery); and the *identification* of the fabric type and the diagnostic *description* (that is, rim, handle etc.). The final two fields contain *habitat* numbers: firstly the box number where each sherd is stored; and secondly the location of the box within the storage system of the National Museum of Ireland. The database is easily searchable for particular types of pottery, vessels, parts etc, and is also appropriate for indicating the diagnostic part of the vessel recovered and the information with regard to contexts linked by reassembled sherds.

FABRIC DESCRIPTIONS

Leinster Cooking Ware (pl. 14)

'Leinster Cooking Ware is the single most widespread medieval pottery type in Leinster' (Ó Floinn 1988, 340). It has been found in varying quantities on both urban and rural sites from Dungarvan to Dublin and further north and west. The fabric contains large plates of mica, quartz grits and other inclusions such as decomposed feldspar (ibid., 327). The sherds represent the typical cooking pots with everted rims, ovoid bodies and sand-marked bases. The latter are characteristic of this fabric type, the probable result of having been placed on a bed of sand during construction (ibid.).

Dublin-type wares

The designation of a fabric with the suffix -*type* is recommended pottery practice to indicate that a ware has been consistently found in a particular area where evidence for a production centre or kiln has not yet been discovered (Blake & Davey 1983, 39–40). The general term London-type, for example, has been adopted to describe wares that share general traditions and clay sources (Pearce et al., 1985, 2). A fuller discussion of the names of the Dublin-type wares has been detailed elsewhere (McCutcheon 2000, 120–3; 2006) and only a general outline is included in this report.

The relative dating of the Dublin-type wares has been developed as a result of consistent recovery in the stratigraphic levels of the Dublin excavations, and the absolute dating is developing by the association of imported wares, and the dating information from coins and dendrochronology. To date no pottery production site has been found in Dublin along Crocker Street at the west of the medieval city. Pottery wasters have been recovered at excavations in the Iveagh Markets to the south of the medieval wall (McCutcheon, in prep.), and ridge tile production, in clay similar to Dublin-type coarseware, has been recovered at the Cornmarket (Wren, forthcoming).

Dublin-type coarseware This is a coarse micaceous fabric. The vessels are generally hand-built, and the production and use appear to date broadly from the late twelfth to the early thirteenth century (McCutcheon 2000, 122).

Dublin-type ware This is a less coarse micaceous fabric. The vessels are generally wheel-thrown, and the production and use appear to date broadly from the early thirteenth to the early fourteenth century (McCutcheon 2000, 122). The principal vessels were the typical strap-handled jugs, with thumbed or plain bases, pulled or pinched spouts and a bevel around the rim. The base sherds had both continuous and spaced thumbing, while some appeared to be plain, although occasionally jugs might have only four 'quartering' thumb marks, which can create considerable ambiguity in the intervening spaces.

There was also evidence of storage jars. These are similar in shape to the cooking jars with ovoid bodies and slightly sagging bases, but the everted rims tend to be shorter and any glaze is also deliberate, mostly around the shoulder. The shortened rim allows for a covering, such as waxed cloth, to be tied securely over the top. From the evidence of the cooking jars, the longer flared rim acts to disperse any flames or sooting from contaminating the food.

Dublin-type fineware (pl. 10) This is a fine, clean fabric. The vessels are wheel-thrown and their use appears to date from the later thirteenth century onwards (McCutcheon 2000, 122). While it is difficult to distinguish between Dublin-type fineware and the contemporary Trim-type ware (below), generally the Dublin-type fineware may be said to be red-firing rather than cream-firing clay and it often contains traces of mica. In addition, the decorative designs on the handles can be used as distinguishing motifs, as a single, rather carelessly incised line is very common on Dublin-type fineware jugs.

Dublin-type cooking ware (pl. 11) This is a generic term used to cover cooking ware from Dublin that is clearly not Leinster Cooking Ware. That is to say, while unglazed and somewhat micaceous, it does not contain large amounts of quartz and the bases are not sand-gritted. The forms are generally the typical medieval cooking pots with everted rims, ovoid bodies and slightly sagging bases. There are also vessels with so-called trumpet handles that are either skillets/dripping dishes or small bowls (Barton 1988, 273–4, fig. 2.9; figs 3.13–15), although both small bowls or cooking jars and larger jars were also recovered at Wood Quay (McCutcheon 2006, figs 35.7–9). These are very closely associated with Dublin and do not appear to be found in other locally-made unglazed wares of the period. The vessels appear to have been both hand-built and wheel-thrown, indicating their overlap with both the Dublin-type coarseware and the Dublin-type ware.

16.1 Dublin-type ware jug from 18 Market Street, Trim (photograph by Richard Johnston)

Trim-type ware (pl. 13)
This is a designation for 'a very uniform group' recognized by David
Sweetman at the excavations at Trim Castle in 1970–4. 'The fabric is a hard-
fired yellowish cream colour and is almost gritless. The glaze can be green,
yellow, black or chocolate' (Sweetman 1978, 171ff). The fabric, while somewhat
similar to the later thirteenth-century finewares from Dublin and Kilkenny,
can still be distinguished visually from these latter types. The simple forms,
however, and the small amount of decoration are paralleled in those
contemporary finewares. It appears that Trim-type ware partially filled the
local niche at the later part of the thirteenth and early fourteenth century that
was filled by Dublin-type fineware elsewhere.

Ham Green wares (pls 8 & 9)
The kiln at Ham Green outside Bristol, and the ware produced there has been extensively described (Barton 1963; Ponsford 1991). Two glazed wares were produced, both of which were hand-built. Ham Green A dates to *c.*1120–60 and Ham Green B dates to *c.*1175–1250. A cooking ware appears to have been contemporary with both glazed wares (ibid., 98).

Saintonge mottled green glazed
The wares from the Saintonge region of south-west France were imported into Ireland and Britain as by-products of the extensive wine trade (Chapelot 1983; Deroeux et al., 1994) and, with the Ham Green wares, are likely to be found on almost every Anglo-Norman site in Ireland. The fabric of the all the Saintonge wares is generally the same – a fine white micaceous fabric with occasional quartz. The mottled green glaze results from the addition of copper filings to the clear lead glaze.

THE POTTERY FROM TRIM TOWN AND CASTLE

The town
Excavations directed by Claire Walsh at the library site on High Street (E404) produced 'a small assemblage', but this included five sherds from south-west France and twenty sherds of Ham Green ware (Walsh 1990/1, 49–51). No Trim-type ware was present. Elsewhere on High Street, excavations by Alan Hayden (01E1146) produced just four sherds of French pottery in an assemblage of over two hundred sherds. Two of these pieces are of particular interest, however, as they are Saintonge green-painted, dating to the later thirteenth to early fourteenth century. Both Dublin-type ware and Trim-type ware were equally represented, with approximately one-third each of the assemblage, but there were no rim/handle fragments, and a figure for the minimum number of vessels represented (MVR) could only be estimated at three each.

A further excavation at 27 High Street (06E0148) by Carmel Duffy (this volume) produced a small group of fifty-four sherds, including Dublin-type ware and Trim-type ware, although there was a minimum of two jugs in the Dublin-type ware.

In contrast to these small assemblages, at Kiely's Yard (Stephens, 'SubUrbia', this volume), a total of 2,051 sherds were recovered. Of these, just five sherds of Saintonge green-glazed ware were recorded. Dublin-type ware accounts for 38% of the assemblage, with the later Dublin-type fineware making up 9%. The balance (18%) of the later thirteenth-century material consists of Trim-type ware. In this assemblage, it was possible to give an accurate minimum number of vessels, at least in the glazed wares, with nineteen jugs represented by rim/handle fragments. In addition, both the Dublin-type ware and the Trim-type ware included storage jars, vessels very similar in shape to cooking jars, but with a considerably shorter rim and often with glaze over the rim and on the shoulder of the jar. It would have been a simple matter to tie a cloth, possibly waxed, over the top of the jar to get a good seal for long term storage.

An excavation at 18 Market Street (02E0671) by Donal Fallon produced a total of 684 sherds of medieval pottery (after reassembly), over 60% of which was Dublin-type ware (fig. 16.1). The later material, consisting of a single sherd of Saintonge ware and one of Saintonge polychrome, dating to the later thirteenth to early fourteenth century, are complemented by five sherds of Ham Green ware, including two possible Ham Green A fragments dating to the early to mid-twelfth century (pl. 8). Trim-type ware and Dublin-type fineware are on a par and together account for only 18% of the overall assemblage.

In a small test excavation on Market Street (05E0744), directed by Carmel Duffy, Dublin-type ware was again predominant, with fifty of the sixty-six sherds present. A minimum of one jug was present in both Dublin-type ware and Trim-type ware, although there were also at least two storage jars of Dublin-type ware. A second similar excavation near Spicer's in Market Street (04E1164), also directed by Duffy, produced just twenty sherds, of which fifteen were Dublin-type ware and five were Trim-type ware.

A further excavation at Haggard Street (99E0142) by Clare Mullins produced a total of 209 sherds of medieval pottery. Here again, Dublin-type ware predominated, with 84% of the total assemblage. A very small quantity of Dublin-type fineware and Trim-type ware sherds were complemented by a Drogheda-type pipkin, or small-handled pot.

At Athboy Gate (E2398), the twenty-two pottery sherds recovered during excavations directed by Matthew Seaver represent most of the typical types. Of particular interest in this assemblage, however, was the radiocarbon date from the basal fill of the ditch, given as 1280–1400 with a 95% probability. A sherd each of Dublin-type ware and Drogheda-type ware were found, with both types dating very broadly to the thirteenth century. The latter was reassembled with another sherd from the overlying back-fill deposit. The medieval pottery from the excavations at Black Friary (Table 15.8), Haggard Street, Mill Street and Navan Gate (also E2398) amounts to 114 sherds in total, of which 59 sherds are Dublin-type ware, 31 Dublin-type fineware and 22 Trim-type ware.

The castle

Two campaigns of major excavations were carried out in the castle. The first was undertaken by David Sweetman in the early 1970s in the area south of the

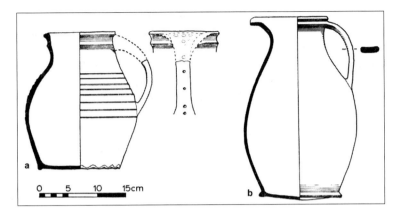

16.2 a) Ham Green jug from Trim Castle (after Sweetman 1978, fig. 14.1); b) Dublin-type ware jug. Green glaze over white slip, pulled spout and plain handle. From late thirteenth-century context at Trim Castle (after Sweetman 1978, fig. 14.3)

keep. The second was directed by Alan Hayden in the mid–1990s, when large areas of the keep, the mint, the Great Hall and the Trim gate-house were excavated. During both of these excavations, substantial sections of the fosse were excavated, and large assemblages of medieval pottery were recovered, both from the fosse and the other excavated areas. Both excavations yielded useful dating evidence based on stratigraphic sequences and associated finds.

Ham Green pottery was found on both excavations. On Hayden's site (1999, 37), two body sherds were recovered from a Phase 1 level that represented pre-Anglo-Norman or very early Anglo-Norman activity in the area of the keep. It was not possible to determine if these sherds were from Ham Green A or Ham Green B wares as they were not diagnostic. Ham Green pottery was found on Sweetman's excavation on features to the south of the keep (Structures L and M; fig. 16a). At the time, Sweetman (1978, 156–60) dated the pottery, and thus the features, to the mid-thirteenth century, based on information from excavations taking place at that time at the Ham Green kiln sites. It now seems possible that these features represented pre-Anglo-Norman or very early Anglo-Norman activity here also, as the interpretation of Ham Green dating has changed over the years (Ponsford 1991, 98). Ham Green A wares were present in the early part of the twelfth century in Waterford (Gahan & McCutcheon 1997, 294). Other English imports recovered by Hayden consisted of very small quantities of Minety ware and Chester ware, while Redcliffe ware, the successor of Ham Green ware, was also found in very small quantities.

The introduction of imports from the Saintonge area of the south-west of France dates to the early thirteenth century (McCutcheon 2006, 88). The sherds from Hayden's site were very fragmentary, but the ware appeared in its greatest bulk in the contexts that dated to the thirteenth and fourteenth centuries. Sweetman found 275 sherds, out of which he was able to reconstruct one almost complete jug and two other less-complete examples. These imports have traditionally been associated with trade in wine, well-established between France and Ireland even before the arrival of the Anglo-Normans. The other medieval Saintonge products, polychrome and green-painted wares, were found on both sites, again in small numbers. These were exported from the region in the later thirteenth to early fourteenth centuries (Dunning 1968, 45). Wares from Normandy were found on both sites (Sweetman 1978, 161; Hayden 1999, 138). One sherd of Merida-type ware, from the Iberian Peninsula, was found in a later-fifteenth-century context on Hayden's excavation (1999, 139).

By far the largest portion of the pottery found on both excavations post-dated the arrival of the Anglo-Normans. On Hayden's excavation, over eleven thousand sherds of green-glazed, locally-produced pottery were found. Much of Hayden's pottery was paralleled to Dublin-type wares, on the basis of the appearance of the fabric and of the vessel forms and their decoration. A sub-group of Dublin-type ware was isolated, comprising at least eight small jugs with squared rims, plain handles and saggy bases. The vessels were small enough to have been drinking jugs, and similar enough to each other to have been made by the same potter (Hayden 1999, 141–2).

A large assemblage of green-glazed pottery was also recovered on Sweetman's excavation. He compared much of it to Dublin wares, and also paralleled the forms to pottery found at Downpatrick (1978, 161). He named one particular sub-group as Trim ware (1978, 171; McCutcheon's Trim-type ware), as it was distinct from the other wares that were found, and he suggested that it was of local manufacture (pl. 6). This suggestion has not been challenged over the years, although no other evidence for pottery kilns in the Trim area has been found, hence the use of the term '-type'. This ware has been found elsewhere in the town (see above). Sweetman indicated a fourteenth-century date for its manufacture (figs 16.3a–c).

As noted above, Dublin-type wares have also been found in the town and generally they were the most numerous of the glazed wares. The range of vessels present at the castle is the same as elsewhere in the town (fig. 16.2b).

As in the town, Leinster Cooking Ware was found at the castle by Hayden. It appeared in small quantities at the end of the twelfth century and remained in the record for approximately two hundred years. Leinster Cooking Ware, identified as micaceous hand-thrown cooking wares, was present on Sweetman's site, and he dated it to the end of the thirteenth century and the beginning of the fourteenth century (1978, 170).

Wares from the Drogheda kilns were identified on Hayden's excavation by Kieran Campbell. Jugs were the only form to be found in contexts dating from the thirteenth century into the early fourteenth century. In view of Hugh de Lacy's connections with Drogheda, and the known trading route along the

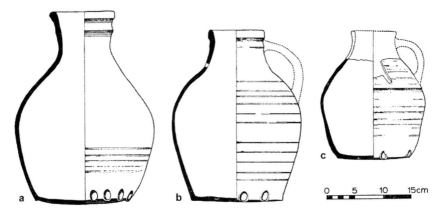

16.3 a) Trim-type ware green-glazed jug from fourteenth-century context at Trim Castle (after Sweetman 1978, fig. 21.1); b) Almost complete body portion of large brown- and yellow-glazed Trim-type ware jug from fourteenth-century context at Trim Castle (after Sweetman 1978, fig. 21.2); c) Body portion of small purplish brown-glazed Trim-type ware jug from fourteenth-century context at Trim Castle (after Sweetman 1978, fig. 21.3)

Boyne between Drogheda and Trim (Potterton 2005, 149), it might have been expected that a larger quantity would have been found, particularly given the volume of production now known to have taken place at the kiln site in Drogheda (Halpin 2007).

A curious feature of Hayden's excavation was the huge quantity of roof-tiles that was found. The fragments numbered several thousand, and probably represented a roofing area equivalent to two of the small side towers of the keep. These tiles were also found on Sweetman's excavation and there are undoubtedly many more remaining in the unexcavated ground. They are concave in section and trapezoidal in plan. They have nibs on their upper surfaces placed in such a way that some would hang in rows from the roof purlins, while the others were placed in overlapping rows, similar in appearance to the roof-tiles used in Mediterranean countries. The largest quantities were found in fifteenth-century contexts, in particular in moat-fill, suggesting that the roof may have been demolished at some time during the fifteenth century. These tiles are not found elsewhere in Ireland. Thin-sectioning suggests a possible origin for the clay in England, but the form has not been recognized there. The closest parallel for the form is in Denmark (Wren 1999, 197–8).

Neither of the two castle excavations produced much post-medieval ware. Sweetman (1978, 175), for example, found only two sherds of North Devon gravel-tempered ware, although there were slightly higher quantities of black-glazed ware and glazed red earthenware. Hayden's excavations produced only 159 stratified post-medieval sherds. It appears that once the activity associated with the military campaigns of the seventeenth century had passed, the environs of the castle were unoccupied and no more pottery came to be deposited there.

CONCLUSIONS

The principal type of glazed ware found in both the castle and the town excavations appears to have originated in Dublin (pl. 2). This fits with the general pattern of Anglo-Norman pottery, with large quantities of wares thought to have been produced in the western suburbs of Dublin, and smaller quantities of pottery produced in Trim itself, probably in the later thirteenth century and with a smaller quantity again from Drogheda. The variations in the medieval pottery assemblages discussed in this paper can be explained by the presence or absence of a Trim-type or a Drogheda-type jug in any particular location. The small quantity of French and English ware dating to the thirteenth and fourteenth centuries also reflects the situation in Dublin where these wares were outnumbered by the locally-made production. It also appears that the same wares and forms were being used in the town and in the castle at the same time.

ACKNOWLEDGMENTS

The pottery assemblages referred to in this paper were analyzed and written up by the writers for the excavators as named. We would like to thank them for permission to refer to their material prior to publication.

BIBLIOGRAPHY

Barton, K.J., 1963, 'A medieval pottery kiln at Ham Green, Bristol', *Transactions of the Bristol & Gloucestershire Archaeological Society* **82**, 95–126.
Barton, K., 1988, 'The medieval pottery of Dublin' in Mac Niocaill, G., & Wallace, P.F. (eds), *Keimelia: studies in medieval archaeology and history in memory of Tom Delaney*, 271–324. Galway.
Brooks, E. St. John (ed.), 1936, *Register of the hospital of St John the Baptist without the New Gate, Dublin.* Dublin.
Blake, H., & Davey, P. (eds), 1983, *Guidelines for the processing and publication of medieval pottery from excavations.* London.
Chapelot, J., 1983, 'The Saintonge pottery industry in the later middle ages' in Davey, P. & Hodges, R. (eds), *Ceramics and trade*, 49–53. Sheffield.
Clarke, H.B., 1998, '*Urbs et suburbium*: beyond the walls of medieval Dublin' in Manning, C. (ed.), *Dublin and beyond the Pale*, 45–58. Dublin.
Clarke, H.B., 2002, *Irish Historic Towns Atlas No. 11: Dublin, Part I, to 1610.* Dublin.
Deroeux, D., Dufournier, D., & Herteig, A.E., 1994, 'French medieval ceramics from the Bryggen excavations in Bergen, Norway', *The Bryggen Papers* Supplementary series No. 5, 161–208. Bergen.
Duddy, C., 2001, 'The role of St Thomas's abbey in the early development of Dublin's western suburbs' in Duffy, S. (ed.), *Medieval Dublin* **4**, 79–97. Dublin.
Dunning, G.C., 1968, 'The trade in medieval pottery around the North Sea' in Renaud, J.G. (ed.), *Rotterdam Papers 1*, 35–58. Rotterdam.

Gahan, A., & McCutcheon, C., 1997, 'The medieval pottery' in Hurley, M.F. & Scully, O.M.B., *Late Viking-Age and medieval Waterford: excavations 1986–1992*, 285–336. Waterford.

Gwynn, A., 1954, 'The early history of St Thomas' Abbey, Dublin', *Journal of the Royal Society of Antiquaries of Ireland* **84**, 1–35.

Halpin, E., 2007, 'Old Mart, Magdalene Street, Drogheda' in Bennett, I. (ed.), *Excavations 2004: summary accounts of archaeological excavations in Ireland*, no. 1085, pp 259–60. Bray.

Hayden, A., 1999, 'Trim Castle, Co. Meath: excavations 1995–8 (95E0077), part II: the finds'. Unpublished post-excavation report.

McCutcheon, C., 1997, 'The pottery and roof tiles' in Hurley, M.F., *Excavations at the North Gate, Cork 1994*, 75–101. Cork.

McCutcheon, C., 2000, 'Medieval pottery in Dublin: new names and some dates' in Duffy, S. (ed.), *Medieval Dublin* 1, 117–25. Dublin.

McCutcheon, C., 2003, 'Pottery' in Cleary, R.M. & Hurley, M.F. (eds), *Cork City excavations, 1984–2000*, 197–235. Cork.

McCutcheon, C., & Johnson, C., 2003, 'Pottery' in O'Donovan, E., 'The growth and decline of a medieval suburb' in Duffy, S. (ed.), *Medieval Dublin* 4, 142–51.

McCutcheon, C., 2006, *Medieval pottery from Wood Quay, Dublin*. Dublin.

McCutcheon, C., forthcoming (a), 'The medieval pottery' in Clinton, M., 'Excavations at Carrickmines Castle, Co. Dublin'.

McCutcheon, C., forthcoming (b), 'The pottery' in Baker, C., 'Excavations at Merrion Castle, Co. Dublin'.

McCutcheon, C., forthcoming (c), 'The pottery' in O'Brien, E., 'Excavations at Dundrum Castle, Co. Dublin'.

McCutcheon, C., forthcoming (d), 'The pottery' in Doyle, I., 'Excavations at Nangor Castle, Co. Dublin'.

McCutcheon, C., forthcoming (e), 'The pottery' in Hayden, A., 'Excavations at Maynooth Castle, Co. Kildare'.

McCutcheon, C., forthcoming (f), 'The pottery' in Cotter, C., 'Excavations at Dunboyne Castle, Co. Meath'.

McCutcheon, C., forthcoming (g), 'The pottery' in Clutterbuck, R., 'Excavations at Cookstown, Co. Dublin'.

McCutcheon, C., in prep., 'The pottery' in Myles, F., 'Excavations at the Iveagh Markets, Dublin'.

Ó Floinn, R., 1988, 'Handmade medieval pottery in south-east Ireland: Leinster Cooking Ware' in MacNiocaill, G. & Wallace, P.F. (eds), *Keimelia*, 325–49. Galway.

Pearce, J.E., Vince, A.G., & Jenner, M.A., 1985, *A dated type series of London medieval pottery part 2: London-type ware*. London.

Ponsford, M., 1991, 'Dendrochronological dates from Dundas Wharf, Bristol, and the dating of Ham Green and other medieval pottery' in Lewis, E. (ed.), *Custom and ceramics: essays presented to Kenneth Barton*, 81–103. Wickham.

Potterton, M., 2005, *Medieval Trim: history and archaeology*. Dublin.

Sweetman, P.D., 1978, 'Archaeological excavations at Trim Castle, Co. Meath, 1971–1974', *Proceedings of the Royal Irish Academy* **78C**, 127–98.

Sweetman, P.D., 1990/1, 'Archaeological excavations at St Johns Priory, Newtown, Trim, Co. Meath', *Ríocht na Mídhe* **8:3**, 88–104.

Walsh, C., 1990/1, 'An excavation at the library site, High St, Trim', *Ríocht na Mídhe* **8:3**, 41–67.

Wren, J., & Hayden, A., 1999, 'Ceramic roof tiles' in Hayden, A., 'Trim Castle, Co. Meath: excavations 1995–8 (95E0077), part II: the finds'. Unpublished post-excavation report.

Wren, J., forthcoming, 'Roof tiles' in Hayden, A., 'Excavations at the Cornmarket, Dublin'.

Meat and craft in medieval and post-medieval Trim

FIONA BEGLANE

This paper discusses the animal bones found during an excavation at Townparks South, and another at 18 Market Street, and compares them with the results of other excavations at Trim and elsewhere in Ireland. The Townparks South excavation was carried out in what were the medieval suburbs, in an area outside the town walls, while the excavation at Market Street was conducted within the town walls, but included a ditch that may have formed an early town boundary. The animal bone assemblages included butchery, food and craft waste dating from the medieval and post-medieval periods. Comparison of the results with those from analyses of faunal assemblages recovered from elsewhere inside the walled town and from the castle revealed interesting differences in activity patterns between the various areas.

INTRODUCTION

Animals were an integral and essential part of past societies. The interaction of individuals in the past with animals depended on their occupation, social status, identity and the nature of the activity they were carrying out. Meat and other animal-derived products were an essential part of the medieval economy and as an aspect of material culture they can also shed light on social and cultural concerns. The careful study of animal bones recovered from excavations can therefore yield information on aspects of past society including diet, craftwork and the economy but also on issues such as leisure pursuits, ceremonial activity and identity (Jones O'Day et al., 2004, xi–xv; O'Connor 2007, 1–9).

Over the past number of years, excavations around the town and castle of Trim have unearthed a wealth of medieval and post-medieval urban animal bone assemblages that have included butchery, food and craft waste. Excavation in the suburban area of Townparks South, outside the town walls, revealed the remains of structures, ditches, pits and hearths, and identified three medieval phases of activity. Phase 1 was dated to AD1027–1290; Phase 2 was dated to AD1250–1400; Phase 2a was dated to AD1400–1650 and, finally; Phase 3 was dated to the post-medieval period (Stephens, 'SubUrbia', this volume). The majority of the bones were recovered from an area now known as Kiely's Yard, where the pattern of the modern property plots is believed to reflect the original layout of the suburban area of the town into burgage plots,

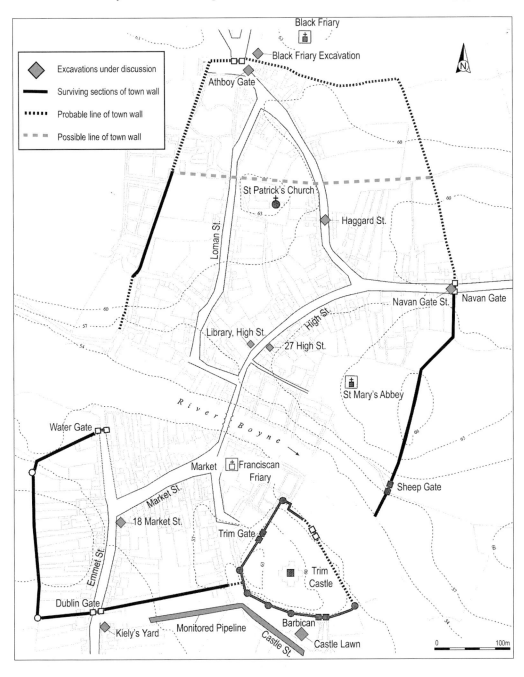

17.1 Map of Trim showing location of sites discussed (base-map courtesy of Ordnance Survey Ireland, Permit 8565 © Ordnance Survey Ireland/Government of Ireland)

outside the town walls (Stephens, 'SubUrbia', this volume). A burgage plot typically had a shop with living accommodation on the street frontage, with workshops and gardens behind, stretching back to the end of a long, narrow plot, and was typically 7.6–9.1m wide (Graham 1999, 133; Potterton 2005, 199–200). In this case, the excavated area appears to occupy the location of two of these properties. A smaller quantity of medieval and post-medieval material was recovered from the castle lawn and Castle Street areas, again outside the walled town, and a deposit of Iron Age pig bones was also identified in peaty deposits under the castle lawn (Beglane, 'Pigs' feet', this volume).

At 18 Market Street, Fallon (this volume) excavated an early metalled surface that pre-dated the layout of burgage plots, a ditch that may have formed an early town boundary, a series of pits and wells to the rear of a burgage plot, that have been dated using pottery to the twelfth-to-fourteenth centuries, and the remains of a structure of probable post-medieval date.

A number of other excavations have taken place in Trim and consequently some comparative faunal data is available. This has been synthesized in order to provide an overview of how animals fitted into the society of Trim and its surroundings. Small assemblages of medieval and post-medieval faunal remains were recovered from the Black Friary (Seaver, this volume), Haggard Street and Navan Gate Street (Seaver 2009a; 2009b) as part of the Trim Street Reconstruction Project (TSRP). These were analyzed by the current author (Beglane 2009a; 2009b) and the results will be briefly discussed here. The Black Friary excavation took place in a lane running west from the Kells Road immediately outside the line of the northern extent of the town wall, while the site at Navan Gate Street lay immediately inside the possible site of the Navan Gate. By contrast, the Haggard Street excavation took place within the core of the medieval town.

The mammal bones from Hayden's unpublished excavations at Trim Castle were examined by McCormick and Murray (undated). Material from the castle came from three phases dating between the twelfth and fifteenth centuries. The remainder of the excavations under discussion were located inside the walled town. McCormick (1991) has published the results of his study of the thirteenth-century animal bones from the High Street library site (Walsh 1991). Monitoring and excavation elsewhere on High Street yielded more medieval remains (Duffy, this volume) and Lynch (2007) examined the human and animal bones from this site. Excavation at Athboy Gate yielded thirteenth- to fourteenth-century material (Seaver, this volume) with Lofqvist (2008) examining the faunal remains. Bird and fish remains found at Trim have also been reviewed. Hamilton-Dyer (2007a; 2007b) examined those found during Hayden's excavation of the castle and at Townparks South. McCormick (1991) included O'Connor's identification of birds at the library site in High Street and those from Athboy Gate were looked at by Lofqvist (2008) as part of her analysis. The locations of all the sites discussed are shown in fig. 17.1.

Results have been compared in terms of the number of identified specimens present (NISP), which is a count of identifiable bones, and the minimum number of individuals (MNI) to which these bones relate. Sheep and goat bones are very similar and, as it is often not possible to separate them, in many cases these have been considered as a sheep/goat category. Where possible, however, elements were differentiated so that changes in husbandry and exploitation of these species could be identified.

OVERALL FINDINGS

At Townparks South, the burgage plots at Kiely's Yard, which lie outside the town walls, yielded over nine hundred bones and teeth dating from the medieval and post-medieval periods, with the Castle Street/castle lawn areas outside the castle, yielding a further 126. During the medieval phases, cattle were generally the most common species of animal present, making up 26–41% of the minimum number of individuals (MNI). This altered somewhat in the much smaller assemblage from the Phase 3 post-medieval period, where sheep/goat (23%) were the most common animal (Table 17.1). In addition to these major species, small numbers of bones from horse, dog, cat, deer, fox, hare, rabbit and rat were identified. Sixty-four bird bones and two fish bones were also recovered from the excavation (Hamilton-Dyer 2007b).

Table 17.1 NISP and (MNI) values from Townparks South

Phase	Cattle	Sheep/ Goat	Pig	Horse	Dog	Cat	Deer	Fox	Hare/ Rabbit	Rat	Total
Phase 1: AD1027–1290	61 (5)	24 (2)	24 (3)	9 (1)	1 (1)	2 (1)	0	0	0	0	121 (13)
Phase 2: AD1250–1400	192 (8)	111 (7)	70 (5)	24 (3)	31 (2)	10 (3)	2 (1)	1 (1)	0	1 (1)	442 (31)
Phase 2a: AD1400–1640	111 (7)	76 (4)	35 (2)	7 (1)	8 (2)	0	1 (1)	0	0	0	238 (17)
Phase 3: Post-medieval	34 (2)	22 (3)	16 (2)	23 (2)	1 (1)	2 (1)	0	0	3 (1 hare 1 rabbit)	0	101 (13)
Castle St/Lawn medieval	58 (4)	15 (2)	13 (3)	16 (2)	2 (1)	1 (1)	3 (1)	0	1 (1)	0	109 (15)
Castle St/Lawn post-medieval	10 (1)	0	5 (2)	2 (1)	0	0	0	0	0	0	17 (4)

Market Street yielded 232 mammal bones as well as ten bird bones, four marine molluscs and three fish bones. The majority of the remains dated to the pre-burgage and medieval phases. Material from the pre-burgage phase was dominated by cattle (71%), mainly horn-cores, with sheep and goat elements, including horn-cores, making up much of the remainder (14–21%), and only small numbers of pig, horse, dog, cat and deer bones. During the medieval phase, the proportion of cattle was much lower (25–40%), and that of sheep/goat much higher (33–42%) than in the earlier phase, but horn-cores continued to make up a significant proportion of the total (Table 17.2).

Table 17.2 NISP, (MNI incl. horn-cores) and [MNI excl. horn-cores] values from 18 Market Street

	Cattle	*Sheep/Goat*	*Pig*	*Horse*	*Dog*	*Cat*	*Red deer*	*Total*
Pre-burgage	51 *(10)[5]*	6 *(3)[1]*	3 *(1)[1]*	1 *(1)[1]*	5 *(2)[2]*	0	1 *(1)[1]*	67 *(18)[11]*
Medieval 12th–14th century	66 *(6)[3]*	47 *(5)[5]*	25 *(4)[4]*	2 *(1)[1]*	1 *(1)[1]*	9 *(2)[2]*	0	150 *(19)[16]*
Post-medieval	8 *(1)[1]*	5 *(2)[2]*	2 *(1)[1]*	0	0	0	0	15 *(4)[4]*

Assemblages from the Black Friary, Haggard Street and Navan Gate Street were much smaller, yielding forty-nine, twenty-four and twenty-one identified countable elements respectively (Table 17.3).

Table 17.3 NISP values from Navan Gate Street, Haggard Street and the Black Friary and (MNI) values from the Black Friary

	Cattle	*Sheep/Goat*	*Pig*	*Horse*	*Dog*	*Cat*	*Total*
Navan Gate Street: Medieval	2	4	1	1	1	0	9
Navan Gate Street: Post-medieval	3	1	2	0	6	0	12
Haggard Street: F114	2	2	1	0	0	0	5
Haggard Street: F130	3	1	0	0	0	0	4
Haggard Street: F125 and F127	9	4	0	1	1	0	15
Black Friary Phase 1 Medieval	4 *(1)*	4 *(1)*	10 *(3)*	0	0	0	18 *(5)*
Black Friary Phase 2 Medieval	4 *(1)*	5 *(1)*	1 *(1)*	0	1 *(1)*	0	11 *(4)*
Black Friary Phase 3 Post-medieval	8 *(1)*	0 *(0)*	4 *(1)*	3 *(1)*	1 *(1)*	3 *(1)*	19 *(5)*
Black Friary Phase 4 Modern	1 *(1)*	0	0	0	0	0	1 *(1)*

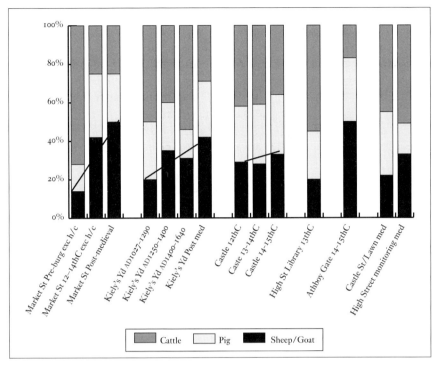

17.2 Percentage MNI of major food species for Trim sites, showing trend in percentage of sheep

FOOD ANIMALS

Among the three major food species at Kiely's Yard, the proportion of cattle and pigs diminished over time and, conversely, sheep rose from 20% in Phase 1 to 42.9% of the MNI in Phase 3, the post-medieval period. This pattern is also noted at Market Street, where the proportion of sheep rose from 14% in the pre-burgage phase to 50% in the post-medieval period (Table 17.4). This data for the three main species was compared across the range of sites available (fig. 17.2). The rise in sheep over time is confirmed in the results from the castle (McCormick & Murray, undated), and it is also notable that the high proportion of pig bones from Castle Street/castle lawn more closely reflect the results from the excavations of the castle than those of the adjacent town, suggesting that the castle inhabitants used this area to dispose of their rubbish.

Cattle
Despite the differences between phases, the actual meat diet of the inhabitants of Trim was predominantly beef, which made up between 72% and 89% of the meat available in the Kiely's Yard area, with the proportion of mutton never

Table 17.4 MNI percentages for three main species from a
range of excavations

Phase	Cattle	Sheep/Goat	Pig
Townparks South, Kiely's Yard Phase 1: AD1027–1290	50	20	30
Townparks South, Kiely's Yard Phase 2: AD1250–1400	40	35	25
Townparks South, Kiely's Yard Phase 2a: AD1400–1640	53.8	30.8	15.4
Townparks South, Castle Street/Lawn (medieval)	44.4	22.2	33.3
Townparks South, Phase 3: Post-medieval	28.6	42.9	28.6
Market Street pre-burgage excluding horn-cores	71.4	14.3	14.3
Market Street pre-burgage including horn-cores	71.4	21.4	7.1
Market Street 12th–14th century excluding horn-cores	25	41.7	33.3
Market Street 12th–14th century including horn-cores	40	33.3	26.7
Market Street post-medieval	25	50	25
Castle 12th century[1]	43	29	29
Castle 13th–14th century[1]	41	28	31
Castle 14th–15th century[1]	36	33	31
High Street Monitoring (Medieval)[2]	51.1	33.3	15.6
High Street Library 13th century[3]	55	20	24
Athboy Gate 14th–15th century[4]	16.7	50	33.3

[1](McCormick & Murray, undated) [2](Lynch 2007) [3](McCormick 1991) [4](Lofqvist 2008)

exceeding 7.2% of the diet. Similarly, at Market Street, beef made up between 67% and 93% of the meat available, with mutton reaching a high of 9.4% in the post-medieval period. On both sites, pork and bacon were the second meat of choice after beef.

Beef production is optimized by slaughtering cattle in the 24–36 month age group, when they have reached approximately full size but the meat is still tender. By contrast, aged animals may be slaughtered once they are no longer useful for traction (in the case of males) or dairying (in the case of females). In Kiely's Yard, the fusion data for all periods shows that the majority of cattle were older animals (fig. 17.3). This is particularly true in the Phase 3 post-medieval deposits, where 83.3% were in this age group. A small peak of animals around 24–36 months is also present in most phases of activity, and a single pre-natal calf was present in Phase 2 (AD1250–1400).

At Market Street, fusion data for cattle also showed a peak of slaughter at 24–36 months and of older, adult animals for both the pre-burgage and medieval phases, whereas the post-medieval phase did not yield sufficient results for analysis. The horn-cores recovered from Market Street provide a different picture from that gained using fusion data. Horn-cores can be used to obtain ages for adult cattle, whereas the other methods group all animals over

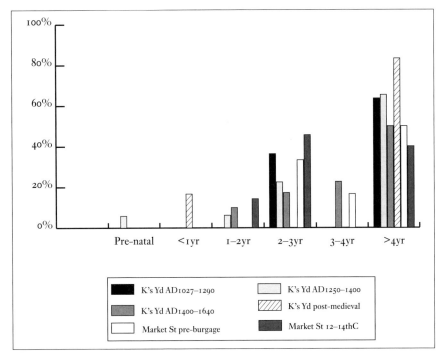

17.3 Townparks South and Market Street: cattle age at slaughter based on fusion data

48 or 50 months into one category. For the pre-burgage phase the horn-core data shows few young animals with the majority being animals over ten years at the time of their deaths. The medieval data is dominated by old animals, but there is also a minor peak of young animals aged less than seven years. Post-medieval data is limited to only two cores, both from relatively young animals (fig. 17.4).

Comparison with data from the Trim Castle excavation (McCormick & Murray, undated) shows a similar situation, where fusion data from all periods suggested that approximately 75% of the cattle were aged over forty-eight months. McCormick and Murray surmised that in the case of the castle itself, a small, permanent household was boosted to a large, temporary population when the lord was in residence, necessitating the purchase of additional meat. At Athboy Gate a juvenile under twenty-four months and a mature adult were identified (Lofqvist 2008) and at High Street both adult and juvenile cattle were present (Lynch 2007).

Since the townsfolk did not control the production of meat, they would have bought surplus animals from the surrounding countryside. It has been noted at other urban medieval sites that the cattle from urban assemblages tend to be predominantly older animals, and it has been suggested that the rural

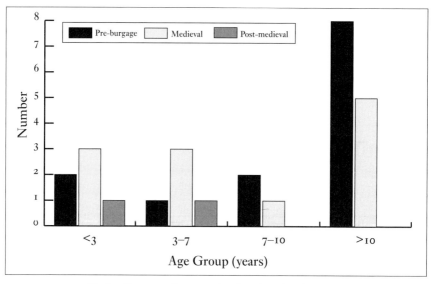

17.4 Market Street: cattle age at slaughter based on horn-core data

producers kept the higher quality meat for their own consumption, only selling the lower quality animals to the town butchers (McCormick 1997, 822; McCormick & Murphy 1997, 201). The data from Trim shows that although the majority of animals were older individuals, 20–40% of the meat being consumed in the town was of high quality.

Sheep and goat
At Drogheda, Co. Louth, Ferrycarrig, Co. Wexford, and various locations in Dublin and Waterford, proportions of sheep in the thirteenth and fourteenth centuries reached up to 56% of the MNI (McCormick 1997). It has been suggested that these very high levels were linked to the development of a wool export trade that resulted in an increase in the availability of excess mutton for sale to urban markets (McCormick 1997). As described above, there is general evidence for an increase in sheep-rearing over time. With the exception of the results from Athboy Gate, however, the proportions of sheep found in medieval Trim were lower than those in the coastal towns. There is a further increase in the proportion of sheep in the Phase 3 post-medieval material at Kiely's Yard, when they reach a peak of 42.9% and at Market Street where, in the post-medieval period sheep reach 50% of the three main species.

The optimum age at which to slaughter sheep for meat is up to thirty-six months, while wool production is optimized by retaining sheep into adulthood and slaughtering them after the age of seven years (Payne 1973). At Townparks South, in all periods, apart from Phase 2 (AD1250–1400), there was a peak of slaughter between sixteen and forty-two months, suggesting that the sheep

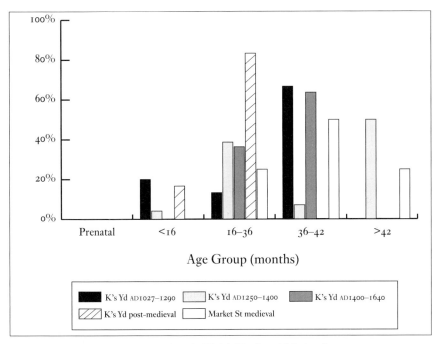

17.5 Townparks South (Kiely's Yard) and Market Street:
sheep/goat age at slaughter based on fusion data

were being reared for meat production. In Phase 2 (AD1250–1400), however, approximately half of the sheep were retained into adulthood, so that during this period there seems to have been a move towards optimizing for wool production. This pattern changed in the post-medieval period, when all of the sheep were killed before they had reached 36 months, at an age to produce prime meat. Interestingly, there was also evidence for a young lamb being killed during the medieval phase, possibly to provide food for a special occasion or feast. At Market Street the medieval mandible data is strongly biased towards young animals aged between one and two years, with six out of eight mandibles being from this age group, one animal aged 3–4 years and one aged 8–10 years. The fusion data also suggests relatively young animals, but with only 25% aged less than 3 years and 50% aged between 36 and 42 months. Fusion data is less reliable than mandible data, since the bones of younger animals are more prone to degradation and destruction, however, despite the differences between the mandible and fusion data, both indicate animals raised primarily for meat (fig. 17.5).

As with many other commodities, there was provision in the murage grant for wool to be taxed, with the rate set at 2*d*. per sack in both 1290 and 1308 (Potterton 2005, 145, 147). The evidence from the relative proportions of the main species and the age distribution at Townparks South suggests some movement away from meat production, towards rearing sheep for wool in Phase 2 (AD1250–1400). Despite rising proportions of sheep over time, this is not borne out at Market Street, however this assemblage was smaller so that patterns may reflect the site rather than the wider economy. When compared to the coastal towns, the relatively modest proportions of sheep imply that Trim was not an important centre for wool production or sale, but instead mainly supplied the local area. As a result, the medieval wool export trade was less developed in Trim than in other, more coastal regions of eastern Ireland. During the medieval period, the Boyne was navigable as far as Trim (Graham 1979), which lies only 40km from the sea. This highlights the importance of a coastal location in the medieval export trade. In contrast to the medieval mixed economy, in which both wool and meat were important, at Kiely's Yard the post-medieval period witnessed a further increase in the proportion of sheep, coupled with a move towards optimizing sheep slaughter to produce good quality meat. This suggests that during this period the inhabitants of the town were driving the market for good quality mutton rather than being passive recipients of agricultural surpluses.

At Kiely's Yard there was evidence for goats being kept in the town to produce meat, which was consumed when the goats reached one to two years of age, suggesting again that this was prime meat for the townsfolk (Beglane, forthcoming). The female goats would presumably have been retained to provide milk, while male juveniles would have been slaughtered for food. It is notable that goats disappeared from the town at the end of the medieval period, with no goat remains found in the post-medieval levels. At Market Street only goat horn-cores were identified, with only sheep identified from the cranial, tooth and post-cranial remains.

Pigs

At Kiely's Yard, there was a clear reduction in the importance of pigs over the course of the middle ages, before the proportion rose again in the post-medieval period. At Market Street, pig gained considerably in significance between the pre-burgage and medieval phases, a feature of the reduction in the importance of cattle on the site. With the exception of the earliest phase at Kiely's Yard (AD1027–1290), the proportions of pig bones identified by McCormick and Murray (undated) from the castle were generally higher than in the town. The deliberate provisioning of castles with live pigs was noted by McCormick and Murray (ibid.) as being a feature of military planning, with documentary evidence for this practice described in medieval documents (Davies & Quinn 1941, 14–15; Sweetman 1875, 1–3, 69). This association of pigs with military activities was of long standing, so that, for example, pork was key to the provisioning of the Roman army (Southern 2007, 221). Pigs can be kept penned and fed on scraps, rather than needing grass or hay. Consequently, they are ideal for holding inside a castle or fort to provide fresh meat even under siege conditions. The meat is also tasty when preserved by smoking or salting, whereas preserved mutton and beef are usually less favoured, making pork the ideal meat to transport with an army on campaign. Pigs do not provide any secondary products, so pork was relatively expensive to produce. This led them to be associated with feasting during the Early Medieval period (Kelly 1997, 358), and this tradition may have continued into the high and late medieval periods, further explaining the higher levels of pig bones found during the excavation of the castle.

Since pigs are kept only for meat, the majority are usually slaughtered as they approach full size, with only a few sows and even fewer boars retained for breeding. Both fusion and mandible data for all phases and sites follow these expected patterns and, furthermore, the mandible data from Kiely's Yard strongly suggests a preference for slaughtering pigs in their second winter, when aged 19–25 months. This suggests that pork and bacon were closely associated with winter food, probably being preserved by smoking or salting. The age distribution was very tight during Phase 2 (AD1250–1400) at Kiely's Yard, whereas by Phase 2a (AD1400–1640) there was a tendency for pigs to be kept until they were older before being slaughtered, and for a wider age distribution of animals being killed. This suggests that while pig-rearing was well-organized in Phase 2 (AD1250–1400), it may have become more *ad-hoc* over time. The figures from Kiely's Yard compare closely with the results from the castle excavations (McCormick & Murray, undated) where slaughter focused on the 17–21 month age group, with a further peak at 23–25 months. Results from the other sites were more limited, but again were broadly similar, so that at Market Street three medieval pig mandibles came from pigs slaughtered at between 17 and 27 months, at High Street, McCormick (1991) found three individuals aged 19–23 months, and Lynch (2007) identified both fused and unfused pig bones. At Athboy Gate, the remains of a piglet, one animal under 18 months, one aged 36–42 months and one adult pig were found, so that at this site a range of age groups were clearly present (Lofqvist 2008).

There is evidence for pigs being kept in the town, with piglet bones being found at Kiely's Yard (Beglane, forthcoming), in deposits in the Castle Street/castle lawn area, at the Black Friary, and in the remains found at Athboy Gate (Lofqvist 2008). Similarly, neonatal bones were found inside the castle, leading McCormick and Murray (undated) to conclude that pig-rearing also took place there. As mentioned above, pigs can easily be kept in a town or a castle as they can be penned and fed on scraps, but interestingly, there were no piglet remains dating from the post-medieval phase, suggesting that this practice had fallen out of favour.

BIRDS & FISH

Sixty-four bird bones were recovered from the excavations at Townparks South (Table 17.5). Domestic fowl (chicken) made up 73–80% of those in the medieval deposits at Kiely's Yard, with goose and duck also featuring. The goose and duck bones were probably domestic, although they could have been from wild species. A number of bird bones were retrieved from a single pit in Kiely's Yard, including several that may have been from a single large cock bird. These included only the mid-part of the wings and lower legs, leading Hamilton-Dyer (2007b) to suggest that the bird may have been cooked in a stew, with these tougher body parts removed before serving. Twelve bird bones came from medieval deposits at Market Street, including fowl, goose (probably domestic) and immature pigeon. Results from the other urban sites were similar, so that at the library site in High Street, O'Connor identified fifteen domestic fowl, three goose and one duck bone (McCormick 1991). At Athboy Gate, there were six bird bones, of which two were from galliformes, one was from a mallard duck and one was possibly from a domestic goose. Galliformes are a group that includes domestic fowl and pheasant (Lofqvist 2008). The castle excavations yielded a much wider range of species (Hamilton-Dyer 2007a, 108), reflecting the interest of the medieval elite in wild fowling and in raising pigeons for food (Murphy & O'Conor 2006; Thomas 2007, 140–1). At the Black Friary, there was one post-medieval fowl bone and two medieval buzzard bones. This raptor was probably wild.

Table 17.5 Bird bone NISP values from Townparks South, Black Friary and Market Street (collated from Hamilton-Dyer 2007b; 2009a, b)

	Goose	Duck	Fowl	Plover	Pigeon	Buzzard	Indet.	Totals
K's Yd Phase 1: AD1027–1290	2	0	9	0	0	0	0	11
K's Yd Phase 2: AD1250–1400	1	0	13	1	0	0	2	17
K's Yd Phase 2a: AD1400–1640	3	0	19	0	2	0	2	26
K's Yd Phase 3: Post-medieval	0	0	1	0	0	0	0	1
Castle St / Lawn: Medieval	1	0	3	0	0	0	0	4
Townparks South: Unstratified	1	2	2	0	0	0	0	5
Market St: Medieval	6	0	4	0	1	0	1	12
Black Friary Phase 2: Medieval	0	0	0	0	0	2	2	4
Black Friary Phase 3: Post-med.	0	0	1	0	0	0	0	1

Two fish bones, one from a large cod over a metre in length and one from an indeterminate large fish, were found at Kiely's Yard (Hamilton-Dyer 2007b). At Market Street, one hake and two flatfish bones (probably plaice) were identified. At the Black Friary, two herring bones (possibly from Scotland), one cod and one ling bone were found. A bone from a salmon or trout was of a size to suggest a freshwater fish rather than a migrating salmon. At the library site in High Street, two fish bones – one from a whiting and one from a turbot – were identified (McCormick 1991). Fish bones are likely to be under-represented in the assemblage due to their small size and to taphonomic problems, but these results suggest that little fish was available in the urban areas of Trim. Again, the results from the Castle were much more extensive, with 597 bones from over ten species, and the earliest identified pike bones in Ireland (Hamilton-Dyer 2007a, 112, 115). It is notable that despite Trim being situated on the River Boyne, almost all of the fish excavated at Trim were sea fish, which McCormick and Murray (undated) suggested had been transported from Drogheda at the mouth of the Boyne. This evidence for the development of trade links between the coastal towns and Trim is significant, especially when compared to the evidence to suggest that the long distance wool trade was relatively limited, despite the fact that wool was an important export from Ireland in the medieval period.

WILD ANIMALS

Wild animals were of little importance as food for the townsfolk of Trim, however at Townparks South deer bones were present in the medieval phases, and hare and rabbit bones were found in deposits dating to both the medieval and post-medieval periods. Furthermore, two possible wild pig bones were identified from Phase 1 and 2 contexts.

Hunting was a high-status activity and venison was often given as a high-status gift, but it was rarely, if ever, sold by the aristocracy (Cummins 1988, 260–5; Murphy & O'Conor 2006; Sykes 2007, 51). The relatively low proportion of deer bones at these sites probably reflects the occupation of this area by people not directly connected with the castle. The presence of deer teeth and foot bones can be interpreted as an indication of leather-working, and the presence of antler indicates artefact manufacturing, but this is not true of the scapula and humerus found at Kiely's Yard. These elements may have been obtained through illicit hunting or poaching (Sykes 2007, 56–7); they could have been a huntsman's share of the carcass; or they may have been individual gifts from castle inhabitants. It is notable, however, that the fore-limb, represented by the scapula and humerus, was traditionally the portion of the deer claimed by non-noble huntsmen employed by a lord (Sykes 2007, 51). At High Street, Lynch (2007) found a single deer metacarpal, again from the fore-foot and a single metatarsal, from the hind foot of a red deer, came from a pre-burgage context at Market Street, but no deer remains were identified in the other urban assemblages from Trim. Several deer elements were recovered from the area outside the castle, and these may be debris from the inhabitants, the townsfolk or a combination of the two. Significantly, this area yielded the only element from the hind limb of a red deer found in the Townparks South excavation. This is the portion reserved for the lord (Sykes 2007, 51), suggesting that these bones may have been castle debris. Similarly, the deposits from the castle excavations included only the rear portions of red deer, but there was a wide range of body parts from fallow deer (McCormick & Murray, undated). In the Kiely's Yard area, it is potentially significant that only male red deer seem to be represented in the assemblage, and that no hind-limb bones were present. This seems to suggest that hunting rather than poaching was the source of the animals. When undertaking high-status hunts, it was important for the hunters to select a worthy opponent, ideally a mature male with a large rack of antlers. This was deemed to provide the best sport and to be of suitable stature so that the successful hunt would enhance the reputations of all involved in the process (Cummins 1988, 33–4). By contrast, poachers would be unlikely to select an animal based on its sex or size, since the aim would be a quick and uneventful hunt. Overall, these results demonstrate the link between the inhabitants of the castle and town, with the castle dependent on the town for employees and craft skills and the town dependent on the castle for work and trade.

As with deer, wild pigs were hunted by the aristocracy (Cummins 1988, 96–109; Kelly 2000, 71–2). The Kiely's Yard material yielded two elements that were towards the bottom end of the wild pig sizes identified by Payne and Bull (1988), but much larger than usual for medieval domestic pigs (ABMAP 2003). An astragalus from Phase 2 deposits (AD1250–1400), was measured as having a GLl of 44mm and a calcaneus from Phase 1 (AD1027–1290) had a GL of 80.5mm. Excavations at the castle uncovered three wild pig bones from late thirteenth- to early fourteenth-century material (McCormick & Murray, undated).

ANIMALS IN THE ECONOMY

Animals were a critical resource for the townsfolk of Trim, providing food, transport and raw materials. Diet has been discussed above, but food would have had economic as well as culinary significance. Some contexts at both Kiely's Yard and Market Street appear to consist mainly of butchery waste, supporting the documentary evidence that professional butchers operated in Trim, selling their meat to the townsfolk (Potterton 2005, 154). This differs from rural sites such as Mountgorry, Co. Dublin (Beglane 2006), where the self-sufficient nature of farming meant that animals were slaughtered and consumed within the household.

Prior to the invention of plastic, animals were a critical source of raw materials, providing bone and antler for tools and artefacts, as well as leather for clothing, harnesses, waterproof covers and bags, skins for vellum production and horn for items such as cups, handles and buttons (Halpin 2000, 172–5; Luik et al., 2005, 11; O'Rourke 2000, 143–58; Reitz & Wing 1999, 7–8). The Townparks

South assemblage provided potential evidence for all of these forms of craftwork taking place within the town. This range of activity suggests that Trim was a vibrant town with specialized craft-workers plying their skills in a market economy. A number of pits and other similar features were found to the rear of the structures in Kiely's Yard, outside the line of the town wall. Some of these contained normal domestic waste or were cess-pits, but others were industrial in character. These included a pit with an associated channel that may have been used for tanning leather or for horn-working, pits that contained butchery or leather-working waste, and pits containing a few waste horn-cores (Stephens, this volume). A metatarsal from a young calf was found in a pit to the rear of Kiely's Yard and could represent the production of vellum or fine calf leather. Plant macrofossil evidence suggests that flax-processing was also being carried out in this area, so that it is quite possible that a number of different crafts used the same pits and yard space, depending on the time of year or the needs of the individuals (Stephens, this volume).

There is considerable evidence from Market Street of butchery and the associated craft activities of tanning and horn-processing. The medieval phase included three large mammal vertebrae that had been chopped through to create 'sides' of meat. This process is typically associated with post-medieval butchery, in which the animal is suspended from a stout post or beam and then split into two sides using a saw or axe. The use of this technique in a medieval context is unusual.

Horn was a popular material for the production of items such as cups, handles, jewellery, buttons, combs and lanterns (Armitage & Clutton-Brock 1976). Horn is very malleable and can easily be moulded into a variety of shapes. The bone cores themselves are a waste product and are discarded once they have been separated from the horn sheaths. The first stage in processing is to soak the horns in water for several weeks or to boil them, or to soak them in a lime solution. The aim of this is to loosen the horn sheath from the core and allow its removal. Three possible sources of horn-cores have been identified on archaeological sites, each of which would result in large numbers being accumulated and then disposed of (Armitage 1990; Armitage & Clutton-Brock 1976): a) butchery waste, b) tannery waste and c) horn-worker's waste. Butchers slaughtered the animals and then supplied tanners with hides, sometimes with the horns still attached. Butchers or tanners could carry out primary processing of the horns to remove the sheath, and then supply the horn sheath to the horn-workers, or, alternatively horn-workers could obtain the sheath still within the cores and carry out this processing themselves. If the processing were carried on by a butcher, one would expect the assemblage to be a proportionate mixture of horn-cores and post-cranial elements. If carried out by a tanner, there is a possibility that the waste might also include foot bones as well as horn-cores, since these were usually, although by no means always, left attached to the hides. Tanners used lime-baths to remove hair from hides and so could easily have processed both hides and cores on the same premises. Where a horn-worker carried out the process in-house, very few post-cranial elements would be likely to be found with the horn-cores (Armitage 1990; Armitage & Clutton-Brock 1976).

For the pre-burgage phase at Market Street, the nineteen horn-cores dominated the cattle elements, so that all other body parts were under-represented. When horn-cores were excluded, the vertebrae, scapula, pelvis and foot elements were present in the expected proportions but, by contrast, the limb bones were still under-represented. This could occur if primary butchery took place on site, with joints of meat subsequently removed, for example to a butcher's shop or stall for sale, or directly to domestic premises. Alternatively, the meat may have been de-boned on site, with the long bones removed elsewhere for use in the craft of bone-working. The dominance of horn-cores in this phase implies that, in addition to those from animals butchered on the site, additional horns must have been brought in. This suggests that as well as slaughtering and butchering animals on site, horn-working or possibly tanning also took place at the site, with the horn-processing being indicative of this.

The medieval phase at Market Street also contained ten cattle horn-cores, and when these were excluded, the vertebrae, scapula and foot bones were grossly over-represented. High proportions of horn-cores and foot elements are typical of waste associated with a tannery. The presence of scapulae and pelvises, in conjunction with low proportions of limb bones, may indicate that, as in the earlier period, butchery also took place on site and that either the meat was de-boned, with long bones removed elsewhere, or the cattle limbs were removed from the site 'on the bone'. For this phase, there is no strong evidence for additional horn-cores being brought to the site. The evidence suggests that while butchery continued on the site, there may have been a shift towards tanning, as there were greater proportions of foot elements present, and horn-core processing was still being carried out, but without additional cores being brought in. Furthermore, one pit to the rear of the burgage plot was filled with lime containing shell and animal hair (Fallon, this volume), so that this may have been a pit associated with the tanning process.

No bone-working debris in the form of off-cuts or partially manufactured artefacts was identified in the Market Street assemblage. This suggests that bone-working was not taking place on site and may explain the lack of limb bones, since it is possible that these were removed to a bone-worker elsewhere in or around Trim.

At High Street, which lies within the walls of the medieval town, McCormick (1991) found evidence of horn-core processing, but no other evidence for craftwork, while Lynch (2007) did not find any evidence of craftwork in her examination of material from the same street. To the north of the town centre, at Athboy Gate, Lofqvist (2008) found no evidence of specialist craft-working, instead stressing the domestic nature of the evidence. McCormick and Murray

17.6 Waste material from button manufacture

(undated) make no reference to craft-working waste at the castle, which is unsurprising since one of the functions of the town was to supply craft products to the castle. The concentration of craftwork in the suburban area of Kiely's Yard, outside the walls, supports the idea that the suburb functioned as an industrial as well as a domestic area. The nearby Leper River would have provided a water source for industrial processing (Stephens, this volume). Similarly, the Market Street site appears to have been at the edge of the original town, and while industrial activities may have been allowed to continue after the building of the town defences, it is likely that any new ventures of this nature would have been located in the suburbs. Activities such as tanning, linen-processing and butchery would have been dirty industries that town authorities would probably have insisted were kept outside the walled town, as they did in urban centres elsewhere (Hindle 1990, 49; Maltby 1979, 86–7).

A number of pieces of worked bone, craftwork off-cuts and discarded artefacts were recovered from Townparks South. One of these provided evidence for button-making during Phase 2 (AD1250–1400). A circular piece of bone approximately 20mm in diameter had been removed from the rib of a large mammal. The bone fragment is now broken and only about half of the hole left by removing the button is still present (fig. 17.6).

Saws were not generally used in butchery until the post-medieval period, but prior to this they were used in craft-working. A partial antler from a red deer recovered from the medieval deposits at Castle Street/castle lawn had had four tines removed using a saw, and can be considered a craftwork off-cut. Tines were often used to make toggles similar to those on modern duffle coats. Other sawn off-cuts included a long bone and a scapula fragment, both from a large mammal.

Bone was also drilled to create artefacts. A drain in Kiely's Yard dated to the earliest phase of activity at the site and contained a cattle metatarsal with a hole drilled approximately half way down the ventral side in the centre of the shaft. This hole was approximately 7mm in diameter, tapering slightly to approximately

6.5mm at its deepest point, which was roughly half way through the bone. A dog had gnawed the bone at the proximal end, and the distal end was missing. It is not clear whether the bone was a partially-made artefact that was rejected for some reason, or whether the bone was used as an anvil or work surface, with the hole being the result of working an artefact on top of the bone. A horse metatarsal from Phase 2 (1250–1400) had been drilled through from the proximal end, to form a sheath or handle, but it seems to have broken during manufacture and then discarded.

A horse scapula from the medieval deposits at Castle Street/castle lawn had evidence of wear in a series of bands over the surface, suggesting that it had been bound to a piece of wood using a thong, probably to form the blade of a spade or shovel (fig. 17.7). The author recently identified a similar, almost complete example from an Early Medieval ringfort at Kinnegad, Co. Westmeath, demonstrating the longevity of this tool type.

At the Black Friary, the fill of a Phase 3 post-medieval pit yielded a metatarsal, a first and a second phalanx from the hind foot of a horse. The metatarsal had evidence of singeing on the shaft, so that it suggests that the foot was initially burnt in a fire before being transferred to the pit whilst still held together by connective tissue. Bones can be burnt to dispose of them, but fresh bone can also be burnt to maintain a high heat in a kiln.

The use of horse bones for craft-working is of great interest. In combination with the evidence for disarticulated and broken horse bones, it suggests that horses were processed after death rather than being disposed of whole, and were valued for their hides and bones. This reinforces the view that horses were seen primarily as working animals that could perform a useful function even in death, and suggests a lack of sentimentality in attitudes towards them.

The importance of animals for traction was also highlighted by the analysis of pathological conditions. A horse metacarpal from Kiely's Yard showed signs of degenerative changes, while horse tarsals from Athboy Gate showed evidence of spavin (Lofqvist 2008), both of which can be related to heavy work or poor shoeing. Horses in the medieval period were important for riding and pulling carts and, from the late thirteenth century, they began to be used for ploughing (Feehan 2005, 81; McCormick 2005, 23). The injuries noted above are consistent with the role of horses as working animals. The horses were generally pony-sized, with those from Kiely's Yard being between 11.9 and 13.6 hands rather than the larger beasts that we are more familiar with today. Horses have a natural lifespan of over 25 years, whereas at Kiely's Yard individuals included a juvenile that died before the age of 3½ years, several animals aged between 7 and 15 years and one older individual aged up to 18 years. Horse remains excavated on Haggard Street were from an individual aged 8½–11½ years, at High Street, Lynch (2007) found an animal aged around 10 years at death and at the castle, the skull of a horse aged 6 to 7 years was found (McCormick & Murray, undated). The evidence suggests therefore,

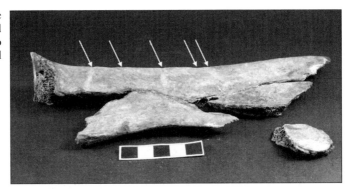

17.7 Horse scapula bound with a thong to create a shovel

that they were killed when they were no longer useful for work, rather than dying of old age.

Cattle were also important for traction of both carts and ploughs. The change from ox- to horse-ploughing was not completed in Ireland until very late. As an example, in nineteenth-century Galway, Dutton (1824, 83–7) was still extolling the advantages of ploughing using oxen rather than horses. Although heavy work would explain the degenerative damage visible on cattle joints, this could also be age-related, since female cattle would have been retained into old age for dairying. A large percentage of the cattle at Kiely's Yard and at High Street (Lynch 2007) had lesions on the proximal articular surface of the metacarpal, a condition that is poorly understood, but may be age-related or associated with degenerative wear caused by use in traction. A cattle proximal phalanx or toe bone from Kiely's Yard demonstrated eburnation consistent with osteoarthritis, again associated with age or heavy work (fig. 17.8). At the castle site and at the High Street library site (McCormick 1991; McCormick & Murray, undated) cattle bones showed that some individuals also suffered from degenerative joint disease or osteoarthritis of the femur and pelvis. McCormick and Murray also identified an individual from the castle with an enthesopathy on the calcaneus, showing that this animal had strained the tendon in the heel. A cattle horn-core from the pre-burgage phase at Market Street was of Age Class 4 (7–10 years) and had a band of differential growth on the underside of the core of approximately 20mm in width, and approximately 8–12cm on the dorsal side. The band was slightly flattened relative to the surrounding material and was notable for the numerous minute pores present. It is possible that the horn was restricted during growth, for example by a rope used as a lead or a halter, and similar examples were identified by Müller (1992) as being due to the pressure of the halter during traction (fig. 17.9). A cattle cranium from an individual aged between 3 and 7 years from a medieval context at Market Street had a large sinus measuring 8.7mm by 6mm on the left hand side of the nuchal eminence of the occipital region, which may have been caused by an infection (Roberts & Manchester

17.8 Cattle phalanx with osteoarthritic changes

17.9 Cattle horn-core with restricted growth: dorsal view (left) and basal view (right)

1997, 126–7). This was very similar to pathologies found at Timberyard, Co. Dublin (Beglane 2007), and at Eyre Square, Galway (Beglane 2008). McCormick (1997b) noted similar pathologies on several cattle from fourteenth- to sixteenth-century Dublin, and suggested that these may be congenital or due to the use of yokes for traction causing injury at that point on the skull.

Other animals also shared the town with the human inhabitants. As well as the pigs and goats, the remains of dogs and cats were found. During the middle ages these were probably working animals that were kept for guarding and vermin control, rather than purely as pets – a subject discussed more fully by Beglane (forthcoming). By the post-medieval period, their role was beginning to change, so that a greater appreciation for companion animals was starting to emerge (Thomas 2005). At Townparks South, dogs of estimated withers height 50–52cm and 62cm were recovered from Phase 2 (AD1250–1400) deposits, and at Market Street a dog from the pre-burgage phase had a height of 55cm. At Navan Gate Street, both medieval and early modern phases provided evidence for dogs of 47cm. The smallest of these was similar to a modern Border collie or a Springer spaniel in height, while the largest was of similar height to a modern Irish setter, so that relatively large dogs were being maintained within the urban environment.

DISCUSSION & CONCLUSION

The faunal assemblages from Townparks South, Market Street and elsewhere in Trim provide an insight into the inter-connected nature of Irish medieval and post-medieval society. The vast majority of the Townparks and Market Street assemblages appear to be the debris of the townsfolk, rather than being related to the occupants of Trim Castle. This is reflected in differences in food choices and availability between these assemblages and that from the castle itself where pork consumption was generally higher than in the town, and where a wider range of fish and fowl were consumed (Hamilton-Dyer 2007a; Hamilton-Dyer 2007b; McCormick & Murray, undated). Nevertheless, the importance of the castle to the economy of the town cannot be overstated, and the presence of red deer and possible wild pig remains in the medieval phases is a reflection of this. In terms of animal-related work, the castle would have provided direct employment for huntsmen, stable-hands and kennel-hands, as well as opportunities for craft-workers to make and sell items of bone, antler, leather and horn.

The connections between the town and its rural hinterland are important, since the townsfolk were solely consumers of beef and mutton rather than being self-sufficient producers. Some meat was produced in the town, but this provided only a small contribution to the diet. Beef made up the vast majority of the meat diet in Trim, and this is a situation that is typical of Irish archaeological sites from all periods and site-types. The age distribution of the animals demonstrates that production of meat for market-sale was not the primary aim of the farmer, but that instead cattle were mainly retained for dairy production and as transport animals, with the meat only being of value as a later by-product. Similarly, meat and wool seem to have been equally important products from sheep-rearing during the medieval period. Townsfolk could not always command premium quality meat for their tables, but could instead receive mutton from sheep that had often been allowed to produce several crops of wool prior to slaughter. This is demonstrated by the results from Kiely's Yard, which show evidence for a partial shift towards rearing sheep for wool in Phase 2 (AD1250–1400). Fragments of wool cloth with a herring-bone weave were also recovered from late thirteenth- to fourteenth-century contexts at Athboy Gate (Seaver, this volume). Wool was produced on rural farms but would have been sold to merchants in Trim, and the additional mutton that was made available as a result of this trade provided an increased variety of meat in the urban diet. Ultimately, any focus on wool over meat declined and, in the post-medieval period, sheep farmers optimized production of good quality meat, which led to an increase in the amount of mutton sold. While goats and pigs were reared in the town during the medieval period, this was no longer the case during the post-medieval phase, and it may be that the increasing availability of good quality mutton reduced the incentive to produce meat within the town.

Comparisons of the assemblages from inside and outside the walled town and from the castle have revealed differences in activity patterns. Inside the walls, the animal bones reflect mainly domestic activity, whereas at Kiely's Yard the assemblage contains a mixture of domestic and industrial waste. The Market Street site is unusual in displaying industrial character within the medieval walls, however the evidence suggests that the initial use of this site pre-dated the demarcation of an early town boundary, and the site seems to have subsequently been allowed to continue in use despite its location. The medieval material from Castle Street/castle lawn resembles the assemblage excavated at the castle more closely than any of the urban or suburban sites, having a higher proportion of pig, deer and horse than the Kiely's Yard material. The pig and deer bones from Castle Street/castle lawn are likely to reflect the higher consumption of these species found during analysis of material from the castle itself (McCormick & Murray, undated) and so represent the waste produced by the castle inhabitants. It is likely that horses would have been more important to the castle inhabitants than to the townsfolk, so that again these bones are probably predominantly linked to the castle.

The faunal remains suggest that Trim was a typical medieval and post-medieval town, where life revolved around trade and craftwork. Meat was mainly produced outside the town to be sold by professional butchers, while fish and shellfish were brought from the coast. The evidence for the development of trade links between the coast and Trim is significant, as it suggests only limited long-distance trading in wool, an important export from Ireland in the medieval period. Instead, to pay for food, wealth would have been generated by manufacturing artefacts for sale and trade with the farmers, other townsfolk and castle inhabitants.

ACKNOWLEDGMENTS

I would like to express my thanks to Mandy Stephens and Finola O'Carroll (CRDS), who excavated at Townparks South, Matthew Seaver (CRDS), who excavated sites at the Black Friary, Navan Gate Street and Haggard Street, and to Trim Town Council, who funded these excavations. I would also like to thank Donal Fallon (CRDS), who excavated 18 Market Street on behalf of St

Loman's Credit Union. Thank you also to Sheila Hamilton-Dyer, Camilla Lofqvist, Patricia Lynch, Finbar McCormick and Emily Murray for the use of unpublished data and to Sam Moore for comments on an earlier version of this text.

BIBLIOGRAPHY

ABMAP, 2003, 'Animal Bone Metrical Archive Project'. University of Southampton. http://ads.ahds.ac.uk/catalogue/specColl/abmap/. Accessed 29 November 2007.
Armitage, P., 1990, 'Post-medieval cattle horns from the Greyfriars site, Chichester, West Sussex, England', *Circaea* **7**:2, 81–90.
Armitage, P.L., & Clutton-Brock, J., 1976, 'A system for classification and description of the horn cores of cattle from archaeological sites', *Journal of Archaeological Science* **2**, 329–48.
Beglane, F., 2006, 'Report on faunal material from Mountgorry, Co. Dublin', licence no. 04E1604. Unpublished.
Beglane, F., 2007, 'Report on faunal material from Timberyard, Coombe Bypass, Dublin 8', licence no. 06E710. Unpublished.
Beglane, F., 2008, 'Report on faunal material from Eyre Square monitoring, Galway', licence no. 03E1786. Unpublished.
Beglane, F., 2009a, 'Report on faunal material from Blackfriary, Trim, Co. Meath', Consent no. C150; licence no. E2398. Unpublished.
Beglane, F., 2009b, 'Report on faunal material from Navan Gate and Haggard Street', Consent no. C150; licence no. E2398. Unpublished.
Beglane, F., forthcoming, 'Suburban husbandry: animals in the landscape of Trim, Co. Meath, Ireland' in Choyke, A. (ed.), Animals as material culture in the middle ages 4: fauna and urban space.
Cummins, J., 1988, *The hound and the hawk: the art of medieval hunting*. London.
Davies, O., & Quinn, D.B., 1941, 'The pipe roll of 14 John', *Ulster Journal of Archaeology* **4** (3rd ser.), 1–76.
Dutton, H., 1824, *A statistical and agricultural survey of the county of Galway*. Dublin.
Feehan, J., 2005, 'Horses: working on the land' in McGrath, M., & Griffith, J.C. (eds), *The Irish draught horse: a history*, 80–90. Cork.
Graham, B., 1979, 'The evolution of urbanisation in medieval Ireland', *Journal of Historical Geography* **5**:2, 111–25.
Graham, B., 1999, 'Urbanization in Ireland during the High Middle Ages *c.*100 to *c.*1350' in Barry, T.B. (ed.), *History of settlement in Ireland*, 124–39. London.
Halpin, A., 2000, 'The small finds: stone metal, wood, bone and antler' in Halpin, A., *The port of medieval Dublin: archaeological excavations at the civic offices, Winetavern Street, Dublin, 1993*, 159–75. Dublin.
Hamilton-Dyer, S., 2007a, 'Exploitation of birds and fish in historic Ireland: a brief review of the evidence', *Environmental Archaeology*, 102–18.
Hamilton-Dyer, S., 2007b, 'Townparks South, Trim, Co. Meath: CRDS 494: bird and fish bones'. Unpublished.
Hamilton-Dyer, S., 2009a, 'Trim: Market Street. Bird and fish bones'. Unpublished.
Hamilton-Dyer, S., 2009b, 'Trim: Black Friary. Bird and fish bones'. Unpublished.
Hindle, P., 1990, *Medieval town plans*. Risborough.
Jones O'Day, S., Van Neer, W., & Ervynck, A., 2004, 'Introduction' in Jones O'Day, S., Van Neer, W., & Ervynck, A., *Behaviour behind bones: the zooarchaeology of ritual, religion, status and identity*, xi–xv. Oxford.

Kelly, F., 1997, *Early Irish farming: a study based mainly on the law-texts of the 7th and 8th Centuries AD.* Dublin.

Lofqvist, C., 2008, 'Osteological report on animal bones from Athboy Gate, Trim, County Meath', C150. E2398. Unpublished.

Luik, H., Choyke, A., Batey, C.E., & Lõugas, L., 2005, *From hooves to horns, from mollusc to mammoth.* Tallinn.

Lynch, P., 2007, 'Human and animal osteoarchaeological bone report: High Street, Trim Co. Meath 06E0148'. Unpublished.

Maltby, M., 1979, *Faunal studies on urban sites: the animal bones from Exeter 1971–1975.* Sheffield.

McCormick, F., 1991, 'The animal bones from High St., Trim' in Walsh, C., 'An excavation at the library site, High Street, Trim', *Ríocht na Mídhe* 8:3, 53–7.

McCormick, F., 1997, 'The animal bones' in Hurley, M.F., & Scully, O.M.B., *Late Viking Age and medieval Waterford*, 819–53. Waterford.

McCormick, F., 2005, 'Archaeology: the horse in early Ireland' in McGrath, M., & Griffith, J.C. (eds), *The Irish draught horse: a history*, 17–29. Cork.

McCormick, F., & Murphy, E., 1997, 'Mammal bones' in Walsh, C., *Archaeological excavations at Patrick, Nicholas and Winetavern Streets Dublin*, 199–218. Dingle.

McCormick, F., & Murray, E., undated, 'The animal bones from Trim Castle'. Unpublished.

Murphy, M., & O'Conor, K., 2006, 'Castles and deer parks in Anglo-Norman Ireland', *Journal of the American Society of Irish Medieval Studies* 1, 51–70.

Müller, H.H., 1992, 'Archaeozoological research on vertebrates in central Europe with special reference to the medieval period', *International Journal of Osteoarchaeology* 2, 311–24.

O'Connor, T., 2007, 'Thinking about beastly bodies' in Pluskowski, A., *Breaking and shaping beastly bodies: animals as material culture in the middle ages*, 1–10. Oxford.

O'Rourke, D., 2000, 'The leather finds' in Halpin, A., *The port of medieval Dublin: archaeological excavations at the civic offices, Winetavern Street, Dublin, 1993*, 143–58. Dublin.

Payne, S., 1973, 'Kill off patterns in sheep and goats: the mandibles from Asvan Kale', *Anatolian Studies* 23, 281–303.

Payne, S., & Bull, G., 1988, 'Components of variation in measurements to distinguish wild from domestic pig remains', *Archaeozoologia* 2:1–2, 27–66.

Potterton, M., 2005, *Medieval Trim: history and archaeology.* Dublin.

Reitz, E.J., & Wing, E.S., 1999, *Zooarchaeology.* Cambridge.

Roberts, C.A., & Manchester, K., 1997, *The archaeology of disease.* Stroud, Gloucestershire.

Seaver, M., 2009a, 'Preliminary report on excavations and monitoring on the Trim Street Reconstruction Project', Ministerial Consent, E2398. Unpublished.

Seaver, M., 2009b, 'Trim Street Reconstruction Project: TSRP 4: archaeological assessment at Navan Gate, Trim, County Meath', Ministerial Consent C150: E2398. Unpublished.

Southern, P., 2007, *The Roman Army: a social and institutional history.* Oxford.

Sweetman, H.S. (ed.), 1875, *Calendar of documents relating to Ireland, 1171–1251.* London.

Sykes, N., 2007, 'Animal bones and animal parks' in Liddiard, R. (ed.), *The medieval park: new perspectives*, 49–62. Macclesfield.

Thomas, R., 2005, 'Perceptions versus reality: changing attitudes towards pets in medieval and post-medieval England' in Pluskowski, A. (ed.), *Just skin and bones? New perspectives on human-animal relations in the historic past*, 95–104. Oxford.

Thomas, R., 2007, 'Food and the maintenance of social boundaries in medieval England' in Twiss, K.C. (ed.), *The archaeology of food and identity*, 130–51. Southern Illinois University.

Walsh, C., 1991, 'An excavation at the library site, High Street, Trim', *Ríocht na Mídhe* 8:3, 41–67.

Management and conservation plans for Trim town walls

The Irish Walled Town Network was established by the Heritage Council of Ireland in 2005 'to unite and co-ordinate the strategic efforts of local authorities involved in the management, conservation and enhancement of historic walled towns in Ireland, both North and South' (Heritage Council of Ireland website). Trim joined the Network in 2006. Conservation and Management Plans for the Trim town walls were commissioned by Meath County Council in 2007. Alastair Coey Architects, Belfast, were appointed as consultants to draw up the plans, and funding was provided by the Heritage Council. A steering group comprising members from Meath County Council, academia, local historical groups, residents, planning and tourist interests and the Department of Environment, Heritage and Local Government was set up. Following the appointments of the steering group and consultants, a public meeting was held to investigate the views and needs of the local community, following which additional members of the public joined the steering group. The consultants carried out their field-work and research in the late autumn of 2007. The first drafts of the plans were presented to the steering group, and subsequently there was further feed-back from the members of the group. At the time of writing, the plans are in the process of being adopted by Trim Town Council; once adopted they will be incorporated into the Trim Development Plan.

THE BURRA CHARTER

The objectives of the Conservation and Management Plans are to strike a balance between the conservation, presentation, access, enjoyment and use, the needs of the local community along with the preservation of the fabric of the site and of the significance of the site for future generations. The objectives are based on the principles of the Burra Charter, which was used as the framework upon which the Conservation Plan was developed. The Burra Charter, more properly known as the 'Australia ICOMOS Burra Charter 1999', is a code of good practice that applies to the management of places of cultural significance. It was published in 1999 by the Australian National Committee of ICOMOS (International Council on Monuments and Sites). Among other matters, it

371

deals with the settings of places of cultural significance and the relevance of such places to the people who live there. Other conservation issues, such as the desirability or otherwise of restoration, conservation, reconstruction, inter-pretation to enhance the enjoyment of the monument, assessment and statement of significance are explained and discussed in the Charter. The participation of people for whom the place has significance is central to the philosophy of the Charter.

TRIM TOWN WALLS CONSERVATION AND MANAGEMENT PLANS

The purpose of the Conservation Plan was to identify the significance of the town walls and potential threats to that significance, and to suggest policies for the protection of the walls. It was recognized that Trim is a thriving, organic town, but that development can be managed in such a way that the character and quality of the walls can be retained and enhanced. The purpose of the Management Plan was to plan for the day-to-day maintenance of the walls and for the organization of events associated with the walls. It aims to co-ordinate the approaches taken by the different agencies who are already involved in the maintenance and management of the walls.

The Conservation Plan

Chapters 1–3 of the Conservation Plan set Trim and its walls in their geographical, historical and administrative contexts. Chapter 4 represents a statement of the significance of the town walls, based on Trim's strategic importance in the Anglo-Norman settlement of Ireland and its connection to one of the leading Anglo-Norman families in western Europe; its geographical location in very good agricultural land and at a crossing point over the river Boyne; and the relationship between the walls and the street layout, the upstanding remains and property plots. The significance of the walls can be increased by investment in conservation of Trim Castle, emphasizing its association with the walled town; and conservation works on the walls, enabling further archaeological research. This conservation will be seen as a mark of civic pride and local identity, thus increasing the image of Trim as a desirable place to live and to visit.

Chapter 4 also lists what are seen as the main threats to the walls. These include lack of knowledge and interest, damage to and decay of the fabric of the walls, inappropriate management and development and anti-social behaviour. Chapter 5 provides a gazetteer of the walls, having broken them down into various zones for ease of description. A more detailed account of the state of the walls is included in the Management Plan.

National Monuments and planning legislation, current at the time of writing, were the main component of the policies listed in the Conservation

Plan; the policies were laid out in chapter 6. The principles and terminology used derive from the Burra Convention. Thirty-eight were proposed, too many to be listed here. The author of the Plans stressed that the higher the level of significance of a monument, the greater care is needed in planning its treatment and that the entire circuit of the walls should be treated as having the same level of significance.

The Conservation Plan proposed the foundation of a management group, under the aegis of Meath County Council. This group will implement a Management Plan, one element of which might be a warden system designed to supervise the walls on a daily basis. Suitably qualified experts should advise on conservation works, which should be carried out according to procedures set down in the Management Plan. New developments should not be permitted in the town where they might impact on the walls and/or their setting. There should be access for all to the walls, including those with disability, and there should be clear and accurate signage. Interpretation should be of good quality and should strive to place the walls in a wider context of Irish and European history. Events should be promoted, but strictly within the confines of an Event Management Plan. There is potential to enhance stretches of the walls; in particular, the Plan suggests a linear park along the west side of the town walls at the back of the properties on Emmet Street. During any such development work, proper attention should be paid to ecological and wildlife factors. Best conservation practice should be observed on any maintenance work to the walls.

The Management Plan
The Management Plan has been drawn up as a policy of the Conservation Plan. It is envisaged in the Management Plan that a management group should be established (see above), with a set lifespan of perhaps five years. It should meet regularly and appoint a Monument Manager. An assessment of the upstanding remains of the walls forms part of the Management Plan. The circuit of the walls is broken down into zones; a description of the condition of the walls in each zone is provided, on both the interior and exterior of the wall. Associated mapping and photography are provided. There are references to structural problems, vegetation cover, modern disturbances and problems such as vandalism and graffiti.

Advice and guidelines on many elements of conservation works are presented, including procedures for the removal of vegetation, re-pointing, consolidation and reconstruction, along with advice on interpretation, signage and access. Priorities that are envisaged for future action include the enhancement of certain zones of the walls that could be improved by way of proper street furniture, signage and interpretation panels, and the provision of a town walking tour. Suggestions are made regarding the elements necessary to achieve a good-quality product.

The costs of repairing and restoring the walls on a zone-by-zone basis are estimated, and the necessity for such works for each zone is prioritized into work that should be carried out as soon as possible, work that should be carried out within five years and work that should be carried out when funding becomes available. The priorities were slightly different for each zone. The legal status of the walls was set out in the Plan, which stressed that actions carried out by the Management Group should comply at all time with all relevant statutory requirements.

SUMMARY

The Plans provide a mixture of sound practical advice allied with a philosophical and ethical approach to the issue. Concepts of significance, as explained in the Burra Charter, provide a framework with which to approach projects such as the conservation, interpretation and presentation of Trim's town walls. Trim is a very particular place, both in Meath and in Ireland. Its upstanding remains are beyond parallel in Ireland, and a systematic programme of conservation, education and presentation must be developed if these remains are to survive and attain esteem in the eyes of Trim's townspeople and the citizens of Ireland, present and future.

Index